Pro Drupal as an Enterprise Development Platform

Jamie Kurtz
Thomas Besluau

Pro Drupal as an Enterprise Development Platform

ISBN-13 (pbk): 978-1-4302-6004-2

ISBN-13 (electronic): 978-1-4302-6005-9

President and Publisher: Paul Manning
Lead Editor: Ewan Buckingham
Technical Reviewer: Anirudh Prabhu, Jeff Pickett
Editorial Board: Steve Anglin, Mark Beckner, Ewan Buckingham, Gary Cornell, Louise Corrigan, Morgan Ertel, Jonathan Gennick, Jonathan Hassell, Robert Hutchinson, Michelle Lowman, James Markham, Matthew Moodie, Jeff Olson, Jeffrey Pepper, Douglas Pundick, Ben Renow-Clarke, Dominic Shakeshaft, Gwenan Spearing, Matt Wade, Tom Welsh
Coordinating Editor: Anamika Panchoo
Copy Editor: Ralph Moore
Compositor: SPi Global
Indexer: SPi Global
Artist: SPi Global
Cover Designer: Anna Ishchenko

Distributed to the book trade worldwide by Springer Science+Business Media New York, 233 Spring Street, 6th Floor, New York, NY 10013. Phone 1-800-SPRINGER, fax (201) 348-4505, e-mail orders-ny@springer-sbm.com, or visit www.springeronline.com. Apress Media, LLC is a California LLC and the sole member (owner) is Springer Science + Business Media Finance Inc (SSBM Finance Inc). SSBM Finance Inc is a Delaware corporation.

For information on translations, please e-mail rights@apress.com, or visit www.apress.com.

Apress and friends of ED books may be purchased in bulk for academic, corporate, or promotional use. eBook versions and licenses are also available for most titles. For more information, reference our Special Bulk Sales–eBook Licensing web page at www.apress.com/bulk-sales.

Any source code or other supplementary materials referenced by the author in this text is available to readers at www.apress.com. For detailed information about how to locate your book's source code, go to www.apress.com/source-code/.

I would like to dedicate this book to my dear wife, and my two lovely daughters, who have been exceedingly patient and understanding with yet another one of my many geeky adventures.

—Jamie Kurtz

To my wife, Jess, for her understanding and support, and to my family, both here and in France, for supporting me in this journey.

—Thomas Besluau

Contents at a Glance

Contents

About the Authors

Jamie Kurtz has over 15 years of experience working in a variety of roles as engineer and solution provider. While working as a developer and tester for an education software company, and working as a developer in a high-temperature super conductivity lab, he received his Bachelor of Science from Western Michigan University—double majoring in Physics and Mathematics and minoring in Computer Science.

From there, Jamie worked in DBA, project lead, team lead, manager, architect, tester, and developer roles in various industries, including telecommunications, fulfillment, manufacturing, banking, and video intelligence/security. He is currently working as consultant and group manager at Fusion Alliance in Indianapolis, IN.

In addition to love and enjoyment of his beautiful wife and two daughters (and dog and two cats), and great times playing drums at an awesome local church, Jamie continually seeks opportunities to share his passion for helping software teams rapidly deliver real and measurable value to their customers.

Thomas Besluau has over five years of experience as a software engineer, most of it as an open source CMS developer (Drupal, Plone, Wordpress) and holds a Master of Science in Information and Communication Sciences from Ball State University as well as a Master of Engineering in Networking and Computer Science from Telecom Bretagne, France.

Thomas moved from software engineer to freelancer to consultant and Drupal preacher and is currently working as a Software Architect at ExactTarget, a Salesforce.com company in Indianapolis, IN.

Having a real passion for automation, polished processes, and not reinventing the wheel, Thomas likes to discover and experiment with a large variety of software, tools, and technologies to add to his toolbox, when not spending time with his lovely wife or his spoiled bulldog.

About the Technical Reviewer

Anirudh Prabhu is a software engineer at Xoriant Corporation with four years experience in web designing and development. He is responsible for JavaScript development and maintainance in his project. His areas of expertise are HTML, CSS, JavaScript, and Jquery. When not working, Anirudh loves to read, listen to music, and practice photography.

Acknowledgments

I would like to thank everyone at Apress for giving Thomas and I the opportunity to share what we believe is a real opportunity for teams to save time and money in building and maintaining software. In particular, Ewan Buckingham for getting yet another book off the ground—even when it first looked like a crazy idea ("another Drupal book?"). And to Anamika Panchoo, who tirelessly worked with Thomas and I, often feeling a bit like pushing a pair of boulders uphill, I am sure, to make sure all of the pieces came together according to the usual Apress excellence.

Thank you, as well, to the technical reviewers: Jeff Pickett and Anirudh, who not only provided great technical feedback, but also brought many years of authorship experience to the table, helping us craft an awesome story about Drupal's strength as a development platform. Jeff even went to so far as to use the techniques in this book on several projects where Drupal provided a great back end for some mobile applications.

Lastly, I want to thank Thomas, for opening my eyes to a whole new world of open source oriented development. Sometimes I feel like I've taken the "red pill." Seriously, I love to learn, and never tire of finding out that a better way exists. Without Thomas's patience in helping me reconcile my nearly two decades of closed source development in the enterprise world with his experience and insight around Linux and open source development, I wouldn't have been able to write this book. So thank you, Thomas. And yes, I just might call you Morpheus from now on. Looking forward to many more years of exploration with you.

—Jamie Kurtz

I would also like to thank all the great folks at Fusion Alliance, particularly Rick Bryson, Mike Gilbert, and David Schroeder, for investing their time and supporting our effort to use Drusal as a solution for an ever increasing variety of projects.

And last but certainly not least, I want to thank Jamie for getting us started on this adventure. It takes quite a bit of energy and a sharp, open mind to not only grasp but quickly adopt a new way of developing software. Jamie's solid experience in software development and relentless challenging of any reasoning shortcut in our process of optimizing application development helped us both better understand how Drupal could be used in the enterprise world. Thank you for your idea to put those thoughts into a book, and your dedication and leadership during the whole adventure. This is but the beginning...

—Thomas Besluau

Introduction

As Vice President of Solutions Delivery for Fusion Alliance, I've found myself dealing with many of the issues facing organizations today. How do you offer more value to your customers in less time for less cost and still meet the robust challenges of developing enterprise-level applications. I've found myself countless times lamenting over ways to improve time to market, reduce cost, maintain quality, while meeting the demands of developers who want to build solutions that challenge their intellect and provide a sense of reward. I am constantly being asked why we have to follow certain procedures and fit into certain roles.

In late 2012, we had begun to look for ways to be faster to market at more competitive costs; our market demanded it. It started with us developing a build and buy strategy, focusing on Content Management Systems (CMSs). We had been working on a number of CMS platforms, but had been hearing really good things about Drupal and its ability to meet enterprise customers' needs. We began by bringing on a Drupal expert, Thomas Besluau. Thomas was passionate about what Drupal could do not only as a CMS but as a solutions platform. I then worked with Jamie Kurtz, our Application Solutions Manager, and Thomas to work on a mid-size Drupal implementation. Soon they began to work together not only delivering the project, but also coming up with a new ways to extend the capabilities of Drupal. We found that we could use it not only for delivering content management solutions but also as a way to quickly develop and deploy services and web sites.

That was what we'd been looking for and finally somebody was doing it. They were practicing what they preached: faster, smarter, and resulting in lower costs and higher value to the customer.

I look forward to using many of the techniques and practices outlined in this book and say thank you to Jamie and Thomas for challenging the status quo.

Rick Bryson
Fusion Alliance, Inc.
Indianapolis, IN

CHAPTER 1

■ ■ ■

A New Era of Software Development

As an experienced software developer, manager, or anyone else involved in building or maintaining software, have you ever found yourself thinking: "There must be a better way?" Are you at a point in your career where you've started so many different projects and code bases on a particular platform that you wonder why you spend at least half of your development budget on the same thing, over and over? Do you find yourself continually seeking out new languages and new tools, because you can't bear the thought of yet again writing the same code for authentication, logging, caching, data access, database tables, startup, shutdown, themes, styles, navigation, data types, validation, auditing, deployment, and testing?

Or, maybe you've inherited some bit of legacy code many times over, and still find yourself puzzling over why it's so hard and risky to add a new attribute to a class or an entity? If all of your code is generally within the same technology, why does adding a simple Surname field to a User entity require three days of specifying, designing, coding, and testing? Why must the new property require adding a new column to a table, adding the new property to a data class, adding the same property to a model class, adding the new property's mapping to your data access layer and/or stored procedures, binding the new property to at least one page or form, adding validation and authorization logic around the new property, writing a database deployment script for the new column, and then updating your test suite to check for any errors introduced by this "small" effort of adding a new entity property?

After all, you say, nearly all enterprise-level applications contain users, pages or forms, validation of some kind, data stored in a database, deployment and configuration, and on and on, right? Sure, you make excellent use of code libraries and various toolkits. These libraries and toolkits keep you from writing framework-level functionality over and over. Hopefully, you're at least not writing loggers or dependency injection containers or encryption classes from scratch. But you know that even wiring together dozens of nice libraries is still a lot of work, and is still done over and over with each new project, and still introduces more than an insignificant quantity of bugs.

If, like us, you are looking to reduce project time and cost, reduce the amount of time and effort spent writing the same basic foundational code over and over, and drastically reduce test surfaces and bugs in new applications, then this book is for you. With much excitement and passion, we believe there is indeed a better way. We believe the practice of software development within IT organizations is on the cusp of a new era, a whole new way of developing enterprise line-of-business applications. And we believe that without this leap forward, without a whole new way of approaching software development, the software craftsman that exists today will be squeezed out. The era of uber geeks forever pouring over miles and miles of really cool code just to help a business department realize some basic value or opportunity is gone. The software craftsman must adapt.

Yes, there is a better way. Yes, you can reduce the time and money it takes to create enterprise applications. Yes, you can reduce the number of bugs in your applications; or, at least, change the nature of the bugs into being more functionally oriented (as opposed to mistakes in the code). Within just a couple of sections in this chapter, you will start to see what we're talking about. And by the end of Chapter 3, Business Application Fundamentals, you will possess the tools needed to quickly create the foundations of an enterprise business application—without writing any code at all. Throughout the remainder of the book, you will explore, one at a time, various aspects of enterprise application development and their corresponding implementations as we see them in this new era.

Although it's rather unlikely, you may still need to write some code. So we'll also show you how to integrate custom code into this new way. And finally, we'll share with you some basic tactics on selling the new way to the rest of your organization. After all, everyone needs to be on board for a change of this kind, even when it results in reduced time and effort and an increase in overall quality and profit.

Let's start with a brief look at the evolution of software languages as they relate to the discipline of application development.

A Brief History of Application Development

This book is all about using the Drupal content management system (CMS) to give you that much-needed quick start in building enterprise-level web applications and services. Shortly, we are going to walk through the ins and outs of what it means to be an enterprise system, and what we demand of a development platform capable of supporting such a system. In short, we believe the Drupal CMS is an excellent platform on which you can build most of the systems that today you build from scratch.

In order to better understand the benefits of choosing a CMS as a development platform, you need to understand a bit about how we got to where we are today. In general, the world of application development is very motivated to reduce time to market, reduce bugs and risk, and increase the happy-factor of both the system's developers and its users.

While a few outliers seem to stumble upon piles of cash, allowing them to ignore any motivation to reduce cost, most IT organizations have to survive in the very real world of ever shrinking budgets yet higher and higher demand for frequent releases of new features and bug fixes. As such, software engineers and their managers have been working hard to improve both the processes involved in application development, as well as the tools and languages used to build the applications.

Language Evolution

Over the past 50+ years, software development languages have been steadily evolving and maturing. Going back to the time of punch cards, languages have always had at their heart the main goal of telling the computer what to do. Even today, with languages much more elegant and efficient than punch cards, the main goal is still simply to tell the computer what to do. These languages have come through several generations and areas of focus, starting with the 1950s and 60s where languages were borne out of both the scientific and business communities. For example, as you can see in Table 1-1, the 50s and 60s saw the birth of Fortran, COBOL, Basic, and Lisp.

Table 1-1. *History of Software Languages*

1950s and 60s - The early years	1955 - Fortran 1958 - Lisp 1959 - COBOL 1964 - Basic
1970s - Laying foundations of object-oriented and other styles of programming	1970 - Pascal 1972 - Smalltalk 1972 - C 1978 - SQL
1980s - Evolving paradigms, building on foundations from previous decade	1983 - C++ 1986 - Objective-C 1987 - Perl
1990s - The Internet, dynamic languages, introduction of virtual machines	1991 - Python, VB, and HTML 1993 - Ruby 1995 - Java, Javascript, and PHP

(continued)

Table 1-1. (*continued*)

2000s - Higher abstractions, AOP, mobile applications, lots of Javascript frameworks	2001 - C#, VB.NET
	2003 - Scala
	2005 - F#
	2006 - jQuery
	2007 - Clojure
	2009 - NodeJS

In the 1970s, language creators—unbeknownst to them—were laying the foundations for various styles of programming for years to come. It was in this decade that object-oriented programming (OOP) was born, as well as the first incarnation of the SQL database querying language. Smalltalk and C were later combined to create Objective-C in the 1980s, which is used today for Mac and iOS programming. The Basic language from way back in the 60s evolved into Visual Basic in 1991. The C language gave rise to C++, and then Java in the late 1990s. In addition to Java, dynamically typed langauges and run-time interpreters running on top of virtual machines typified advances made in the 90s. Many of today's Internet-oriented scripting languages were created in the 1990s, with PHP, HTML, Javascript, Ruby, and Python leading the way.

After the turn of the millennium, Microsoft followed in the footsteps of Java and C++ to create the .NET Common Language Runtime (CLR). C# was influenced most heavily by both those languages, with VB.NET being a next-generation .NET-based Visual Basic.

Beyond the statically typed languages introduced in the 1990s and 2000s, it might not be an overstatement to say that the first couple of decades of the 2000s will be most remembered for a tidal wave of Javascript libraries, packages, and toolkits. The most prominent, of course, will likely be the jQuery library, built to help us overcome the shortcomings and complexities of both JavaScript and a variety of browsers.

Programming languages have certainly come a long way in the past 50+ years. Most developers would agree that they can get new features and bug fixes into users' hands much faster with languages and toolkits such as Ruby, C#, and Javascript than one could do with Basic or C—especially given the distributed and security-focused nature of today's business applications. But in the end, it's all still centered on writing code. And for anything other than samples and "Hello World" applications, programmers write lots of code—even with the nice languages and libraries available to us.

Libraries, Toolkits, and Packages

Early on in the history of programming languages, programmers learned to bundle common code into libraries. As you probably know, these libraries allowed code to be shared across different applications. For example, one programmer might write a logging library, used to add debug or performance log entries to an application. Programmers would import shared code files into their applications and compile them into a single executable file. These days, programmers can import already-compiled packages, DLLs, gems, and other similar files. In fact, one of the latest technologies to invade the world of software development is what is commonly known as a package manager. These tools, usually driven from the command-line, let a programmer simply enter a command similar to the following to download and import a library directly into their system and/or application.

```
gem install json        // to install the Ruby json gem
npm install json        // to install the NodeJS json package
Install-Package json    // to install the JSON package into a .NET project
```

Programmers also learned to combine libraries and packages and other tools into toolkits—essentially, a tool box for software engineers. Sometimes these toolkits just contain a bunch of libraries. Other times they include libraries as well as scripts, helper utilities, emulators, debuggers, and many more such tools.

These libraries and toolkits help the modern-day programmer save time by not having to write and test basic infrastructure functionality every time they start a new project, or develop a new feature. The loggers are already written and hardened; the user controls have already been written and vetted through various user groups; and security libraries have already been built by smart people that know all the ins and outs of Internet-age security. As such, the programmer not only saves time, but hopefully reduces risk and bugs by virtue of leveraging already-tested libraries. And as today most of these libraries are published within the open source community, much of their vetting and fixing is spread across many developers with varying backgrounds and experience.

Even so, and per the point of this book, programmers still have to write a lot of code in order to stitch together all those libraries into a working application. And where there's code, there must be tests. Further, where there's new code, there will be bugs. So while the programmer is saving time and risk by using existing libraries, there is still a large untested gap between those libraries and a fully functional application. As we'll explore throughout this book, there actually is a big difference between code libraries and application-level modules—like those found on the Drupal platform.

When it comes to building applications faster, meeting users' needs better, and delivering with higher quality, we need a bigger leap than better languages and more libraries can offer.

The Real Cost of Developing Applications from Scratch

If you're reading this book, you've likely had to deal either directly or indirectly with the large up-front effort required in starting a project from scratch. That is to say, a certain amount of mental and emotional depression sets in when you, either as programmer or manager, have to once again create a new source tree from scratch, find and install a dozen or more libraries, create all of the new application's code projects and associated references, wire up the truly mundane components like authentication, logging, application startup and shutdown, caching, user access, navigation, on and on.

Those tasks can be fun the first and maybe second time you have to do them. But any time you, as a programmer, aren't adding real measurable business value, you feel it. And deep inside, you can't shake that feeling that configuring a logger yet again isn't adding a whole lot of value.

To avoid those depressing feelings of both working in a rut and of not delivering value quickly, we programmers tend to run toward new and trendy ways of doing the same old thing. We find a great new logger. Or a new library that helps us write tests just a little bit better. Or we jump into a whole new language—just to give us something new to play with. At least some fun and excitement can momentarily distract us from the lack of value being delivered. Then when project managers or customers come knocking, we say something to the effect of "we'll save lots of time if we use new library ABC instead of old library XYZ."

An Example of Libraries

As an illustration, let's walk through a quick collection of libraries and how we might use them for the case of building an application from scratch. In Table 1-2, you can see a short list of libraries typical in most applications. These are not specific to any one platform,such as Java, .NET, or PHP, but rather kept fairly generic on purpose.

Table 1-2. *Sample of Library Usage for Typical Enterprise Applications*

Library Functionality	Typical Implementation
User authentication	Custom code dealing with credential validation, "forgot password" feature, secure storage of user sign-on information; use of libraries for password encryption, password policies; building user interface for all related functionality
Content or entity types	Hand-written code classes representing each entity; need to build database tables to store entity data; also need to create mapping between classes and database, write data access or CRUD code, provide some bit of validation (both in the database and in the data access layer)
Data entry pages or forms	Web pages, desktop forms, Javascript UIs—all must be coded from the ground up; use of toolkits such as jQuery, WPF, or Java Forms provide base functionality and controls; required to custom write models for binding, controllers for user interaction, and presentation code or markup
Display pages for searching, reporting, information	Similar to data entry pages and forms, only less validation and more presentation code; must write custom layout; code must be written or imported to enable paging, sorting, grouping, and filtering of lists; reporting and exporting of page data typically relies on custom usage of third-party libraries—for example, export page to PDF
Image and file storage	Typically dealing with byte arrays, file/folder organization, and securing the image and file data; large data must be scrubbed or reduced; code must be written to archive or purge image and file data after a certain period of time; must write code to deal with thumbnails of images; typically still have to create all UI code
Business rules	Plenty of rules-related libraries available, but must be plugged into some host for execution; dealing with rule evaluation, binding, fail-fast, forward chaining, and so forth, not trivial; rule language itself must be learned, even sometimes defined and built from scratch; business rules must typically be configurable or parameterized, adding even more complexity
REST API	Once all data has been defined, another layer must be added to enable REST API access; must write code dealing with resource URLs and routes, access permissions, different media-types, service activation

You can see from the table that there's a lot of code to write just to enable the most basic application functionality. More likely than not, all of those pieces of functionality will be present in every application you write—especially when dealing with enterprise-level business applications.

Of course, so far we're only looking at the relative cost of code libraries. Even more important, writing code creates bugs; the more you write, the more bugs you will have. Period. So we must test, and test, and test some more. And not only are we testing business functionality, but we're largely testing all of that written-from-scratch code—all that code that surrounds those nice libraries.

Cost of Quality

You may have heard the term Cost of Quality mentioned on an application development project at one time or another. It's actually not strictly a software engineering term, but applies to most all types of engineering disciplines. It essentially helps us associate a cost (either relative or absolute) with efforts and consequences related to good and poor quality.

For example, the cost of finding a software bug early in the release process is orders of magnitude cheaper than finding it later in the release cycle. And, of course, letting customers find bugs not only introduces an even higher cost to fix the bugs, but typically includes with it some cost in terms of lost relationships, loss of trust, lost sales, and diminished reputation and referencability.

It is the aspect of this cost—dealing with tested, hardened, and complete functionality—that relates most directly to the topic of this book. When you as a programmer have to write a lot of code to assemble and configure a bunch of libraries, you are introducing risk and most certainly introducing bugs. Therefore, the cost of quality increases in two ways. First, more time and effort must be spent on prevention of customer-discovered bugs. And second, because you are introducing more code, which introduces more bugs, the cost of quality after release necessarily goes up; that is, time and money will be spent to remediate issues and repair relationships on account of bugs in the code.

Instead of having to write all that basic foundational code just to expose some library functionality, what if you could simply "turn on" authentication, or "turn on" business rules? Your bug count immediately drops significantly. This is especially true if the act of turning on authentication or business rules also includes the complete user interface components needed to support that functionality. So rather than having to write all the "glue code" around libraries, and then also create (from scratch) all of the user interface, a simple flick of a switch completely enables this functionality.

Much more will be said about the topic of enabling complete pieces of functionality in this manner. That is, after all, the crux of this book. But before we move on to what we believe to be a better way of developing software, ask yourself a few basic questions.

- In a typical release cycle, how much time do you and your team spend writing code, writing tests, testing the code, then fixing the code?

- Of that time, how much is spent on value-add business functionality, versus dealing with code-level or framework issues?

- How much time do you and your team spend learning new libraries on new projects?

- What kind of exposure and vulnerability come from your code? In other words, with all the code you write, what might happen if it doesn't work as planned —that is, there's a bug?

- What foundational functionality are you building from scratch today that has already been written, packaged, and published?

- How many common tasks of a development project—initial code base setup, releases, backup—have you been able to automate efficiently?

- Are you extremely competitive in bidding for projects that are architecturally close to some you've already done?

Answer these questions honestly. We believe such an honest examination will lead you to at least wonder if there's a better way.

A Better Way

Even though it may make sense to start an application from scratch for very specific use cases, for example, R&D, scientific research, or something no one has ever thought of before—as far as enterprise development is concerned, there is likely a quicker and more efficient way.

Most applications developed from scratch have the same set of components: authentication, user management, permissions, views, search, and so forth. As a developer or development manager, you know that if a set of tasks must be repeated for every project, it should be automated. Or, in the case of application components, packaged. Chances are someone else has already made a package for those. You can even jump one step higher in the automation process and have a platform easily manage those packages for you. This is where CMSs come in.

Ranking Application Development Approaches

Let us consider a scale ranking development automation. On one end of the scale, we have building an application from scratch. And on the other end, we have an advanced CMS like Drupal.

1. Custom development, from scratch.

2. Advanced IDEs, toolkits. Everything is still completely custom, but the use of IDEs like Eclipse, or toolkits like jQuery, make the development more convenient and quicker.

3. Packages, modules, libraries. If you find a package out there that does just what you're looking for, you don't need to code it all. For enterprise-level web applications, using packages only gets you a portion of the way there.

4. Web application frameworks. As opposed to packages that you import and use directly in your existing code base, frameworks are an existing code base to which you will add your custom code. Such platforms, like CodeIgniter, Tornado, or Ruby on Rails, allow you to have a vanilla application up and running right away and customize it progressively.

5. CMS. A CMS is either a particular type of web application framework, or layered on top of one. It brings a few core features to the table, like the ability to create, edit, and publish content (pages, blog posts, news articles). It often lets you manage users, roles, and permissions, as well as specific content workflows.

6. Advanced CMSs. A few CMSs, like Drupal, offer many features that are a step above normal content management. Instead of a platform that manages content, you can see them as a platform that can even manage its ability to manage content, making almost everything possible from a configuration perspective. In addition to this, an impressive community is supporting Drupal and contributing thousands of modules (pluggable packages that can be enabled and managed from the user interface and add features to Drupal) to make it harder everyday to find something Drupal cannot do.

The diagram in Figure 1-1 shows how those different methods compare based on two critical criteria: how quickly a new feature can be implemented using the method, and how early in the development process a working, presentable, and testable application can be released (regardless of completion).

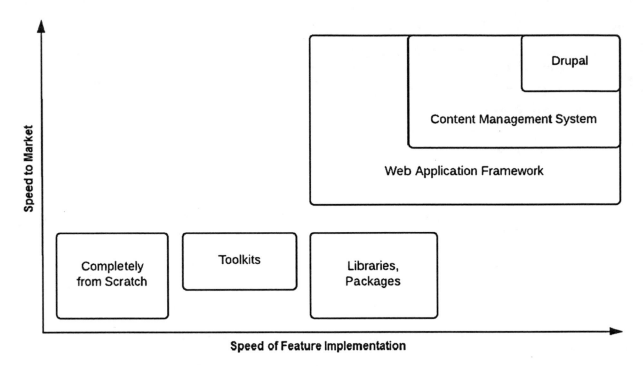

Figure 1-1. *Application development tools scale*

Advantages of Using a CMS

There are many reasons why you should consider using a CMS for your enterprise application development needs over starting development from scratch.

Competitive Edge

The most obvious advantage of using a CMS for a project instead of starting from scratch in .NET, Java, or PHP, is the time that you will save overall. You can have a fully functional web site up and running in minutes. Add the proper modules and your whole application's code base is complete. From there it is a simple matter of configuration and content.

Due to the shortened time required for putting together and deploying your site, you will also save on the overall project cost. Not to mention that with Drupal being an open source project, you won't have to pay a dime for it or any of its add-ons. If there is a metric that every single one of your clients or bosses will understand, it is certainly the total implementation cost of a project.

Whether you are building this web application for a customer or convincing your own managers of its need for your own company, coming up with such extremely diminished cost and implementation time will give you a boost in competitiveness over a custom-coded project. Even some improvement, cleanup, or bugfix related projects for an existing code base that was built from scratch could end up being cheaper if the entire system is rebuilt using the proper platform.

As you may not be the only person in town to think of using Drupal to reduce cost and time, keep in mind that your competitors may come up with application solutions that are built around CMSs. They would likely seriously underbid any attempts to compete by building the same application from scratch.

Being more competitive will also give you additional flexibility when pricing your solution. If your company is busy enough and lowering your bidding prices is not a priority, consider using CMSs to increase your profit instead. If time is of the essence, you can leverage this additional time you have to improve your processes, do more quality assurance, and add high availability considerations to deliver an end product that is far more polished.

More Stability, Security, Reliability

CMSs are not bug free, and every so often, a patch or security update has to be applied. Their overall stability and security is very high, however, and errors are handled properly. With a custom application, it will take quite a bit of extra time and effort to ensure appropriate security and ensure possible errors are properly contained.

A common issue with custom-made applications is that the more features you add over time, the messier they get. You need to make sure the new features you're adding are not breaking older ones or introducing security vulnerabilities.

If your application is designed with the ability to add features from an admin perspective, you don't have to worry about breaking something every time you make a change to it. Adding new features in Drupal is a key component of its architecture. The only time you would be in this situation is when you add a new module, which if you plan ahead shouldn't happen often at all.

An Up-to-Date Product

Libraries and toolkits change over time. New releases offer bug fixes and additional features, and some features become obsolete. And even if you were to maintain a code base with many aspects of your application already developed, you would need to keep it up to date with the latest changes in the toolkits and libraries you are using. Updating such libraries, of course, requires a significant investment in research, test regression, and deployment.

When using a CMS, updates and upgrades also matter. The difference is that for an open source CMS, there is a whole community of people taking care of this for you. Not only are they constantly releasing new versions of the CMS, they also relentlessly work on making more and better modules for it, so you will have even less work to do to put together your application (and subsequent updates) using the CMS.

Easier Processes

Who doesn't wish for more predictable software development projects? By using an enterprise-level CMS, you can put together solid development and management processes specifically designed for it. Not only will it make it easier on the person in charge of defining processes and best practices, it will also give you better control over your timelines and make your dependencies more predictable.

By starting every project with the same code base, you will be able to automate your code foundation creation, regression testing, deployment processes, and so forth. You could have an initial release up and running for the client to see in as little as one hour.

More Power to the User

Have you ever deployed a new release because of a missing comma or a letter to capitalize or a spelling mistake? With CMSs, the main objective is to keep the content well separated from the platform's functionalities and features, allowing for site administrators or authors to easily manage content without a developer having to jump in each time. Changes to content are not necessarily cause for a new release, and they don't need to involve the development staff.

Even if the required changes are a little too complicated for your client to make, there is a good chance you won't need to do a new release for it. It could be a new field to add to a content type, a font to change in the theme, or even adding a new element to the information displayed in a custom view. Most changes will be doable from the CMS's admin interface.

In the end, this represents substantial savings for the user and can easily be turned into a sales argument. Your clients will appreciate the fact they are not dependent on you to make any slight change to their site. You would be surprised to see how often what seems to be a major new feature can easily be implemented from the admin interface in a few clicks.

Quick Library Comparison

Let's take a quick look at the list of libraries found in Table 1-1 from the previous section, "An Example of Libraries," and see if those are already covered by a basic Drupal setup with a few modules (see Table 1-3).

Table 1-3. *Drupal Comparison with Basic Libraries*

Library Functionality	Equivalent Drupal Functionality
User authentication	Part of the core. That's the least you would expect from a CMS.
Content or entity types	Part of the core. You can create any new content type you want or edit an existing one with a variety of fields. More field types can be available with some additional modules.
Data entry pages or forms	There's a module for that: Webforms. Not only does it provide you with easy-to-make customizable forms, but it also stores the user input for you, or emails it to you.
Display pages for searching, reporting, information	The most popular Drupal module of them all: Views. Let's put it this way: it can grab any data you want from any content within the application and display it the way you want based on static and dynamic conditions. No querying, templating, or rendering work for you!
Image and file storage	Depending on what type of file you want Drupal to handle (images, pdfs, videos,and so forth) it can be part of the core or in stable modules. Again, you just need to turn the feature on.
Business rules	There's a module for that: Rules. Based on the proven "Event Condition(s) Action(s)" concept, you can automate a variety of business rules. And these business rules can be associated with user data entry, internal events, or even REST service endpoints.
REST API	There's a module for that: Services. Enables web services for Drupal, allowing you to create REST endpoints to login, manage users, query and updated content, and more!

Our Demonstration Enterprise Application

In this last section of this chapter, we will introduce the fictitious development project being used to showcase Drupal. This particular project was fabricated to best demonstrate all of the features we feel most enterprise-level applications would require.

What is Enterprise?

Before we jump into the project's subject, let's briefly discuss what we mean by "enterprise." This entire book is predicated on the idea that you can implement real enterprise applications with Drupal, so we should start by describing what that means. While no formal definition exists, we want to at least get ourselves on the same page with respect to the types of applications we are talking about.

In his famous book, *Patterns of Enterprise Application Architecture* (Addison-Wesley Professional, 2012), Martin Fowler states that "enterprise applications are about the display, manipulation, and storage of large amounts of often complex data and the support or automation of business processes with that data." Key in that statement, for our purposes, is the part about "business processes." We aim to address real business process problems, solving them in the context of an application built on Drupal.

In this book, we draw a clear distinction between consumer-level applications and those built to support lines of business. Indeed, throughout this book, we cover concepts that could also be described as "line of business." That is, we are not attempting to provide new or better ways to build marketing web sites. Nor are we trying to talk you into using Drupal to build a mobile application. And we're also assuming that you are not reading this book because you need a simple CMS. Though many people use Drupal for all of these reasons, and many more, our desire for this book is that you see Drupal as a platform on which you can go about building enterprise business applications.

Enterprise applications often have to deal with more difficult security concerns; it isn't unusual to require LDAP integration with Windows Active Directory, or similar. Enterprise applications typically require complex and robust business rules, data entry screens, and data validation. Such applications also tend to benefit from options, plug-ins, and a wide array of configuration settings. It's also very common in enterprise-level applications to alter navigation and layout according to user roles and domain groups. And while a simple web site might include two or three roles for users, an enterprise application may contain hundreds or thousands of different roles and groups.

Another key aspect of enterprise business applications is system integration. While simple marketing web sites and other single-purpose consumer applications typically stand alone, most enterprise applications require a significant level of integration with other applications in the enterprise. This means constructs such as SOAP and REST services, data imports and exports, scheduled jobs, flexible data formats, and batch processing are critical to its success. These applications rarely run in isolation. In this book, we will show you how to integrate Drupal into a larger enterprise infrastructure.

As we progress through this book, you will be introduced to implementing other line-of-business–oriented features in Drupal, including: business continuity, data migration, policy compliance, reporting and analytics, scaling up and down, globalization and localization, security, auditing, and much more.

Bottom line: remember that this book is about using Drupal to address those complex concerns that typically drive you to build applications from scratch. We believe there's a better way, even when building and maintaining large enterprise-level applications.

The Demo Project

Throughout the book, we will be using a single enterprise-level example in order to have some consistency. As we walk through different concepts, we will discuss and show how they apply to this example.

K&B Restaurants is a fictitious restaurant franchise, with about 25 locations in 4 states. The company was leaving it to every branch to make their own web site and recently decided to centralize their whole web presence into a single web site while leaving the possibility for branches to promote special offers and events locally.

The new site must include the following features:

- User management with four types of users:

  - Visitor (anonymous)

  - Customer/user account (can choose a preferred location and can set up preferences to receive special offer coupons and events)

  - Branch manager account (can edit own branch information and create local events and special offers)

  - Site Administrator (can manage the whole site, edit all branches, and create global events and special offers)

- Special offers: branch managers must be able to easily create and manage special offers. They will be specific to a given location and be accessible to users based on location and special offer preferences. Additionally, web site administrators will be able to create global special offers that are honored by every location, and can be automatically emailed to users based on preferences.

- Special offer printing and emailing: special offers and events must have an option to be emailed to people on a certain date based on their preferences. This should be an option when creating a special offer and the emailing should be handled automatically by the site.

- Reporting dashboard to customer preference metrics

- Creating, pulling, and updating any user or content on the site, as well as running batch updates of content and rules from an external REST client

- Nightly maintenance database backup

- Pulling updated list of employees from an external REST service

- Ability to import large amount of content from external sources

- Gathering site use analytics and customer satisfaction

Summary

In this chapter, you were presented a brief history of application development, starting with the first software languages introduced well over 50 years ago. The evolution of these languages, including libraries and toolkits, was discussed in light of incremental progress toward reducing cost and time in building applications.

We then discussed the "real" cost of developing applications from scratch, including the concept of Cost of Quality—which speaks to the increasing cost of maintaining software quality before and after a release. This cost was used to introduce what we believe is a better way of building software: using Drupal as an enterprise application development platform, instead of assuming you need to build software from scratch.

Finally, you were presented our sample project for this book, which you can follow along and build with us as we go. This sample project will include most of the concerns faced today when building enterprise business applications.

In the next chapter you will begin learning about the Drupal CMS, its main features, architecture, and step-by-step instructions on installing a complete Drupal system.

CHAPTER 2

The Drupal Content Management System

It's time to start talking about Drupal. Thus far, we've focused more on general software development, its history, and a (hopefully) convincing argument against building applications from scratch as a matter of practice. While the two of us certainly consider ourselves developers at heart, we have an interest in providing business solutions as quickly and efficiently as possible. And if it's not clear already, it is our belief that Drupal offers one of the best development platforms for doing so.

In this chapter, you will be introduced to the Drupal Content Management System (CMS) as a platform for enterprise application development. As you read about Drupal's capabilities, we will introduce you to a few of the most compelling reasons to choose it as your platform of choice.

As you read through this introduction to Drupal, and all that we believe it offers, remember that this book is not about writing code in PHP. What it is about is doing as much as you can without writing any code. As such, there is a focus in this chapter and beyond on Drupal as it relates to core features, modules, themes, and other such platform-related capabilities. If all goes well, you won't have to write any code at all. But if that scenario does come up, we'll show you near the end of the book how to integrate a Drupal-based application with other custom applications and components. And in that case, you can build them in whatever tool and technology you feel most comfortable with. You are certainly not constrained to write PHP applications directly in Drupal.

Introduction to Drupal

Drupal is an open source CMS, written in PHP, that runs on Windows, Mac, or Linux. As you'll see shortly, it is highly modularized, encouraging the development of small, single-purpose components, each adding a small piece of application functionality. It was originally developed in 2000 by a Dutch student named Dries Buytaert as a small news site with a built-in webboard. The software was later released as an open source project in 2001.

Drupal picked up steam a few years later, and is now competing with Joomla as the second most used of all CMSs—second only to the immensely popular WordPress. At the time of this writing, millions of web sites around the world are running Drupal.

Before we explore some basic features in Drupal, you need to understand that Drupal is, at its heart, a CMS. That is, it was designed to facilitate the publication and maintenance of content. Of course, and as you will see shortly, the concept of content can be applied to just about any piece of data—that is, not just web pages or blog posts. Content in Drupal can be used to track all kinds of enterprise business data. And all of this data is indexed and can be searched with a variety of powerful search features built into the system and available as downloadable modules.

In addition to storing data, a CMS typically offers version control of that data. This means that all changes to the content are tracked, and can be viewed in a log of changes that details the user who made the change, the date they made it, the actual changes made, and optionally a comment provided by the user.

Finally, like most CMSs, Drupal supports fully customizable layout and styling of the stored content. By default, the content's fields are displayed in a simple list or table. But by leveraging various capabilities within Drupal, including a set of layout rules and custom CSS, a user can create just about any desired user experience. This also includes, as you will see later on, the ability to create custom calculated fields, where a field used for display can be calculated from some combination of other fields and some business and formatting rules.

Overview of Core Features

Drupal really isn't meant to be packed with features in its out-of-the-box core version. While the core's objective is to be limited to a small set of very stable and basic features, there are plenty of modules available to add additional features and capabilities. Recall from Chapter 1 that the Drupal community provides more than 20,000 different modules—not including additional themes and distributions.

In this section, you will learn about the basic set of core features on which nearly all applications are built. As we progress through building our sample application, additional modules will be added that fulfill specific functionality needed.

User Management

In Drupal, like in most good CMSs, the basic user account is not directly associated with a set of permissions regarding what they can or cannot see or do. Permissions are associated with roles, and users belong to one or more roles.

Permissions

A permission in Drupal is a simple task that is either allowed or not. It is purely binary and is represented through the default management interface by a checkbox. They are accessible from the "people" tab, under the "permissions" subtab. There you will see a list of all permissions with a check box per role per permission. There are quite a few of them in the core, and most modules you install will add new permissions to the list. It is very important as a site administrator that you keep an eye on those permissions, as they are what differentiate a simple anonymous user from an all-powerful administrator. Figure 2-1 shows you a few examples as you will find them on the site.

Figure 2-1. *Sample of Drupal permissions*

Roles

Roles are an abstract concept used only to hold a given set of permission settings. Users can then be assigned a role and will automatically get the permissions of the role. When a user has several roles, he or she will get all permissions that are enabled for each role. Meaning the most restrictive role will be overridden by the most powerful.

You can also think of roles as groups or categories of users. They are usually a simple yet important part of the application's design. Table 2-1 shows the three roles that Drupal comes with by default.

Table 2-1. *Explanation of default Drupal roles*

Name	Description
Anonymous	Every user visiting the site without authenticating falls automatically into this role. By default, it has the most restrictive permissions.
Authenticated user	You got it, it's the role automatically assigned to everyone who has logged in. A simple use-case for it compared to the Anonymous role would be for news sites where logged-in users have access to more content than simple visitors. You could even have a third role called "Paid user" that designates users who have paid to see even more content or specials.
Administrator	The site's ruler. Administrator has all permissions. It is a good idea to create sub-admin accounts with less power when delegating some of the site administration. As a rule of thumb for securing just about any resource, a user should possess only the minimum permissions they need. Adding a user to the Administrator role simply because they need to edit some content is a really bad idea. Instead, create a "Content editor" role that has the same permissions as Authenticated, with an additional one: "edit own content" or even "edit any content."

Users

Drupal's user account can be assigned one or more roles. It holds information about the user: user name, password, e-mail address, and so forth. As shown by Figure 2-2, there are ways to easily filter through users; and several batch operations are possible, such as blocking users or unblocking them, and adding or removing a role to the selected users. In other words, the user administrative interface allows you to update many users with a single update.

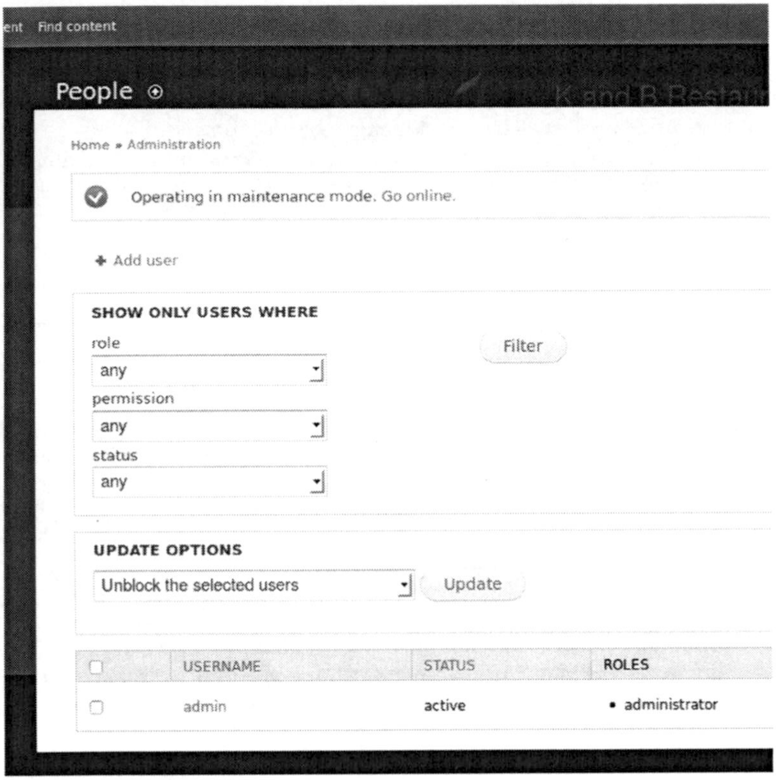

Figure 2-2. People page

In addition to basic user management, Drupal also allows you to add additional attributes to a user account. And as you'll see later, the fields you add can be of any type, not just text fields.

Content, ownership, workflows

A priori, a CMS is all about content. But what is this content and how is it organized?

Content Type

Its name is right on! A content type is a type of content; for instance a page, or an article, or anything you want, really. Drupal lets you create and customize any content type you need, like promotional pages, events, clubs, slideshows, and so forth. It is very similar to the concept of a class in object-oriented programming. Indeed, a good Drupal architect certainly has a good object-oriented approach.

Content Item

A content item is an instance of a given content type. For example, your "about us" page would be a content item, of the "page" content type. And your latest blog post is an item of the "blog entry" content type (by the way, blogging is part of the Drupal core and just needs to be enabled).

Field

Fields can hold pretty much any kind of data: a number, a date, html code, a novel, a list, a simple binary value, a password, a file, an image, and much more. They are defined at the content type level and Drupal lets you customize your content types with as many fields as you want, with the option to make them mandatory—in which case a content item will force the user to fill in the field in order to create or update the item.

Some modules make additional fields available, as well as additional widgets, that are associated with a field and allow for different user experiences when filling up the field—for example, having a nice date picker instead of a simple text field to enter a date.

In Table 2-2, you can see how these constructs in Drupal are very similar to certain constructs in an object-oriented language.

Table 2-2. *Similarity between Drupal and OO constructs*

CMS/Drupal concept	Object-Oriented equivalent
Content Type	Class
Content	Instance
Field	Attribute
Reference Field	Relationship

Modules, Themes, and Libraries

Instead of trying to be a do-it-all CMS, Drupal has a very sane and pluggable approach to adding new features. You can use an independant package, completely separate from the core's code base, called a module, to make an additional feature available. You can place the module in the site's file system under a dedicated folder where you put all your site's modules. Once added to the Drupal folder structure, the module becomes immediately visible to the Drupal site, under the "Modules" tab. From there, you simply click a check box to enable the module.

In a very similar way, under a different folder, you can add themes to your Drupal site. Themes are the look and feel of the site, and are more of a graphical design concern, whereas modules are an architectural concern. They work the same way, though: you drop their code into a dedicated folder and they become available to your site under the "Appearance" tab.

Finally, libraries are typically third-party products that are required for a module to work. But because they are not specific to this module, they can be used by other modules, as well. They are a separate piece of software, and they are stored in a separate location from the modules that use them. Examples of libraries would include PDF generation or HTML editor libraries.

In the Age of Apps

As discussed in Chapter 1, the general approach of building applications from scratch is getting ever more expensive. All of the well-tested functionality available to developers on platforms such as Drupal continues to make building it yourself a losing proposition. The key to all of this functionality is actually something very familiar to just about everyone in the developed world these days: apps.

The concept of apps has been around for a while, of course. In this context, we're talking about discrete pieces of software that you can download and install into your system, and that provide a specific piece of functionality. If you've ever used a computer, you've certainly used apps of one kind or another. Office-related applications, graphics editing suites, accounting packages, browsers, calculators, and so on. Those are all considered apps. However, one thing forever changed the landscape of apps. That is, the manner in which apps are discovered and delivered.

In mid-2008, to support their revolutionary new iPhone, Apple introduced the App Store—a single online location where any iPhone owner could easily select and download thousands of utility, business, productivity, and gaming applications. Suddenly, installing apps became much more than something only highly trained IT professionals did. The app store meant that literally anyone could quickly and easily (and cheaply) add new functionality to their iPhone. As it turned out, the apps concept—with its ease of discovery and super-simple approach to buying and installing—became a key driver in propelling the iPhone into technology stardom.

There's a Module for That

You've no doubt heard the iPhone commercials repeating the phrase "there's an app for that." In this book, we're going to make a slight update: "there's a module for that." In Drupal, the unit of deployment used for adding specific pieces of functionality is called the module. And similar to the iPhone and its apps, these modules—and their supporting architecture—are what make Drupal such a powerful enterprise development platform.

From the beginning, when Drupal was originally built as a small collaboration tool back in 2001, the system was architected with a modular "core." And to this day, only a handful of features are built into the Drupal core, with everything else being implemented in separate modules. In fact, per Drupal extensibility practices, modules are kept completely isolated from the core, stored in separate folders and interacting with the core and other modules using a strong developer-centric API.

This strong consideration and support for modularity meant that developers could easily extend the platform. Further, the Drupal community maintains a central web site from where you can discover and download nearly all modules. At the time of this writing, the Drupal.org web site lists over 20,000 such modules. Of course, as the number of modules has increased over time, the need for developers to create new modules in order to support particular business needs has slowly decreased. In other words, thanks to its extension-friendly architecture, Drupal has created a massive community where so much functionality is available by way of modules that one rarely finds the need to actually create a new module.

The Drupal core itself is modular as well. The only difference being what ships with Drupal, and what doesn't. Let's look at some of the modules included in the 7.x release of the Drupal core. Table 2-3 lists a sampling of the more popular modules that are included by default. These descriptions were taken directly from a 7.19 version install of Drupal. Note that previous major releases of Drupal—such as Drupal 6, are quite a bit different architecturally. Table 2-3 really only applies to version 7.x. However, minor releases within the 7.x lineage, such as 7.19 or 7.22, will be the same as far as the modules involved.

Table 2-3. *Sample of Drupal core modules*

Module	Description
User management	Manages the user registration and login system
Search	Enables site-wide keyword searching
OpenID	Allows users to log into your site using OpenID
Blogs	Enables multi-user blogs
Forums	Provides discussion forums
Taxonomy	Enables the categorization of content
Menus	Allows administrators to customize the site navigation menu
Field type: text	Defines simple text field types
Field type: list, options	Defines list field types; use with Options to create selection lists
Field type: file	Defines a file field type

The 7.19 version of Drupal contains a little over 40 modules that ship as the core. These alone are sufficient to build most basic web sites, blogs, collaboration portals, and the like. But to turn your Drupal system into a real working enterprise application, you will likely need to install at least a few non-core modules.

THERE'S A MODULE FOR THAT

As developers, it's very natural (and quite fun, really) to immediately start thinking of how you might design and code a certain piece of functionality. Most of us have made a decent living doing exactly that. But in this book, we want to challenge you to get in the habit of thinking maybe "there's a module for that"— TAMFT. Similar to Apple's phrase "there's an app for that," we believe that on the Drupal platform, most functionality has already been built.

It will take some work, some self-discipline, and some quality time just turning on some modules before a TAMFT mindset will take its place at the forefront of your daily thoughts. But eventually, if you stick with it, you will find yourself liberated. You will find that simply downloading and turning on some small discrete feature will free you to become a true solution provider. And that is, after all, what we are first and foremost— above developers or designers or managers. We are solution providers.

No doubt as you begin working with Drupal to create enterprise applications, you will find that the core modules are not quite enough. This is where the 20,000+ modules available on Drupal.org come in. In Table 2-4, you will find a sample of the more popular non-core modules available for your Drupal system.

Table 2-4. *Sample of Drupal.org non-core modules*

Module	Description
CKEditor	WYSIWYG HTML editor for use on any text field in your application
Views	Allows you to design a page with any layout you want, showing any data you want— static or dynamic/calculated— and put it anywhere you want within the site
Rules	Define conditionally executed actions based on occurring events
Captcha	Those little blocks of hard to-read text that attempt to differentiate a human from a computer.
Google Analytics	Adds the Google Analytics web statistics tracking system to your web site
Printer, e-mail and PDF versions	Generates printer-friendly, PDF, and e-mail versions of any content in Drupal
Calendar	Displays dates as a calendar
Commerce	Full-blown shopping cart for an eCommerce application
Filedepot	Document management with locking, versioning, tagging, keywords, and organization (similar to document libraries in Microsoft's SharePoint)
REST service	Expose a REST endpoint for any content type in the application, with configurable permissions and allowed operations
Backup and Migrate	Easily back up and restore part or all of your Drupal application's data
Various field types	Extend Drupal with field types for e-mail addresses, embedded Youtube videos, images,and so forth
OpenID Provider	Allows users of your site to log in to any other OpenID-enabled site using their Drupal password and identity
LDAP	LDAP integration for user authentication and authorization
Antivirus	Provides antivirus scanning for files uploaded to your Drupal system

As you can see, the modules available to you cover a wide range of features and functionality. Many such features also provide enterprise-level business functionality, such as LDAP integration, filedepot, antivirus, and various backup and restore modules. Throughout this book, we will be using these modules, and many more, to create a sample enterprise application on Drupal.

Assessing Module Quality

With over 20,000 modules available for Drupal, it can be a little overwhelming to find something that both fits your business need, and is also of sufficient quality for the given enterprise environment. In this section, you will see a few key metrics available on the Drupal.org site's module page that can help you assess the module's relative quality. Leveraging these metrics is, of course, a subjective process. But they can certainly help you obtain some sense of historical quality as well as ongoing maintenance and stability.

Releases

Nearly every module on Drupal.org will include a table of releases. They are generally broken up into recommended, development, and "other." It is important, of course, that the module provide a version that runs on your version of Drupal. The versioning scheme of modules will give you this information. A module's version is specified in the format Drupal_version-module_version. For example, if a module is on its 4.6 release, which runs on any version of Drupal in the 7.x lineage, the module's full version will be 7.x-4.6. If it can only run on a given version of Drupal, you will see something like this: 7.19-4.6.

Not only is it important to make sure a module version is available for your version of Drupal, but it should also be a non-development version. Most modules will include a "dev" release— used for ongoing development activities, and also a stable release or "recommended" release. If a module only provides a dev release, it should serve as a warning for you— the module has never been released and is still undergoing development and/or testing. It's possible that the module will never provide a stable release. Or, it could be that the module is simply very new and hasn't reached stable status yet.

If the module doesn't provide a stable release, another metric you can use is the release dates. If the only release is a dev release, and the last date listed is only a few weeks ago, then it is likely the module is well on its way to providing a stable release. However, if the last date is a few years ago, then it's likely the module has been abandoned.

Commit History

Because Drupal modules are open source, you have full access to view source code commit history. And similar to viewing commit history on any other open source project, you can use a module's commit history to determine whether or not the module is under active development. Of course, a module doesn't need to be under active development to be of high quality or of use to you. But, it is certainly an indication of intent to maintain the code, fix bugs, and add new features. If the last commit was made two or three years ago, you might want to think twice before installing the module.

Number of Downloads and Installs

The number of times a module has been downloaded is also available to you for review. This number will vary widely across modules, and a lower number doesn't necessarily mean lower quality. The popular Views module has been downloaded near 4 million times, which tells you it is definitely being used heavily and has been thoroughly tested by the community.

Additionally, the number of reported installs is an indication of active use— even beyond the number of downloads. A healthy number of installs is certainly an indicator of quality, in that many people use the module and are actively contributing to its overall test coverage.

Distributions

A quick word about distributions. They are available on the Drupal.org web site as well as many other open source and commerical sites. Simply put, distributions are a mechanism for packaging up multiple modules and themes into ready-made Drupal-based applications. For example, one of the most popular distributions is called Commerce Kickstart, as it combines the Drupal Commerce module with a bunch of smaller required modules, a demo database, and a custom built back office user interface. As another example, the OpenChurch distribution includes many modules and default configuration options that most churches would need when building a public web site. Out of the box, the distribution includes a blog, event calendar, charitable giving page, a sermon podcast page, and a page formatted to list church staff members.

Community Support

As with any platform that prides itself on modularity and extensibility, the key to Drupal's success as such a platform lies in its community support. In the previous section, we discussed the large ecosystem of modules and themes available to Drupal users. All of those modules and themes come by way of the open source community surrounding Drupal. And with open source, the size of the community matters a great deal. Indeed, with any platform built to be an "app platform," a large community and a large number of apps or modules defines its success.

And so it is with Drupal. In terms of a CMS, its community size of over 25,000 developers is second only to that of WordPress. At over 20,000, it boasts more modules than any other CMS outside of WordPress. Drupal has long since passed that critical point, where lots of people got involved to offer more functionality and capability through modules, making the platform a better choice for web sites and enterprise applications, which brought more people to the platform, which resulted in more modules being developed, and so forth.

In addition to great community support, quite a few companies also offer enterprise-level support for Drupal. This is similar to Red Hat and its support offering for Linux. This kind of support can be very important for corporate enterprise installations of Drupal.

Drupal Setup

Drupal can run on Windows, Mac, or Linux. Most enterprise installations of Drupal are indeed on Linux, but knowing how to install and configure a Drupal site on Mac and Windows can be very beneficial within a team of developers and testers. In this section we walk through the details of installing a Drupal site on Windows and Linux, starting with some prequisites and then moving into Drupal itself and the awesomely powerful Drush command line tool.

The AMP Stack

People often wonder if Drupal is cross platform, and the answer to that is: wrong question! Drupal doesn't run on a given operating system but on top of an AMP (Apache, MySQL, PHP) stack. Therefore, Drupal will run on any OS that can handle an AMP stack. This includes Windows, Linux, and Mac OSX. In the next few sections, we will walk you through the Windows and Linux AMP installation and configuration. The Mac version of this process is only briefly described.

Once you have your AMP stack configured and Drupal installed, nearly everything else related to Drupal will be the same regardless of your platform. Thus we are spending a bit more time right now to make sure your foundation is configured properly. But once we get into the Drupal install itself, we will rarely make any reference to Windows, Linux, or Mac.

In addition to the AMP stack itself, you will also install Drush. Drush is going to be your time-saving tool for a lot of different operations, from a Drupal install to adding and enabling modules, not to mention migrations and whole-system backups. And since Drush is a command-line tool, it is perfect for all of those system batch jobs, installs, and upgrades needed in most enterprise environments.

WAMP Server (and Drush)

Before you even get started on this, note that you don't even need a real AMP stack on Windows, since Drupal will run with IIS as its web server application (instead of Apache) and SQL Server as its database (instead of MySQL). That said, we recommend starting with a true WAMP configuration, and then tweaking that later as you learn the system.

You can download a WAMP stack install from numerous sources. For this book, we used the 64-bit Apache 2.4.2 version from `http://www.wampserver.com`. The download itself is only about 30 MB, and you can simply accept the defaults when going through the installer.

Once installed, you can start the WAMP stack by finding the "Start WampServer" shortcut in the Windows Start menu. Once started, a small green WAMPSERVER icon will appear in the Windows Notification Area (bottom right-hand corner). Assuming you didn't already have IIS or another application using port 80, you can then use your browser to navigate to the WampServer's home page at `http://localhost`. If everything is working properly, you will see a page similar to Figure 2-3.

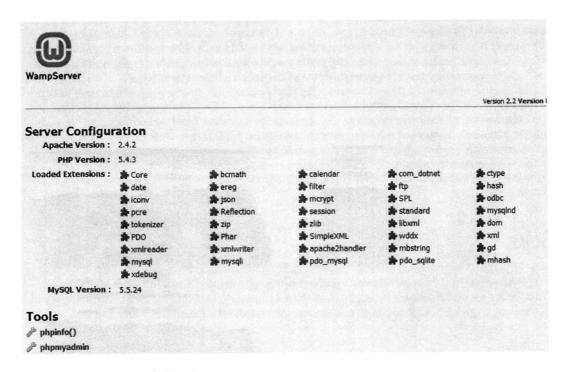

Figure 2-3. *Home page of WampServer*

CHANGE APACHE PORT WITH WAMP SERVER

If you need to update the port being used by Apache— for example, if IIS is already running and listening on port 80— you can simply use WAMP Server's notification icon to make the change. In the Windows status bar, in the lower right-hand corner of the desktop, click on the WAMP Server icon. Then select the Apache ➤ httpd. conf option. Once the file opens in Notepad, navigate to about line 58 where you should see the text Listen 80. Go ahead and change the port to something else, such as 8080. Save and close the file, and then use the same WAMP Server icon to restart the Apache server. This option is found under the Apache ➤ Service menu.

Note that if you accepted all defaults, the local folder being used for Apache web sites will be `c:\wamp\www`. Use this path when following the Drupal install instructions.

WINDOWS PATH FOR MYSQL

As a matter of good practice, you will likely need to have quick command-line access to the MySQL command-line client tool. This is true especially if you intend to use Drush, as described in the next section. By default, the WampServer install does not put the path to the MySQL command-line tool in your Windows PATH environment variable. As such, we strongly recommend that you do so now. The path to MySQL should be something like: `C:\wamp\bin\mysql\mysql5.5.24\bin`.

To install Drush on Windows, follow the instructions and downloads at `http://drupal.org/project/drush`. Note that in order to follow the Drush-based instructions below, and indeed to ensure Drush works properly, you will need to enable the "Register Environment Variables" option during the Drush installation.

LAMP Server (and Drush)

Installing an AMP stack on Linux can be done with just a few command-line statements. This approach utilizes the Tasksel package configuration tool. There are, of course, many different options for configuring a LAMP server. We've simply chosen one of the simplest options for this book. Also, note that throughout this book we've used Ubuntu 12.10 as our Linux distribution of choice.

Run the following commands in your Linux (Ubuntu) terminal. You will be prompted to enter a password for the root user in MySQL. Remember what you enter, as you'll need it later.

```
sudo apt-get update
sudo apt-get install tasksel
sudo tasksel install lamp-server
sudo apt-get install php5-gd php5-curl php-db
```

Those four commands are all that you need to get an AMP-based web server running. At this point, you can navigate your browser to `http://localhost`, and you should see a simple web page verifying that the install worked. If you changed the port to something other than port 80, be sure to enter it here —for example, `http://localhost:8080`. The web folder being used to store web site content is `/var/www`— which is where you will place the Drupal files in the next section.

Before we call it completely done, you can go ahead and install phpmyadmin. This will give you a nice web interface for administering the MySQL database. Run the following command. If prompted, select apache2 to run phpMyAdmin.

```
sudo apt-get install phpmyadmin
```

Be sure to choose the apache2 web server when given the option. And when prompted for the MySQL administrator user's password, enter the password you used when installing the LAMP server. Finally, for the phpmyadmin MySQL password, feel free to just hit Enter— accepting to let the installer generate a random password.

This will install and configure phpmyadmin against the MySQL database installed when you ran the previous statements. The only minor issue is that it will place the phpmyadmin files in a folder that is not actually used by apache. Remember from above that the lamp-server package install configured apache to run out of the `/var/www` folder. But the phpmyadmin install places its files in the `/usr/share/phpmyadmin` folder. Therefore, to make sure you can access the phpmyadmin site, run the following command to create a symbolic link from `/var/www` to the newly configured phpmyadmin folder:

```
sudo ln -s /usr/share/phpmyadmin /var/www/phpmyadmin
```

Now you can navigate your browser to `http://localhost/phpmyadmin` and you should see a login page. Use the root user, with the password you provided during the lamp-server install/configuration, to log into the site.

Lastly, install Drush by running the following command:

```
sudo apt-get install drush
```

Your LAMP server and Drush install should now be fully operational. Read on to install Drupal.

MAMP Server

Installing an AMP stack on Mac is very similar to the Linux install process. Please reference the `Drupal.org` site for further assistance.

Drupal Download and Install

Now that your AMP server is all set up, it is time to get the latest Drupal version to install. The best resource to get it is naturally the `Drupal.org` site itself. At `http://drupal.org/start`, you will find a link to a downloads page that contains the latest stable release of Drupal. This is the release you want to install. Newer releases are available, but they are not yet as stable as the recommended one. This link will take you to a page where you can select in what format you want to get the code's compressed file, as shown on Figure 2-4.

Downloads

Recommended releases

Version	Downloads	Date	Links
7.22	tar.gz (3.04 MB)	zip (3.47 MB)	2013-Apr-03	Notes
6.28	tar.gz (1.05 MB)	zip (1.22 MB)	2013-Jan-16	Notes

Development releases

Version	Downloads	Date	Links
7.x-dev	tar.gz (3.04 MB)	zip (3.48 MB)	2013-Apr-05	Notes
6.x-dev	tar.gz (1.05 MB)	zip (1.22 MB)	2013-Jan-17	Notes

View all releases

Figure 2-4. Stable and development releases of Drupal on Drupal.org

In this situation, you would select the `tar.gz` or zip file for Drupal 7.22 and download it to the machine you want to work on. Once extracted, you can rename the drupal folder to anything you want and place it in any directory served by Apache. For example, if you installed a WAMP server using the instructions in the previous section, and accepted all the defaults, you would place the unzipped Drupal folder into `c:\wamp\www`. For the purpose of following along in this book, you can rename the folder to `kbr`. If you followed the Linux instructions in the previous section, you would place your `kbr` folder in `/var/www`.

You can also download the latest stable Drupal release using Drush— which, honestly, is the easiest way to go. Simply run the following command from within the AMP www folder - `c:\wamp\www` on Windows, and `/var/www` on Linux:

```
drush dl drupal
```

(On Linux, you will likely need to prefix the command with sudo. And on Windows, you will likely need to make sure you're running the console in Administrative mode).

After the Drupal folder is downloaded, we recommend you rename it to kbr— in order to follow along with the example in this book.

Now that the code is in place, you will need to create a database for Drupal and configure the new site. There are several ways to do this. The most efficient and recommended way is to use Drush. But you can also utilize myphpadmin and then follow the Drupal configuration wizard pages. Both are described next.

Create Database Using Drush

Once you have Drush installed, open a terminal and navigate to your Drupal directory. Then use the following command, where USERNAME and PASSWORD are new credentials to be generated for this DBNAME database. None of those need to be pre-existing, Drush will create them for you.

```
drush site-install --db-url="mysql://USERNAME:PASSWORD@localhost:3306/DBNAME" --db-su=DBROOTNAME
--db-su-pw=DBROOTPASSWORD --site-name="SITENAME" --clean-url=0
```

For this book's example, you should run the following:

```
drush site-install --db-url="mysql://kbr:PASSWORD@localhost:3306/kbr" --db-su=root --db-su-
pw=DBROOTPASSWORD --site-name="K & B Restaurants" --clean-url=0
```

For the first PASSWORD value, make up a password that the Drupal site will use to connect to its MySQL database. And for the DBROOTPASSWORD, be sure to enter the MySQL root user's password, as entered in the previous section during the LAMP/WAMP/MAMP install.

It will ask you to confirm creation of a database (or dropping all tables if database already exists). After the process is done, it will output the admin name and password. Use them to log in to the site at SERVED-ADDRESS:PORT/PROJECT — for example, http://localhost/kbr.

Create Database Using PhpMyAdmin

You can also manually add a database through web phpmyadmin. If you used the WampServer instructions from above, this tool is already installed. If not, you can download it from http://www.phpmyadmin.net. In this book we will focus primarily on using Drush for system and administrative activities. But some basic instructions for creating a new user and database are described next.

Using your browser, navigate to http://localhost/phpmyadmin/. Once you are in the phpmyadmin homepage, click on the Privileges link. You should then see a link for "Add user"— click it and enter the new user's username and password, along with entering localhost for the host name. Under the "Database for user" section, select the second option, which is to create a new database with the same name. This option is shown below in Figure 2-5.

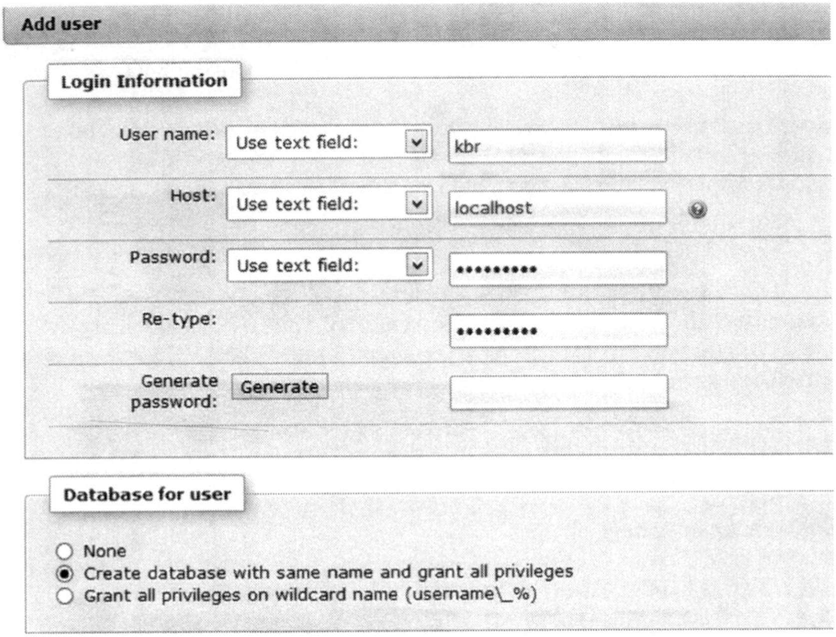

Figure 2-5. *Creating a new user and database*

Once the new user and database have been successfully created, you can move on to the Drupal install and configuration, as described next.

Using your browser, navigate to the Drupal Configuration wizard by going to an address that represents the folder you extracted after downloading Drupal. In our example here, that URL would be http://localhost/kbr. Walk through the wizard pages, entering various site information. As seen in Figure 2-6, we are using a site called "kbr"— sans quotes.

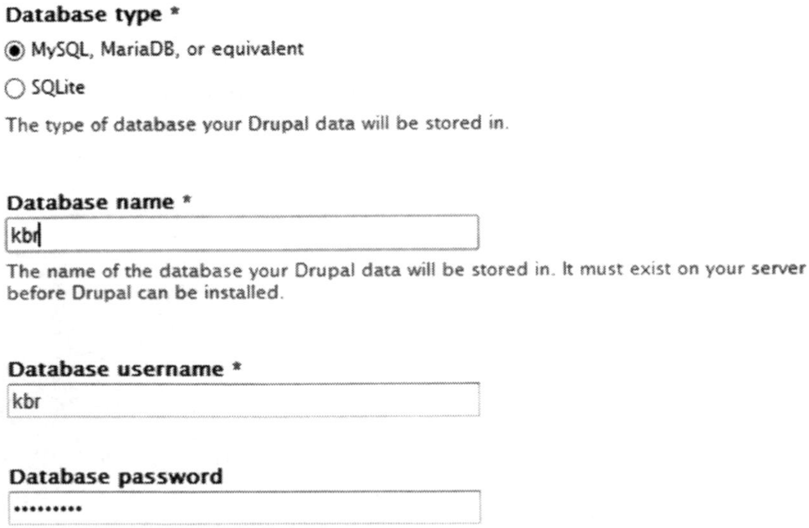

Figure 2-6. *Creating a new database for a new Drupal site*

Once the wizard is completed, your new site is up and running. You can log into the site using the username and password you entered for the Maintenance account.

How to Add a Module or a Theme

Using the `views` module as an example (as taken from `http://drupal.org/project/views`), let's walk through the process of adding a module to your Drupal site. You have three options here. From the URL above, identify the recommended download compatible with your version of Drupal. We're using Drupal 7, so it should be the version 7.x-some.version.

Using Drush

Using Drush is our preferred approach for installing modules. The following command is similar to `apt-get` on most Linux platforms, where it will download the latest stable release from a centralized online repository, install the module, and then enable it for you.

```
drush -y dl viewsdrush -y en views
```

Again, you don't need to enable the module after running this command, as it is already taken care of.

Manually

If you don't want to use Drush, and instead prefer to manually configure your module, you can essentially copy the module into the Drupal site directory, and then enable it from within the Drupal modules page.

To start, grab the recommended download compatible with your version of Drupal. This will download a compressed file. You will then extract the content of this file into your Drupal site in, for example, `kbr/sites/all/modules`. If instead you are adding a theme (as opposed to a module), put the extracted directory into `kbr/sites/all/themes`. Finally, if you are adding a library, add it to `kbr/sites/all/libraries`. Once the module's code is in this directory, you are good to go to the next step.

Through the Drupal site

Clicking the administrative "Modules" tab will take you to the modules administration interface, at the top of which there is an option to add a new module, as shown on Figure 2-7.

Download additional contributed modules to extend Drupal's functionality.

Regularly review and install available updates to maintain a secure and current site. Always run the update script each time a module is updated.

✦ Install new module

▾CORE			
ENABLED	NAME	VERSION	DESCRIPTION

Figure 2-7. *Modules tab in Drupal*

Click on "+ install a new module," then go to the module's URL (`http://drupal.org/project/views`) and right-click on the recommended download you picked. Select "copy link location," then paste this link into the "Install from a URL" field, and Install - as shown in Figure 2-8.

27

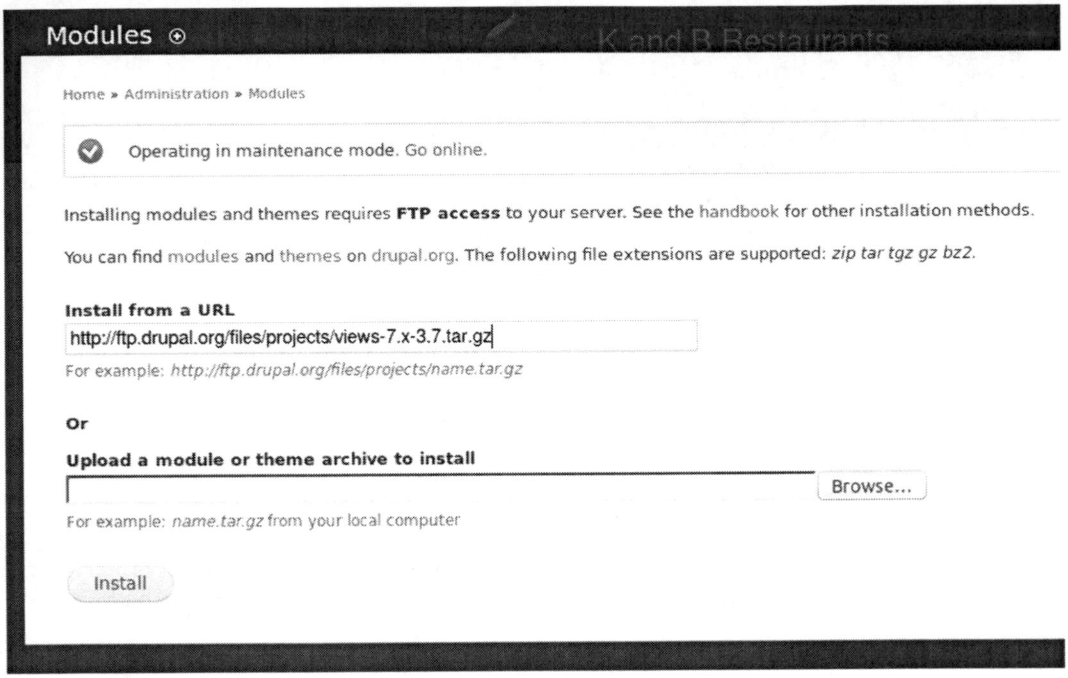

Figure 2-8. *Installing a module from the* Drupal.org *FTP address*

If you wish to add a theme through the site, use the exact same process, starting from the "Appearance" administrative tab instead of "Modules"

Enabling Your Module or Theme

After you have completed the addition of the module, you still need to enable it (unless you used Drush). You will need to go on the site's administrative Modules tab and click the check box in front of the newly added module, and then click save.

If you added a theme, go to the site's administrative Appearance tab, find the theme you just installed, and click "enable and set default."

Summary

In this chapter, you were introduced to the Drupal CMS. We discussed how much of Drupal's power as an enterprise development platform arises from its highly modularized architecture, and subsequent contribution by the Drupal community. Indeed, in an era where building software from scratch is becoming more and more a losing proposition, having over 20,000 modules already built and tested at your disposal is a sure strategy for lowering cost and reducing bug surface area.

This chapter also started you from a clean Windows or Linux (Ubuntu) machine and successfully installed and configured an AMP server, Drush, and the latest stable release of Drupal. On Linux, this was all done with a few simple commands. On Windows, a few installers were used. Then we rounded out the Drupal setup by installing and enabling an example module.

It's now time to start building our enterprise application on Drupal. In Chapter 3, we'll dive right in and design our site, and begin building our content types and their relationships.

CHAPTER 3

■ ■ ■

Business Application Fundamentals

Now that you've got an instance of Drupal up and running, it's time to start building an application. In this chapter, we will explore the fundamentals of using Drupal to build a business application, starting with the task of defining what the application will do. In a real software project, the process of gathering requirements would generally take some time and be done by one or more qualified analysts. For our example application, though, we aren't really concerned with the quality or coverage of these requirements. We just need to make sure we're all on the same page with what we're building. As such, we'll cover the requirements quickly—just enough to get an idea of our application's basic functionality.

The next step in building the application will be to map our requirements to existing Drupal modules. Indeed, one of the main points of this book is that most functionality will be available to you in the form of pre-existing modules. Therefore, this exercise of mapping features to modules will be something rather easy to do, and something that you will find becomes second nature rather quickly. As discussed in Chapter 2, anyone with an iPhone, Android device, or recent Windows phone knows the power of the app. And they've also come to expect that for some desired bit of functionality or need, there is most likely "an app for that." So it will be with Drupal—you will quickly learn to search through modules whenever a new piece of functionality is required.

Once the modules are selected, you will walk through the process of modeling your content types and their relationships. As with any data modeling, you need to define your entities, as well as their attributes and relationships. In fact, a lot of what we'll be doing throughout this book will feel very similar to typical software development practices. For example, in the previous paragraph we talked about mapping features and requirements to existing modules. This is exactly what any seasoned architect or developer would do when building a new application. The main difference being that instead of choosing code-level libraries, components, and controls, we're now using Drupal to select entire sets of functionality— packaged as a module. And as you'll see shortly, creating content types is nearly identical to creating classes in object-oriented programming (OOP).

Lastly in this chapter, you will take a quick look at the Features module. As we all know, when it comes to software, you can't claim credit and make any money if the user or customer can't get their hands on your work! The Features module allows you to combine your work into packages that can be exported and then re-applied to one or more separate Drupal instances. Think of this module as enabling the delivery of enhancements and bug fixes. After all, you certainly don't develop this stuff directly on the production server. So we need a mechanism for moving changes out of development, through various stages of testing, QA, and into production. Features is your module of choice for this practice.

Designing Your Application with Drupal as the Platform

As with any application development project, the first thing you need to do is define what the application is supposed to do. So let's briefly do that now—to make sure we're all on the same page as to the requirements of the application.

The Restaurant Application's Requirements

In this section, we will list the various requirements of our K&B Restaurant's application. The more obvious functional requirements are listed in Table 3-1.

Table 3-1. The application's functional requirements

Title	Description
Login	User should be able to provide username and password and log into the application as an administrator.
Anonymous login	Users should be able to view the restaurant's menus and other information without logging in.
Menu Item	Will store individual items on a menu. Each item can belong to zero or more menus. The item will need to store a title, some descriptive text, a price, and a picture.
Menu	A collection of menu items, grouped according to the type of menu item referenced. For example, should be able to list as an appetizer, an entree, a dessert, and so forth.
Branch	An individual restaurant in the franchise —that is, a branch. In addition to basic store information, should also identify the store's owner, its hours, and a menu.
Special	For a given period of time, groups a set of menu items for a given set of locations.
Google Maps	Show a map of a store's location.
Google Analytics	Used to track usage of the K&B web site.
HTML Editor	Allows the user to build nice HTML content for the menu items, the menu, and the store itself.

Now we need to list the non-functional, or system-level requirements. In this case, we're less concerned with things like performance and uptime, and more concerned with functionality needed by the system but not directly used by its users. You can see requirements of this type in Table 3-2.

Table 3-2. The application's system-level requirements

Title	Description
Backups	Back up the system on a regular basis.
Date and Period	Be able to specify a date in terms of a period —that is, start and end dates.
Entity Reference	Create references between entities—similar to a relationship in class or data modeling.
Configuration, Feature, and Bug Fix Export and Import	Need to be able to move configuration settings, new features, and bug fixes through the deployment pipeline and into production, applying the changes to various Drupal instances along the way.
Data import	Be able to import data from an external system —for example, employees out of an ERP or CRM.
Jobs, scheduling	Ability to schedule jobs, such as backups, e-mails, and so forth.

(*continued*)

Table 3-2. (*continued*)

Title	Description
Password policies	Be able to enforce password complexity and username and password history.
Business rules	Be able to define rules (and associated actions) throughout the system.
Custom displays/pages	Be able to define, from scratch if needed, custom pages to display data and then export those to PDF.
Polls/surveys	Be able to publish surveys to users, and manage the results.
Application settings	Be able to specify certain key-value pairs that will be used throughout the system. For example, a slogan or catch-phrase that is repeated all over the web site. Need to be able to change it in one place, not multiple copies.

That takes care of most of the application's requirements. Now we need to map those requirements to actual modules in Drupal.

Requirements Mapping to Modules

The easiest approach to finding modules is just to Google them. The Drupal.org site includes a modules search feature, but it isn't very good. In our experience, it is much faster to utilize Google to match features and requirements with potential modules. And 9 times out of 10, you end up on the Drupal.org site anyway, since that's where most modules are published. Optionally, you can add site:drupal.org to your search box in Google to limit the module search to those found on the official Drupal site.

In Chapter 2, you learned how to assess the relative health or feasibility of a module. That information, combined with good old Google searching, is all you need to go about finding an appropriate module for a given requirement. Of course, we've already done that for the requirements in this book. Table 3-3 lists each requirement along with its best choice for a module. Note that some modules support more than one requirement.

It's important to remember that, in addition to gaining exposure to a sampling of Drupal modules and all that they offer, you need to learn the simple process and habit of trying to find a module that meets your needs. Remember, "There's a module for that!" We encourage you to try doing some Google searches for modules based on the requirements in Tables 3-1 and 3-2. See if you arrive at the same modules we did.

One more note. In Table 3-3, the names of the modules are specified with their official name as stated on Drupal.org. For each of them, you can simply append the name to http://drupal.org/project/ to get the module's information. For example, the password_policy module can be found at http://drupal.org/project/password_policy.

Table 3-3. *Requirements mapped to modules*

Requirement	Module(s)
Login	core
Anonymous login	core
Menu Item	core, entity, entityreference
Menu	core, entity, entityreference
Branch	core, entity, entityreference
Special	core, entity, entityreference
Google Maps	gmap, location

(*continued*)

Table 3-3. (*continued*)

Requirement	Module(s)
Google Analytics	google_analytics
HTML Editor	ckeditor
Backups	backup_migrate
Date and Period	date
Entity Reference	entityreference
Feature and Bug Fix Export and Import	features
Data import	feeds
Jobs, scheduling	job_scheduler
Password policies	password_policy
Business rules	rules
Custom displays/pages	views, views_pdf
Polls/surveys	webform
Application settings	token
(dependencies, other)	ctools entity login_security

Only a few of these modules will be covered in this chapter. But they will all be used eventually in this book. Let's go ahead and add the first set now by running the following commands from within the root of your Drupal KBR site folder.

```
drush dl views features entityreference date
drush en views features entityreference date
```

Starting with Drupal 7, site administrators can create and edit content types and fields directly out of the box, without having to install a module. The module that was previously used for this kind of manipulation, CCK, has been integrated into the core and is now unnecessary. An important addition to the content management features, however, is found in the "Entity Reference" module. It allows for fields of a content type to be references to other content types, or a list of other content types, much like in OOP when a class references another class by having an attribute that holds an instance of another class, or a list of such instances.

Using the content type creation core feature and the Entity Reference module, we will now start the design of our site's content types. We will also use the Features module to export our work into a module so it is easier and safer to deploy and promote content type definitions, a key aspect of the design, in the form of version controlled source code.

Content Types

To determine the content types needed for the site, a solid object-oriented approach is advised. Try to identify every possible entity you might need and how they relate to each other. For each entity, you should also identify their attributes—including the type of data being stored in each attribute. Whereas in an object-oriented approach you might pick from simple/native or complex software data types, when identifying Drupal entities you will choose the data type as viewed by the user. For example, a valid data type could be a simple list or e-mail address, or it could be a file, or even an embedded media type, such as a Youtube video. In other words, your content type's attributes are "closer" to the user than class attributes, and so their data types should be, as well.

Also similar to OOP, you can even use UML diagrams—particularly class diagrams—to help you visualize the components. And when modeling a REST service in Drupal, along with its supporting content types, you might find a sequence diagram useful. Remember, even though we are working with a CMS, we are building enterprise software, so those same architecture tools apply. The CMS is simply our platform of choice—but architecture is still architecture, and software is still software.

Content Type Definition

Next, let's examine the content types for the K&B Restaurant site from the bottom up. Again, remember that the types and their attributes will be closer to the user experience in definition, versus class definitions.

Menu Item

Any food or drink served by the restaurant. It can be a beer, a pasta plate, some appetizer, and so forth.

- Title
- Body Text - a text area field to be edited with an HTML editor, to write any information/details about the item
- Picture
- Price

Menu

Just like a physical menu, it will group several Menu Items and sort them between Appetizers, Entrees, Drinks, and so forth.

- Title
- Body Text
- Appetizers (Any number of Menu Items)
- Entrees (Any number of Menu Items)
- Desserts (Any number of Menu Items)
- Drinks (Any number of Menu Items)

Restaurant Branch

Corresponds to a physical branch of the K&B franchise.

- Title
- Body Text
- Owner
- Hours
- Menu (1 Menu)

Special

For a given time, at select locations for some menu items, you can have a special price or some perks that you want to advertise.

- Title
- Body Text
- Locations (Any number of Restaurant Branch)
- Menu items (Any number of Menu Items)
- Date (start—end)

A good idea after figuring out your content types is to make a simplified UML class diagram—or content type diagram, to be exact. Figure 3-1 illustrates what we get for our example project. We have four content types, and we show how they relate to each other through reference fields with arrows and a number for the relationship. For instance, an arrow with a 1 would indicate that the field will reference exactly one other item, while an arrow with a '*' means any number, and '1-*' means at least one, up to any number.

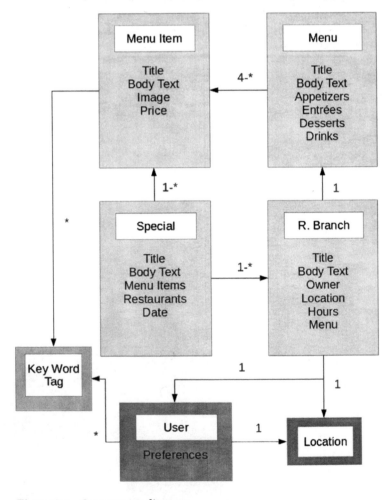

Figure 3-1. *Content type diagram*

Note that Tag, User, and Location data are built into the Drupal core. But we can still reference them from our own content types.

Creating your Content Types in Drupal

We hope you're excited—this is the first hands-on activity for your newly created Drupal site. We are now going to create every content type we need and every field in those content types. From an architectural perspective, this is the most important part of the implementation, since the better you define your content types, the easier it will be to maintain your site properly and to scale. A poor content type definition will lead to a multiplication of workarounds and hacks over time, and if any step deserves some extra time and scrutiny, it's definitely this one. This is not at all unlike modeling a database or object model.

Content Type Creation and Editing

From the administrator menu, select the Structure tab. It will take you to the screen as shown in Figure 3-2. Don't worry if your page looks a little different—at this point you've installed the modules you'll need.

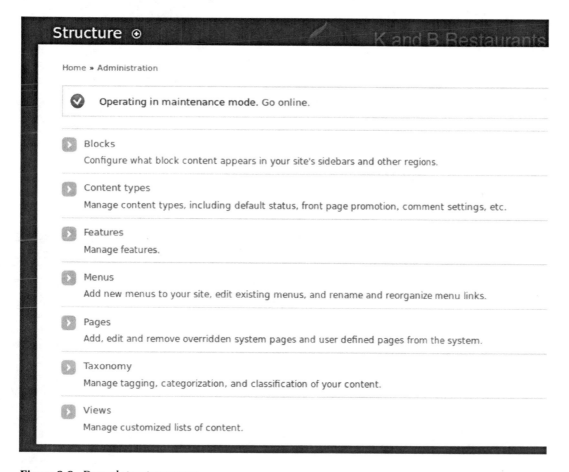

Figure 3-2. Drupal structure menu

Select the Content Types option to access the Content Type creation and modification page shown in Figure 3-3.

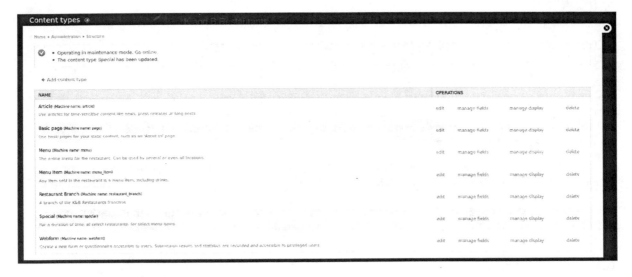

Figure 3-3. *Content types menu*

On the top of the page, you can click the "+ Add content type" link and get started with your first content type. Figure 3-3 shows you how it will look after all your content types are defined. Right now, you most likely have a couple out-of-the-box content types only.

Menu Item

The first step in creating a content type is quite basic. Enter a name, such as Menu Item—then a quick description of what a menu item is and when it should be created. This description will appear to content creators when they are selecting a content type for content about to be created. Also, add a Title field label, if one isn't already present on the "Submission form settings" tab.

You can leave the rest of the options as-is right now, and click the "Save and add fields" button. It will take you to the important part of content type creation: defining fields. By default, the Title and Body Text will already be created; you will have to add the other fields for the Menu item.

As shown in Figure 3-4, click "Add new field" in the second to last row, type the label (or name) of the field, such as Picture, then select the type of field it will be. For the picture, you will want an image field, and for the price, a decimal field. Their default widgets will do for now.

Figure 3-4. *Menu Item content type fields*

You have to add fields one by one, and when you save them, you will be taken to additional screens where you can input additional information and rules. For example, on the the price, field you will probably want to define a minimum price for food items, to prevent typos that will put a steak on sale for $0.16. We used $1 in our example. You can also define a prefix for the field. Because we will be using dollars for the price field, we prefixed the field with a dollar sign ($). You can always come back later and modify any field you want from this field addition/editing screen.

Menu

Now that our Menu Item is ready, let's get to the next content type. Note that we don't have any "love triangle" situation where you have to come back to an earlier content type and edit it with a reference field to a content type you have since created. But this happens sometimes and that's why having a UML diagram done is a good idea. The Menu type, as shown in Figure 3-5, is going to have several reference fields.

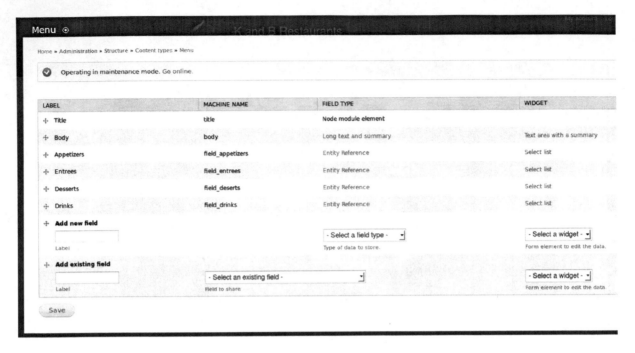

Figure 3-5. *Menu*

The first reference field is Appetizers. The field type is Entity Reference and you will have to set a Node target type with Menu Item selected as the only possible choice for the field. Because your Appetizer field is going to be populated by many different menu items, we need to set the number of values for this field to Unlimited, as shown on Figure 3-6. Alternatively, if you want to make sure your restaurants are not offering too many options, you can set a fixed number, like 5 or 10. You can see all of these options in Figure 3-6.

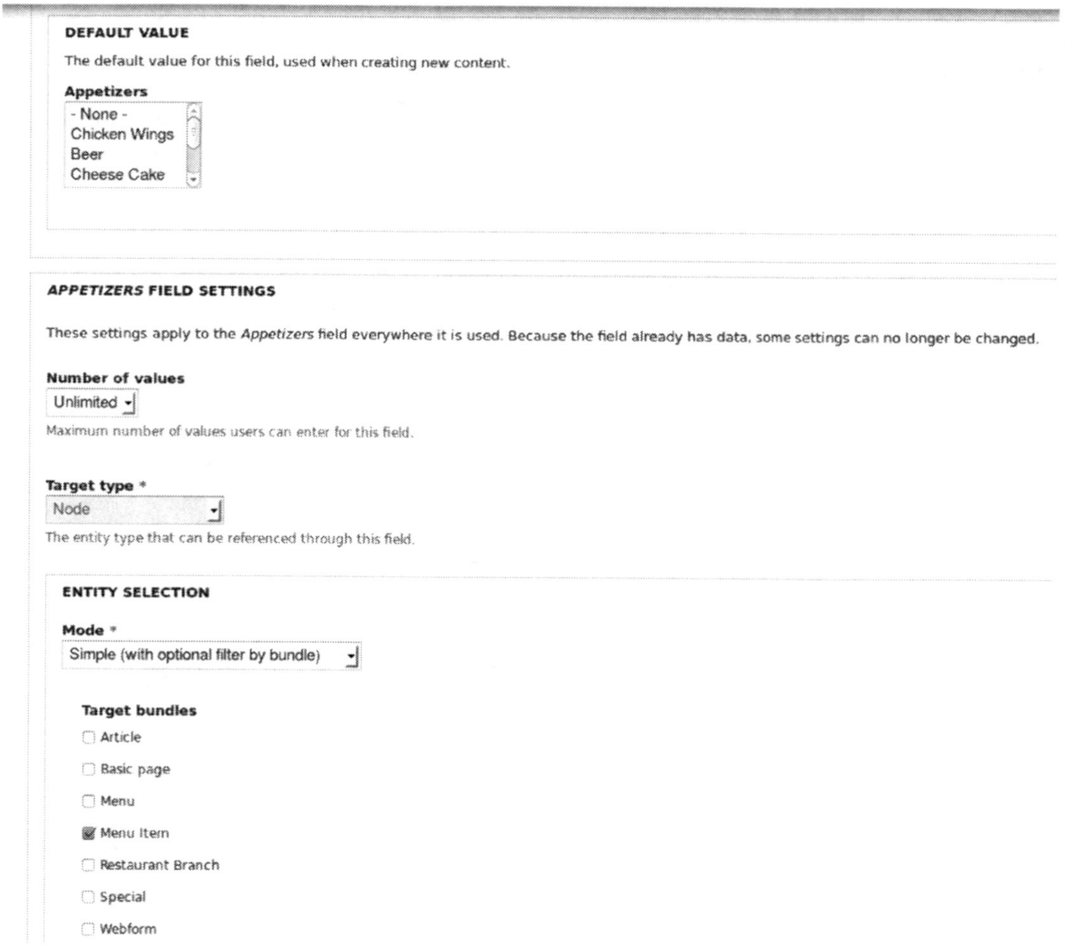

DEFAULT VALUE

The default value for this field, used when creating new content.

Appetizers

```
- None -
Chicken Wings
Beer
Cheese Cake
```

APPETIZERS **FIELD SETTINGS**

These settings apply to the *Appetizers* field everywhere it is used. Because the field already has data, some settings can no longer be changed.

Number of values

Unlimited ▾

Maximum number of values users can enter for this field.

Target type *

Node ▾

The entity type that can be referenced through this field.

ENTITY SELECTION

Mode *

Simple (with optional filter by bundle) ▾

   Target bundles

   ☐ Article

   ☐ Basic page

   ☐ Menu

   ☑ Menu Item

   ☐ Restaurant Branch

   ☐ Special

   ☐ Webform

Figure 3-6. *Reference field definition*

Picking the right widget for the reference field is always challenging. A widget defines the UI control the user will see to edit the field. You have the following options available for list-oriented fields:

- Checkboxes: Every possible entity choice is going to be displayed with a check box on the side. Checking the box will select the item as the referenced item, or add it to the list if you have selected more than one Number of values, as shown on Figure 3-6. This widget is appropriate when there are only a few options, say less than 10, or even less than 5. We could use this for the restaurant branch selection on the specials, or the menu selection on the restaurant branches.

- List: A drop-down with all the possible choices to scroll through. There again, based on the ability to select several options with the Number of values set to more than one, you will be able to hold CTRL (or CMD on the mac) down and click several items on the drop-down. This widget is appropriate when the number of choices is too large for check boxes but can still be scrolled through in a reasonable time. This would work for a number of choices between 10 and 50, for instance, so in our example, we can use this widget for the Appetizers reference field on the menu.

- Autocomplete: It looks like a simple text field, but it will autocomplete as you start typing. Very useful when you have too many options to be listed, such as in a reference field that lets you pick a user from a list of potentially hundreds or thousands. Also quite handy when the name of the item you would want to list is predictable—for instance, if you named your users based on their real name, and you have a list in hand of who needs to be referenced where. In our case, it's hard for an admin to anticipate how a menu item would be called, so autocomplete doesn't seem ideal for the Menu content type.

Last but not least, we need to choose how a reference field will be rendered when a user views an item of the Menu content type. The options, as shown in Figure 3-7, are:

- Hidden: If you simply don't want this field to show but have to use it for some administrative purpose, or for specific rules (we'll get back to this later).

- Label: Will display the title of the item, either as plain text or as a link, which you can edit on the right hand side of the row.

- Entity id: Relatively useless for our site, it will render the node id of the referenced item.

- Rendered entity: Shows the full referenced node inside the parent node; very useful in our case where the menu will be able to display all its menu items, with their body text and images. You can disable links in the rendered entity, and you can filter down the fields rendered using the config button on the right hand side of the row.

Figure 3-7. Menu display

Restaurant Branch

That should do for the menu. Now let's get started with the Restaurant Branch content type. Every branch should have an owner or manager. So let's make an owner reference field and make its target type a user. Because usernames are likely going to be the same as real names, an autocomplete widget will be appropriate, as shown in Figure 3-8. We may or may not want to display the name of the branch owner, so select your field display as hidden or label as appropriate.

Figure 3-8. *Restaurant Branch content type fields*

Next, you should add a property called Hours. This will be a simple Long Text field that will be used to specify a restaurant's operating hours.

Each restaurant will need a menu. In practice, there will most likely be only one menu for every restaurant, but some may be specialized with more seafood or a selection of different drinks, for instance, so maintaining menus and restaurants separately is a good practice. A menu reference field limited to the menu content type with a list widget will be perfect here. Because we want the user to be able to click on the menu from the restaurant page and get redirected there, we need to make the menu field display clickable by selecting label and checking the link check box from the display options, as shown in Figure 3-9.

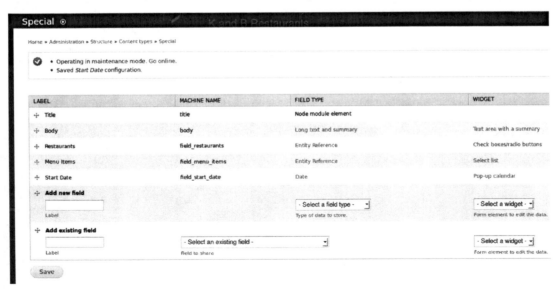

Restaurant Branch ⊙

Home » Administration » Structure » Content types » Restaurant Branch

✓ Operating in maintenance mode. Go online.

Content items can be displayed using different view modes: Teaser, Full content, Print, RSS, etc. *Teaser* is a short format that is typically used
Here, you can define which fields are shown and hidden when content is displayed in each view mode, and define how the fields are displaye

✓ Operating in maintenance mode. Go online.

FIELD	LABEL	FORMAT
⊹ Body	\<Hidden\> ▾	Default ▾
⊹ Owner	Above ▾	Label ▾
⊹ Menu	Above ▾	Format settings: **Label** ☑ Link label to the referenced entity Update Cancel
⊹ Hours	Above ▾	Default ▾

Figure 3-9. *Restaurant Branch menu label configured as a link*

Special

A special is a time-limited offer on a selection of menu items that can be valid at every branch or just a selection
of them. It needs to hold reference fields to the restaurants, using a Check boxes widget if you have few locations, or
a select list. It also needs to reference the menu items, using a select list, as shown on Figure 3-10.

Special ⊙

Home » Administration » Structure » Content types » Special

✓ • Operating in maintenance mode. Go online.
   • Saved *Start Date* configuration.

LABEL	MACHINE NAME	FIELD TYPE	WIDGET
⊹ Title	title	Node module element	
⊹ Body	body	Long text and summary	Text area with a summary
⊹ Restaurants	field_restaurants	Entity Reference	Check boxes/radio buttons
⊹ Menu Items	field_menu_items	Entity Reference	Select list
⊹ Start Date	field_start_date	Date	Pop-up calendar
⊹ **Add new field** [ ] Label		- Select a field type - ▾ Type of data to store.	- Select a widget - ▾ Form element to edit the data.
⊹ **Add existing field** [ ] Label	- Select an existing field - ▾ Field to share		- Select a widget - ▾ Form element to edit the data.

Save

Figure 3-10. *Special content type*

The only new thing here is the date field we are using to set the start and end date for the special. Figure 3-11 shows the options we have regarding the precision in the date information we collect, and the fact that we require an end date as well, making this field more of a period field than a simple date field. This period will be the period of validity of the specials.

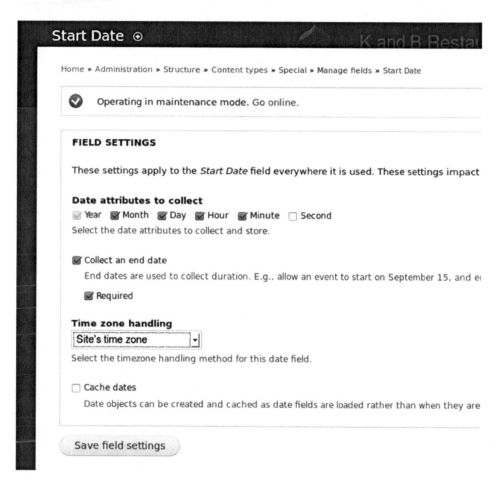

Figure 3-11. *Date field*

Note that this is an example of a data type that is much higher-level than a simple DateTime data type in a class definition. The data types in Drupal have been created to allow such configuration of common user-oriented fields, including in this case, the date's time zone, whether or not an end date is required, and the format and elements of the value collected.

At this point, you should have all of the content types created for the K&B Restaurant example project. This includes each content type's fields, as well as its relationships to other content types. Further, each field defines the UI widget the user will use to edit its value. The last section in this chapter will focus on a Drupal capability called Features—used to import and export various pieces of a Drupal configuration.

Features Module

Features provides you with an interface to export work you have done on the site from the administration interface, such as creating content types, fields, relations, defining permissions, adding roles, changing the site's name, and so forth. It puts all of this configuration into a Drupal module, called a feature set, that you can download from the features interface. You can then run this module on a different Drupal site and it will reproduce the work you have done. Think of it as a replay of all your configuration activities.

Why Do We Need These Features?

Every configuration you make on the site is stored in the database. Using the previous example of our content types, now that you have them all created, they "live" in the site's database. Given that we are building an enterprise application, you will have to promote this configuration data to testing environments, staging, and production servers to have those content types available.

Not only can this be a pain, but without Features it is also relatively unsafe because data can be compromised, lost, erased, and so forth.

Further, the code for your site is under version control. If not, stop reading this, press the big red panic button, and do not rest until it is! And since your code is under version control, you should try and move as much as you can from the database into the code—to be stored in version control. Think of using Features as a means of scripting out database and configuration changes into code files that can be versioned and used for deployment.

Of course, Features also makes your configuration reusable in any other site started from scratch. This might be your own test or development servers. Or it might be a Drupal system owned by a client of yours.

Bottom line, Features is a powerful packing and deployment mechanism for just about anything you can configure in Drupal.

How Do I Use Them?

Assuming you have the Features module installed, select Features from the Structure administrative menu. Then click on the Create Feature tab to create a new feature. It will take you to a seemingly complex interface. Start by entering a name and a description for the feature. In our example, we named it "K & B Content Types"—because the feature set will hold the content types for the project.

Now take a look at the options to the right. Because we just created content types, let's simply go in the Content Types section and select all the content types. Notice that Features will automatically select the appropriate dependencies and fields that are necessary to reproduce our content type definition and add them to the feature. If all of the module dependencies aren't present —for example, Entity Reference, Date—click on the Refresh button in the Advanced Options section. Then proceed to select them all. All of the selected components are shown in Figure 3-12.

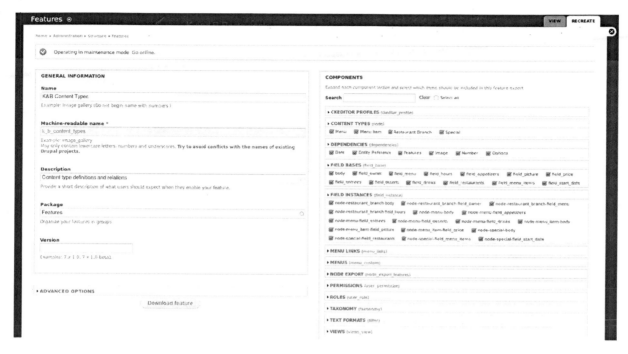

Figure 3-12. *Feature creation*

That's it, we're done with Features. You can either download it and place it in the site in /kbr/sites/all/modules/, or, let Features do it for you in the advanced options, leaving everything empty and just clicking the Generate feature button. Note that because the Generate feature button will, by default, write the feature's files out to the sites/all/modules folder, you will need to ensure that the folder is writable to at least the web server's service account.

Voila! You just exported the whole content type model and all of their module dependencies!

How Do I Test the Feature?

Obviously, you can't test a feature on the site you used to make it, because you are basically exporting the state of this site (or a select portion of it).

The best way to test a feature is to create another site with the same code as your first site and either no data (start from scratch), or an image of the database your site had before you started the work you have exported into a feature. Now add the feature as a module to this new site, and enable the module. This will automatically run the feature set on the site and recreate your work. Alternatively, you can find and run this feature with more information from the Features interface.

I Didn't Create the Content Types Myself; Can I Get Your Feature Set?

Well, of course! This feature set has been included in our sample code, so if you deploy a Drupal site with our sample code at https://github.com/EnterpriseDrupalBook/LoadedSiteFinal or using git: https://github.com/EnterpriseDrupalBook/LoadedSiteFinal.git, you will find this feature already available from the Features menu or the modules. Additionally, you run this feature set on its own as explained in the project's README.md or at https://github.com/EnterpriseDrupalBook/LoadedSiteFinal.

Summary

In this chapter, you learned one of the most important practices with any Drupal system—that of finding modules to match application requirements. This really is the crux of the message in this book: that you don't need to first think about writing code to solve a particular problem. Instead, we intend that you will first think "There's a module for that!" and subsequently consult Google to go find that module.

You also spent some time modeling out the various content types and their relationships needed to support the K&B Restaurants application, including the various attributes associated with each content type. We hope you noticed that this exercise was very similar to modeling classes and relationships in more traditional OOP.

And then, finally, we took a very brief look at the Features module—which facilitates feature and bug fix promotion through the various Drupal systems by way of converting those changes into source code.

At this point in the book, you should now understand how to:

- Install Drupal on to Windows or Linux
- Use Drush to configure Drupal and its modules
- Define requirements in terms of Drupal modules
- Search for modules and assess them for quality and health
- Model your application's entities and their relationships and attributes
- Use the Features module to move changes around the enterprise

You've certainly come a long way in relatively short order! In the next chapter, you will continue the build-out of the K&B Restaurant application, dealing specifically with pages, custom views and layouts, and the wonderful world of Drupal business rules.

CHAPTER 4

■ ■ ■

Implementing Application Behaviors

Now that your content types and their relationships are defined, you have the basic structure you need to create and manage content. If the purpose of your site is to simply hold well-structured information, your work is mostly done. If, however, you want to add some custom features or displays to your site, this chapter will show you a few must-have modules and how to use them.

At this point in the development of the K & B Restaurants web site, you should have completed the following:

- Configured a LAMP, MAMP, or WAMP server

- Installed and configured Drupal

- Installed the Drush command-line tool

- Mapped the site's features to Drupal modules

- Modeled the site's content types

- Created those content types

- Installed the Features module

With all of those activities out of the way, you could actually start creating content—that is, the menus, the menu items, the store locations, and so forth. However, in this chapter we are first going to explore a few powerful Drupal modules related to custom display and business rules. When doing so, it is not uncommon to realize you need additional attributes or entities (that is, changes to your content types). Similar to building an application from scratch, we want to make sure the data is modeled as best we can before we start loading too much data. As such, this chapter will focus on various rules around and usages of the content types we created in Chapter 3. Then in Chapter 5 you will learn how to import content.

Before going forward, think for a minute about the activities completed in the previous chapters (listed above). Ask yourself:

- How much time would it have taken to code from scratch the foundations of a web site that you have now (including the database, data access, and domain model)?

- How much time would you have spent fixing bugs related to authentication, permissions, navigation, database structure problems, and data access mismatches?

- Isn't this essentially the same set of things you do for nearly all web application or mobile back-end projects?

- How much time and energy would you have spent designing, building, and testing a deployment architecture —that is, the ability to install modules, configure them, and automatically update them?

As you progress through this book, we will continue to draw these types of parallels to the build-from-scratch model of application development. Because we're not working down in the code, it's very easy to lose sight of all the design, build, test, and deployment work you are bypassing. And not only do you need to understand the savings, but you will likely need to convince others within your organization of the same. Thus it is good practice, at least while you develop some momentum around Drupal-based development, to keep tabs on the cost comparisons of building your applications.

The feature we are going to develop now is the automatic emailing of specials to people with matching preferences. This will essentially be a cron job that runs every day on the Drupal server. For every special that will start within a week and that hasn't been emailed yet, the site will send an email to every user of the site that has defined preferences matching the special's interest tags. We will utilize a few very powerful modules to implement this feature—without having to write any code whatsoever. Everything you need to build this emailing feature is available through existing Drupal modules.

Modules for Specials Custom Behavior

In this section, you will learn about four modules that will be needed by nearly all web applications and mobile back-end services. They are: taxonomy, views, rules, and views_rules. Each module plays a key part in implementing custom business rules.

Taxonomy

Part of the core and shipped with out-of-the-box Drupal, the taxonomy module lets you define site-wide vocabularies—lists of words—and make them available to your content types as a field. This can be useful when you want items in your site to have tags—or keywords, as they are usually called.

For our example, we are going to use Taxonomy to make a vocabulary of tags that will be used on some of the content types you created in Chapter 3: menu items, specials, and users. This will allow us to easily associate users with menu items or specials that have tags matching the user's preferences.

If you've ever read a blog post, you no doubt have seen various keywords and categories associated with the post. That's exactly what we're talking about here—taxonomy is simply a mechanism for listing important aspects of a "thing" such that it can be indexed and searched.

Views

Views is the single most downloaded and used Drupal module available today. In short, this module lets you display any part of any data in the site, filtered and sorted anyway you want, including contextual elements. This module essentially allows you to build custom web pages for your site. Only, in this case, you aren't required to write raw HTML pages. Instead, the views module handles all of the plumbing related to rendering and templating, as well as binding the requested data to that template.

Think of views as a custom query builder that can get anything from your Drupal database, including traversing reference fields to grab anything from the referenced item (or collection of items), and so on, paired with a custom template builder that lets you choose what part of the result you want to display and how. This might be similar to an ASP.NET Razor view (in ASP.NET MVC Framework), an ERB template in Ruby, or a view in the CodeIgniter PHP toolkit. In other words, the views module behaves very much like an MVC-based web application framework: you define the view and the model, and the module itself acts as a controller.

To better understand what views can do, look at the following examples:

- Display a table with the name and email address of all users in the site that have logged in during that last 48 hours.

- Show a list of all restaurants branches in the site that have no menu assigned yet.

- Make a jump menu (select an item from a drop-down, then click a "Go" button to go to the item you just selected) of menu items that have no image yet, sorted by price from most to least expensive.

Rules

Business rules are arguably the most difficult part of an application's customization. They require a basic understanding of algorithmic concepts, such as conditional expressions, loops, inclusion, and forward chaining. And they typically must be editable by someone not writing code. Many a project over the years has attempted to build a configurable business rules engine. And many code-level libraries exist that help implement some of the basics. But ultimately, configurable business rules must include storage, rule execution code, and a well-designed user interface. This is where the Drupal rules module comes in.

Business rules are one of the the most powerful features of Drupal, as they allow you to automate a number of actions and "code" using your site's graphical interface. There are three components in a rule: triggers, conditions, and actions (or loops).

Trigger

First, a trigger is an event that sets the whole rule in motion. When the event defined as the trigger happens, and if the conditions of the rule are verified, then the rule's actions will be executed. Example events that Drupal can use as triggers are:

- Creating or deleting content (this can be any type of content: a user, a content type, a product, a taxonomy term or vocabulary,and so forth)

- Before or after updating existing content

- When a content item is viewed

- When a cron job executes

Many modules also add their own triggers, conditions, and actions, as well. For instance, the commerce module can trigger a rule when an item is purchased or added to the cart.

Condition

Second, the condition is a simple verification made by the rule. If the condition or set of conditions is verified, the rule will execute its actions. If not, it will simply terminate without doing anything. Example conditions include:

- Data comparison (equal, different, greater than, less than, is one of)

- Item is part of a list

- Entity is of a given type

- Entity has a given field

- Current user is in a given role

Additionally, you can make complex conditional statements using AND and OR condition groups. You would place an item inside a group by simply indenting it one step compared to the group's indentation and placing it below the group. You can also negate a group's conditional evaluation. This is all accomplished within the rules module user interface.

For instance, if you want the condition to be:

```
(VariableA > VariableB and VariableA > 5) or VariableC is set to "No" or VariableD is set to
anything but not empty
```

You will have a condition section looking like:

```
OR
    AND
        Data Comparison (Between VariableA and VariableB, using "greater than")
        Data Comparison (Between VariableA and 5, using "greater than")
    Data Comparison (Between VariableC and "No", using "equals")
    Data value is empty (Checking VariableD, negated)
```

Action, Loop

The final and most important part of a rule, the actions will be executed sequentially in the order in which they are set in the action section. Example actions include:

- Add a variable to be worked on to the context of the rule

- Add or remove an item from a list

- Set a variable to a given value

- Create or delete an entity

- Unpublish content

- Send an email

- Block a user

You can drag and drop actions higher or lower, and you can use loops as well.

A loop is the equivalent of a "for" loop in an algorithm. You pass it an item that can be looped through, like a vocabulary or a list field, or any field with more than one allowed value, and it will iterate through all the values to execute an action for each of them. For instance, if you have a list of email addresses, you can create a loop, pass it the list, and use a mail action for each element of the loop. You can have loops inside of loops, as well.

To draw a parallel to the build-from-scratch approach, this is very similar to the basic code constructs of if/then/else blocks, conditional and logical operators, and for and iterator loops.

Finally, instead of a simple action, you can have what is called a component triggered by a rule. A component can be another rule or set of rules (without a trigger because we don't need it), or an additional set of conditions that would be used to apply to some actions (instead of the rule's conditions that apply to all actions). Think of this capability as nesting and partitioning rules, and making them available for reuse by other rules.

In the end, you can build extremely complex rules with the rules module. You can define conditional expressions for the whole rule, just a loop, and for loops inside of loops. The inner loops can have their own conditional expressions to trigger specific actions or rules inside the rule, which can also have their own loops, and so forth.

The only limitation of rules is that they are not able to access all of the data in the site like views can. Based on what trigger was used, only a few contextual variables will be available. For instance, if your trigger is a content item being saved, you will have access to that item and its fields inside the rule, but not to the users of the site, or other items of the same content type that you may need to use to compare fields or other logic.

However, there is a way around this limitation: by using the "Fetch entity by property" action. This feature allows you to create a variable—which can potentially be a list of items—based on a given property. This can return all items of the site of a given content type, for instance. Think of this action as a lookup, where you can fetch another entity or set of entities by any property—including, of course, the entity ID. The fetched entity or entities are then available to subsequent actions.

That said, we found it much quicker and more convenient to use the views_rules module to allow us access to other pieces of data (that is, data not directly attached to the rules context). This module essentially lets you use the whole querying power of views to define models used by rules, instead of the limited queries provided by rule fetching.

Views_Rules

To make up for the context-available limitation of rules, we are going to use a small yet powerful module called views_rules. It creates an additional display option on the view definition called "rules" that will be available as a loop for every rule in the action section.

QUICK NOTE ON RULE NAMES

As discussed in Chapter 1, the easiest and most efficient way to find a Drupal module is simply to use Google. For example, to find the views_rules module, simply Google something similar to "Drupal views_rules module." This should lead you to the URL `http://drupal.org/project/views_rules`. The `drupal.org` web site is the location of nearly all Drupal modules. Their names vary widely, of course. But one thing common across all module names is the URL used to identify them. Note that in this example, the URL ends with `views_rules`. Interestingly, this is also the name that can be used by the Drush command —for example, `drush dl views_rules`. In other words, regardless of the human-friendly name given to a module, its URL on `drupal.org` will always end with a unique key of a name, which is also its identifier when using Drush.

In other words, it makes all data a view can return available to the context of any rule! Think of this capability as giving you total control over and total access to the entire database for defining the data used by a rule, lifting the context limitation, and virtually multiplying the scope of what rules can achieve ten-fold. Remember all that views can access (any piece of data in the system) and all that rules can do (execute any action on any event in the system). Being able to access any data, and then subsequently execute any action is what makes the combination of views, rules, and views_rules so powerful in creating custom business rules in Drupal.

Getting back to our example, that of emailing people interested in a given special's menu items, let's start by defining the taxonomy for the specials and the users' interests.

Creating your Taxonomy Terms

In the Structure administrative menu, there is a link to the Taxonomy menu. Once you get there, notice how there is already a vocabulary defined by default, called Tags. If you need several vocabularies on your site, you will want to name them appropriately. For this example, we'll just use the Tags one (see Figure 4-1).

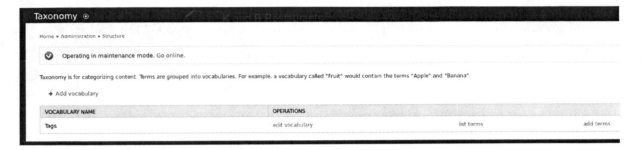

Figure 4-1. *Taxonomy screen*

We have the option to list the items of the vocabulary or add a new one. Figure 4-2 shows you an example of a list you might have on the K&B Restaurants site. Of course, right now you should have nothing in there. To add a new term, just click on the Add term button, enter a name and a description, and click Save. This term you just created will become available sitewide as part of the Tags vocabulary. You should add a few more terms that seem relevant as special item tags or user preferences. Feel free to simply copy the terms from Figure 4-2.

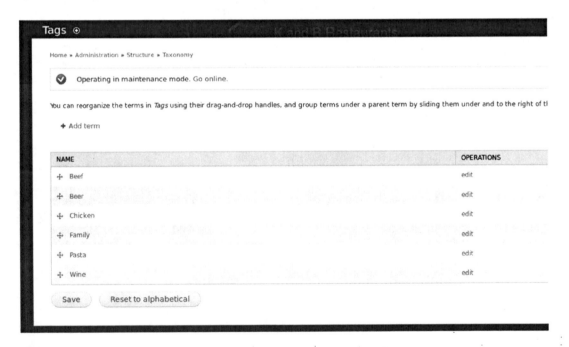

Figure 4-2. *Vocabulary terms*

Preparing Entities for Rules

One of the main concepts we are trying to communicate throughout this book is that you rarely need to develop your own module for Drupal because you can "develop" most custom behaviors directly in Drupal, using the right content types, entity references, views, and rules. Going back to our object-oriented analogy: sometimes when programming, you need a class to have an attribute that will be used to store values for various calculation and comparisons, but will never be modified by the users or displayed to them. For instance if you had a class for specials and wanted to know for every instance of specials whether or not it has already been emailed, you would add a boolean attribute to the specials class to store this information. We are going to do exactly the same to the specials content type. We will need the following fields:

- For each special, a taxonomy term reference field

- For each special, a list of users' email addresses to be emailed based on the user preferences matching the special's taxonomy items

- For each special, a boolean stating whether it still needs to be emailed or it has been emailed already

- For each user, a taxonomy term reference field

Let's start with the account settings to add a taxonomy term that lets the user indicate their interests. In the Configuration administrative tab, select the account settings, and go to the Manage Fields tab. From there, you can add fields to the user entity just like for your own content types. Add a new field that is of type Term reference, and click Save (see Figure 4-3).

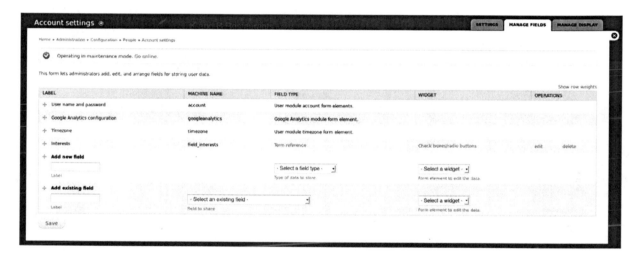

Figure 4-3. *Account fields*

To configure your newly created field, you will have to choose the vocabulary you want to use. Select the vocabulary you created in the taxonomy section. Because we will only have one vocabulary in this site, we used the default one called Tags. In addition to that, you will want an unlimited number of values for this field, so users can select any interest term they want. See Figure 4-4 for an illustration. Ultimately, this will be limited by the total number of terms in your vocabulary.

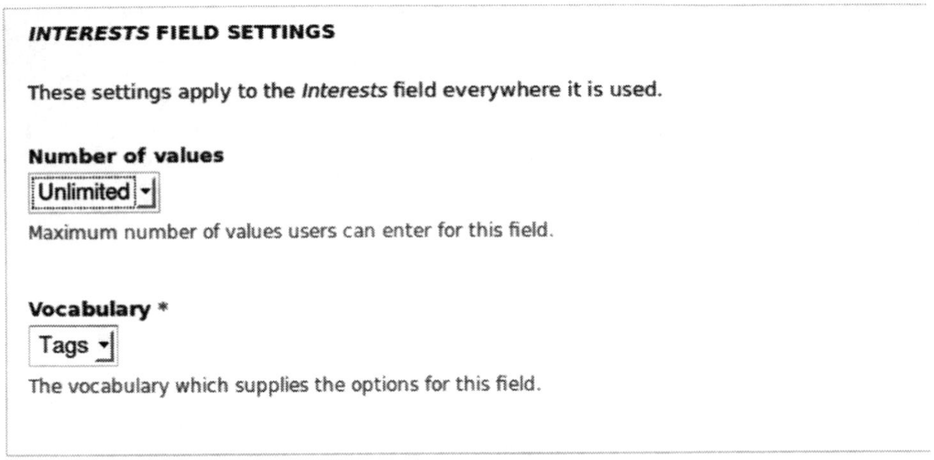

INTERESTS FIELD SETTINGS

These settings apply to the *Interests* field everywhere it is used.

Number of values

Unlimited ▾

Maximum number of values users can enter for this field.

Vocabulary *

Tags ▾

The vocabulary which supplies the options for this field.

Figure 4-4. Interest field settings

This is all we need to do for the account settings.

Going back to our content type definition (as a reminder, use the Structure administrative tab and select Content Types), we will add the very same field we just added to the account. As shown in Figure 4-5, we simply called it Tags.

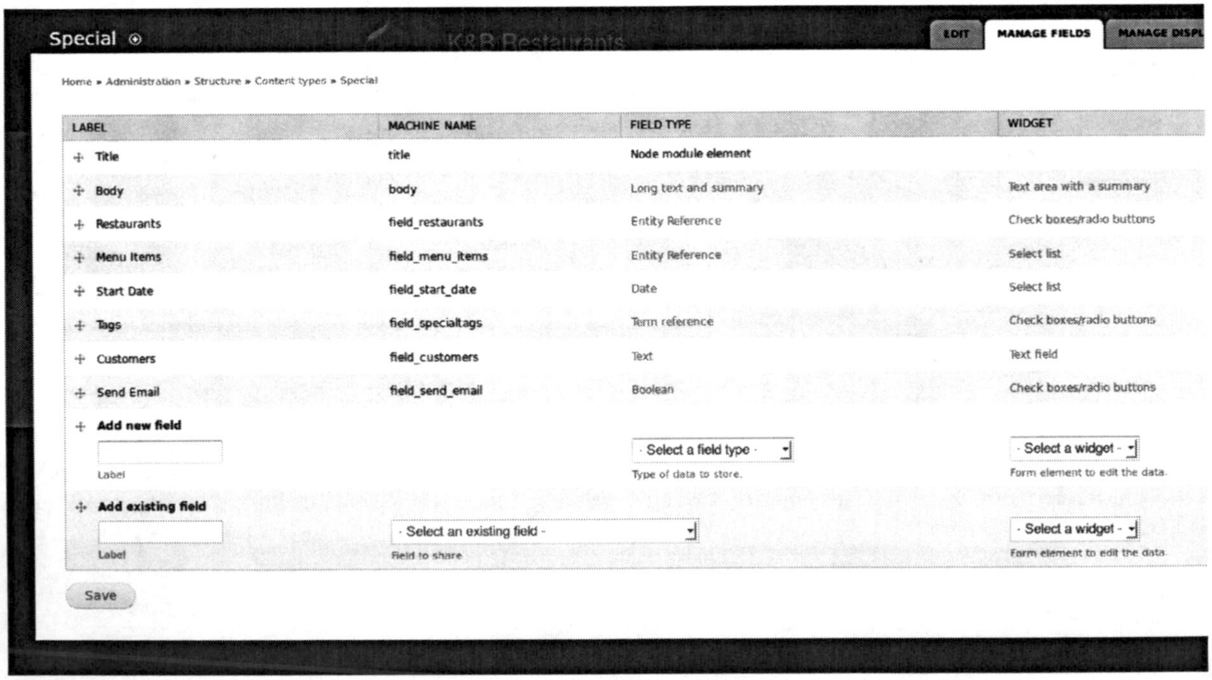

LABEL	MACHINE NAME	FIELD TYPE	WIDGET
✛ Title	title	Node module element	
✛ Body	body	Long text and summary	Text area with a summary
✛ Restaurants	field_restaurants	Entity Reference	Check boxes/radio buttons
✛ Menu Items	field_menu_items	Entity Reference	Select list
✛ Start Date	field_start_date	Date	Select list
✛ Tags	field_specialtags	Term reference	Check boxes/radio buttons
✛ Customers	field_customers	Text	Text field
✛ Send Email	field_send_email	Boolean	Check boxes/radio buttons
✛ **Add new field**			
		· Select a field type · ▾	· Select a widget - ▾
Label		Type of data to store.	Form element to edit the data.
✛ **Add existing field**			
	· Select an existing field - ▾		· Select a widget - ▾
Label	Field to share.		Form element to edit the data.

Save

Figure 4-5. Special fields

The second field we need is the list of customers to be emailed. Because we only need the address, we will use a text field, and make it hold unlimited values.

Last, the Send Email field will be a simple Boolean, assigned to either Yes or No—indicating whether or not an email has been sent for that special. This field is shown in Figure 4-6.

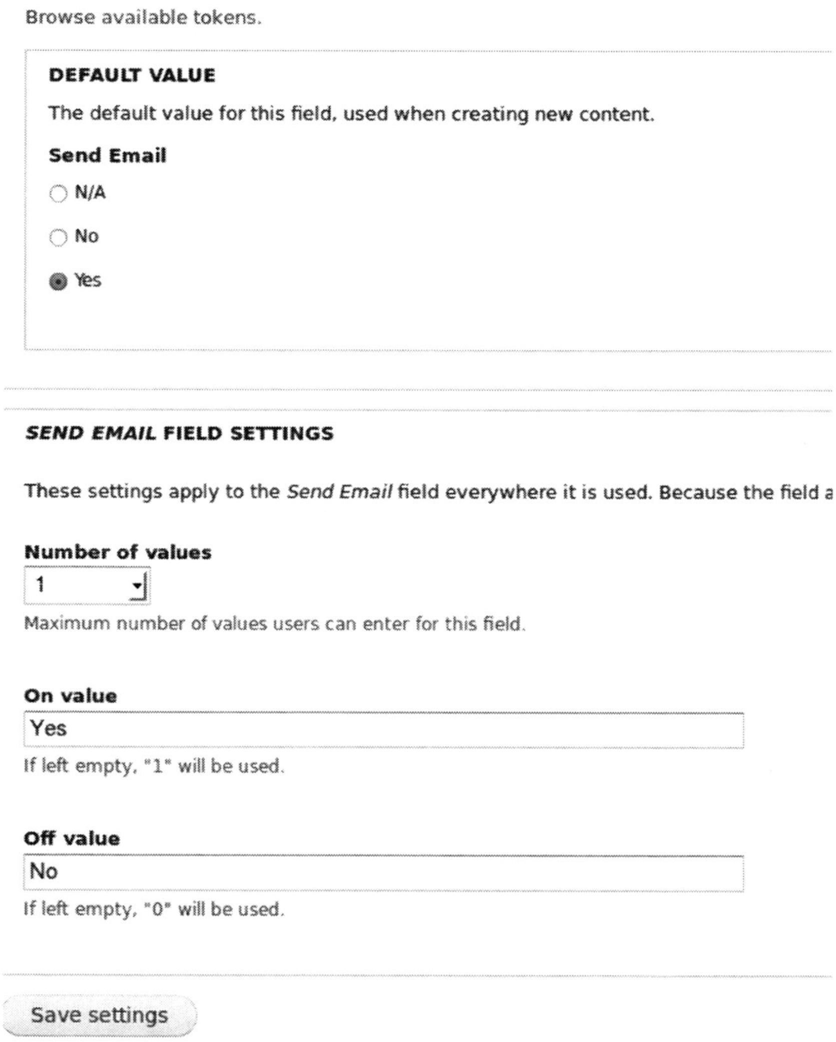

Browse available tokens.

DEFAULT VALUE

The default value for this field, used when creating new content.

Send Email

◯ N/A

◯ No

◉ Yes

SEND EMAIL **FIELD SETTINGS**

These settings apply to the *Send Email* field everywhere it is used. Because the field a

Number of values

| 1 ⌄ |

Maximum number of values users can enter for this field.

On value

| Yes |

If left empty, "1" will be used.

Off value

| No |

If left empty, "0" will be used.

Save settings

Figure 4-6. Boolean field

At this point, we've added fields to our content types—and the user account type—necessary to both track the users' interests as well as process the specials email rule. Next, we will define the views —that is, the models used for getting the data we need to run the process.

Defining the Views and Views_Rules

As explained earlier, we need some magic from the views_rules module to make data available in the context of our custom business rules that would normally not be available. The items we need will become more obvious as we get to the next part: defining the rules, but when you will work on your own application, this will be part of your design. We need two separate lists of data:

- A list of all the customers that have preferences defined

- A list of all the specials that are a week away or less from being in effect

We will need those lists available to loop through in our rules, which is where the views_rules module comes in. It essentially provides a bridge between the views and our rules —that is, the data model and our business logic.

Views are available through the Structure tab of the administrative menu. As usual, you can just click the little Add new view link on the top left-hand corner of the Views menu (see Figure 4-7).

Figure 4-7. *Views menu*

When creating a view, you have to fill up a few fields for what you want to query, and how to display it. Note that you will be able to customize both aspects in greater detail on the view overview screen. Right now, since our first view is about fetching all users on the site, let's just show Users and display a list of fields. As shown in Figure 4-8, you can leave the default values for everything else and click on Continue & edit to get to the actual view configuration screen.

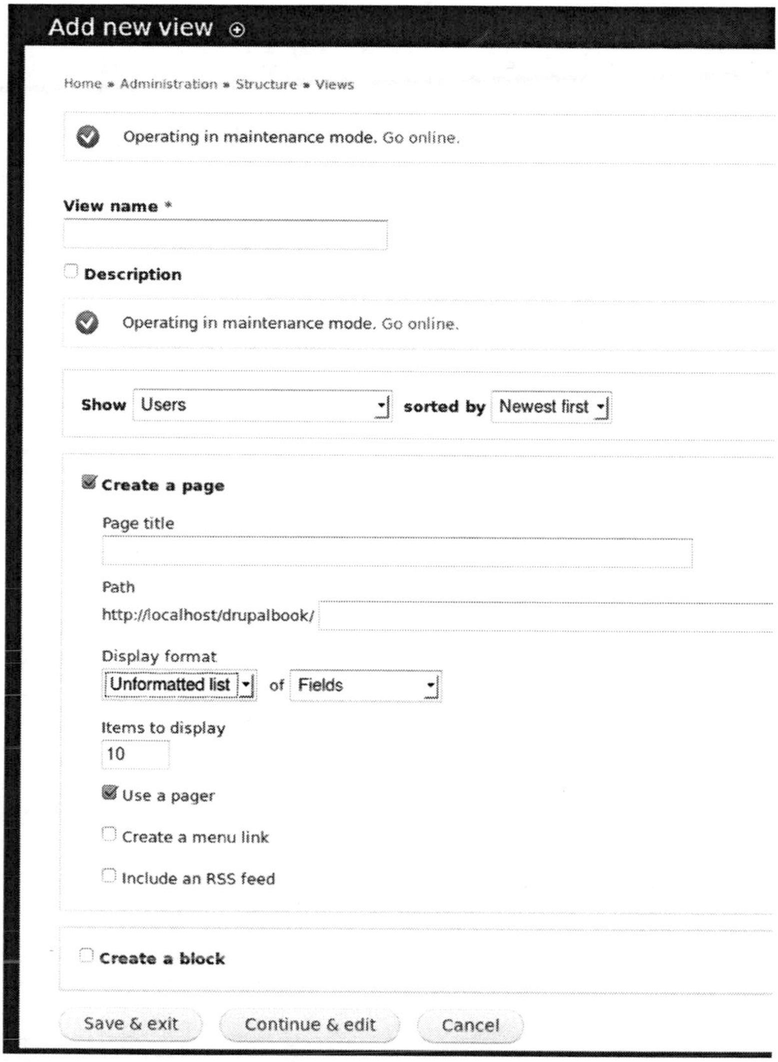

Add new view ⊕

Home » Administration » Structure » Views

✓ Operating in maintenance mode. Go online.

View name *

▢ **Description**

✓ Operating in maintenance mode. Go online.

Show | Users   ▾ | **sorted by** | Newest first ▾

☑ **Create a page**

Page title

Path
http://localhost/drupalbook/ [   ]

Display format
| Unformatted list ▾ | of | Fields   ▾ |

Items to display
[10]

☑ Use a pager

▢ Create a menu link

▢ Include an RSS feed

▢ **Create a block**

(Save & exit)   (Continue & edit)   (Cancel)

Figure 4-8. *New customer view*

The screen shown in Figure 4-9 is one of the most configuration-intensive screens you will find in Drupal. First, a view is all about querying data and displaying it in a certain way. For each view, you can then define several types of displays:

- As a page on the site: This display type is used to create a page of dynamic content that will be shown in the usual Content region on the site.

- As a feed: This display is used to expose a view as an RSS feed. In this way, people can use RSS aggregators to consume a Drupal view's data.

- As a block: This display allows you to create a specific block for your view that can then be placed within a region (using the Blocks configuration page).

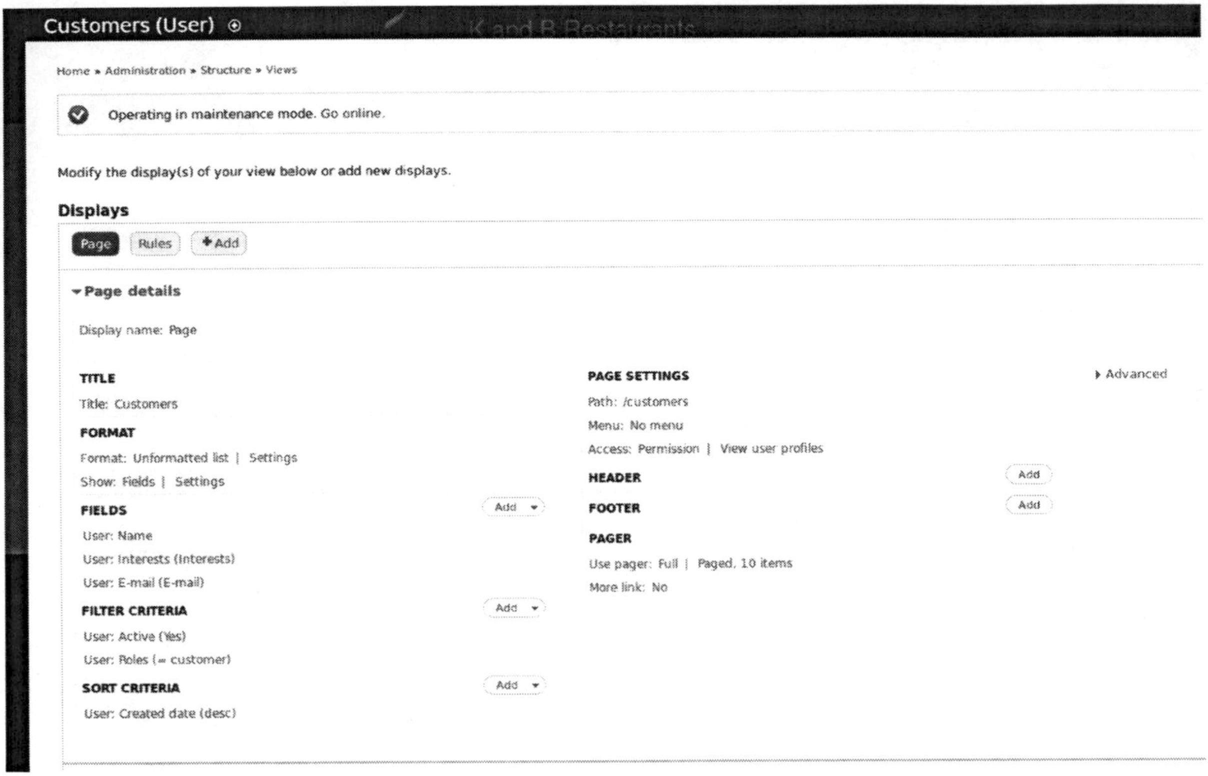

Figure 4-9. *Customers view*

And if you have additional modules installed, they can also add more display types:

- As a PDF page

- As a service query

- As a rule's view loop

Displays are shown on the top bar, and each display will have its own additional configuration. Think of these displays as kind of views for the view —that is, different ways to output the same data. Each display is similar to a database view on top of a table, which is essentially a layer of abstraction for that table. The displays are similar, in that they provide a layer of abstraction over the underlying content types. Not all of them are related to users viewing the data with their browser.

Let's stay on the Page display for now and configure the data we are querying a bit more. Because this is a Page display type, it will define how the user will see the data in their browser. By default, in the Filter criteria section, there should already be a filter to grab only active users.

We are going to add a new filter criteria based on type, because we're only interested in customers, not site admins or managers. To add the filter, click on the Add button, then check the box that says User: Roles and click Save. Then select Customer as the role you want to use for this filter. Because there is no need for us to loop through customers with no interests, let's also add a filter on User: Interests, set to "Is not empty." That should do for the view's filters.

The second part of the configuration of this view is about the fields we want to show or use for each result. We really only need the user's interests and email address. We can add the name in there for good measure in case we want to add it to the rules later. In the Fields section, you can click add for each of those three fields: User: Name, User: Interests, and User: Email. These fields are shown in Figure 4-9.

There are several ways to go about defining how we want to display the Interests field, but the most useful option for the rest of our views/rules configuration is to display it as a basic textfield. Even though it is a list, you can click on the Settings link to the right of the Interests field in the Fields section and expand the Multiple Field Settings configuration. There, you can just check to display all the values in the same row with a simple comma separator. This is standard for tags and other taxonomy inputs.

Congratulations, you have just built your first view! You've essentially configured a set of items to query and defined what fields of the items to show.

Now let's add a new display to this view so it can be used by our rules (this is what is enabled by installing the views_rules module). In the Displays section, click the Add button and select Rules. It will show you a screen that is quite similar to the Page display, except for the Rules settings section on top of the middle column. This section contains the Row variables configuration, which is where you will define the the subset of fields available to rules, including their field names. Note that in order to make a field available to rules, the field must defined in the first column of the Display configuration.

Within the Row variables configuration for our example, let's enable all three of them. The display will require you to at least edit those row variables once, even though they will most likely be properly auto-configured when you click on the "edit field info" link. Their configuration can be seen in Figure 4-10.

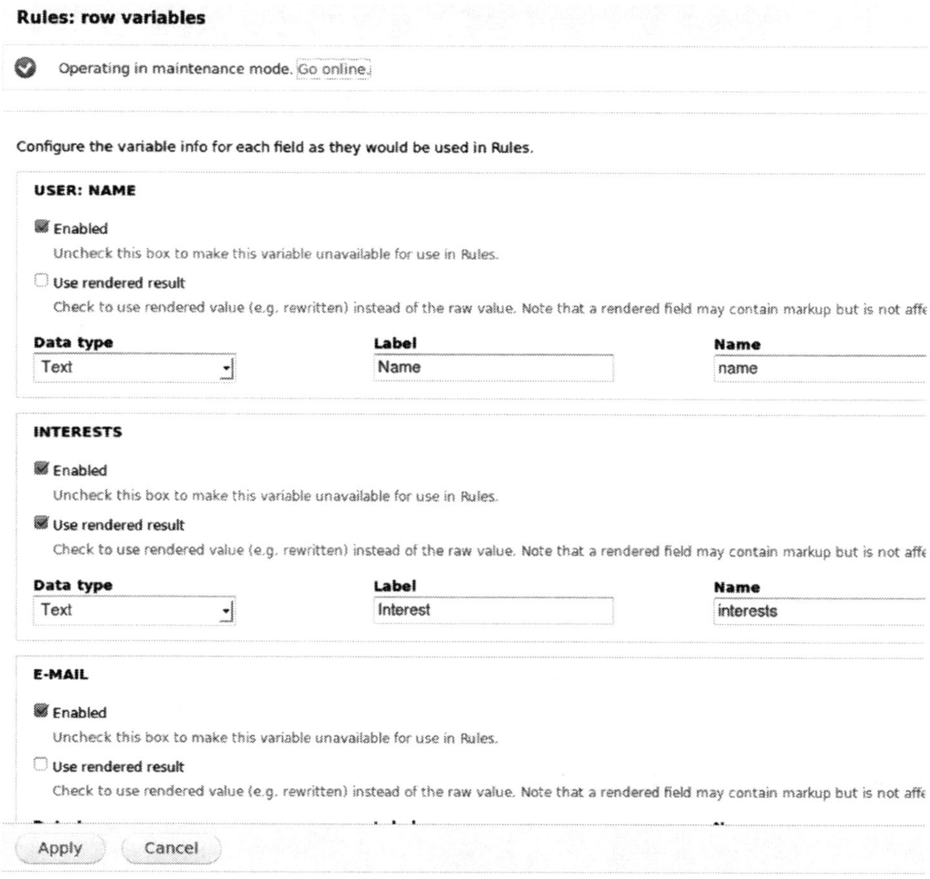

Rules: row variables

✓ Operating in maintenance mode. Go online.

Configure the variable info for each field as they would be used in Rules.

USER: NAME

☑ Enabled
Uncheck this box to make this variable unavailable for use in Rules.

☐ Use rendered result
Check to use rendered value (e.g. rewritten) instead of the raw value. Note that a rendered field may contain markup but is not affe

Data type	Label	Name
Text	Name	name

INTERESTS

☑ Enabled
Uncheck this box to make this variable unavailable for use in Rules.

☑ Use rendered result
Check to use rendered value (e.g. rewritten) instead of the raw value. Note that a rendered field may contain markup but is not affe

Data type	Label	Name
Text	Interest	interests

E-MAIL

☑ Enabled
Uncheck this box to make this variable unavailable for use in Rules.

☐ Use rendered result
Check to use rendered value (e.g. rewritten) instead of the raw value. Note that a rendered field may contain markup but is not affe

Apply   Cancel

Figure 4-10. Customers view row variables

Finally, because we don't want to miss any user, we will have to set the Pager in the middle column to show all items, by clicking on the "Paged, 10 items" link and selecting "Show all items". Remember that a rule will be consuming the output of this view's Rule display, not a human using a browser. So there's no need to page the items. In fact, in this case, paging will cause us to not email all of the desired users.

That concludes our first view for now. The view has two displays defined: one for viewing by users of the site, and another specifically for making its data available to our business rules. You don't actually need to define a Page display for those cases when you only need the view for the purpose of exposing data to rules.

For the second view, we want to list all specials in the site that are within a week of their start date. Let's create another view and show content of the Special content type, sorted however you want. There again, we will show an unformatted list of fields and click on Continue and edit, as shown in Figure 4-11.

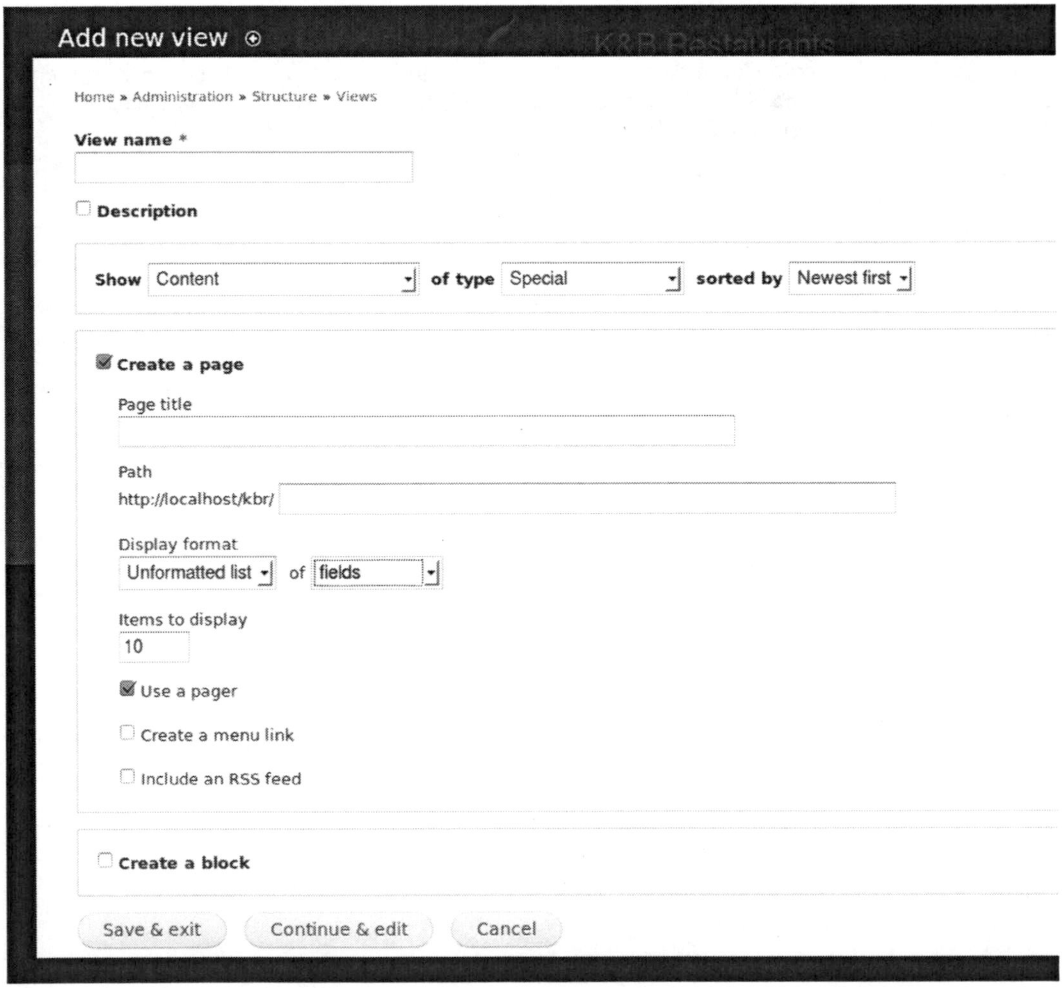

Figure 4-11. *Adding the specials view*

Once on the view screen, notice that the filter criteria have already defaulted to Published content of the special type. We need to add a couple more filter criteria, as show in Figure 4-12.

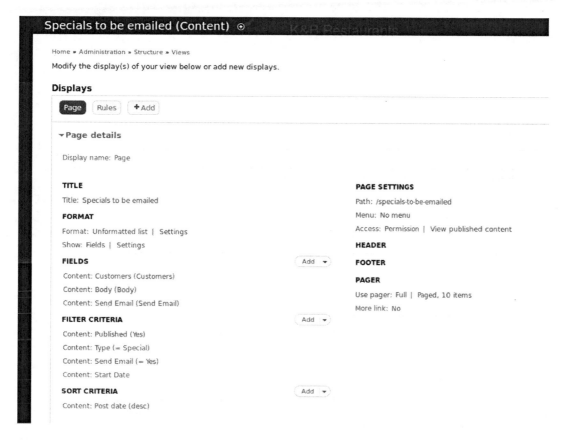

Figure 4-12. *Specials view*

Our Send Email Boolean should be filtered to only those with Yes, and the Start Date field should be configured as shown on Figure 4-13—that is, within seven days of the date.

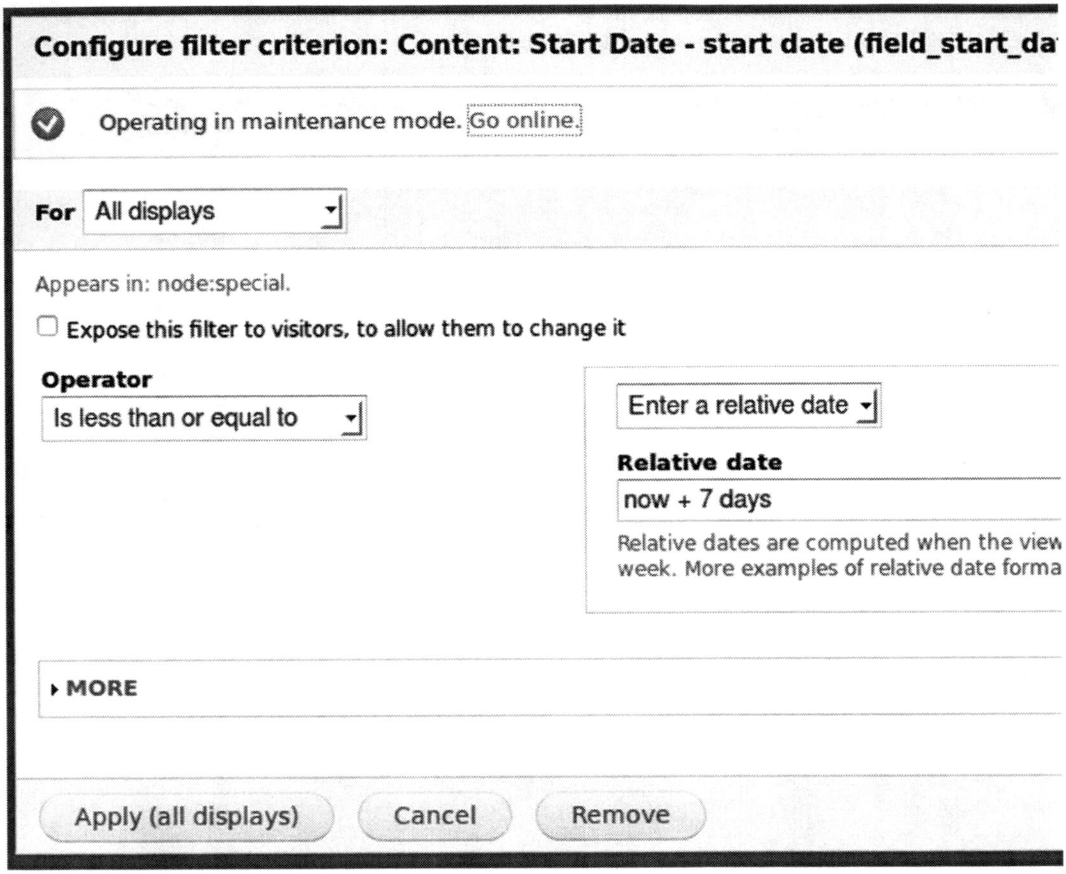

Configure filter criterion: Content: Start Date - start date (field_start_da

✅ Operating in maintenance mode. ⸢Go online.⸥

For | All displays ▾ |

Appears in: node:special.

☐ Expose this filter to visitors, to allow them to change it

Operator

| Is less than or equal to ▾ |

| Enter a relative date ▾ |

Relative date

| now + 7 days |

Relative dates are computed when the view
week. More examples of relative date forma

▸ **MORE**

(Apply (all displays))　(Cancel)　(Remove)

Figure 4-13. *Start Date criterion*

The operator needs set to "Is less than or equal to" because the start date needs to be less than in a week. Then the value to compare with needs to be a relative date, set to "now + 7 days".

After this, we need to also set the pager to show all the items instead of limiting to only 10, and we will be ready to get to the list of fields we want to use.

Because we plan on using this view in a rule to send an email about the special item returned by the view, we need to make every field we want to use in the email or in the rule in general visible on the view in the Fields section. In other words, if a field isn't in the Rule display for the view, it won't be available for use by the rule. For this example, we used the list of customers to email, the body of the special, and the Send Email Boolean. If you designed a richer specials item with a lot of relevant fields, such as descriptions, teasers, and so forth, you would want to add them here, too, so that they can be used in the construction of the email for the rule.

Finally, let's create a Rules display and make sure the row variables look okay, as shown in Figure 4-14. This should be similar to the first view we created. Don't forget to save your changes!

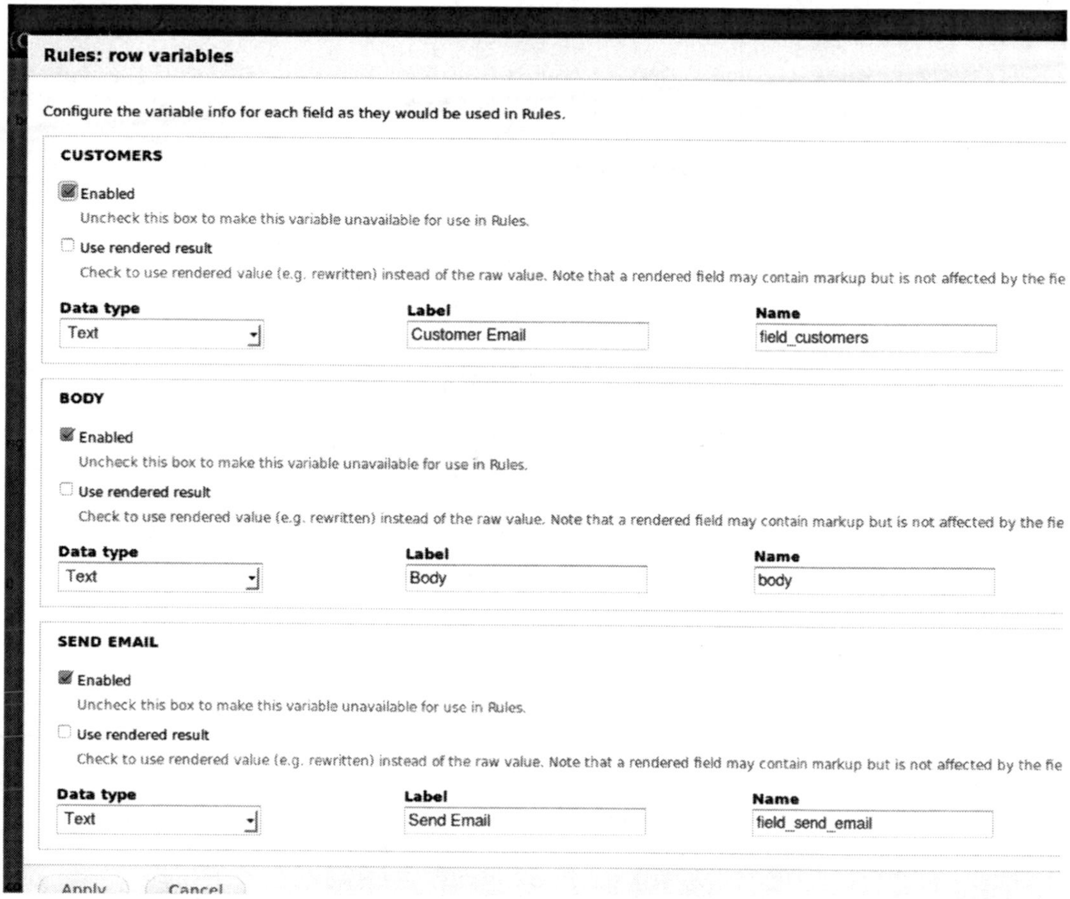

Rules: row variables

Configure the variable info for each field as they would be used in Rules.

CUSTOMERS

☑ Enabled

Uncheck this box to make this variable unavailable for use in Rules.

☐ Use rendered result

Check to use rendered value (e.g. rewritten) instead of the raw value. Note that a rendered field may contain markup but is not affected by the fie

Data type	Label	Name
Text	Customer Email	field_customers

BODY

☑ Enabled

Uncheck this box to make this variable unavailable for use in Rules.

☐ Use rendered result

Check to use rendered value (e.g. rewritten) instead of the raw value. Note that a rendered field may contain markup but is not affected by the fie

Data type	Label	Name
Text	Body	body

SEND EMAIL

☑ Enabled

Uncheck this box to make this variable unavailable for use in Rules.

☐ Use rendered result

Check to use rendered value (e.g. rewritten) instead of the raw value. Note that a rendered field may contain markup but is not affected by the fie

Data type	Label	Name
Text	Send Email	field_send_email

Apply   Cancel

Figure 4-14. *Specials view row variables*

Going back to the views configuration page, notice that there is a simple URL associated with the Page display for each of the views you created, for you to go to the actual display of the view. You can use it to see the output of the view and check that everything works fine with a little bit of placeholder content.

That does it for defining the views, or data model, for the email specials business rules. Nex,t we will use these views to configure the rules themselves.

Defining the Rules

Now that we've defined the data model that will be used by the rules (that is, using views specially created just for consumption by some custom rules), let's get to the most impressive part of advanced Drupal configuration: the rules definition! Recall from previous sections that the Rules module lets you create from simple to complex business rules, including loops, if/then/else logic, and conditional grouping, all triggered on any one of many events in the system, resulting in some action(s) being executed. Whereas the Views module provides support to display any data in the system in any way needed, the Rules module lets you create just about any business rule (including an action). Again, think of these rules as "writing code," only in this case we are working within a higher-level "language" —that is, that of the Rules module's rule definition.

Further, if you recall from Chapter 3, you installed the Features module to let you promote configuration from one Drupal environment to another. The configuration data contained within Rules falls into this category, of being able to export the rules as features, and install them on one or more target Drupal systems. This would be very similar to writing business logic in code, and then deploying that code to an application server.

You can get to the rules menu under the Configuration administrative tab. As shown in Figure 4-15, this menu shows you the rules you currently have, with the option to enable/disable them, and to create new ones.

Figure 4-15. *Rules screen*

The first rule is about keeping a list of email addresses of customers to be emailed for each special. The right moment to check and update this list is when a special is being created or edited. As shown in Figure 4-16, you can select a trigger on the rule creation screen.

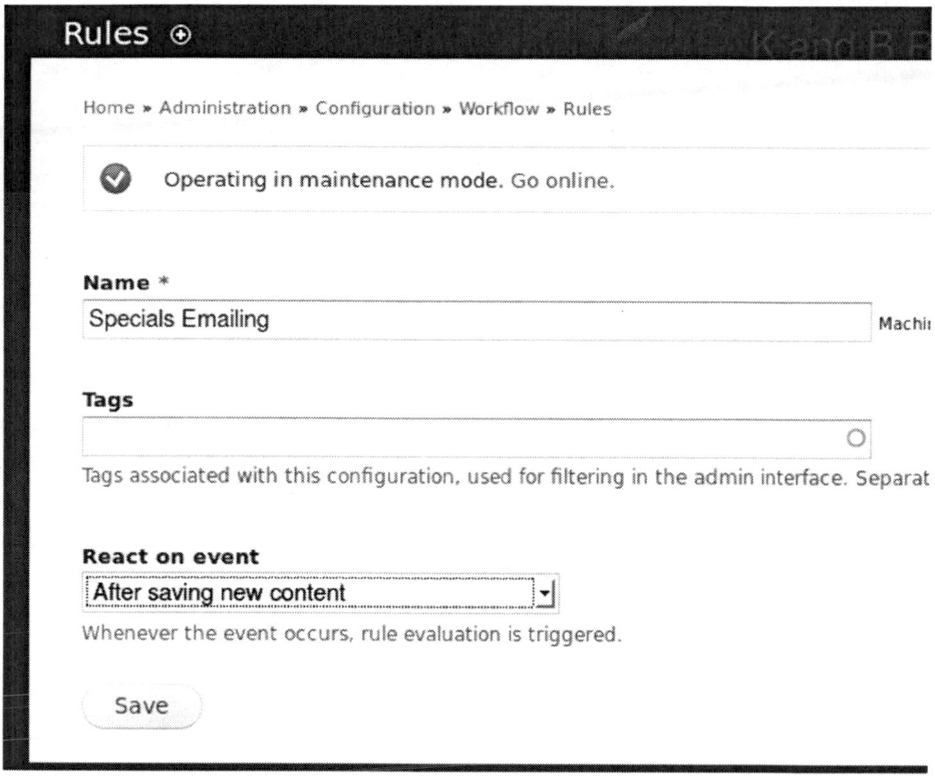

Rules ⊕

Home » Administration » Configuration » Workflow » Rules

✔ Operating in maintenance mode. Go online.

Name *

Specials Emailing   Machir

Tags

○

Tags associated with this configuration, used for filtering in the admin interface. Separat

React on event

After saving new content   ▾

Whenever the event occurs, rule evaluation is triggered.

Save

Figure 4-16. *New Rule*

After you name your new rule and select one of our two events as the trigger (the other can be added right after the rule is created), simply save the rule to navigate to the rule editing screen. As shown in Figure 4-17, there are three sections on there. The first one is to define the events that will trigger the rule. We already added the "After saving new content" event as a trigger, so let's also add the "After updating existing content" one. This means that the rest of the rule will be processed every time either of those events happens —that is, creating a new special or updating an existing one.

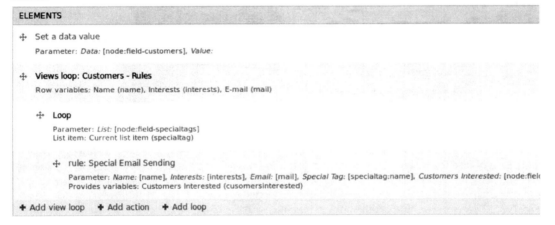

Events

EVENT
After saving new content
After updating existing content
✚ Add event

Conditions

ELEMENTS
⊹ Content is of type
Parameter: *Content:* [node], *Content types:* Special
⊹ Entity has field
Parameter: *Entity:* [node], *Field:* field_customers
✚ Add condition   ✚ Add or   ✚ Add and

Actions

ELEMENTS
⊹ Set a data value
Parameter: *Data:* [node:field-customers], *Value:*
⊹ Views loop: Customers - Rules
Row variables: Name (name), Interests (interests), E-mail (mail)
⊹ Loop
Parameter: *List:* [node:field-specialtags]
List item: Current list item (specialtag)
⊹ rule: Special Email Sending
Parameter: *Name:* [name], *Interests:* [interests], *Email:* [mail], *Special Tag:* [specialtag:name], *Customers Interested:* [node:fielc
Provides variables: Customers Interested (cusomersinterested)
✚ Add view loop   ✚ Add action   ✚ Add loop

Figure 4-17. *Rule overview*

Next are the conditions that, if verified, will let the rule execute its actions.

Our first condition will be to check if the updated item is a special. A simple "Content is of type" condition will do. It will lead you to a screen where you can select what content type you are talking about. The autocomplete selection of content seems a little bit unintuitive at first, but our simple use case is a good opportunity to understand how it works. The autocomplete will show you all the variables available to the current context of the rule. Meaning that you don't have access to more "things" than what is shown in the selector. Possible selections are usually followed by a brief description of what they represent. In this case, we want to select the item we just saved, called node, as shown in Figure 4-18.

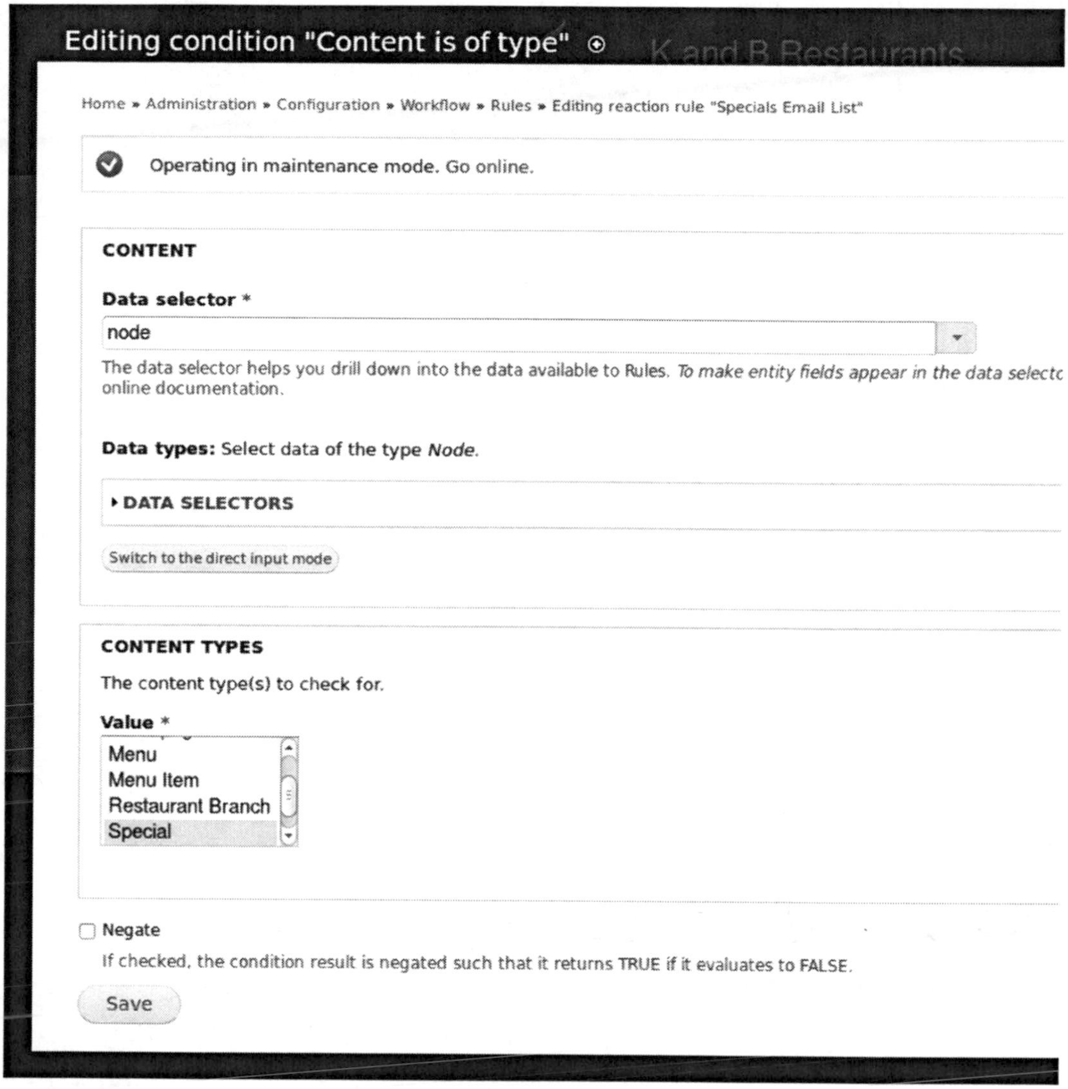

Figure 4-18. *Content is of type condition*

Then we select what content type we want to match our selection with. In this case: Special. We also have the option to negate the expression, to match our item against all content types but one, for instance, which in our case is not required.

Our second condition is purely "programmatic." We need the list of email addresses held by the special to be made available to the context of this rule —that is, we will need to access it later on during the actions section. In order to add a field to the context of a rule, we simply check for its existence in the conditions section. As shown in Figure 4-19, all we have to do is add the condition "Entity has field," select our node again as the entity, and choose the customer_emails text list we created earlier as the field to check for. From now on in this rule, this field will be accessible to data selectors.

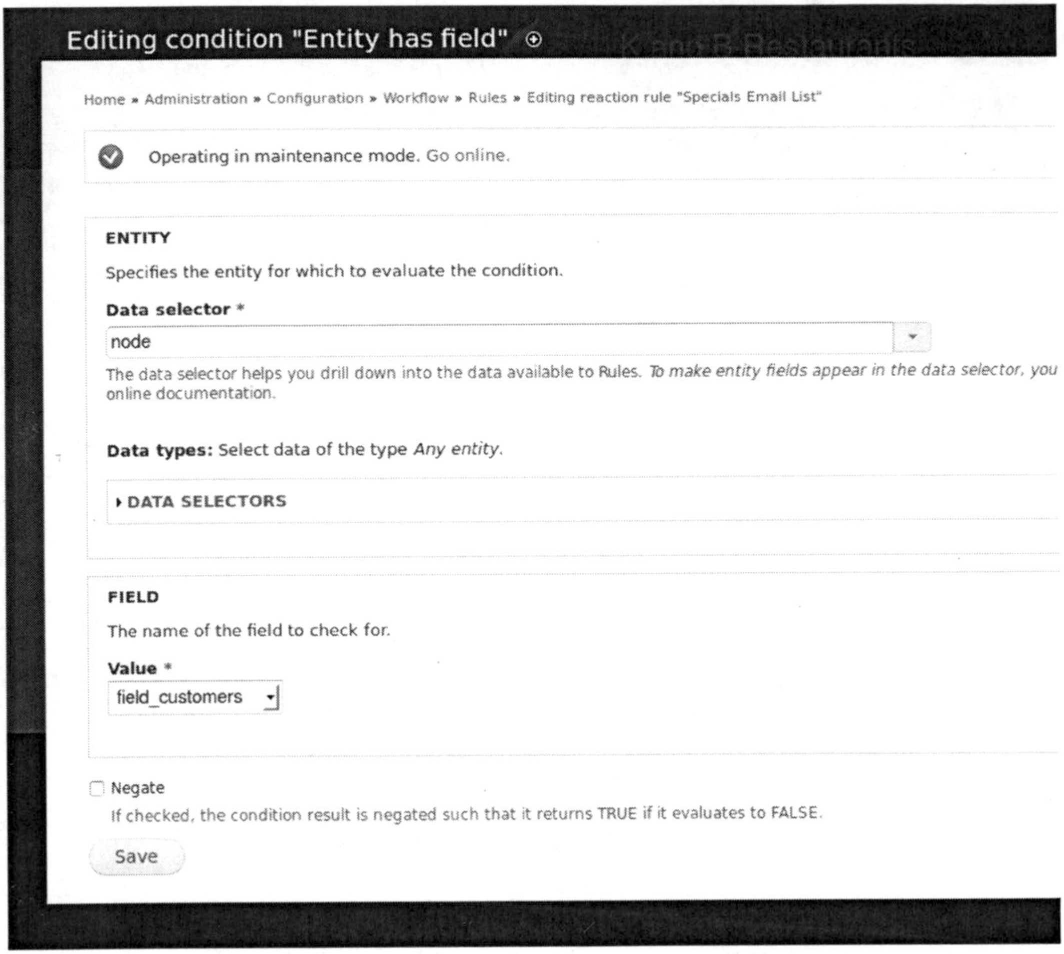

Figure 4-19. *Entity has field condition*

FIELD AVAILABILITY

Just to clarify what we're doing with the customer_emails field, the actions associated with this rule won't have access to the field if that field is not included in a condition. That's why we need to add a somewhat bogus condition—which is to simply check that the entity in question has the customer_emails field. Doing so will make sure that field is available within the data selectors for the rule's actions.

This whole rule is about re-building the list of email addresses to be contacted about the special. So the first thing we're going to do is clean it up. To do this, we are going to add an action, of the "Set a data value" type. Because we just made the customers field of our special available to the rule, it will show on the data selector, and we can just leave the value we want to set it to empty (see Figure 4-20). This means that the first thing the rule is going to do once it validates its condition is empty the customers list of the special item.

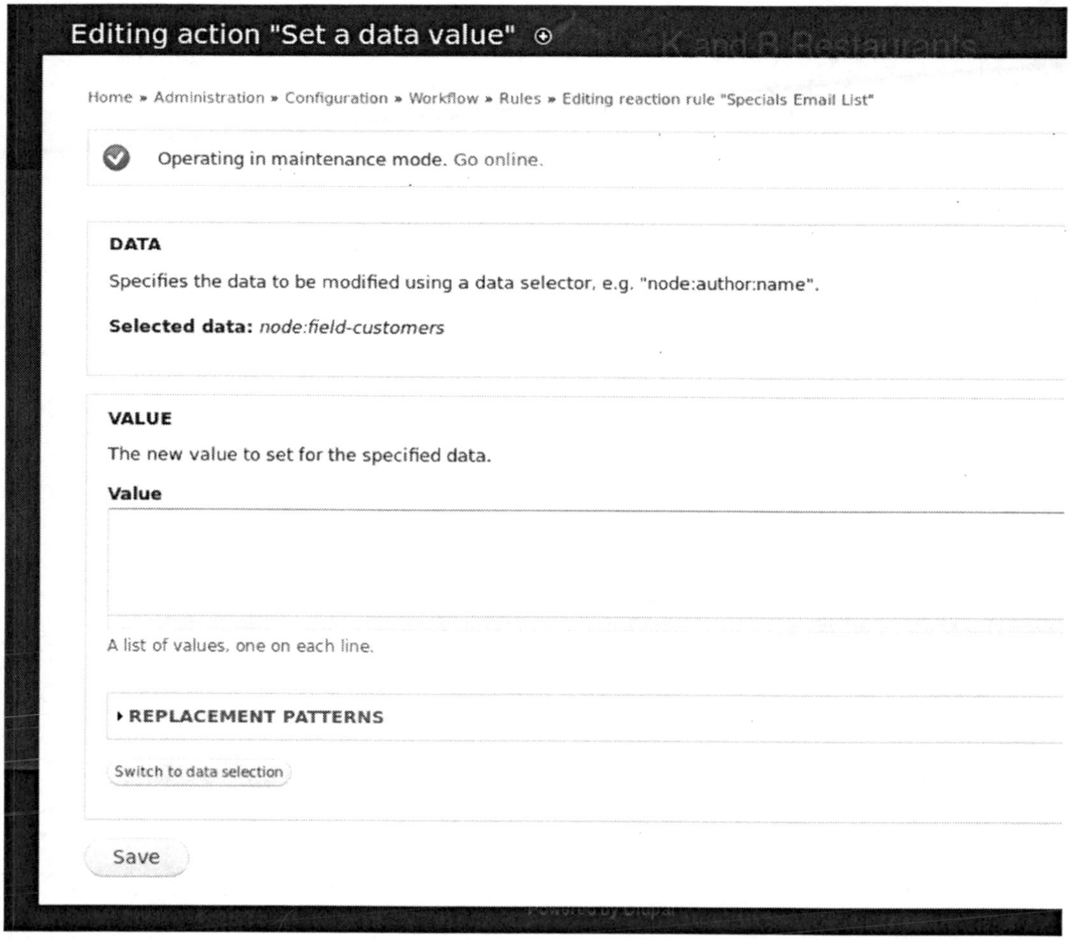

Figure 4-20. *Set data value to empty action*

Now we need to re-populate this list, by looping through all the users of the site with defined preferences and adding them to the customers list we just emptied. Normally, we wouldn't be able to just loop through customers, but we have defined a views_rules display earlier in the views section that we can now use in rules. Remember, the views_rules module lets us bridge the power of views with the power of rules, giving rules access to any data within the system.

In the action section, select a views loop, and pick the customer loop. Remember that you had to define row variables on the Rules display of the view, as shown in Figure 4-21. These fields will now be available to the rule's loop.

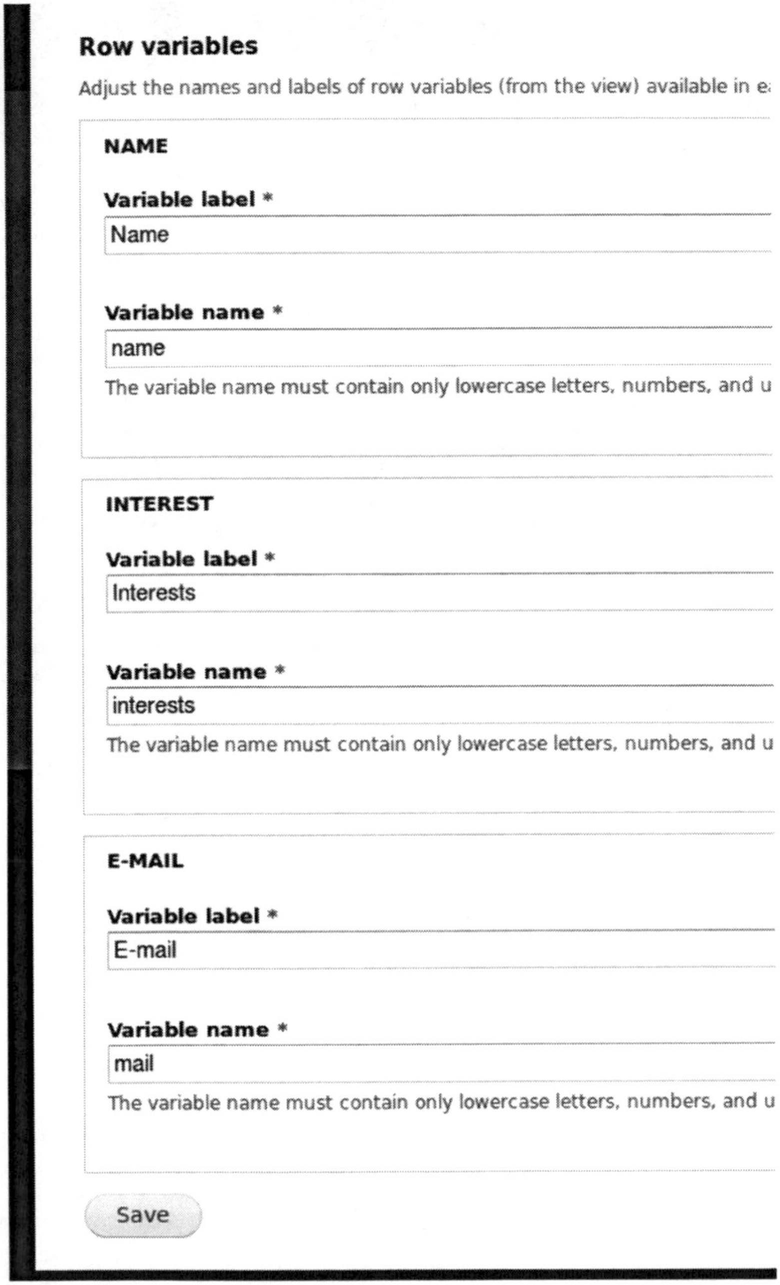

Row variables

Adjust the names and labels of row variables (from the view) available in e:

NAME

Variable label *

Name

Variable name *

name

The variable name must contain only lowercase letters, numbers, and u

INTEREST

Variable label *

Interests

Variable name *

interests

The variable name must contain only lowercase letters, numbers, and u

E-MAIL

Variable label *

E-mail

Variable name *

mail

The variable name must contain only lowercase letters, numbers, and u

Save

Figure 4-21. Views loop row variables

We are now looping through all customers in the site that have set preferences. And we want to compare those preferences with the tags on the specials. So we will loop again, this time using a normal loop because we're going through values of a field accessible to the current rule context: the special's specialtags field.

To differentiate between actions or loops that are meant to happen inside a loop, and the ones that need to happen after, we use indentation. Indenting actions or loops one more level than the loop before them means they will happen inside the loop that is indented one less level. If they have the same level of indentation, they will happen after the loop. This is very much like the way indentation is used for loops in proper syntax of all major programming languages. You indent while you loop and unindent once you're done looping.

When defining a rule's loop, you will have to select the data you want to loop through and how you want to name the element currently being iterated by the loop, as shown in Figure 4-22. This is very much like a for-each loop within most modern programming languages. These are also known as iterators, because they allow you to iterate through a list. In our case, because we're looping through specialtags, our element is called specialtag. This element will be available to all the actions falling under this loop (that is, actions that follow the loop and are indented more than the loop itself).

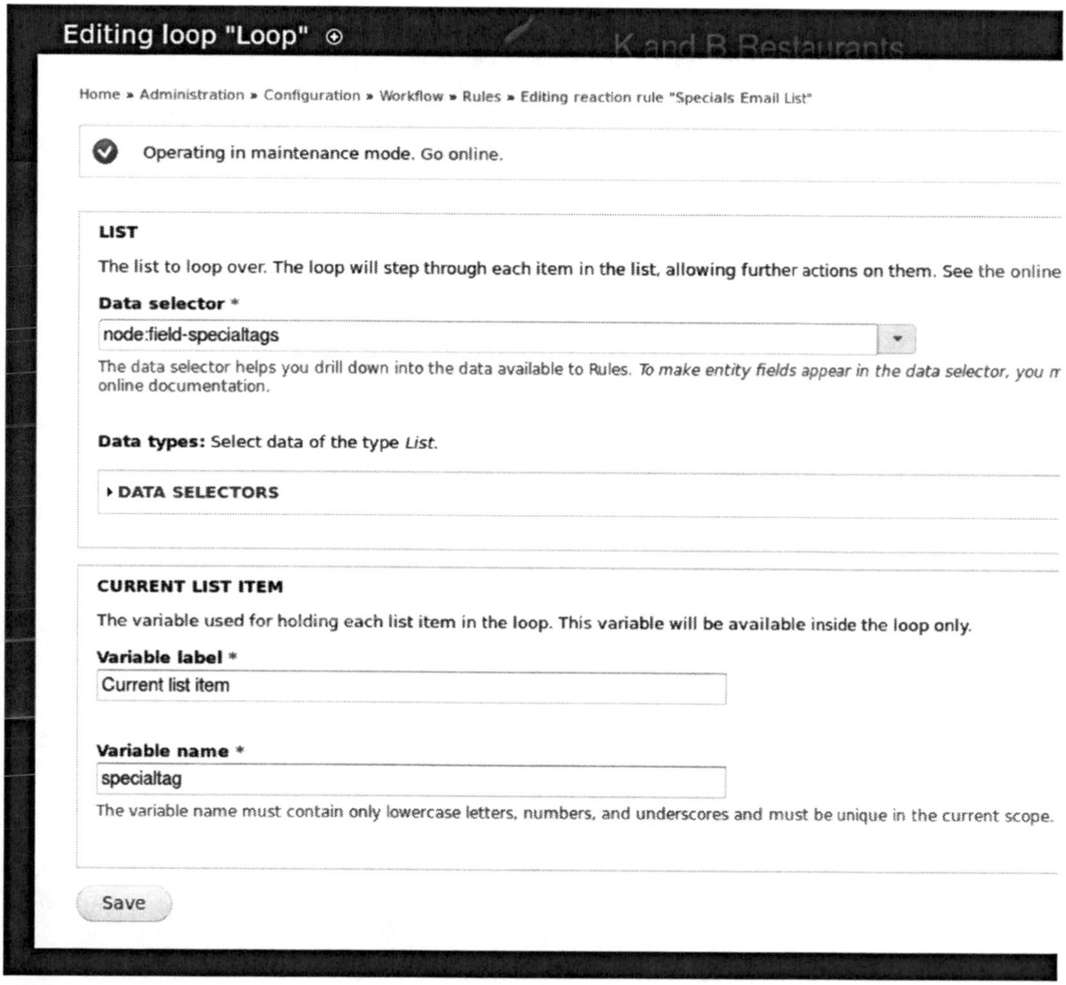

Figure 4-22. *List loop*

Now that we have both our loops, we need to compare the tags of our first loop with those of the second, and add the user's address to our list if we have a match. Since we just said *if*, we will need an additional condition before we can take action. This means we're going to have to create a rules component as an action of our rule, as that's the only way we can add a condition within the loop of an action.

Let's go back to our rules menu and select the components tab to the right. This will take us to a menu quite similar to the rules one, where we can define special actions to be used by other rules or rule actions (among other things). Click on "Add new component" then select a Rules component (see Figure 4-23).

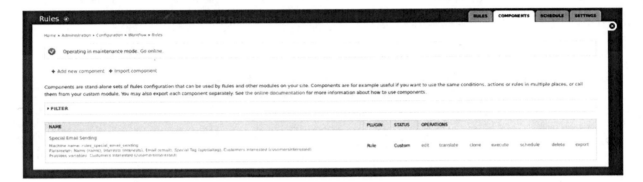

Figure 4-23. *Components screen*

A rules component is quite similar to a rule, except it has no trigger. It will be called by another rule automatically, thus there is no need for a trigger with the component. In our case, the component will be called on every iteration of our normal loop. Having no trigger also means the rules component needs to be given some context to work on. Usually the context available to the rule depends on what type of trigger you have. If your trigger is saving an item, then the item and its fields will be available to the context, for instance. See Figure 4-24 for a view of the component you're going to create.

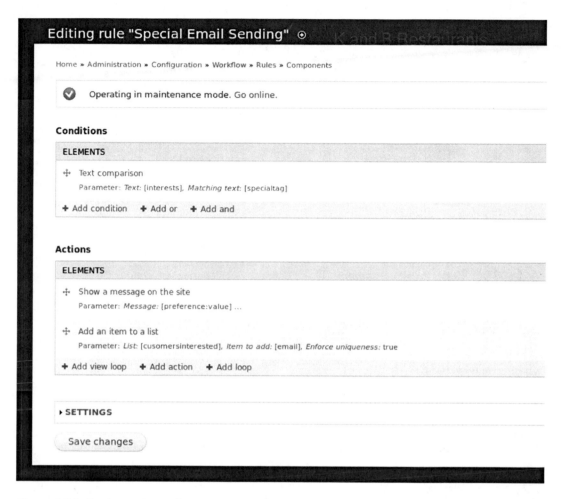

Figure 4-24. *Component overview*

First things first, though. We want to create variables to be mapped to our rule component. To do so, just edit your rule component and expand the "Settings" section. There you will need to add five variables, as shown in Figure 4-25. Those are the variables you need to have in the newly created rule component.

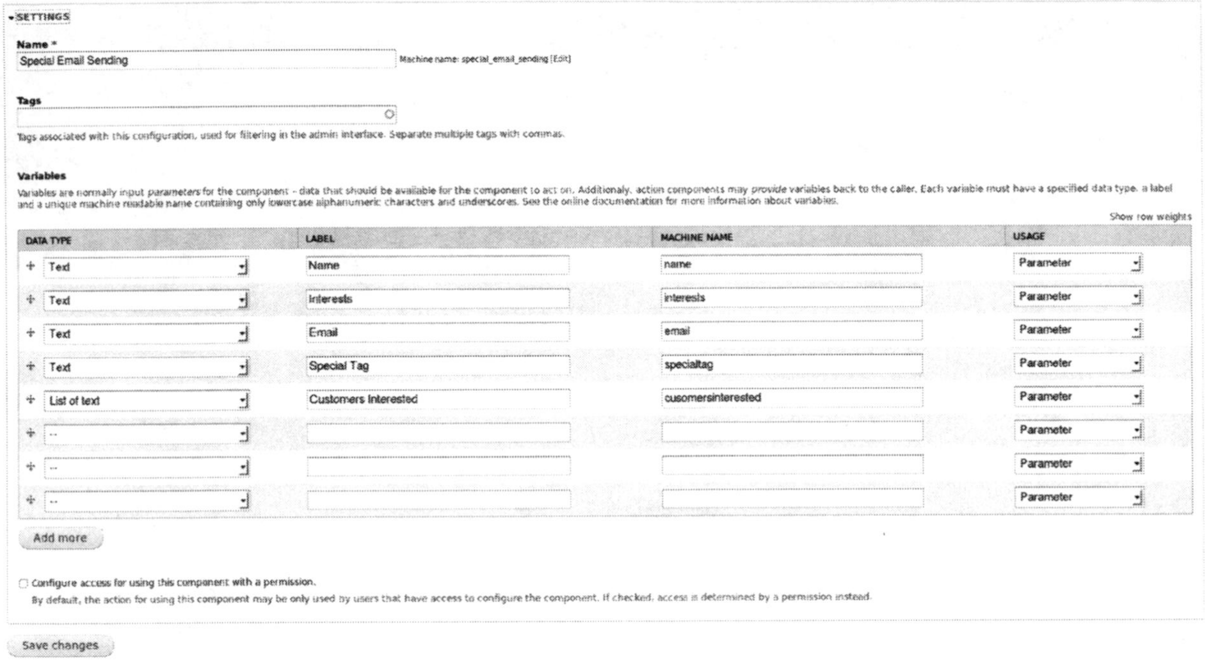

Figure 4-25. *Rule component variables*

Now that those variables are defined, let's map them from our main rule. As shown in Figures 4-26 and 4-27, the mapping is fairly straightforward. The hard part is to figure out what variables you need for your rule component. The good thing with configuring those rules from a user interface is that it's very easy to go back and forth between your component and your main rule to add and match variables as you realize you need them for the rule component.

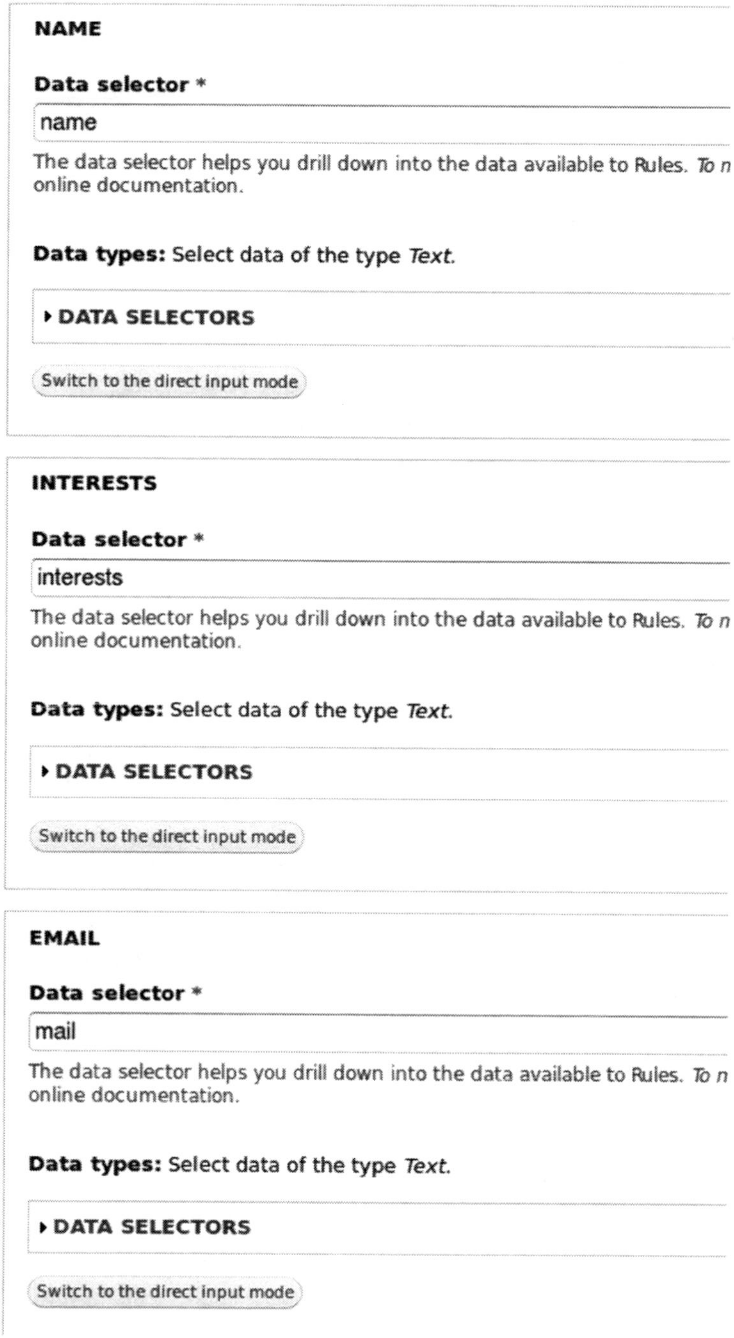

NAME

Data selector *

name

The data selector helps you drill down into the data available to Rules. *To n* online documentation.

Data types: Select data of the type *Text*.

▸ **DATA SELECTORS**

(Switch to the direct input mode)

INTERESTS

Data selector *

interests

The data selector helps you drill down into the data available to Rules. *To n* online documentation.

Data types: Select data of the type *Text*.

▸ **DATA SELECTORS**

(Switch to the direct input mode)

EMAIL

Data selector *

mail

The data selector helps you drill down into the data available to Rules. *To n* online documentation.

Data types: Select data of the type *Text*.

▸ **DATA SELECTORS**

(Switch to the direct input mode)

Figure 4-26. *Component variable mapping 1*

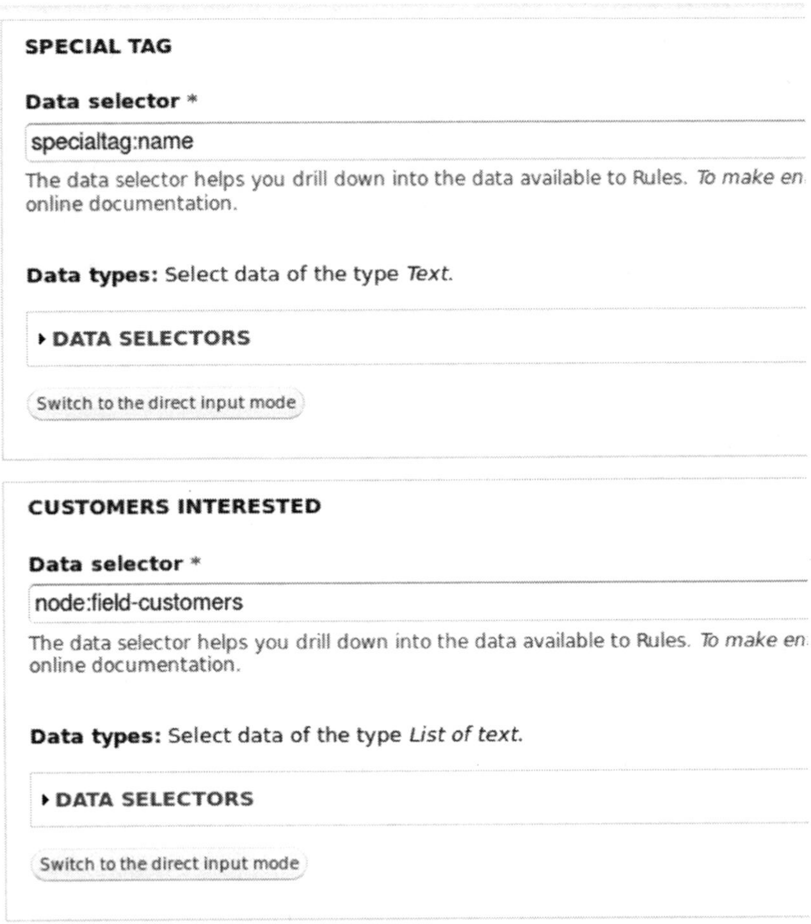

SPECIAL TAG

Data selector *

specialtag:name

The data selector helps you drill down into the data available to Rules. *To make en*
online documentation.

Data types: Select data of the type *Text*.

▸ **DATA SELECTORS**

(Switch to the direct input mode)

CUSTOMERS INTERESTED

Data selector *

node:field-customers

The data selector helps you drill down into the data available to Rules. *To make en*
online documentation.

Data types: Select data of the type *List of text*.

▸ **DATA SELECTORS**

(Switch to the direct input mode)

Figure 4-27. *Component variable mapping 2*

Now that everything is mapped, it's time to configure the rule component. Even though we don't need a trigger, we still have conditions and actions to set up.

Our condition here is to compare the current special's tag we are looping through with the user's comma-separated list of interests (also tags). We can do that using a "Text Comparison" condition, as shown in Figure 4-28. We will select the user's interests field and match it with the specialtag using a `contains` operator, meaning that we are checking if the specialtag is part of the comma-separated list of interests of the user.

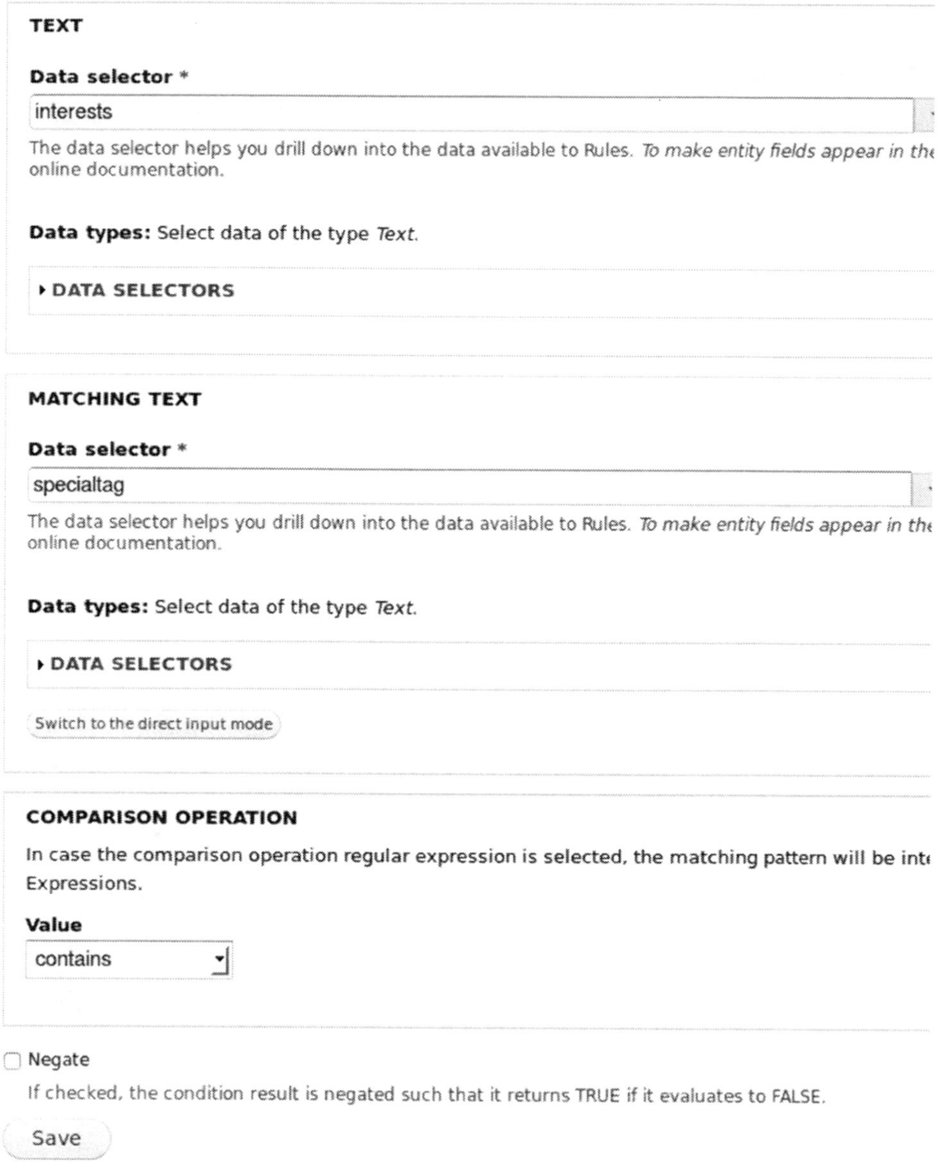
TEXT
Data selector *
interests
The data selector helps you drill down into the data available to Rules. To make entity fields appear in the
online documentation.
Data types: Select data of the type Text.
DATA SELECTORS
MATCHING TEXT
Data selector *
specialtag
The data selector helps you drill down into the data available to Rules. To make entity fields appear in the
online documentation.
Data types: Select data of the type Text.
DATA SELECTORS
Switch to the direct input mode
COMPARISON OPERATION
In case the comparison operation regular expression is selected, the matching pattern will be int
Expressions.
Value
contains
Negate
If checked, the condition result is negated such that it returns TRUE if it evaluates to FALSE.
Save

Figure 4-28. *Variable contains condition*

If it is (that is, if the condition is verified), then it's time for the component's action to be executed. What we want to accomplish here is to build a list of user email addresses to be stored back on the special item. Our action will simply be "Add item to a list." Our item will be the email of the user we're currently evaluating in the loop, and we will add it to the customers list of the special. Note how there is a very convenient option to enforce the uniqueness of each item of the list, which in our case is very useful because there could be many duplicates. In other words, we may match a specific user more than once based on their interests, but we don't want to add the same email address to our list of addresses more than once. Figure 4-29 shows the resulting screen.

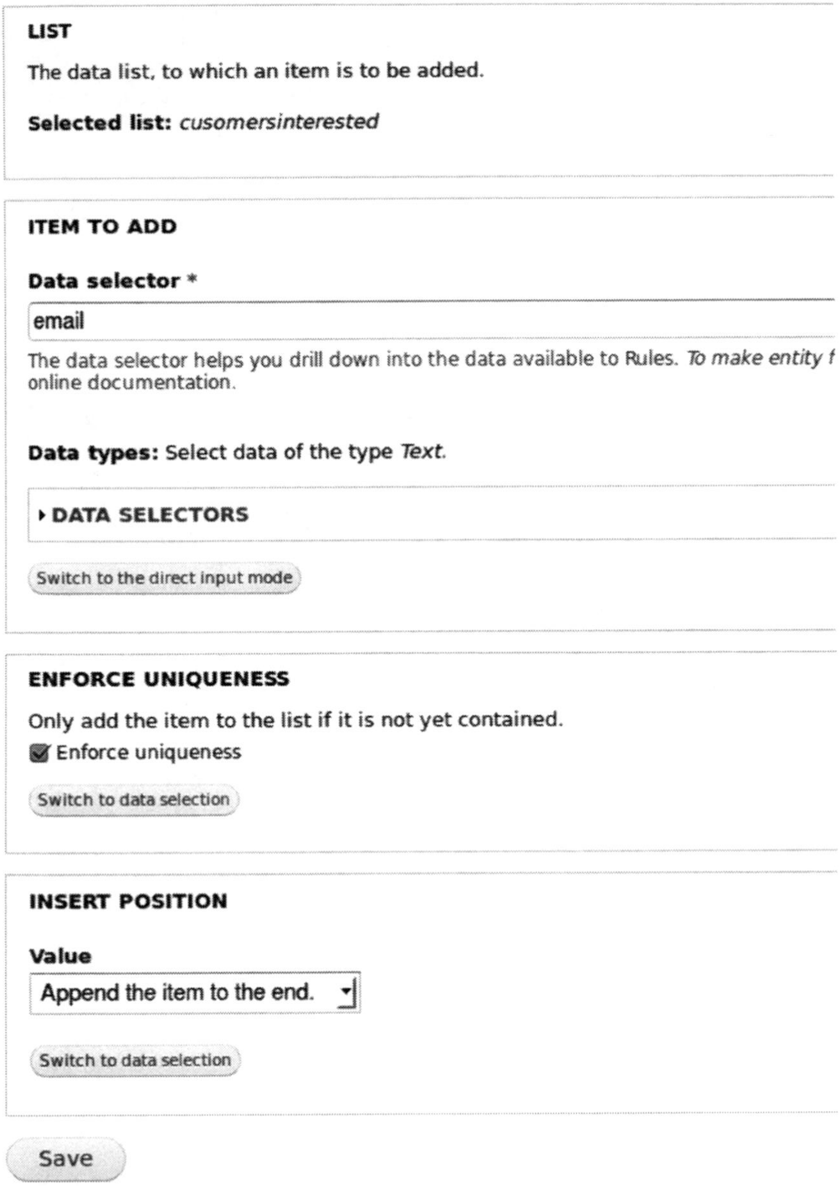

LIST

The data list, to which an item is to be added.

Selected list: *cusomersinterested*

ITEM TO ADD

Data selector *

email

The data selector helps you drill down into the data available to Rules. *To make entity f* online documentation.

Data types: Select data of the type *Text*.

▸ **DATA SELECTORS**

(Switch to the direct input mode)

ENFORCE UNIQUENESS

Only add the item to the list if it is not yet contained.

☑ Enforce uniqueness

(Switch to data selection)

INSERT POSITION

Value

| Append the item to the end. ▾ |

(Switch to data selection)

(Save)

Figure 4-29. Add item to list action

This concludes our first rule. Now every time a special is created or modified, it will automatically update its customer field to hold a list of all the customer email addresses that will need to be emailed about this special.

At this point, the special will have the list of email addresses ready for emailing. We will now use a second rule to actually send those emails. The best way to do this is to periodically check on the specials in the site and email those that are relatively close to beginning. For this example, let's email the list whenever the current date is within a week of the special's start date.

The trigger for this new rule will be "Cron maintenance tasks are performed." Cron operations run every few hours on your site. You can change this on the Configuration admin tab, under Cron. This rule will be triggered every 3h in our case. Figure 4-30 shows the completed rule.

Events

EVENT
Cron maintenance tasks are performed
✦ Add event

Conditions

ELEMENTS	WEIGHT
None	
✦ Add condition ✦ Add or ✦ Add and	

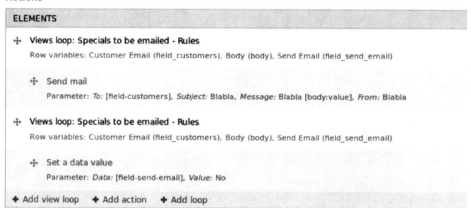

Actions

ELEMENTS
✛ Views loop: Specials to be emailed - Rules
Row variables: Customer Email (field_customers), Body (body), Send Email (field_send_email)
✛ Send mail
Parameter: *To:* [field-customers], *Subject:* Blabla, *Message:* Blabla [body:value], *From:* Blabla
✛ Views loop: Specials to be emailed - Rules
Row variables: Customer Email (field_customers), Body (body), Send Email (field_send_email)
✛ Set a data value
Parameter: *Data:* [field-send-email], *Value:* No
✦ Add view loop   ✦ Add action   ✦ Add loop

Figure 4-30. Emailing rule overview

There is no condition for this rule. Every time the cron job runs, we will grab all the specials in the site that need to be emailed. For this, we are going to use another views loop. Remember our second views_rule view grabs all the specials with a start date within seven days from now. Those are exactly the ones we need. Figure 4-31 shows the row variables used for this particular views loop.

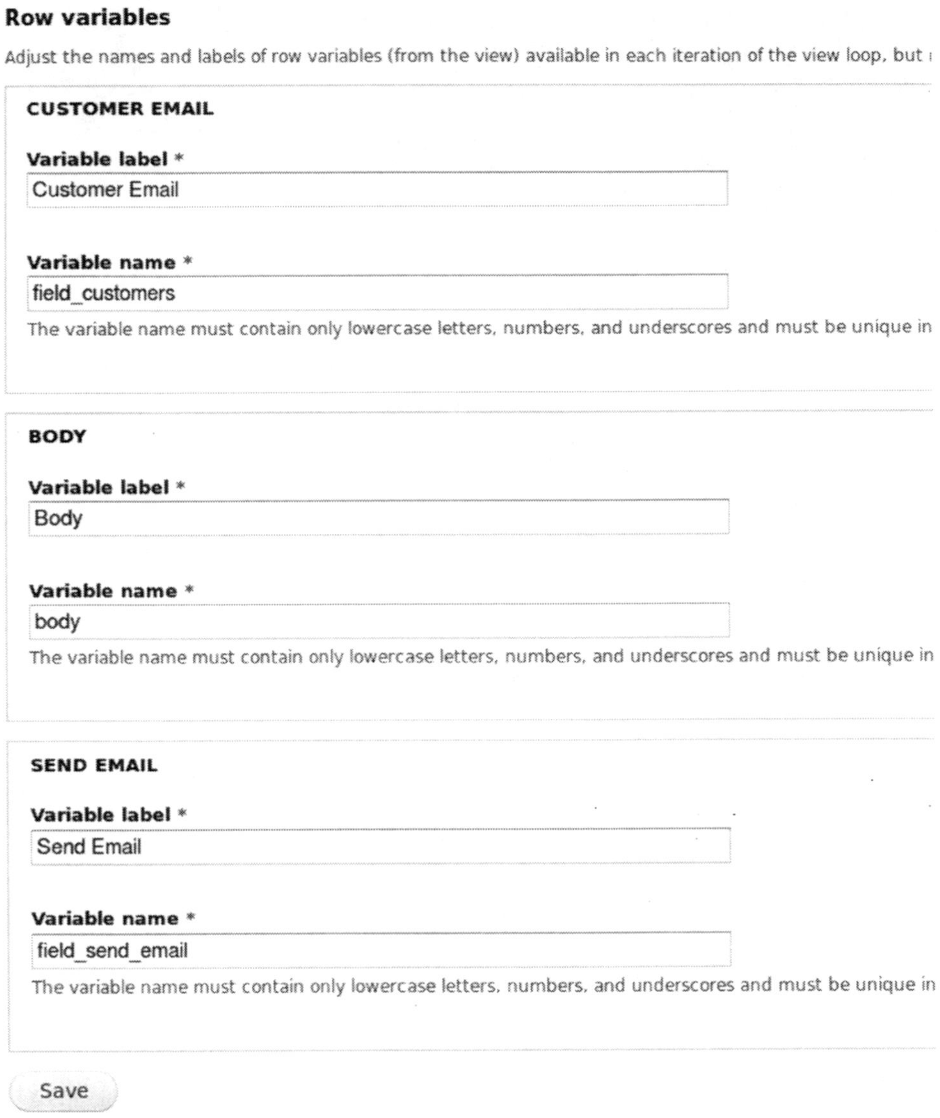

Row variables

Adjust the names and labels of row variables (from the view) available in each iteration of the view loop, but

---

CUSTOMER EMAIL

Variable label *

```
Customer Email
```

Variable name *

```
field_customers
```

The variable name must contain only lowercase letters, numbers, and underscores and must be unique in

---

BODY

Variable label *

```
Body
```

Variable name *

```
body
```

The variable name must contain only lowercase letters, numbers, and underscores and must be unique in

---

SEND EMAIL

Variable label *

```
Send Email
```

Variable name *

```
field_send_email
```

The variable name must contain only lowercase letters, numbers, and underscores and must be unique in

---

Save

Figure 4-31. *Views loop variable mapping for sending specials email*

Finally, the actual "Send mail" action! You will have to define the destination field, the subject line, and the content of your email – as shown in Figure 4-32. Depending on your marketing strategy, the email body may be simple or more complex, with lots of HTML and graphics. And typically, you will want to include in the email some information from the special items. To grab more fields from the special item, you will have to edit the views_rules view we created earlier to display more fields and add them to the row variables.

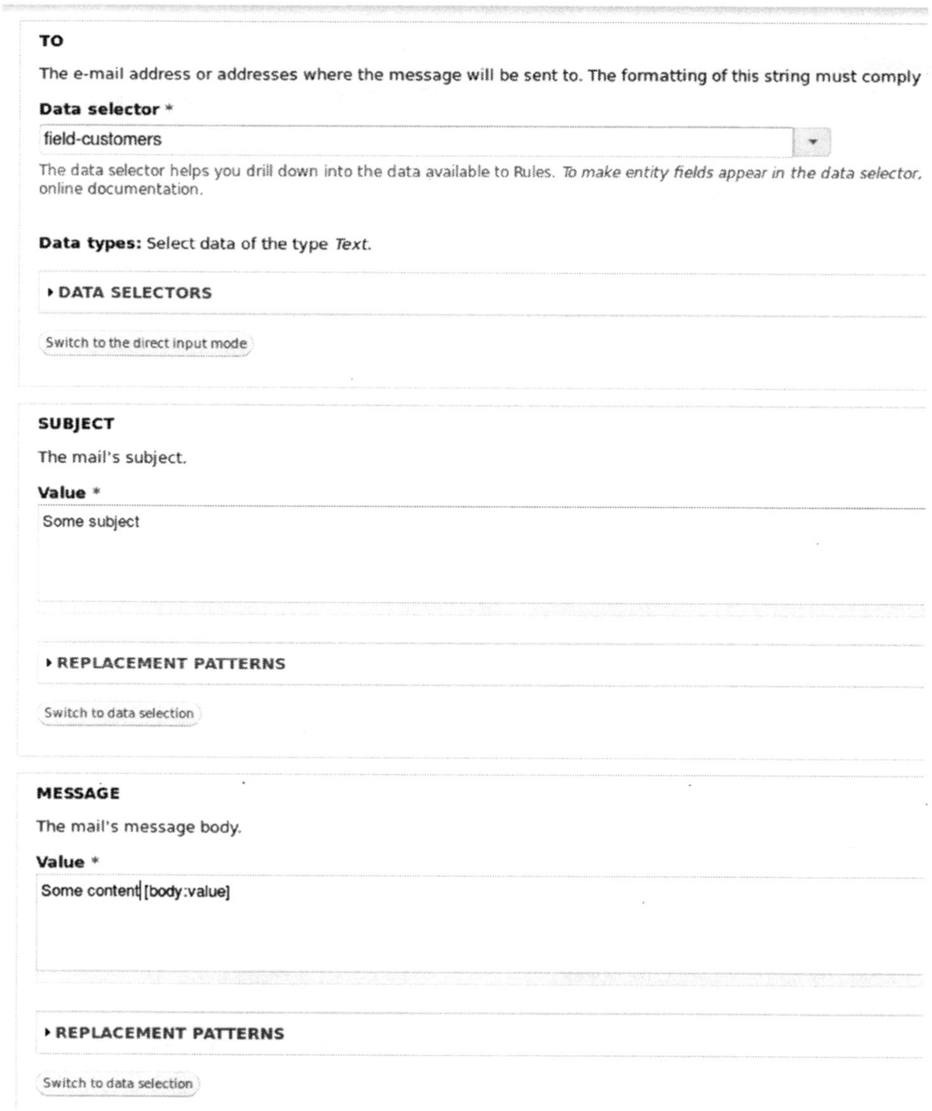

TO

The e-mail address or addresses where the message will be sent to. The formatting of this string must comply

Data selector *

field-customers

The data selector helps you drill down into the data available to Rules. *To make entity fields appear in the data selector,* online documentation.

Data types: Select data of the type *Text*.

▸ **DATA SELECTORS**

Switch to the direct input mode

SUBJECT

The mail's subject.

Value *

Some subject

▸ **REPLACEMENT PATTERNS**

Switch to data selection

MESSAGE

The mail's message body.

Value *

Some content [body:value]

▸ **REPLACEMENT PATTERNS**

Switch to data selection

Figure 4-32. *Send email action*

Now that our email is sent, we just have to make sure we mark the special as emailed, by setting the "Send email" field to No. This means it won't be grabbed by our view anymore—and thus be considered done, as shown in Figure 4-33.

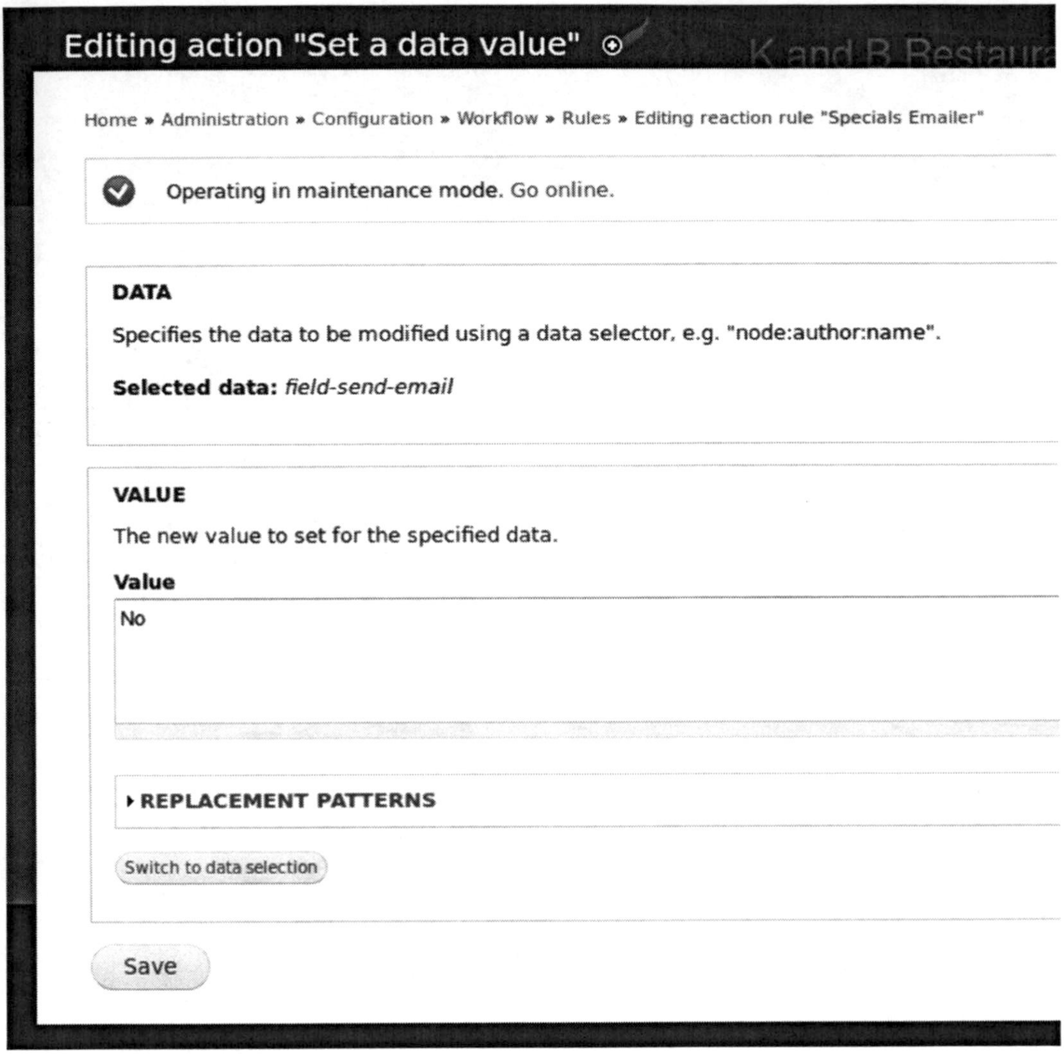

Figure 4-33. *Mark special as emailed*

That's it for our two rules. This required quite a bit of effort and preparation, but those rules would require expensive, error prone, and time-consuming custom development for most content management systems out there. These rules—including their configurability, data context, conditions, actions, and if/then/else and loop control flow constructs—would require even more time and bug fixing if developed from scratch. Drupal's ability to deal with custom actions using rules, all from the user interface, will ultimately save you a lot of time, money, and risk.

Summary

Hopefully, at this point, you're thinking "wow! I can do all that through the UI, without having to write and test any code? Without having to spend hours fixing bugs related to general rules architecture?" If you're not yet thinking something along these lines, feel free to come back to this chapter and read it again anytime as you progress through the project.

Seriously, rules is one of the most powerful features in Drupal. In this chapter, you learned how to configure views to act as the model (or, row data) for one or more rules. Then you learned how to create new rules, including their triggers, conditions, and corresponding actions. We even threw in some job scheduling for good measure.

Having thus far modeled our entities and their relationships, defined some taxonomy, and created a set of example business rules, we are well on our way to building a fully functional web application. For the remainder of this book, we will be focusing on those features of Drupal that turn our standard web application into an enterprise-class business system, starting with security in Chapter 5.

■ ■ ■

Securing Your Application

Building an enterprise-level web application will nearly always involve solving for a consistent set of security concerns. Users will need to be able to log in, you will need to enforce password policies, and users will certainly forget their passwords. You, of course, also need to deal with various types of authentication credentials, different roles and permissions, single sign-on, and even different options for API authentication.

Building these from scratch generally involves using a code-level library, and then building the various business rules, user interface, and configuration settings by hand. Sure, you can readily find a library to handle such activities as hashing, encryption and decryption, regular expressions for password complexity, and even library-plus-data solutions that bear some of the burden of authentication and user management. Within the Microsoft .NET world, a common approach is to use the ASP.NET Membership provider. But again, all of these methods (and many others) still require the developer to write the bulk of the actual implementation—including test code. Not only does this involve the developer himself, but those screens and UI widgets must be designed and styled, and all of it must be fully vetted through some sort of QA process. After all, lines of code written from scratch will certainly have bugs. And so the more lines of code written, the more bugs lie waiting to be discovered and fixed.

As should be plenty obvious by now in this book, the Drupal way offers much more comprehensive and complete solutions for these security concerns. In the end, we want to avoid writing a bunch of code for security, and instead just install and configure a set of modules that have already been tested and used by hundreds or thousands of others just like us. And, as we've already seen, these modules include everything needed to implement security: code, business rules, UI, configuration, and even deployment and updating.

Standard Security Concerns

Before we jump into Drupal's security-related offerings, let's walk through the list of concerns we need to address. These are, of course, not specific to Drupal or any other system; they are common across nearly all web applications. The concerns we're going to cover are:

- Authentication
- Single sign-on and API tokens
- Password encryption
- Forgotten password
- User registration, CAPTCHA, and new user emails
- Password policies
- Disabling accounts

- Login protection

- Auditing

- Roles and permissions

The following sections briefly describe each of these concerns, enough to make sure we're all on the same page. Then we will explore how Drupal implements each of them, including various configuration options available.

The specific topics of service security, and of calling a Drupal service from a mobile application, will be covered in detail later in this book.

Authentication

In order to log into a web site, users need to provide two things: a claim of who they are, and some form of evidence that proves the claim. Typically, this is a username and password. That is, the username provides a key to the identity of the person they claim to be, and the password is proof that they are indeed that person. If the user can't provide the correct password, then we consider their claim false—that is, as far as the application is concerned, the user isn't who they claim to be.

This is the main idea with authentication—the user claiming to be someone and then providing proof of that claim. These days, there are many different types of information being used for those of pieces of data. Rather than a username, the user might want to provide an email address. Or, maybe they provide a phone or Social Security number. Those types of data typically require passwords in order to verify the user's claim of identity.

Beyond a username (or other form of identity claim) and a password, recent advances in authentication have given us more choices and better security. For example, in addition to a username and password pair, some systems support two-factor authentication. Essentially, the username and password pair represents something you *know*, and then you must also present something you physically have in order to sign on. This is typically accomplished with a smartphone application or SMS text message. When the user attempts to log in with their username and password, they must also submit a numeric code (or similar) as provided by the app or text message. The codes change frequently—that is, every few seconds or minutes—or are sometimes single-use codes. This means that just knowing the username and password is not sufficient; the user must also physically possess a configured smartphone, RSA key fob (you can read about these at http://www.rsa.com), or something else pre-configured to provide the correct code. Figure 5-1 shows one of the RSA SecurID fobs.

Figure 5-1. *RSA SecurID key fob (taken from www.rsa.com)*

The user would carry the key fob in their pocket or on their keychain, and would supply the number shown on the fob during the login process (in addition to their username and password).

Single Sign-on and API Tokens

Many times, a user doesn't want the burden of creating yet another username and password. With so many web sites and applications requiring logins these days, it can be quite overwhelming to have to remember so many different passwords. Of course, one way users minimize the headache of many unique passwords is to just use the same password for all sites. This is quite risky, as a compromised password will grant someone access to all of the user's sites, without any mechanism for quickly and reliably disabling that access.

As a result, various single sign-on technologies and techniques have been developed to not only lessen the burden of many passwords, but also increase the default security offered to users. An in-depth exploration of these options is well beyond the scope of this book, but suffice it to say that quite a few options do exist. All of them are designed around the concept that some site or service provides authentication, so that your application doesn't have to. Many times your application won't even take the user's username and password, but instead it will trust a third-party authentication service to actually authenticate the user. Your application will then grant access to any user that presents a token from the trusted service. In short, you delegate the burden of secure authentication to another application, relieving you of the responsibility of storing passwords and of providing username and password validation.

The two most popular and recent standards for such single sign-on behavior are OpenID and OAuth. OpenID allows a user to always use a single application, along with a single username and password pair, to authenticate against. The various sites into which the user is seeking access then trust that application to provide secure access tokens that represent its users. For example, you can use a Google GMail account for OpenID authentication. You can also create your own OpenID account at sites such as www.myopenid.com. More and more web sites these days are providing OpenID-style sign on.

OAuth, while similar in its use, is actually quite different in intent. While OpenID provides authentication for a user, OAuth is meant to allow one application to talk to another on the user's behalf. For example, I might want my LinkedIn account to be able to read and post to my Twitter feed. Rather than requiring me to authenticate every time LinkedIn calls Twitter to read or post, I would simply grant access to LinkedIn once and for all, thereby letting LinkedIn act as me for a limited set of Twitter operations. This approach is very popular in social networking applications, since so many of them cross post and collaborate on your behalf.

EVOLUTION OF OAUTH

It doesn't take much effort to find controversy and dissent related to OAuth on the Internet. Originally conceived in 2006, with the 1.0 version being published in 2007, the specification has been rapidly evolving to try to accommodate today's changing web and social application needs. Although its original intent was to simply allow web applications to talk to each other (on a user's behalf), OAuth has also been used as a mechanism for authenticating users. Some refer to this as pseudo-authentication. In some ways, it competes with the OpenID specification, which was created to handle only such sign-on authentication scenarios.

Most of the team members that originally incepted the OAuth specification have since resigned from the effort. Some of them claimed that their goal of providing an easy-to-use and safe framework for API-based authorization was replaced by corporate and enterprise agendas, resulting in a specification that, as of version 2.0, is more complicated, harder to implement, and thus inherently less secure than it should be. The 2.0 version is also not compatible with the 1.0 version, leaving early adopters in a place of having to rework their implementations.

Suffice it to say, although something OAuth-like is very much needed in our very connected world of Internet and mobile applications, we are far from a settled approach to single sign-on and API-based authorization. The specification is still a work in progress, and you should expect to not only see security-related, configuration, and other such bugs, but also find yourself chasing a moving target. So it goes with web application development these days.

And finally, a very popular option for many enterprise environments is to integrate the login process with Windows Activity Directory. Or, more generally, integrate with any LDAP server. This allows users to log in to a web site using their domain credentials, rather than having to create yet another username and password pair.

To summarize this and the previous section, most web applications need to provide some sort of authentication process. There are many options available today, and you need to be prepared to support the latest and greatest being demanded by your users. Relying solely on username- and password-based credentials for sign-on is not really an option anymore.

Password Encryption

Any system storing user credentials (that is, username and password) must, of course, make sure the passwords are stored in a secure manner. Generally speaking, storing a hash of the user-provided password is the most secure, as it cannot be decrypted. That is, typical encryption allows for decryption—something you clearly need when protecting things like documents, files, pictures, and sorth. After all, not being able to ever read a document once it's encrypted would be rather inconvenient. However, when it comes to securing passwords, the most secure method is to one-way hash them—that is, no one can ever retrieve the actual decrypted value. This works for passwords because we really don't care what the original value was, as long as we can compare the stored hash with a hash of the password value submitted during login. If the hashes match, then we know the supplied password is correct—without ever needing to decrypt its stored value.

There are many options available for hashing and/or encrypting passwords. The algorithms themselves have been evolving and improving over the last few decades, as have the libraries that implement those algorithms. Some of the first hashing algorithms—such as MD5—are no longer considered secure enough for today's connected applications. At the time of this writing, a very popular algorithm involves deliberately introducing delays and/or extra loop iterations into the calculation of the hash, so as to prevent brute-force hash matching. The only way a password cracking program can effectively guess a hashed password is to loop through thousands and thousands of guesses. So if the hash algorithm itself relies on small delays and time-consuming loops, then such brute-force attempts are rendered useless. If you are interested in learning about this particular algorithm, we encourage you to read up on the bcrypt algorithm.

As we'll see shortly, Drupal has followed the general trend of increasingly more secure encryption and hashing, with version 7 being substantially more secure at storing encrypted passwords than the previous version.

Forgotten Password

If it weren't for users, or if your users weren't human, you wouldn't have to worry about them forgetting their passwords. But, because we are dealing with less-than-perfect humans, we need to provide a mechanism for them to be able to reset their password should they forget. Note that, per standard security practices, you do not want to send the user an email containing their current password.

Your passwords should be hashed, and therefore unrecoverable. But even if you can decrypt your users' passwords, you should never email a plain-text password. Ever. The best practice is to send the user an email containing a link to reset their password. This works well, and is secure, because the user must be able to access the supplied email account in order to reset the password. The assumption being, of course, that someone trying to hack or assume someone else's identity would not have access to another user's email account.

The email itself should also be templatized. That is, administrators of the web applications you create should be able to customize the email subject and body that is sent to users needing to reset their passwords. And the customized text should use standard templating techniques, allowing for substitutions such as: first name, last name, current date and time, reset URL, site or company name, and so forth.

Lastly, the email's reset URL should expire after some short amount of time—for example, a few hours or a couple days. Further, it should only be allowed to be used once. This prevents the URL from finding its way into the wrong hands and being used to gain access weeks or months or years later.

In short, to support the "forgotten password" functionality, your web application must provide:

- A "request new password" link on the login page

- Emailing to the user's email address

- Email templates

- A web page for editing the templates

- A web page to which the user navigates in order to reset their password

- Link expiration and one-time use

There are, of course, other ways to deal with users forgetting their passwords. But this is by far the most common and secure approach used today. If you're following the overall theme of this book, you should guess that Drupal handles this scenario and the different features listed in this section out of the box—requiring no configuration for it to just work.

User Registration

At some point, you need to be able to either add new users to your web application, or allow users to register themselves. In either case, there are—again—standard practices to follow. First, newly registered users should receive an email with a link they can use to activate their account. This should include setting a password. The link, similar to resetting their password, should expire after a short amount of time, and should be allowed to be used only once. This new user registration email must be sent regardless of who actually registers the user—that is, an administrator, a site manager, or the user himself.

Second, it should be a simple configuration option to allow or not allow user self-registration. In other words, the process should be the same—that of new user emails, setting a password, and so forth. But setting exactly who is allowed to register new users should be easily configurable.

Third, when users are allowed to self-register, integrating CAPTCHA. This is the feature that prevents bots and other automation from programmatically registering thousands of fake accounts. It typically requires the self-registering user to read and type some barely readable text contained within an image. A simple example is shown in Figure 5-2.

Figure 5-2. *Example of CAPTCHA functionality*

And finally, most web sites (and mobile applications) these days require some form of single sign-on with Twitter or Facebook. This means that a user shouldn't have to create a new username and password. But instead, the self-registration process should allow the user to link their Twitter or Facebook account to a new account in your web site, thus allowing for single sign-on.

Of course, all of these features and capabilities are readily available with some simple options in Drupal.

Password Policies

Closely related to user registration, all web applications should allow their administrators to specify and tune the username and password complexity policies. For example, a password should have at least 8 characters, include at least 1 number and 1 symbol, and should expire every 60 days. Further, no password should be re-used within a six-month period. This not only helps your users maintain a higher level of protection over their account(s), but also reduces your vulnerability to a "front page security event"—the kind that can kill a company.

Disabling Accounts

Just as the ability to register new users should be part of any modern web application, deleting or disabling them should, too. Whether through self-deletion or by a system administrator, an account should have the ability to be deactivated (or blocked). Further, when deactivating an account, what happens to the user's published content? That also needs to be configurable.

Login Protection

When creating a brand new web application, it may not seem terribly important to protect your sites and your users from evil-doers. But it doesn't take much of an "event" to kill any size company, small or large. And with the ease at which you can apply extra protection to a Drupal site, you really have no excuse. The types of things we include in this category of security concerns include the following:

- IP address blocking

- Locking an account after a certain number of failed login attempts

- Detecting and preventing brute-force login attempts

- Keeping login failure messages vague, so as to not give the evil-doer any information that might help them guess valid usernames and passwords

- Showing users their last login attempt and successful login, helping them detect if anyone else has attempted to login with their account

All of these standard security capabilities dealing with login protection are available to you as a Drupal module that just needs to be installed and enabled.

Auditing

For many enterprise systems, just allowing users to make changes to data is only part of the story. These systems need to track who changes certain pieces of data, both to help maintain integrity with the data, and also to adhere to various compliance policies in the industry. For example, many of the provisions in the Sarbanes–Oxley Act of 2002 require extensive logging and auditing of any changes made to systems, machines, and data within applications. As such, you must be able to record select data changes—that is, who made them, when they were made, and exactly what changed. Sometimes this auditing is handled with database-level triggers and procedures. Sometimes it is implemented within a web service. Regardless, auditing is a capability that must be available to you on whatever platform you choose. Of course, given the book you're currently reading, we're happy to tell you that auditing is built into Drupal.

Roles and Permissions

So far, most of the security concerns we've discussed have dealt with authentication—that is, the process of logging in and related concerns. Last on our list is the general concern of authorization, which deals with what an authenticated user (or, sometimes, an unauthenticated anonymous user) is allowed to do or not do. By far the most standard approach to this aspect of security is to utilize roles—sometimes called "groups"—to which permissions are assigned. Then we simply assign users to one or more roles.

For example, a role called Content Manager might be granted permissions related to creating, publishing, editing, and deleting content for a web site. Certain users of the site are then added to the Content Manager role, thereby granting those users the role's permissions.

Think of it this way:

- A resource is any object (such as page, user, menu) in the system that can be protected
- Permissions define things that can be done to a resource
- Roles are granted permissions to certain resources
- Users are added to those roles, inheriting the permissions of the role

This is a very standard approach to implementing authorization—which, again, is all about configuring what a user is allowed and not allowed to do.

To summarize this entire section of dealing with security in web applications, there are about a dozen different concerns that must be addressed. And there are standard approaches to dealing with those concerns. Throughout the rest of the chapter, you will learn how to provide solutions for each of them within a Drupal-based web application.

Implementing Security in Drupal

Now that we've walked through several common security concerns of enterprise-level web applications, let's dive into their configuration in Drupal. Note that while we're going cover most of the fundamentals, some of these concerns can include a fair amount of configuration options. We will not necessarily cover the breadth of all this configuration.

Authentication

Let's start back at the top with user authentication. For the default and typical method of users supplying their usernames and passwords, Drupal simply handles it out-of-the-box; just install Drupal per the instructions in Chapter 2, and, once registered, users will be able to log in to your site.

Beyond basic username and password, you can also enable two-factor authentication. As discussed in the previous section, this means your users will have to supply a second form of evidence that is not their password—and, that they physically possess. To do this in Drupal, there are a few different modules available. Let's look at the module supplied by the folks at Duo Security (https://www.duosecurity.com/). They've published a module called "Duo Two-Factor Authentication"—or, "duo", for short. This module integrates into the various two-factor service integrations Duo Security offers. You can install and enable the module with the following Drush commands. Remember to run these commands from the root of your Drupal site—where the install.php and index.php files exist.

```
drush dl duo
drush en duo -y
```

Once enabled, you can access the Duo configuration options by finding the entry for Duo on the Modules page. Click on Configure, and you should see the options shown in Figure 5-3.

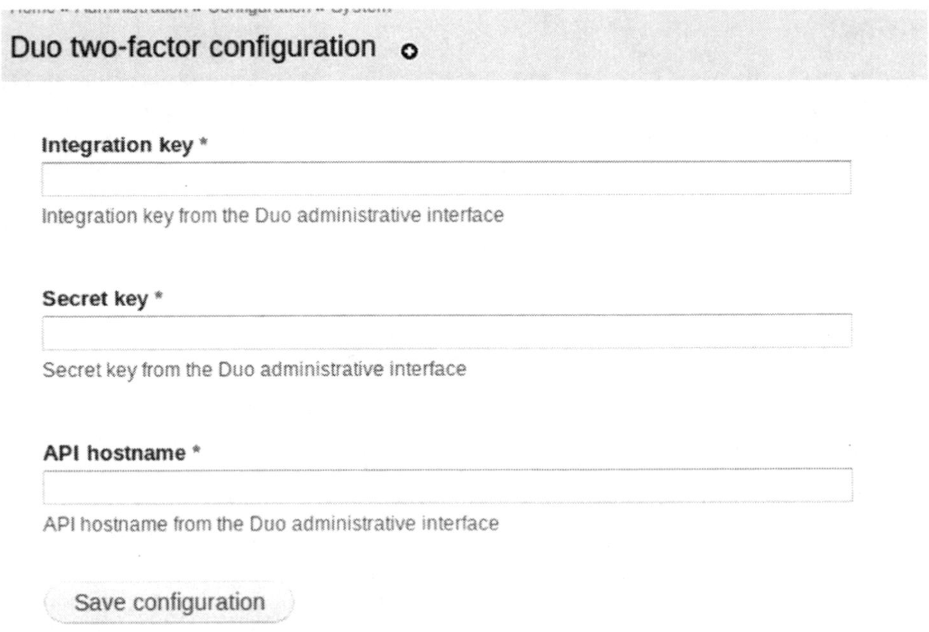

Duo two-factor configuration ⊙

Integration key *

Integration key from the Duo administrative interface

Secret key *

Secret key from the Duo administrative interface

API hostname *

API hostname from the Duo administrative interface

Save configuration

Figure 5-3. *Duo Security configuration options*

You might be wondering, where does one obtain those values? As most services offering two-factor integration, you need to create an account before you can use the services. Once created, you will be able to obtain the required configuration values.

The other piece of configuration made available by installing the Duo module is shown in Figure 5-4.

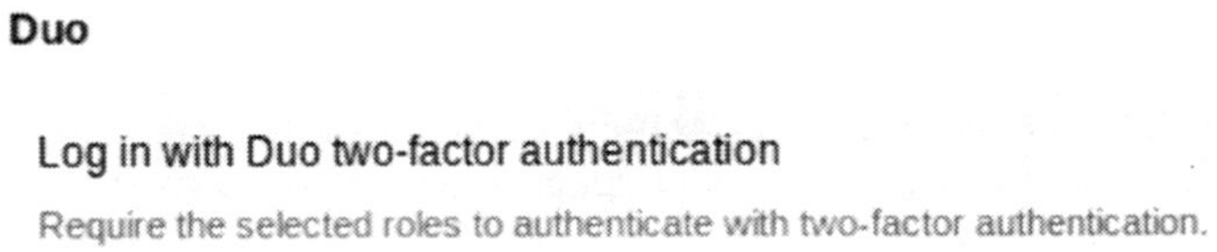

Duo

Log in with Duo two-factor authentication

Require the selected roles to authenticate with two-factor authentication.

Figure 5-4. *Duo role permissions*

The Duo module adds a new permission to the system, allowing you to require two-factor authentication for specific roles. You can find more information on this module in the usual Drupal location: https://drupal.org/project/duo.

Single Sign-on and API Tokens

Now let's look at enabling a few different options for single sign-on. First, and most straightforward, is the OpenID module, which happens to be built into the Drupal Core. To enable the module, navigate to the Modules page, and find the OpenID module within the Core section. Once enabled, users will see a new option under the username and password login fields. The new "Log in using OpenID" link is shown in Figure 5-5. And Figure 5-6 shows what the OpenID login screen looks like.

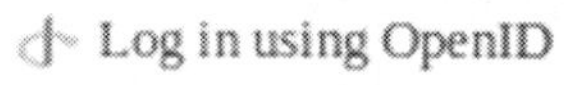

⏏ Log in using OpenID

Figure 5-5. *OpenID login option*

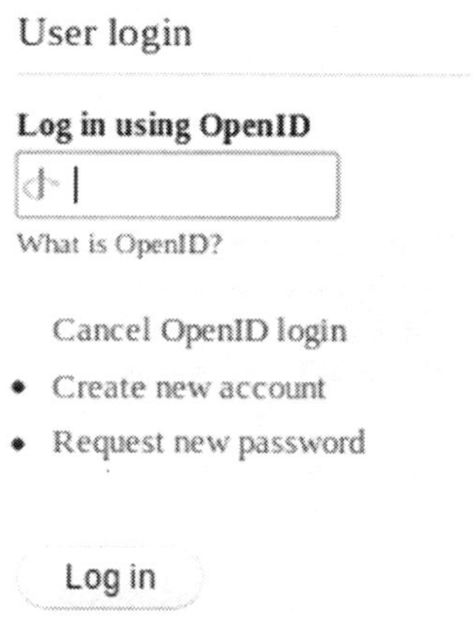

User login

Log in using OpenID

⏏ |

What is OpenID?

Cancel OpenID login

• Create new account

• Request new password

Log in

Figure 5-6. *OpenID login screen*

In order for new users to be able to register themselves, thereby creating new accounts in your site, you need to make sure the account settings are configured to allow visitors to self-register. You can find this configuration setting by navigating to the ➤ Settings. The available options are shown in Figure 5-7.

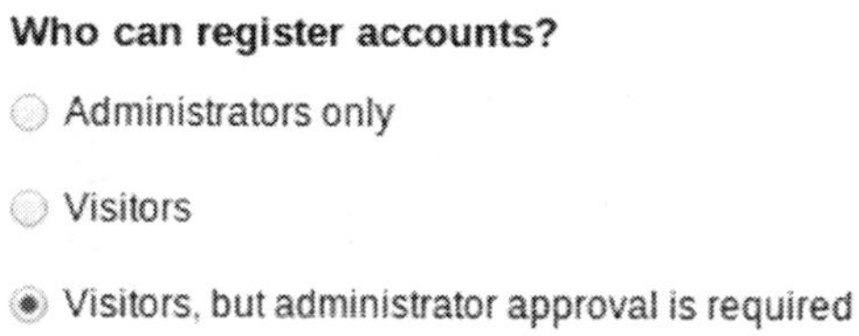

Who can register accounts?

◯ Administrators only

◯ Visitors

◉ Visitors, but administrator approval is required

Figure 5-7. *Allowing users to self-register*

The OpenID module not only allows new users to register with their OpenID account, but existing users can also associate one or more OpenIDs with their Drupal account. In Figure 5-8, you can see the new tab that appears on a user's account information page.

Figure 5-8. *OpenID account information tab*

After clicking on the new tab, a user will see a list of existing associated OpenIDs. They will also have the option of adding additional associations, as shown in Figure 5-9.

OpenID

Add an OpenID

Figure 5-9. *Associating additional OpenIDs*

OAuth

If you want to allow your users to sign on to your site with their Twitter or Facebook accounts, you can install the Twitter and Facebook OAuth modules. Both Twitter and Facebook support single sign-on via OAuth, which, as described previously, provides a pseudo-authentication capability. This essentially means that their Twitter or Facebook account will set up a limited trust relationship with your site's Twitter or Facebook account. Thus, you will need to create a company or site-based Twitter or Facebook account—one that is associated with (at least) your web site.

Let's look at installing and configuring the Twitter module. Run the following Drush commands (again, from the root of your Drupal web site folder):

```
drush dl oauth
drush dl twitter
drush en twitter -y
drush en twitter_signin -y
```

Once enabled, navigate to the Twitter configuration via the Modules page. Once there, notice that you need to enter your Twitter-provided OAuth Consumer Key and OAuth Consumer Secret. You can obtain both of these by visiting https://dev.twitter.com/apps. Log in using the Twitter account associated with your web site, and then select the option to create a new Application. The application must represent your Drupal web site, including the URL where you want users returned once they've granted access to their own Twitter account. This is typically just the home page or root URL for your site.

Once the consumer key and secret are saved, you need to click on the Twitter tab and add your web site's Twitter account. By default, you should see something similar to Figure 5-10, which is telling you to add an authenticated Twitter account.

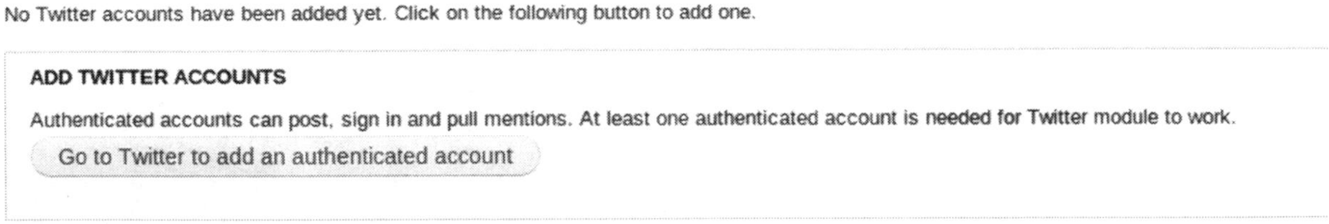

No Twitter accounts have been added yet. Click on the following button to add one.

ADD TWITTER ACCOUNTS

Authenticated accounts can post, sign in and pull mentions. At least one authenticated account is needed for Twitter module to work.

Go to Twitter to add an authenticated account

Figure 5-10. *Add a Twitter account*

Click on the big button, and then use your web site's Twitter account to grant Twitter access to your web site.

You will also want to click on the Sign-in tab (within the Twitter configuration page), and optionally change a couple options. Most importantly, if want to avoid making new users also register on your web site, you need to enable the option to "Automatically register new users."

Once this is completed, your users should see the "Sign in with Twitter" button on your web site's login page.

Password Encryption

Starting with the 7.0 release of Drupal, passwords are much more securely encrypted—as compared to Drupal 6. Where in version 6.0 passwords were hashed with MD5, and without a salt value, in 7.0 Drupal the much stronger hash algorithm SHA512 is used. Additionally, a salt value has been introduced. These two improvements alone increase the security of the Drupal account passwords by several orders of magnitude.

But Drupal 7 actually goes one step further: it leverages the concept of "stretching." This is essentially a technique whereby the hash is generated by either deliberately introducing a timed delay (such as one second) into the hash algorithm, or running the algorithm hundreds or thousands of times in a loop. Either way, the time it takes to crack a single password increases dramatically —for example, being able to guess 2 million passwords per second down to maybe 1,000 passwords per second. This effectively eliminates the possibility of a brute-force attack guessing a given password in a Drupal 7 system.

This feature in Drupal is completely hands-off. There's nothing to install or configure.

Forgotten Password

As discussed in the previous section on security concerns, users inevitably forget their passwords. When this happens, the process of requesting a password reset should be completely self-service for your users. The last thing you want is people emailing or calling you and your staff for something as simple as requesting a new password.

A side benefit of giving your users the ability to reset their password is that no one, including the IT staff, will be tempted to create a password and email it or write it down anywhere, or even know it. Remember, when it comes to passwords, the only person that should ever know a user's password is the user. A completely self-service password reset process keeps everyone out of the loop—except for the user himself.

In Drupal, the password reset request process is simply part of the core install. By default, users will be able to change their password if they are already logged in; or, they will be able to request a password reset if they can't log in. As shown in Figure 5-11, the user is presented a "Request new password" link right under the username and password fields on the login page.

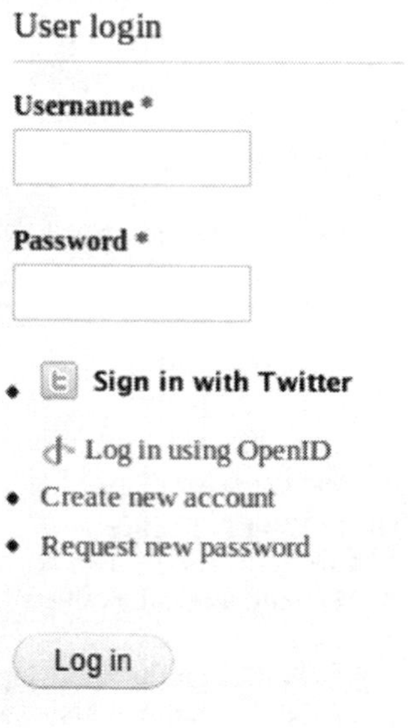

User login

Username *

Password *

- ⧉ **Sign in with Twitter**

  ⧉ Log in using OpenID
- Create new account
- Request new password

Log in

Figure 5-11. *Login screen showing link for requesting new password*

The one piece of configuration with password reset that can be modified is the email sent to users when they request a new password. Navigating to the Configuration ➤ Account Settings page, and scrolling to the bottom, you will see a tab titled "Password recovery"—in the E-mails section. Figure 5-12 shows the default email template.

E-mails

Welcome (new user created by administrator)	Edit the e-mail messages sent to users who request a new password. Available variables are: [site:name], [site:url], [user:name], [user:mail], [site:login-url], [site:url-brief], [user:edit-url], [user:one-time-login-url], [user:cancel-url].
Welcome (awaiting approval)	
Welcome (no approval required)	**Subject**
	Replacement login information for [user:name] at [site:name]
Account activation	
Account blocked	**Body**
	[user:name],
Account cancellation confirmation	A request to reset the password for your account has been made at [site:name].
Account canceled	You may now log in by clicking this link or copying and pasting it to your browser:
Password recovery	[user:one-time-login-url]
	This link can only be used once to log in and will lead you to a page where you can set your password. It expires after one day and nothing will happen if it's not used.
	-- [site:name] team

Figure 5-12. *Password recovery screen and default email template*

The email template contains several features worth pointing out. First, it is a template in which you can substitute several different variables. Second, these variables indicate a few other nice features. The [user:one-time-login-url] variable references a page provided by Drupal where the user actually resets their password. This URL is, as the name suggests, available only one time, to prevent the link from being used days or weeks or months later to gain illegal access to an account. Of course, the very fact that we're working on an email template implies that Drupal will automatically email the message to the user, allowing you to completely avoid writing code dealing with SMTP servers, formatting email messages, sending email on a background thread, and so forth.

Bottom line once again: Drupal's got you covered. Without doing anything beyond installing the system, users are empowered to securely reset their passwords—all on their own.

User Registration

Similar to the forgotten password scenario covered in the previous section, registering new users should be drop-dead simple—out-of-the-box. As we're sure you've guessed, Drupal delivers here, as well. By default, users are allowed to self-register. Of course this is optional, and can be turned off on the Configuration ➤ Account Settings page.

When users are registered, whether by an administrator or via self-registration, an email is sent and the user is required to perform a one-time login to set up a password and activate their new account. The emails sent by Drupal are also customizable templates, similar to the password reset email.

You can also install a module to enable the ever-popular CAPTCHA feature for self-registrations. Run the following commands to install and enable the reCAPTCHA module. Note that at the time of this writing, the 7.x version of the CAPTCHA module (a dependency of the reCAPTCHA module) is in beta and not marked as a recommended release, so you need to select it after running the first command. Just enter the appropriate number at the command line, and hit Enter.

```
drush dl captcha
drush dl recaptcha
drush en recaptcha -y
```

Once installed and enabled, you can access the configuration options via the Configuration ➤ CAPTCHA page. On it, you will need to enable the feature for the user registration process. Do this by finding the user_registration_form Form in the table on the configuration page, and select challenge type from the drop-down. Note that you can use the default behavior—which is set in the drop-down above the Forms table, or you can override that default with another option.

The default challenge type is to use a math problem to verify the user self-registering is indeed a human. But you can also enable the typical reCAPTCHA interface, which needs a little more configuration. As shown on the reCAPTCHA configuration tab, you need to first create a free account at recaptcha.net. Once that is done, you can enter key information into the configuration page, and save the configuration. Then you will be able to present new self-registering users with the typical reCAPTCHA snippet. You can even alter some of its look and behavior on the configuration page, as shown in Figure 5-13.

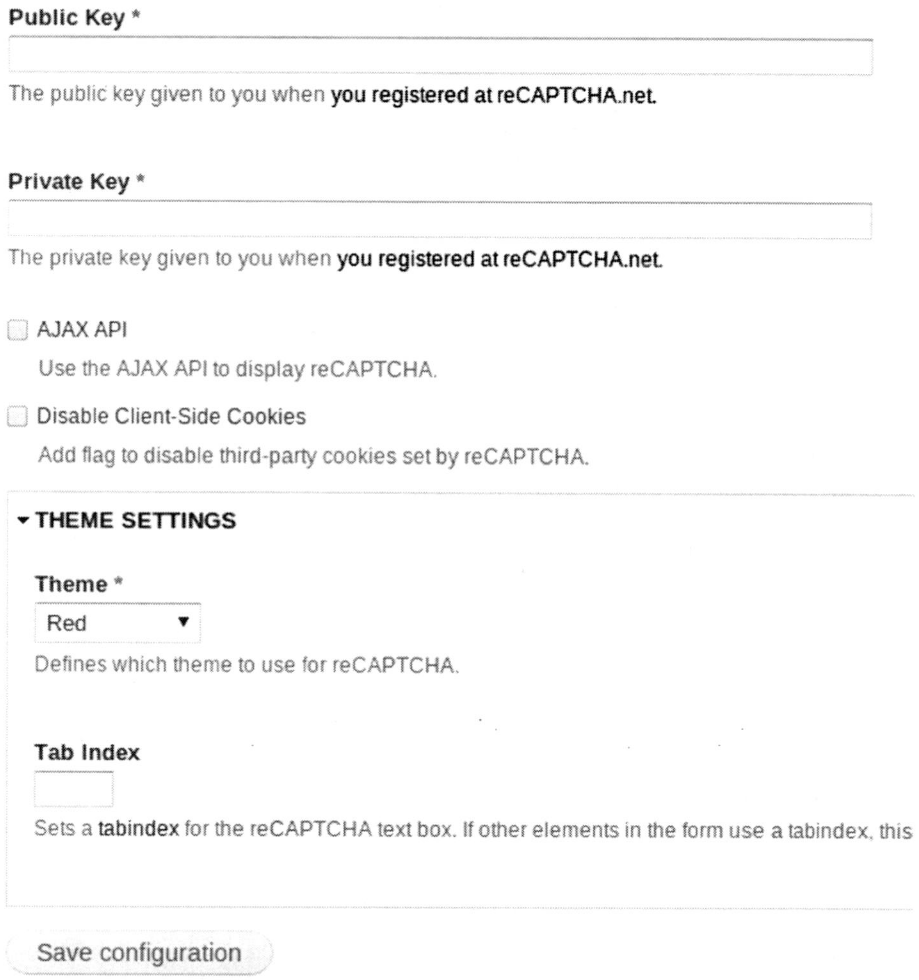

Public Key *

The public key given to you when **you registered at reCAPTCHA.net.**

Private Key *

The private key given to you when **you registered at reCAPTCHA.net.**

☐ AJAX API

Use the AJAX API to display reCAPTCHA.

☐ Disable Client-Side Cookies

Add flag to disable third-party cookies set by reCAPTCHA.

▾ **THEME SETTINGS**

Theme *

| Red ▾ |

Defines which theme to use for reCAPTCHA.

Tab Index

Sets a **tabindex** for the reCAPTCHA text box. If other elements in the form use a tabindex, this

Save configuration

Figure 5-13. *ReCAPTCHA options in Drupal*

One interesting feature of the CAPTCHA module is that you can actually enable this verification behavior on just about any page or form in the system. For example, maybe you want to add the CAPTCHA feature to an order entry page, or maybe a page used for submitting blog post comments. In other words, the act of making sure the user submitting data is human doesn't have to exist only on the self-registration page.

Password Policies

It is very easy to implement password policies in Drupal. Let's go ahead and add the appropriate module, using the following commands:

```
drush dl password_policy
drush en password_policy -y
drush en password_policy_password_tab -y
```

Note that we enabled two separate modules with one download. This is because the password_policy_password_tab module is actually contained within the password_policy module, and so doesn't need to be downloaded separately. That second module just puts the user password change form on a separate UI tab from the rest of the account information, making it clearer and easier to change a password.

The password policy module includes lots of great password complexity and other security features. We're not going to cover them in great detail, as we're assuming that anyone reading this book knows what these different policies mean. For example, we're not going to explain the business definition of "password must contain at least 2 digits".

You can access the password policies configuration via the Configuration page, clicking on the "Password policies" option. You are then presented with five different tabs, as shown in Figure 5-14.

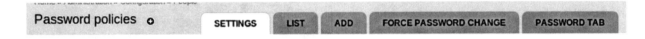

Figure 5-14. *Password policies options*

The SETTINGS tab contains global options for all password policies. For example, you can turn on an option that makes the built-in administrator account adhere to the password policies (by default, it does not).

There is also an option to show the user a list of all the policies, and which ones are met/not met, on the password change page. Figure 5-15 illustrates this option.

▾ VISIBILITY SETTINGS

☑ Show restrictions on password change page.

Should password restrictions be listed on the password change page.

Figure 5-15. *Password policy option to list policies when user changes password*

On the SETTINGS tab is also where you can customize the warning email that gets sent to users when they password is about to expire.

The LIST tab simply lists all of the password policies you've created. The module allows you to create one or more policies, and assign them to different roles. This means you can assign one set of policies to, say, administrators or content managers, and another set of policies to regular users. You can also use this tab to enable and disable policies—without having to permanently delete them.

The ADD tab is to—you guessed it—add a new policy. It is on this tab where you can see the bulk of the features and capabilities of the Password Policy module. The following list illustrates a sample of the password policy options available:

- Selecting one or more roles on which to apply the policy

- The expiration period (in days) for a password

- The number of days ahead of expiration that a warning email will be sent; can be more than once—for example, "10,5,2" would send an email 3 times: 10 days before, 5 days before, and 2 days before the user's password expires

- About eight different options related to the number of digits, uppercase, lowercase, password length, the use of punctuation,and so forth

- Password delay, which sets the minimum number of hours between password changes

- Password history, which sets the number of previous passwords a new password cannot match

All of those rules are contained within a single policy, of which—as stated previously—you can create one or more, and assign them to different roles. Very powerful indeed! Think of the amount of time it would take you to write all of the code for rule and policy management, rule execution, and all of the UI for editing rules and policies, as well as the UI the user sees when setting new passwords and being told of policy violations. Per the theme of this entire book, this module saves you possibly weeks or months of development and testing—all by simply running a couple Drush commands.

The fourth tab, FORCE PASSWORD CHANGE, simply allows you to force password changes—either on first login or immediately. The immediate option is available on a per-role basis. Figure 5-16 shows you what this would look like if you haven't created any custom roles.

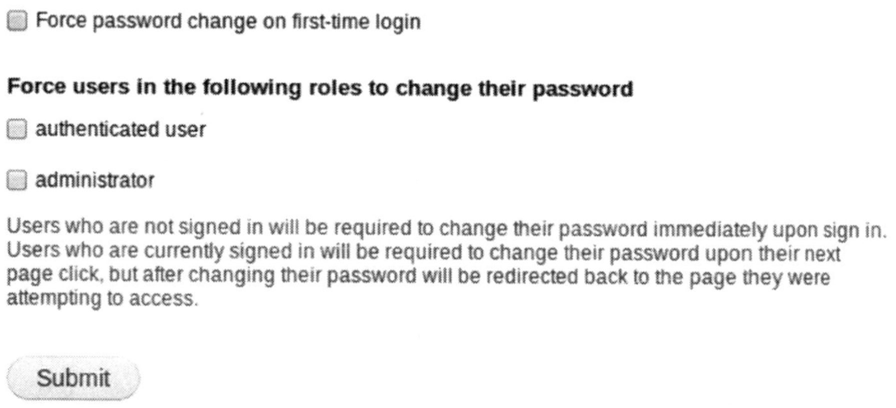

☐ Force password change on first-time login

Force users in the following roles to change their password

☐ authenticated user

☐ administrator

Users who are not signed in will be required to change their password immediately upon sign in.
Users who are currently signed in will be required to change their password upon their next
page click, but after changing their password will be redirected back to the page they were
attempting to access.

Submit

Figure 5-16. *Force password change options*

The last tab, called PASSWORD TAB, lets you enter an alternate URL that is used as the page the user is taken to after they've created or changed their password. By default, the user is taken to a view page of their account. But you can enter a different URL; for example, maybe you want to take them to a "Thanks for changing your password" page. Or, this option also accepts substitution tokens. So a value of user/%uid/edit would take the user to a page where they can edit the rest of their account information.

One last feature that we didn't see on the configuration page relates to individual accounts. The module adds a new option to the account settings page that lets you force a password change to an individual account. Figure 5-17 shows this new option.

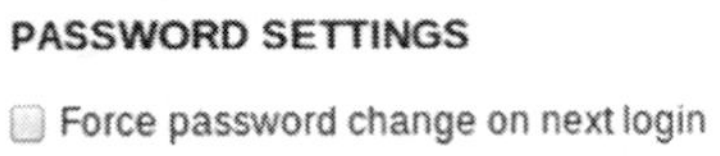

PASSWORD SETTINGS

☐ Force password change on next login

Figure 5-17. *New option for forcing a password change on a single account*

All in all, this module is packed with very useful password security-related features. And these are particularly useful in enterprise settings, where system administrators must ensure that employees' passwords follow corporate policies.

Disabling Accounts

The ability to disable an account, either manually or automatically, is very important in enterprise web applications. Manually means, of course, that some administrator edits a user account by setting the option to block the account, as shown in Figure 5-18.

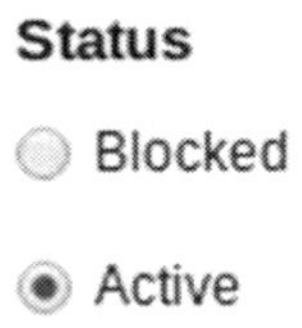

Status

⦾ Blocked

◉ Active

Figure 5-18. *Option to manually disable an account*

Accounts can also be disabled (or, blocked) automatically based on a few conditions. These are handled by the Login Security module, discussed in the next section.

Login Protection

In this section, we'll briefly explore a module called Login Security. This module only provides a few relatively small features, but they are incredibly important when it comes to keeping an Internet-facing web application secure. As described on the Login Security project page (https://drupal.org/project/login_security), this module "improves the security options in the login operation of a Drupal site." Essentially, this module protects from various username and password guessing scenarios, including brute-force attempts and hiding the little-too-informative default login failure message that Drupal provides.

You can install this module per the usual pair of Drush commands:

```
drush dl login_policy -y
drush en login_policy -y
```

Once installed and enabled, you can access the various rules and options via the Configuration page, clicking on the Login Security option. There you will find about a dozen different configuration values, ranging from numbers to email addresses to email subjects and message bodies.

At this point, we'd like to just show a few screenshots of the various options and their descriptions, as that seems like the easiest way to understand what the module can do for you. This is also a testament to a well-designed module, as each option's description is sufficiently informative for understanding what they do.

The first option available to you deals with the number of hours to use for the time window for security violations. Think of it as a sliding window, where login failures are kept in a list for that amount of time. Other options, described next, rely on this list of failures for detecting and responding to perceived security events. For example, if this time is set to five hours, and the number of failed attempts reaches the defined threshold within that five hours, then a notification email is sent. Figure 5-19 illustrates this first option.

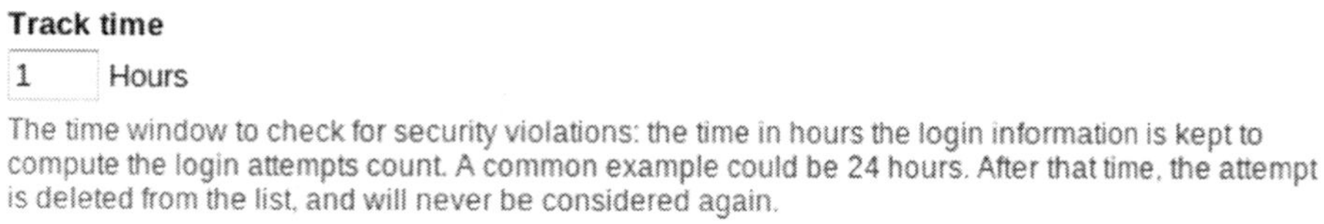

Track time

| 1 | Hours |

The time window to check for security violations: the time in hours the login information is kept to compute the login attempts count. A common example could be 24 hours. After that time, the attempt is deleted from the list, and will never be considered again.

Figure 5-19. *Option to set number of hours to "remember" failed login attempts*

Next, in Figure 5-20, you can see two options that let you add a delay in the login process for failed attempts. This would obviously make it much more difficult for anyone to attempt a brute-force login attack.

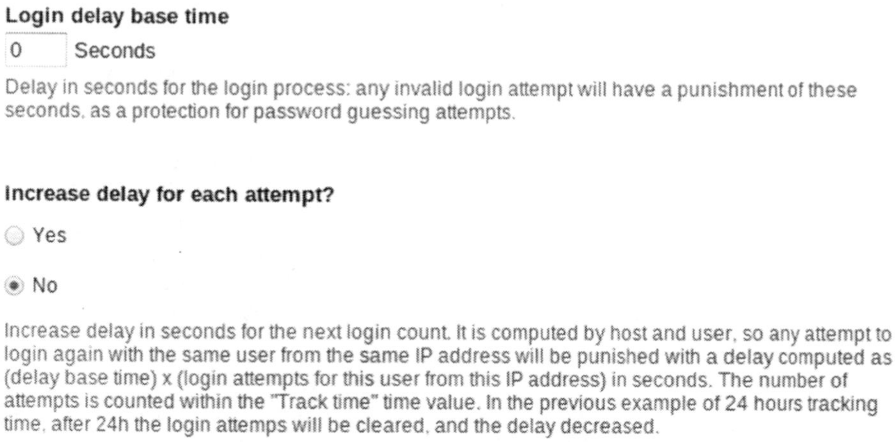

Login delay base time

| 0 | Seconds |

Delay in seconds for the login process: any invalid login attempt will have a punishment of these seconds, as a protection for password guessing attempts.

Increase delay for each attempt?

◯ Yes

◉ No

Increase delay in seconds for the next login count. It is computed by host and user, so any attempt to login again with the same user from the same IP address will be punished with a delay computed as (delay base time) x (login attempts for this user from this IP address) in seconds. The number of attempts is counted within the "Track time" time value. In the previous example of 24 hours tracking time, after 24h the login attemps will be cleared, and the delay decreased.

Figure 5-20. *Options for adding delay to failed login attempts*

Next, you can set any of four different options that control account and/or IP blocking on failed attempts. Figure 5-21 illustrates these next four options.

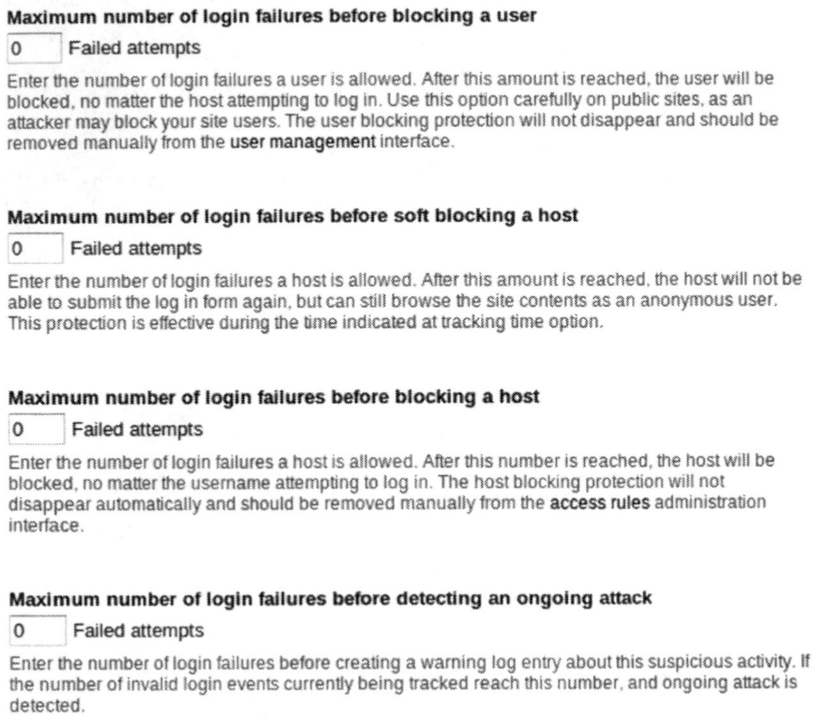

Maximum number of login failures before blocking a user

| 0 | Failed attempts

Enter the number of login failures a user is allowed. After this amount is reached, the user will be blocked, no matter the host attempting to log in. Use this option carefully on public sites, as an attacker may block your site users. The user blocking protection will not disappear and should be removed manually from the **user management** interface.

Maximum number of login failures before soft blocking a host

| 0 | Failed attempts

Enter the number of login failures a host is allowed. After this amount is reached, the host will not be able to submit the log in form again, but can still browse the site contents as an anonymous user. This protection is effective during the time indicated at tracking time option.

Maximum number of login failures before blocking a host

| 0 | Failed attempts

Enter the number of login failures a host is allowed. After this number is reached, the host will be blocked, no matter the username attempting to log in. The host blocking protection will not disappear automatically and should be removed manually from the **access rules** administration interface.

Maximum number of login failures before detecting an ongoing attack

| 0 | Failed attempts

Enter the number of login failures before creating a warning log entry about this suspicious activity. If the number of invalid login events currently being tracked reach this number, and ongoing attack is detected.

Figure 5-21. *Options to detect and respond to brute-force login attempts*

The first three options allow you to block a user or the host from which the attempt originates. Note that the options differentiate between a "hard" block and "soft" block.

The fourth option is quite interesting, as it is used to set the number of failed login attempts that can occur within the number of hours set for the "Track time" option (shown in Figure 5-19) before an attack is detected. At this point, the system is considered under attack, and notification emails are sent (if an email address is configured).

The next four options deal with what information is shown to a user logging in. As you can see in Figure 5-22, the first two affect the messages shown to the user for failed login attempts. In general, you don't want to give the user of a failed login attempt any information that might help them gain access to the system. For example, displaying a message indicating the submitted password is invalid would inform the user that they have entered a valid username.

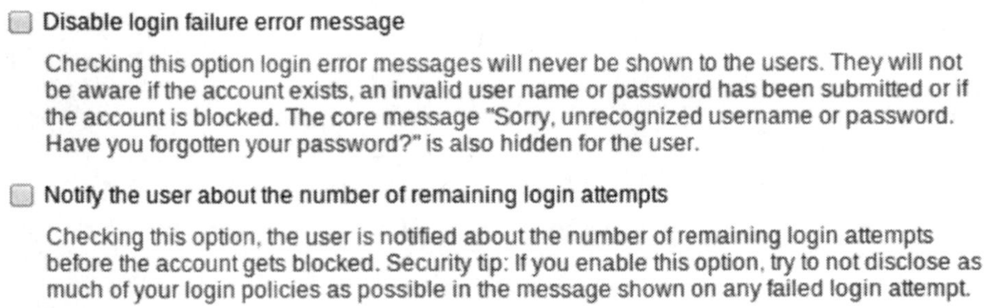

☐ Disable login failure error message

Checking this option login error messages will never be shown to the users. They will not be aware if the account exists, an invalid user name or password has been submitted or if the account is blocked. The core message "Sorry, unrecognized username or password. Have you forgotten your password?" is also hidden for the user.

☐ Notify the user about the number of remaining login attempts

Checking this option, the user is notified about the number of remaining login attempts before the account gets blocked. Security tip: If you enable this option, try to not disclose as much of your login policies as possible in the message shown on any failed login attempt.

Figure 5-22. *Modifications for failed login attempt messages*

The second option simply informs the person attempting the login of the number of failed attempts they have left before the account is blocked.

Figure 5-23 shows the next two options, which, when enabled, displays extra information to a user upon successful login. It is this type of information that can clue a user into someone else potentially attempting to gain access with their account.

☐ Display last login timestamp

Checking this option, when a user successfully logs in, a message will display the last time he logged into the site.

☐ Display last access timestamp

Checking this option, when a user successfully logs in, a message will display the last site access with this account.

Figure 5-23. *Options to display additional login information to a user*

The remaining options, which we won't show here, all deal with configuring various aspects of notification messages and emails. This includes emails for a detected attack, and emails letting someone know that an account has been blocked as a result of too many failed login attempts. Note that similar to other email and notification messages we've discussed, the messages in this module are templatized, too. The list of tokens is actually quite extensive, as shown in Figure 5-24.

- %date : The (formatted) date and time of the event.
- %ip : The IP address tracked for this event.
- %username : The username entered in the login form (sanitized).
- %email : If the user exists, this will be the email address.
- %uid : If the user exists, this will be the user uid.
- %site : The name of the site as configured in the administration.
- %uri : The base url of this Drupal site.
- %edit_uri : Direct link to the user (based on the name entered) edit page.
- %hard_block_attempts : Configured maximum attempts before hard blocking the IP address.
- %soft_block_attempts : Configured maximum attempts before soft blocking the IP address.
- %user_block_attempts : Configured maximum login attempts before blocking the user.
- %user_ip_current_count : The total attempts for this user name tracked from this IP address.
- %ip_current_count : The total login attempts tracked from from this IP address.
- %user_current_count : The total login attempts tracked for this user name .
- %tracking_time : The tracking time value: in hours.
- %tracking_current_count: Total tracked events
- %activity_threshold : Value of attempts to detect ongoing attack.

Figure 5-24. *Placeholder tokens used for Login Security messages*

The Login Security module lets you greatly enhance the security of your Drupal-based web application, by simply installing the module and setting a few configuration values. As you have been doing all along in this book, think for a minute how much time and effort you'd spend building this functionality from scratch; not to mention the level of risk you'd expose you or your company to on account of bugs in such security-related code.

Auditing

Next on our list of security concerns to look at in Drupal is auditing. It is not uncommon in enterprise-level web applications to require all changes to certain pieces of information to be stored—including who changed the data, when it was changed, and a record of old and new values. This is particularly important when it comes to Sarbanes–Oxley compliance.

Fortunately, Drupal has you covered here, too. The concept of revisions is baked into the core of Drupal, and can be used to track all changes to any piece of content in the system. More on revisions will be covered in Chapter 6, but for now look at Figure 5-25 to see the setting—included on every content type—that you can enable to track all changes to content items.

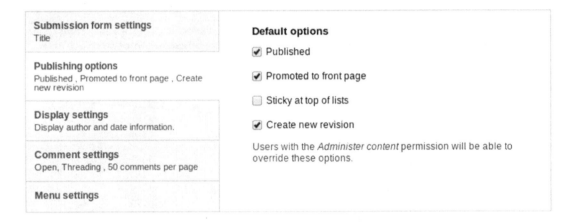

Figure 5-25. *Option to create new revisions on every content item update*

The revision data is available to use with views, for example, or simply viewing the revision history on the Revisions tab of a content item.

Another option, and possibly more powerful, offering broader reach, and less likely to get repurposed for other business needs, is to utilize rules for tracking changes. The rules module was covered in detail in Chapter 4, and you can use it, for example, to create a new content item every time a change is made to an account. In fact, you can trigger content item creation for a change to any entity type in the system, be it a user, a content item, taxonomy data, or even comments.

Last on our list of security concerns is the ever-important topic of roles and permissions. This particular aspect of security is extremely well-implemented in Drupal, being highly extensible, allowing modules to add to the set of permissions available in a base install. This allows those modules to provide very granular protection over the data they add to the system. The remainder of this chapter is dedicated to exploring roles and permissions in Drupal.

Roles and Permissions

With our content types defined, it's quite easy to lay down permissions for our different roles. In our example projects, the admin has default admin rights (all the rights, in short), and the customer as well as anonymous users have the same rights (which would be by default). So, we really only need to define the branch manager permissions.

But first, let's define this content manager role. In the "People" administrative tab, select PERMISSIONS on the top right corner then Roles right below this. As shown in Figure 5-26, you just need to enter a name for the role and click "Add role." A role requires no specific configuration as it is, you just create it and then you can assign users to the role as well as define permissions for it.

Figure 5-26. *Publishing options for Restaurant Branch*

As shown in Figure 5-27, for every content type you create, a set of five permissions will automatically be added to the permission management screen:

- Create new content: Users with a role with this permission enabled will be able to create an item of the given content type and fill up all of its fields. The item will then be considered their own, with regard to with the following permissions. Please note that even if users don't have this permission on, they can still be given ownership of an item (by the item's actual owner or a site admin), which will apply to the following permissions.

- Edit own content: Users will be able to edit and make any changes to an item that they created beforehand, or somehow got ownership of (through an automated assignment by a rule, for instance).

- Edit any content: The same permission as the previous one, except it applies to every item of the given content type, regardless of ownership. It is quite a powerful permission that should be given carefully.

- Delete own content: Allows users to delete content they have ownership of.

- Delete any content: Allows users to delete of any item of a given content type. Should only be given to site-wide content editor or not at all except for admins.

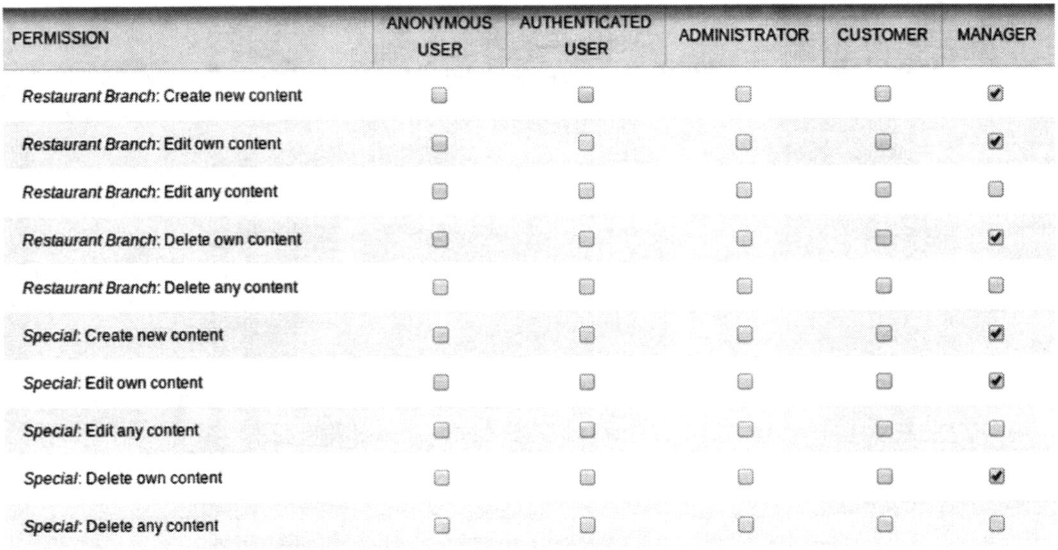

PERMISSION	ANONYMOUS USER	AUTHENTICATED USER	ADMINISTRATOR	CUSTOMER	MANAGER
Restaurant Branch: Create new content	☐	☐	☐	☐	☑
Restaurant Branch: Edit own content	☐	☐	☐	☐	☑
Restaurant Branch: Edit any content	☐	☐	☐	☐	☐
Restaurant Branch: Delete own content	☐	☐	☐	☐	☑
Restaurant Branch: Delete any content	☐	☐	☐	☐	☐
Special: Create new content	☐	☐	☐	☐	☑
Special: Edit own content	☐	☐	☐	☐	☑
Special: Edit any content	☐	☐	☐	☐	☐
Special: Delete own content	☐	☐	☐	☐	☑
Special: Delete any content	☐	☐	☐	☐	☐

Figure 5-27. *Permissions per content type*

In our example, we will give branch managers all permissions regarding their own branches and specials, and no permission to edit or delete someone else's branches or specials. Note that we could also revoke the permission to delete their own content for the branch, as it is unlikely a branch manager would need their branch just deleted without a site admin having a say. This type of permission could be given at first when the site gets populated and such a case can easily arise, but deleted later on.

Another interesting aspect of permissions is the simple workflow you can configure by separating content creation and content publishing powers. For our example, I might want to let managers create and edit their restaurant branches freely, but its publication would only be done by a site administrator after review. This allows your web application to easily provide an approval process around new and modified content.

To do this, we need to edit the content type we want to control: the Restaurant Branch (see Figure 5-28). In the "Structure" administrative tab, under content types, click the edit link for Restaurant Branch.

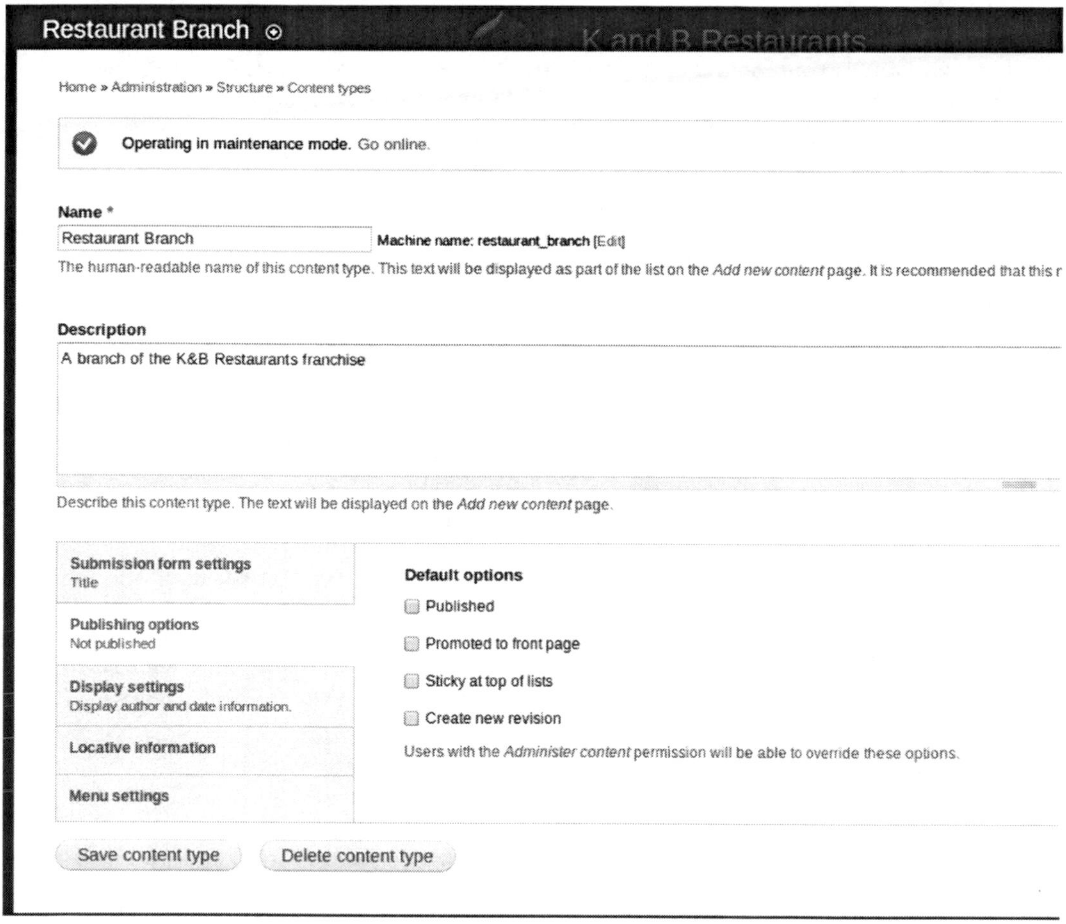

Figure 5-28. *Publishing options for Restaurant Branch*

At the bottom of the edit screen, click on the "Publishing options" tab and uncheck all boxes. This will make sure that content created by a user without the "Administer content" permission will not be public until a user with the permission edits it to be public.

After this, let's go back to our permissions and set them up as shown in Figure 5-29 to only have administrators with the "Administer content" permission. In addition to that, in order to let Managers see what they are creating, we need to enable the "View own unpublished content" permission.

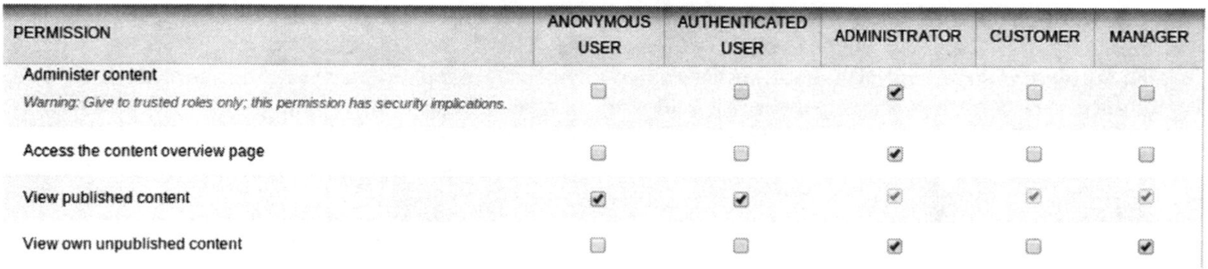

PERMISSION	ANONYMOUS USER	AUTHENTICATED USER	ADMINISTRATOR	CUSTOMER	MANAGER
Administer content *Warning: Give to trusted roles only; this permission has security implications.*	☐	☐	☑	☐	☐
Access the content overview page	☐	☐	☑	☐	☐
View published content	☑	☑	☑	☑	☑
View own unpublished content	☐	☐	☑	☐	☑

Figure 5-29. *Administer content permissions*

Now we have a simple yet efficient way to make sure no content makes it to the public without administrative approval, but managers can still create and edit content as usual. There is a module for much more advanced workflow requirements, if needed by your application: https://drupal.org/project/revisioning. This module allows for much finer-grained control over the implementation of a document approval workflow.

Additional Security Considerations

In this final section we wll cover a few additional aspects of security in Drupal. These aspects are specifically related to content, content format, and exposing content via REST services.

HTML Types

In addition to only being able to edit their own content, we want to make sure our managers can't include security threats in the content they create.

Drupal's textarea fields, best edited using an HTML editor and its module, such as CKEditor in our case, offer two different levels of control: full HTML and restricted HTML.

The first simply means that there is no control over what a manager will put in a field that will ultimately be rendered to a user as HTML.

The second will have some security control, preventing users from using HTML tags that can introduce malicious code, such as scripts and iframes. In our case, we want to make sure managers can only edit fields that are using restricted HTML.

Full HTML should only be authorized for expert content managers who know the security implications of it, and on a per-needed basis (for instance, if a given page needs to have a trusted third-party survey iframed into it).

Menus

We often hear people ask how to make sure content items are hidden or removed from menus for users who don't have the right to use them. There is no need for this. By default, Drupal only displays links in menus if the current user has the permissions to view them, so there is no additional work required on menus, they will adjust as you edit your content items.

Services

Another aspect of permissions that you should know about: they can also apply to Drupal's services when using Drupal as an endpoint for mobile applications, for instance. We will get back to this point in detail when discussing Drupal's REST services, but for now just know that this means that for any application using Drupal as a backend service, you can use Drupal's simple user/role/permission system.

Views

Last but not least, you can control the ability to view a view's display by mapping it to an existing permission. For instance, view published content, or view a specific content type. In Figure 5-30 you can see the three different permission types for restricting access to a view.

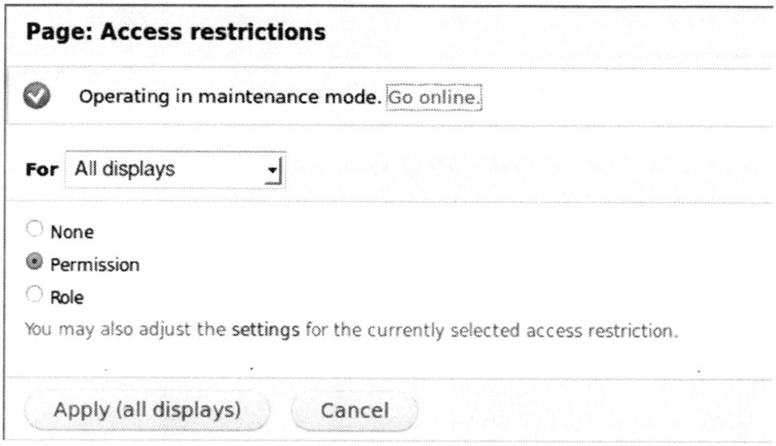

Page: Access restrictions

✔ Operating in maintenance mode. Go online.

For | All displays ▾ |

○ None
◉ Permission
○ Role

You may also adjust the **settings** for the currently selected access restriction.

(Apply (all displays)) (Cancel)

Figure 5-30. *View access restrictions*

Additionally, you can simply let a set of roles see the view, or force it to be visible to anyone. By default, the ability to see a view will default to the "view published content" permission which should be enabled for anyone by default.

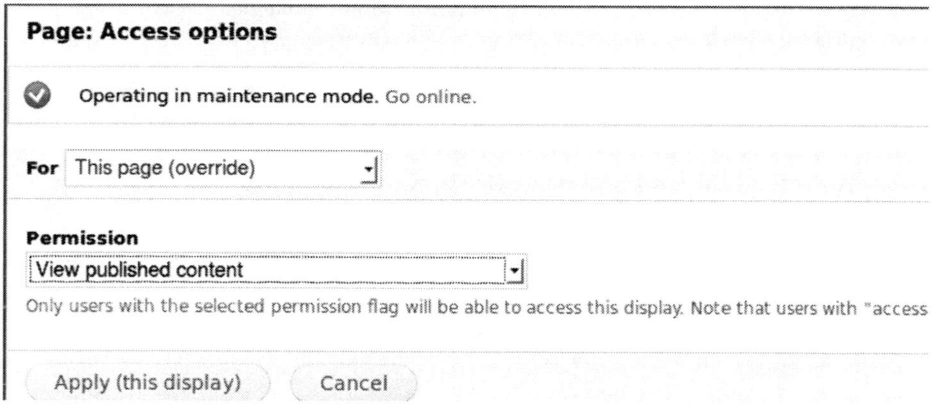

Page: Access options

✔ Operating in maintenance mode. Go online.

For | This page (override) ▾ |

Permission
| View published content ▾ |

Only users with the selected permission flag will be able to access this display. Note that users with "access

(Apply (this display)) (Cancel)

Figure 5-31. *View permission mapping*

It is also good to note that turning this permission off for some anonymous users will force them to log in before they can access the site's content or views (unless the views are forced to be public).

Summary

This chapter was entirely about securing a Drupal-based web application, bringing it up to the standards being demanded by today's web and mobile consumers. We covered about a dozen aspects of security that you must implement on nearly all of your web sites. To recap, these different aspects are:

- Authentication
- Single sign-on and API tokens
- Password encryption
- Forgotten password
- User registration, CAPTCHA, and new user emails
- Password policies
- Disabling accounts
- Login protection
- Auditing
- Roles and permissions

We showed you how to quickly and easily install various Drupal modules, most of which provide the above capabilities with little or no configuration. Even integrating your user registration and sign-on with Twitter requires only setting a few configuration options.

In the last section, you learned how to leverage one of the most powerful features in Drupal security—roles and permissions. Implementing a pattern very common in nearly all types of applications, the combination of roles and permissions allow ultimate flexibility and security for the resources in your web site.

Next up, Chapter 6 will show you how to really work with content in Drupal, whether in the system itself, or importing from or exporting data to other systems.

CHAPTER 6

■ ■ ■

Working with Content

To take a step back again, we are about half way through this book, and have yet to formally work with content. Back in Chapter 3, you learned how to create content types—that is, model your data—but we only loosely alluded to creating the site's menus, menu items, and so forth. In this chapter, you will learn the details of manually entering content, as well as how to script and automate batch imports.

We also want to show you how to export content—to be used for importing into other instances, to be shipped with your site's code, and to facilitate testing and data migration. Manually adding content is quite trivial. The interesting work when it comes to content centers around site deployments and automated migrations. And so you will learn how to leverage the Feeds and Node Export modules to do so.

Closely associated with content entry, of course, is content validation. If you've built at least one web site in your career as a software engineer, you know that user-supplied data must be validated. Some of this validation is provide to you out-of-the-box with different field types in Drupal. For example, a decimal field will only allow decimal entry. And setting the length of a text field will prevent data being longer than the specific value. However, any respectable line of business enterprise application will require more customized validate. And so in this chapter, you will learn how to use the Field Validation module to create field-level validation rules.

The hardest and most critical part of your site configuration is behind you. Now that the site's structure, rules, and permissions are defined, it's time to get started building the site itself—that is, the content.

Let's start with quickly exploring how to manually add content. Then we'll look at importing a large comma-separated value (CSV) file of entities.

Manual Entry

The most natural way to enter some content is to simply use the Drupal interface to add items manually (see Figure 6-1).

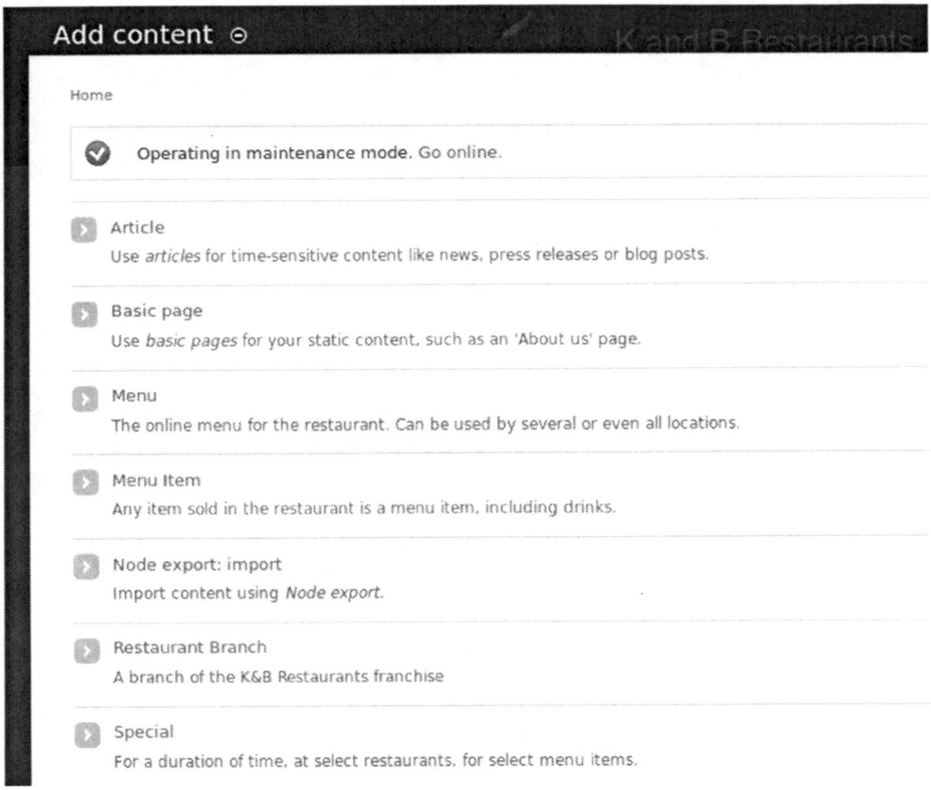

Figure 6-1. *Adding content*

There are several links throughout the site to lead you to this Add content menu. For instance, in the Content administrative tab, use the "Add content" link on the top left corner. Once you get there, you can select what content type you want to be using for the item, and then fill up all the fields you need and save. There are a few additional options at the bottom of the content creation page that are common to all content types: the menu, revision, URL path, authoring, and publishing settings.

You can also provide a link that takes the user directly to the screen where they can add a specific type of content item. For example, the HTML shown in Figure 6-2 will display a link the user can click to directly create a new Menu Item in our K&B Restaurants site.

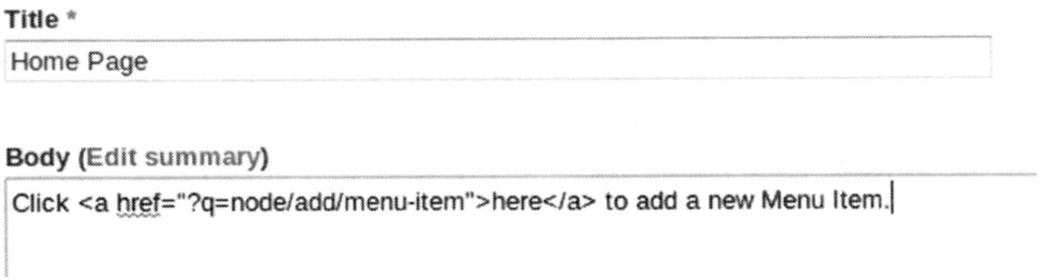

Figure 6-2. *HTML providing a link to create a new Menu Item*

This example is quite simple—just creating a small home page, of sorts. The ability to create links to manipulate and add new content items is the main point.

Menu Settings

If you want your new content item to be easily accessible using one of several menu systems Drupal has to offer, you can simply check the "Provide a menu link" box on the editing screen of the content item itself, as shown in Figure 6-3. Locate the content item you wish to link to from a menu and click edit. In the bottom section under Menu settings, click the check box to quickly add the item to a menu. It will ask you for a title as it will display in the menu and a description that displays when the user hovers their mouse over the item in the menu. You also need to decide which menu or menu item the new item will be under. The choices will depend on the theme that is currently active. For example, as shown in Figure 6-3, you can select the main menu in Drupal. You can also make the new item be a child of another content item.

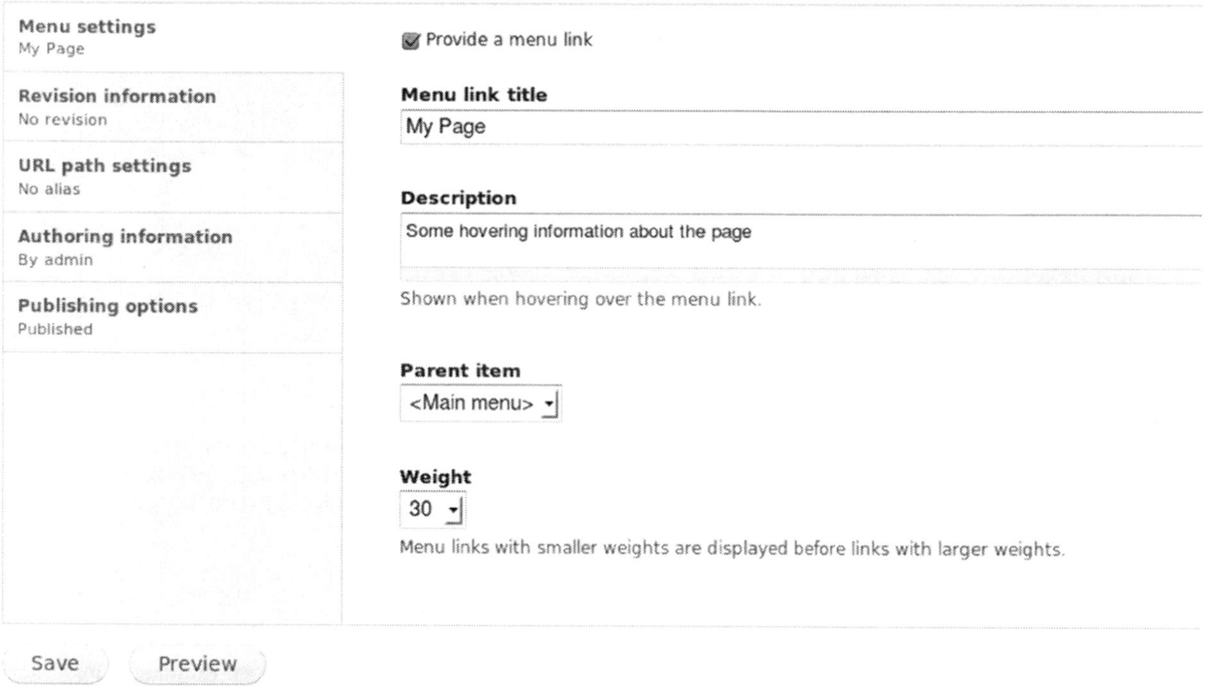

Menu settings
My Page

Revision information
No revision

URL path settings
No alias

Authoring information
By admin

Publishing options
Published

☑ Provide a menu link

Menu link title

My Page

Description

Some hovering information about the page

Shown when hovering over the menu link.

Parent item
\<Main menu\> ▾

Weight
30 ▾
Menu links with smaller weights are displayed before links with larger weights.

Save   Preview

Figure 6-3. *Menu settings*

Lastly, the weight of a menu item indicates how far from the beginning or top of the menu it will show. For pages like "Contact us" or "Directions" that are traditionally at the end of a menu, you will want a high weight, as opposed to a front page, for example.

You can find more information about menus at `https://drupal.org/documentation/modules/menu`.

Revision Information

Drupal allows you to keep track of all changes made to a content item in order to show a full history of who's changed what, and when they changed it. You can also revert to a previous revision, if necessary. We will get to this in greater detail later in this chapter, in the section entitled "Revisioning and Content Checkout." For now, you can see in Figure 6-4 how to enable revisions for a specific content item. When on the editing screen for a given content item, you will find the revision information option at the bottom, right after the Menu settings.

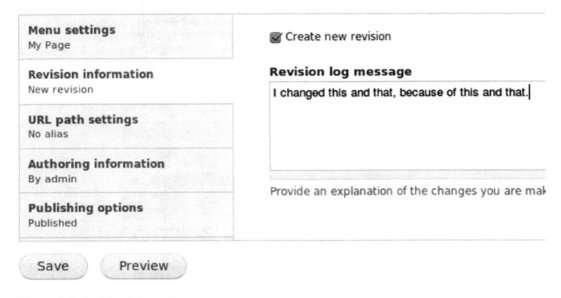

Figure 6-4. *Revision information*

For the purpose of auditing, as would be required in many enterprise-level applications, you can turn on revisions for all content types in the system. You can also disable the ability to turn revisions off, thus allowing for complete auditing and policy compliance across the entire system and with all changes to all data. We'll deal more with auditing and compliance in Chapter 10.

URL Path Settings

By default, Drupal will map nodes to a URL using the node id. For instance, you can access node number 34 by navigating to the /node/34 address. This, of course, isn't very good-looking or user-friendly. If you want the URL to be more appealing, you can specify an alias in the URL path settings, as shown in Figure 6-5.

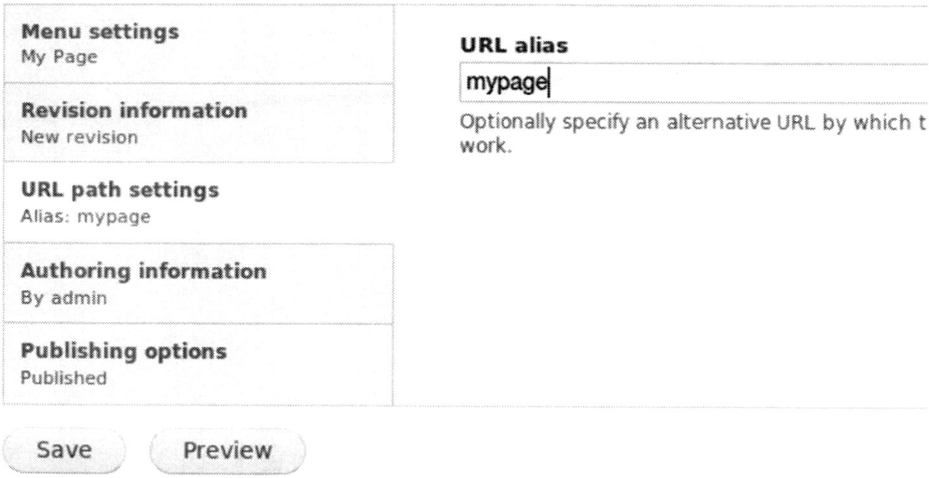

Menu settings
My Page

Revision information
New revision

URL path settings
Alias: mypage

Authoring information
By admin

Publishing options
Published

URL alias

mypage|

Optionally specify an alternative URL by which t
work.

Save   Preview

Figure 6-5. *Url path settings*

Authoring Information

With the Authoring information tab, you can force the author to be someone else if you need to. Otherwise it will default to the person who actually created the page. And as you can see in Figure 6-6, you can also override the date the content item was created.

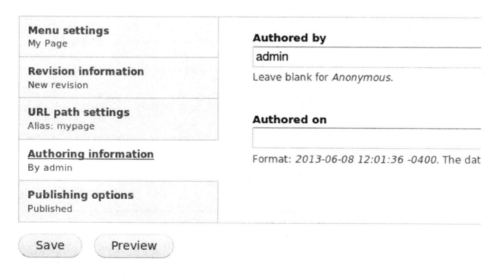

Menu settings
My Page

Revision information
New revision

URL path settings
Alias: mypage

Authoring information
By admin

Publishing options
Published

Authored by

admin

Leave blank for *Anonymous.*

Authored on

Format: *2013-06-08 12:01:36 -0400.* The dat

Save   Preview

Figure 6-6. *Authoring information*

Publishing Options

The Publishing options tab allows you to specify whether or not the new content item is published or private (see Figure 6-7). You can decide to keep a new item private if it's not yet ready for the public to see, or if you mean for it to be seen only by users who have permissions to bypass access control.

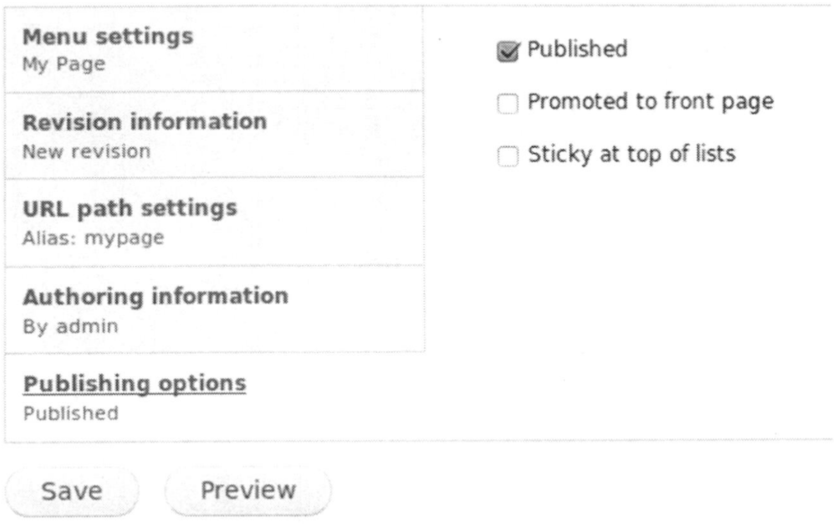

Menu settings My Page	☑ Published
Revision information New revision	☐ Promoted to front page
URL path settings Alias: mypage	☐ Sticky at top of lists
Authoring information By admin	
Publishing options Published	

(Save)   (Preview)

Figure 6-7. *Publishing options*

The publishing options in Drupal—or, more specifically, the ability to have a piece of content either private or public—allows you to build web sites that include a bit of approval workflow. You can accomplish this with role permissions. You simply remove the ability of a certain role to publish content, thereby requiring someone in a higher role to approve and actually move the content into a published state.

Adding, updating, and deleting content in Drupal is really quite simple. In addition to the power of defining your own content types (and their fields), Drupal provides many site-related options on top of each piece of content for navigation, auditing, reverting to a previous version, and making items public or private.

One last note: through the proper application of permissions, you can hide any or all of these content item options. For example, a user without either of the "URL aliases"-related permissions will not see the "URL path settings" tab. The same applies to the rest of the tabs—that is, they are associated with different permissions.

Comment Options

If you have the Comment core module enabled, you will see an additional option, Comment settings, at the bottom of an item's edit screen. Unless user comments are part of your site's design and you plan on using those, we recommend you simply disable the Comment module from the Modules administrative tab. Otherwise, please refer to the last section of this chapter, "Comments, Forums, and Blogs," to see how to configure comments.

THE SIMPLIFY MODULE

One of the more useful modules found in Drupal that can help you clean up your user interface, and make it more web application–like, is the Simplify module. Once installed, you will be able to globally hide a lot of the non-content options normally shown to the user when creating or editing content items. For example, you can hide the comments section, or the revision information. These bits of information are useful to see in certain scenarios, but can clutter up your UI for the average user.

We use this module quite often just to hide the text format options for long text and HTML fields. Once we configure the system to allow a certain type of data—such as plain text or full HTML—we really don't want create or edit content pages to provide options to the user for picking a text format. Thus, you can hide the entire block of HTML, shown in Figure 6-8.

Text format Filtered HTML ▼

- Web page addresses and e-mail addresses turn into links automatically.
- Allowed HTML tags: <a> <em> <strong> <cite> <blockquote> <code> <ul> <ol> <li> <dl> <dt> <dd>
- Lines and paragraphs break automatically.

Figure 6-8. *Text format block (that you can hide with the Simplify module)*

You can find this module at `https://drupal.org/project/simplify`.

Check out the module—we're pretty sure you will like it!

Now that we've covered the basics of manual content management, let's move on to exporting and importing.

Export

When it comes to exporting data and content from your application, it makes sense to separate the data into two main categories:

- Reference Data—shipped with your application's code (for example, lookup values, ZIP codes, site names, and so forth)

- Content—Data that is used for testing, sample sites, or migration (for example, training content, performance test data, test users, and so forth)

In the first category, we have content such as reference and lookup information. When measured by the number of tables, nearly half of any enterprise database consists of reference data—for example, types, categories, dropdown list values, ZIP codes, and so forth. This category of content is an integral part of your application, and thus must ship and be deployed with it right out of the box. Without this reference data, your application would not function.

The content in the second category does not typically ship with your web site. Instead, we use exporting and importing of this type of data to facilitate test data, demo sites, data migrations, stand-by systems, reporting instances, and the like. While the files for these exports might be stored somewhere in version control, they don't typically ship with your web site. They might instead be offered out of band, maybe as a separate download; or, they might be created for a particular client or project.

Both of these categories deal with exporting content. But we will treat them a little differently, to make sure your application's reference content lives with your application's source code. Further, we want to make sure it's easy to deploy and enable this reference content, by utilizing the Drupal deployment mechanism found in a couple modules. For this, we will use the Features module and its integration with the Nod Export module.

To prepare for this section of the chapter, run the following commands to install and enable the required modules. Note that the Node Export module requires the Universally Unique Identifier module.

```
drush dl uuid node_export -y
drush en uuid node_export node_export_features -y
```

You can also get the UUID module from `https://drupal.org/project/uuid` and the Node Export module from `https://drupal.org/project/node_export`.

Let's get started by looking at some simple export and import procedures.

Simple Export and Import

With the Node Export module enabled, you will notice that a new tab appears—next to the View and Edit tabs—when viewing a content item. For example, suppose you have a Menu in our K&B Restaurants site called "Lunch Menu." When you click on a link to view the menu content item, you will see the Node Export tab, as shown in Figure 6-9.

Node export of Lunch Menu

| View | Edit | Node export |

Download file

Node export code

```
array(
  (object) array(
    'vid' => '16',
    'uid' => '1',
    'title' => 'Lunch Menu',
```

Figure 6-9. *Menu node export tab*

The text contained in the big text box is all you need to import this particular menu into a new or different instance of Drupal. You can click on the Download File button to create a file that can be checked into your version control repository. Or, you can simply copy and paste the text, as shown next.

To create a new content item from the copied text, navigate to the Add content page, and click on the link titled "Node export: import". As shown in Figure 6-10, you will see two options for importing the content.

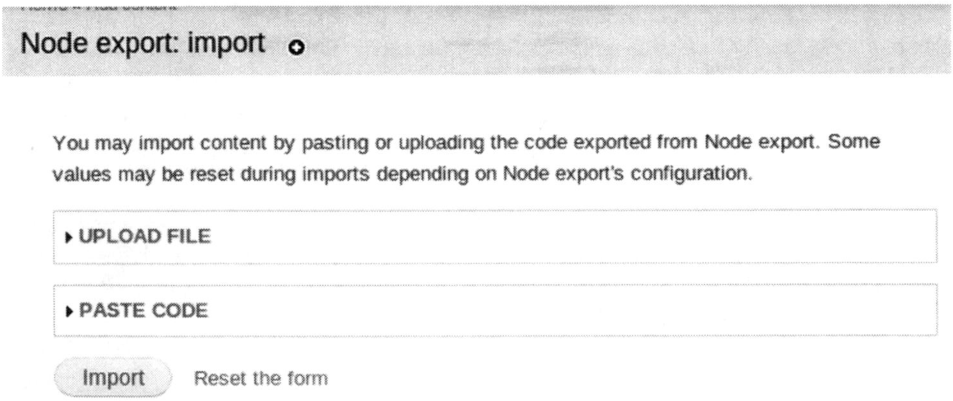

Node export: import ⊙

You may import content by pasting or uploading the code exported from Node export. Some values may be reset during imports depending on Node export's configuration.

▸ UPLOAD FILE

▸ PASTE CODE

Import   Reset the form

Figure 6-10. *Import screen for Node Export*

Simply click on the Paste Code link to expand that section, and paste in the text you copied from another system's content item Node Export tab. Of course, you can also upload the file obtained, if you used the Download File button when exporting a content item.

When importing, it is important to consider what happens if and when the item already exists. By default, the Node Export module, which handles the import process, will create a new node if it finds that a node with the same NodeID already exists. What this means, though, is that if you are using the Node Export module to deploy content items to other systems—for example, test instance, production instance—and you deploy more than once, you will end up with duplicate content items. In fact, you'd get a new copy of the content items each time you run your deployment. This would certainly be more than just an inconvenience if supporting a continuous integration and delivery environment!

To modify this behavior, navigate to the Modules page, find the Node Export module, and click on its configure link. Part way down the page, you will see a section titled "When importing a node that already exists." There are three options, as shown in Figure 6-11. If you want imports of nodes that already exist to merely update the node (rather than create new ones), make sure the second option is selected.

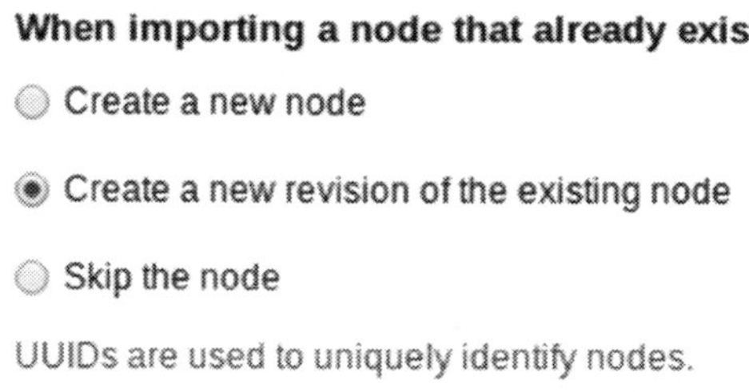

When importing a node that already exists

○ Create a new node

◉ Create a new revision of the existing node

○ Skip the node

UUIDs are used to uniquely identify nodes.

Figure 6-11. *Node Export import behavior*

Doing so will allow you to deploy all of your reference content over and over, knowing that existing items will be updated—not duplicated. Note that if a particular content type has revisions turned off, then the item will simply be updated during import without creating a revision history.

Bulk Export and Import

There are times, of course, when you need to export and import more than one item at a time. Fortunately, the Node Export module provides this ability. Simply navigate to the Find Content page, select the content items you want to export, select "Node export" from the Update Options drop-down, and then click the Update button. In the same way we saw with an individual item's Node Export tab, you will be taken to a page where you can either download a file or copy a long string of text that represents all of the content items you selected to export.

To import the batch, simply use the same Add Content option we used previously—that is, the "Node export: import" link—and either paste in all of the items' text or upload the downloaded file. Simple as can be with the Drupal Node Export module!

To help automate the import process, you can use a simple Drush command to import content from a file that was downloaded from the Node Export tab. For example, if your file was named node-export01.export, you can run the following command to import all of its content into the current Drupal instance.

```
drush ne-import --file node-export01.export
```

You can place this command into any Linux, Mac, or Windows deployment script. We'll talk more about deployment in Chapter 10 including how to use the Features module to package up exported content along with a bunch of other configuration data to create a deployment package.

119

Now that we've covered basic export and import of content items, let's take a deeper dive into the more complex world of importing data from other systems.

Feeds

A recurrent need when building a web application is the import or migration of data into the newly created site. Sometimes it is just about importing a few dozen pages, sometimes you need to migrate a hundred thousand users. The good news is: there is a module for that! It's called Feeds, and it allows you to import content from a variety of sources into a variety of entities. You can find the Feeds module at `https://drupal.org/project/feeds` or using drush:

```
drush dl feed -y
drush en feed -y
```

Feeds is one of those vastly used, high-value modules that are designed to allow for pretty much any type of import you could think of directly from the user interface by configuring a few options. Data population or migration is often a significant part of a web application's cost, and Feeds alone can make Drupal a vastly superior choice as a platform when data migration is involved.

Accepted sources include:

- XML feeds in RSS 1, RSS 2, and Atom format, from a file or a url to a feed or a page with a feed

- CSV files; This also means the ability to quickly import from any Excel document or any SQL-type database after converting content to CSV

- Node export documents, to migrate data from one drupal site to another, or to use during deployment

- OPML files

- Sitemap XML format feeds

Content to be created includes:

- Nodes (content item from any given content type)

- Taxonomy terms

- Users

For our example, we would like to migrate a lot of users from an older system to our newer Drupal site. Let's say our marketing team did a very good job and we have plenty of subscribers (10k for instance) stored in our previous system's database.

Using an entry-level database manager query, we can retrieve the information we need from users and populate a CSV file with it:

```
SELECT Name, Email, Password
FROM users
INTO OUTFILE 'somepath/users.csv'
FIELDS TERMINATED BY ','
ENCLOSED BY '"'
LINES TERMINATED BY '\n'
```

Once you have all your users exported to a CSV file, we'll configure Feeds for the import. Going to the Structure administrative tab, select "Feeds Importers" from the menu and add a new importer. If you don't see this option on the Structure page, make sure you have the "Feeds Admin UI" module enabled (provided with the Feeds module). You will start by entering a name and description for the feed, as shown on Figure 6-12.

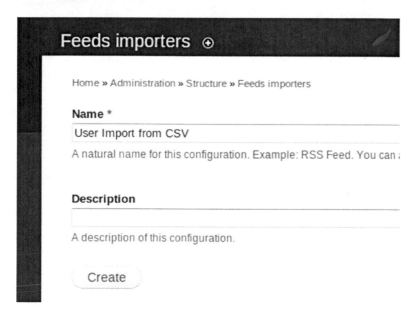

Figure 6-12. *Feeds importer creation*

Click the Create button to start the configuration. It looks quite complicated at first, but most of the pre-configured options are already what you want, so the work here will be limited. In the basic settings, as shown in Figure 6-13, we will start by choosing "Use standalone form" in the "Attach to content type" drop-down. You can make other choices when you wish to import items of a given content type to provide an import form on the content type creation page. Periodic import should be set to Off, since this is a one-time import. This option actually allows you to run the import on a schedule, using Drupal's job scheduling system.

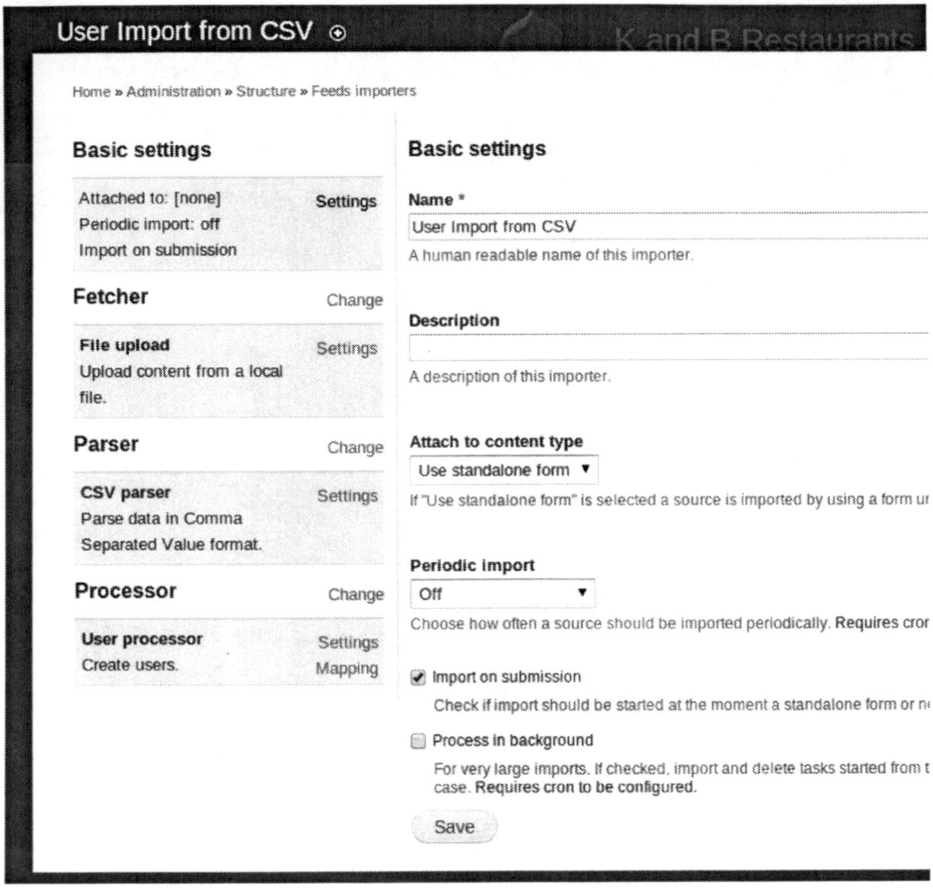

Figure 6-13. *Feeds importer basic settings*

We want the import to begin upon CSV file submission and run in the foreground for our test. In production, you would typically adjust your settings to import during the night, in the background, in order to minimize the impact it could have on the site (slowing down smaller servers, for instance).

Since we have a file ready, we will pick a "File upload" fetcher, as shown on Figure 6-14. You can use an HTTP fetcher to import content directly from an RSS feed, for instance.

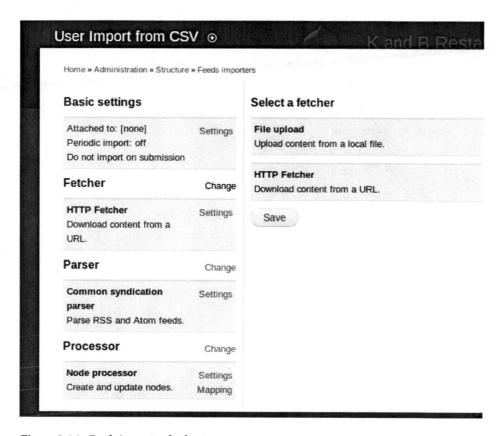

Figure 6-14. *Feeds importer fetcher type*

By default, CSV will be an accepted format for file upload fetchers (see Figure 6-15). We will just leave this section as is.

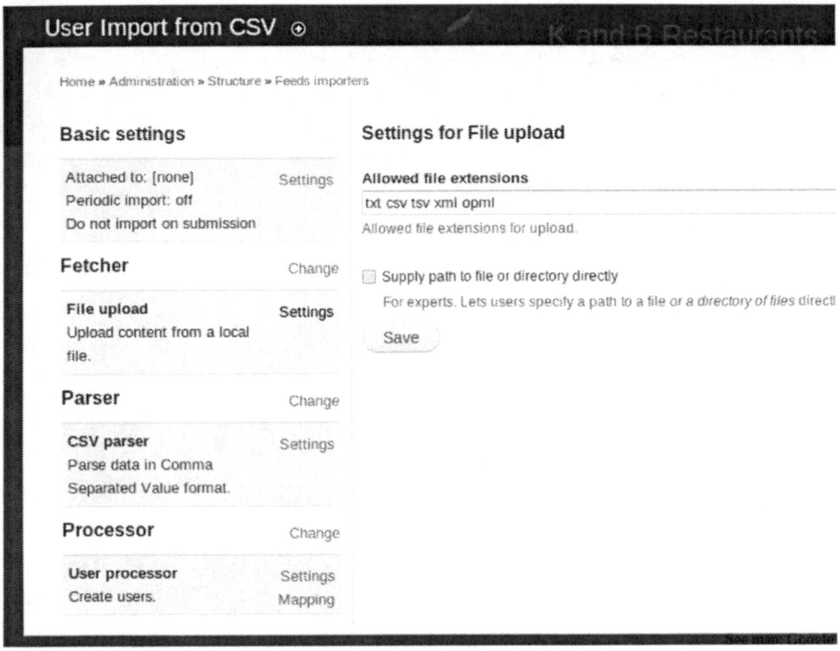

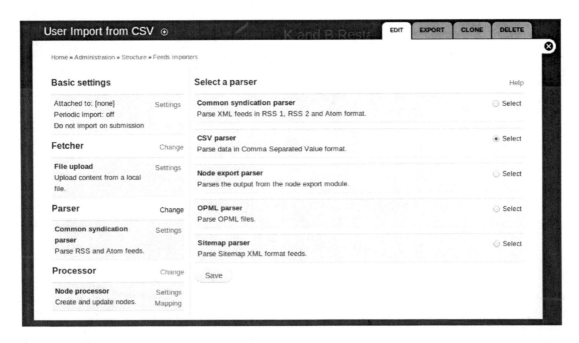

Figure 6-15. *Feeds importer file upload fetcher*

Another easy configuration: the type of parser you plan to use to read and interpret data in your file. As shown in Figure 6-16, we will just select CSV.

Figure 6-16. *Feeds importer parser selection*

Depending on your CSV file's options, you will separate data with a comma, a tab, or a semicolon. Select the right option for your file in the CSV parser options section. Note that you will be able to modify this setting on the upload form right before you start the import, so if you have different CSV files, there is no need to convert them or to make several importers. There will also be an option to check if your CSV files have no header (see Figure 6-17), meaning they start directly with data as opposed to starting with column names. This will influence the mapping step, as you will have to map column numbers to fields instead of column headers to fields. Let's say for our example that we added column headers for clarity.

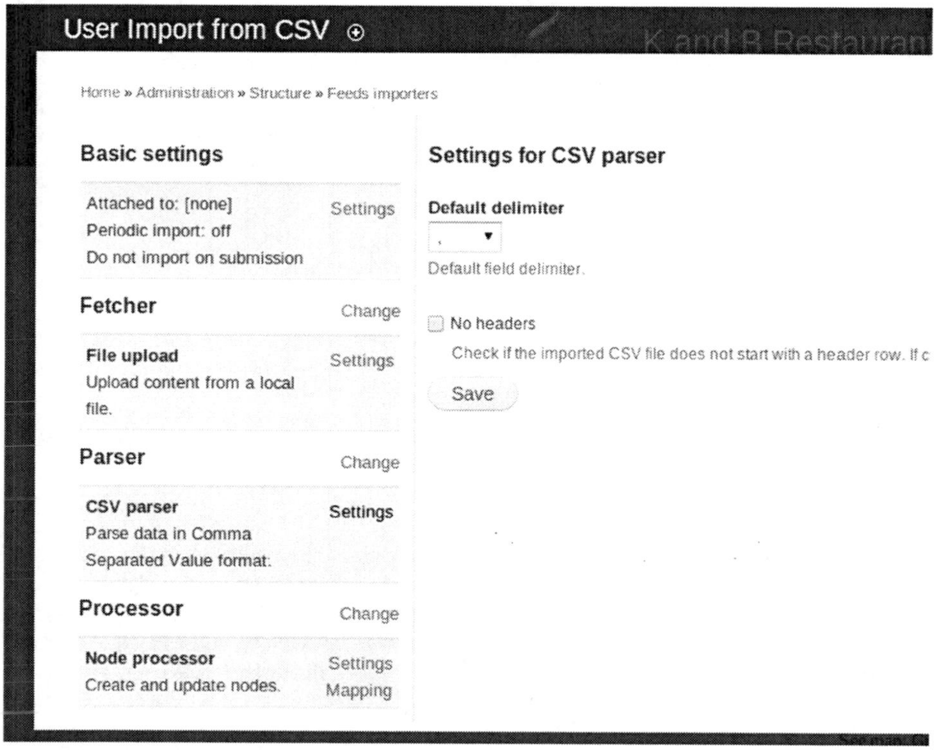

Figure 6-17. *Feeds importer CSV parser settings*

Now that we specified what file to import from, it's time to configure what we want to create upon import. In our case, as shown in Figure 6-18, we want to import users. Most of the time, you will be importing content items or users.

125

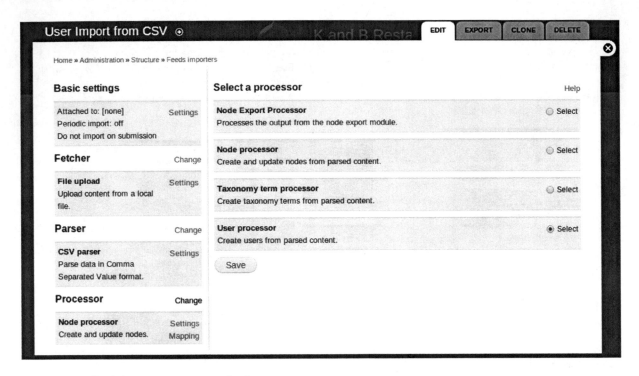

Figure 6-18. Feeds importer processor selection

The last section to configure is for the selected processor that will effectively create items based on your source (see Figure 6-19). You will have the option to replace items when trying to import content that already exists in the site. In addition to that, you can force replacement even if the items are identical. This could be useful if you have added some additional validation or rule based on the items being created or modified. Finally, you will get to choose some entity-specific settings; in our case: if a user is enabled or disabled upon import, the default role users should get, and so forth.

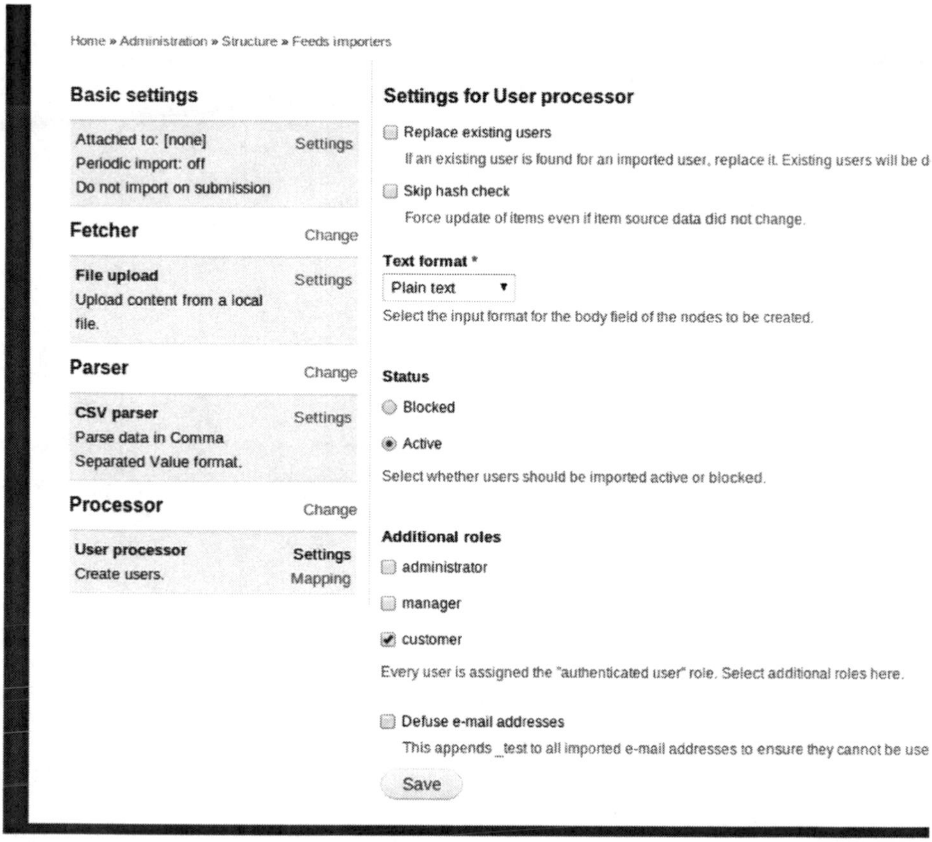

Home » Administration » Structure » Feeds importers

Basic settings

Attached to: [none]	Settings
Periodic import: off	
Do not import on submission	

Fetcher   Change

| File upload | Settings |
| Upload content from a local file. | |

Parser   Change

| CSV parser | Settings |
| Parse data in Comma Separated Value format. | |

Processor   Change

| User processor | Settings |
| Create users. | Mapping |

Settings for User processor

☐ Replace existing users

   If an existing user is found for an imported user, replace it. Existing users will be d

☐ Skip hash check

   Force update of items even if item source data did not change.

Text format *

[Plain text ▾]

Select the input format for the body field of the nodes to be created.

Status

○ Blocked

◉ Active

Select whether users should be imported active or blocked.

Additional roles

☐ administrator

☐ manager

☑ customer

Every user is assigned the "authenticated user" role. Select additional roles here.

☐ Defuse e-mail addresses

   This appends _test to all imported e-mail addresses to ensure they cannot be use

[Save]

Figure 6-19. *Feeds importer user processor settings*

One very nice feature (among many!) of the user processor is that you can have email addresses "defused." This means the Feeds import process will append "_test" to all addresses. If you've ever done data imports for the purpose of testing, you know how important it is to make sure you don't accidently send out production-looking emails from a test system. This is one way in which you can protect yourself from making such a mistake—that is, change all email addresses to something bogus.

The second step of the user processor—and last step of our configuration—consists of mapping CSV columns to their corresponding user field. In our example, we only have three fields to map, as shown in Figure 6-20. You will have to enter the column header name as displayed in the CSV file, or column number in the CSV file if there is no header. Then, select what user field it corresponds to. You must specify at least one field that should be unique, for instance the email address in a user import. This helps ensure you don't import duplicate users.

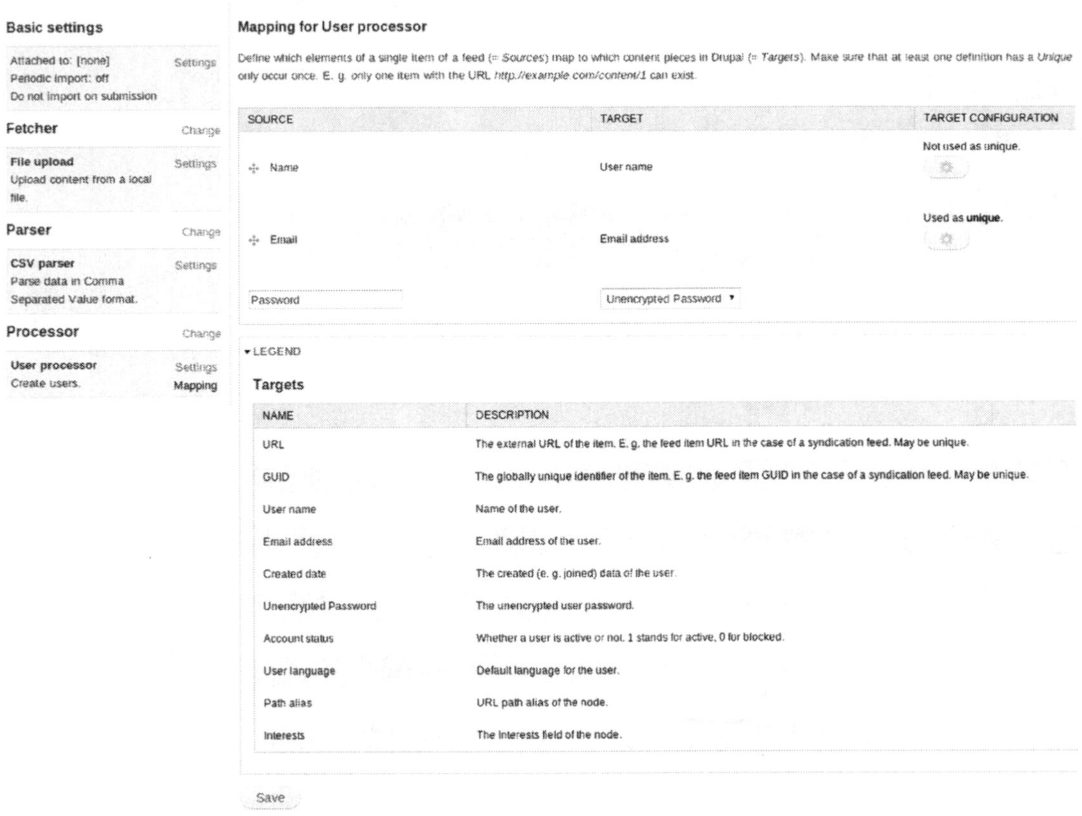

Basic settings

Attached to: [none]	Settings
Periodic import: off	
Do not import on submission	

Fetcher — Change

File upload	Settings
Upload content from a local file.	

Parser — Change

CSV parser	Settings
Parse data in Comma Separated Value format.	

Processor — Change

User processor	Settings
Create users.	Mapping

Mapping for User processor

Define which elements of a single item of a feed (= Sources) map to which content pieces in Drupal (= Targets). Make sure that at least one definition has a *Unique* only occur once. E. g. only one item with the URL *http://example.com/content/1* can exist.

SOURCE	TARGET	TARGET CONFIGURATION
⊹ Name	User name	Not used as unique. ⚙
⊹ Email	Email address	Used as **unique**. ⚙
Password	Unencrypted Password ▾	

▾ LEGEND

Targets

NAME	DESCRIPTION
URL	The external URL of the item. E. g. the feed item URL in the case of a syndication feed. May be unique.
GUID	The globally unique identifier of the item. E. g. the feed item GUID in the case of a syndication feed. May be unique.
User name	Name of the user.
Email address	Email address of the user.
Created date	The created (e. g. joined) data of the user.
Unencrypted Password	The unencrypted user password.
Account status	Whether a user is active or not. 1 stands for active, 0 for blocked.
User language	Default language for the user.
Path alias	URL path alias of the node.
Interests	The Interests field of the node.

Save

Figure 6-20. *Feeds importer mapping*

Congratulations, you just created your feeds importer. Now time to test it by importing those ten thousand customers. You can use our example file for this in the **Github repository that accompanies this book**, titled TestCustomers.csv.

Go to your site's import menu (see Figure 6-21) at /import and you will see a list of all the available feeds importers. Select your newly created user importer.

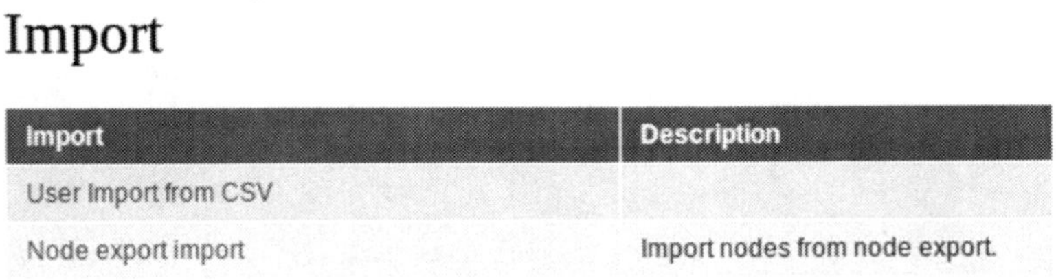

Import

Import	Description
User Import from CSV	
Node export import	Import nodes from node export.

Figure 6-21. *Import menu*

This will take you to a form where you can pick a delimiter for your CSV file (TABs for our sample file, to see that we can change from the original comma configuration), confirm whether or not the file has column headers, and upload the actual file to be used for the import (see Figure 6-22).

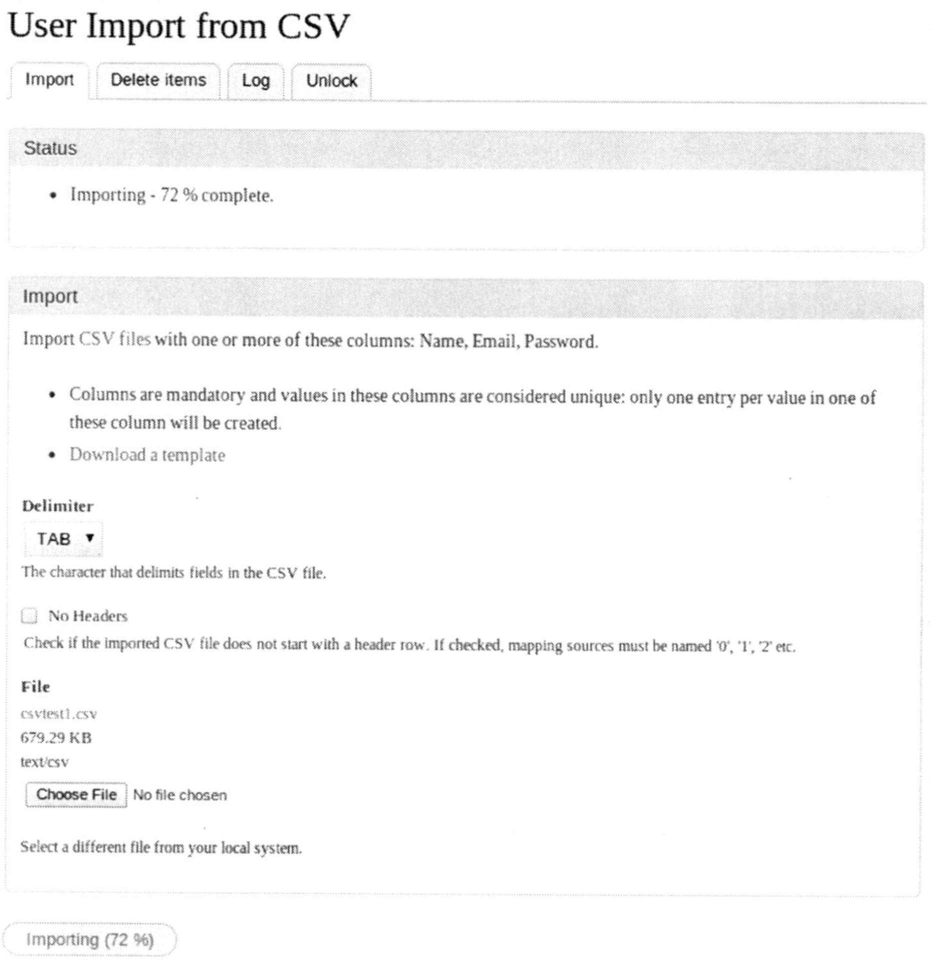

User Import from CSV

Import	Delete items	Log	Unlock

Status

- Importing - 72 % complete.

Import

Import CSV files with one or more of these columns: Name, Email, Password.

- Columns are mandatory and values in these columns are considered unique: only one entry per value in one of these column will be created.
- Download a template

Delimiter

TAB ▼

The character that delimits fields in the CSV file.

☐ No Headers

Check if the imported CSV file does not start with a header row. If checked, mapping sources must be named '0', '1', '2' etc.

File

csvtest1.csv
679.29 KB
text/csv

Choose File No file chosen

Select a different file from your local system.

Importing (72 %)

Figure 6-22. *Import process*

Click Import to start the import process. It will take you to a progress bar. On our local machines, importing those 10k users took about 10 minutes.

The Feeds module is incredibly powerful for migrating data from one system to another, or for restoring data on a regular basis—for example, a reporting system, a test server, and so forth. You can also use this import process along with exported files from the Node Export module, to automate the deployment of lots of data. This is especially useful when the data being imported requires a customized importer, which the Node Export import process does not offer.

Next, we're going to cover the topic of data validation—using an awesome module called Field Validation.

Data Validation

Nearly every application in the world needs to provide some sort of data or field validation. As we covered earlier, most apps have users, most users are humans, and most humans make mistakes. Ultimately, of course, you need to protect the integrity of the data in your application. For that, we can apply rules of one kind or another to the update of any content type. For example, an email field should represent a valid email address. And a postal code should be a valid (and existing) postal code. Here are some other field-level validation scenarios:

- Valid URL

- Required or non-empty value

- Value must be numeric

- Value must be between a min and a max

- Text field must have least a certain number of words

- Minimum and/or maximum length for text fields

- A date field must be within a given date range

- Field cannot contain any blacklisted words

- Text must match on a given regular expression

The list goes on and on. And, of course, using a regular expression provides pretty much any field-validation possible. If that doesn't work for you, the validation module we're going to look at allows you to write your own custom validators that simply plug into the module and are then shown on the Validation screen. This can be very useful when your web application needs to provide custom validation to its users, whereby those users can use your validators by setting a couple of options and associating them with content type fields.

Let's implement a simple field validator for our K&B Restaurants site.

Field Validation

To get started with field validation, you need to install the Field Validation module. To do so, run the following commands (from the root of your Drupal site). Note that we need to first install and enable the ctools and entity modules. Don't worry if they're already installed; installing them again won't hurt anything.

```
drush dl ctools entity field_validation -y
drush en ctools entity field_validation field_validation_ui -y
```

Let's add a date range validator to the Start Date field on the Special content type.

1. From the Structure ➤ Content Types page, click the Manage Fields link for the Special.

2. Click the edit link for the Start Date field.

3. Since you just enabled the field_validation and field_validation_ui modules, you should now see a Validation tab, as shown in Figure 6-23.

Home » Administration » Structure » Content types » Special » Manage fields » Start Date

Validation ●

| EDIT | FIELD SETTINGS | **VALIDATION** |

Figure 6-23. *Validation tab on field settings page*

4. To add the validator, click the link titled "Date range2."

5. Name the new validation rule "Special Start Date Range"—sans quotes.

6. In the Column setting, select "value" from the drop-down. Leave the "Cycle of date" value set to Global.

7. Then in the "Minimum date" field, enter the word "now"—sans quotes again. This instructs the rule to enforce that the special's start date be greater than now.

When finished, the rule should look like Figure 6-24.

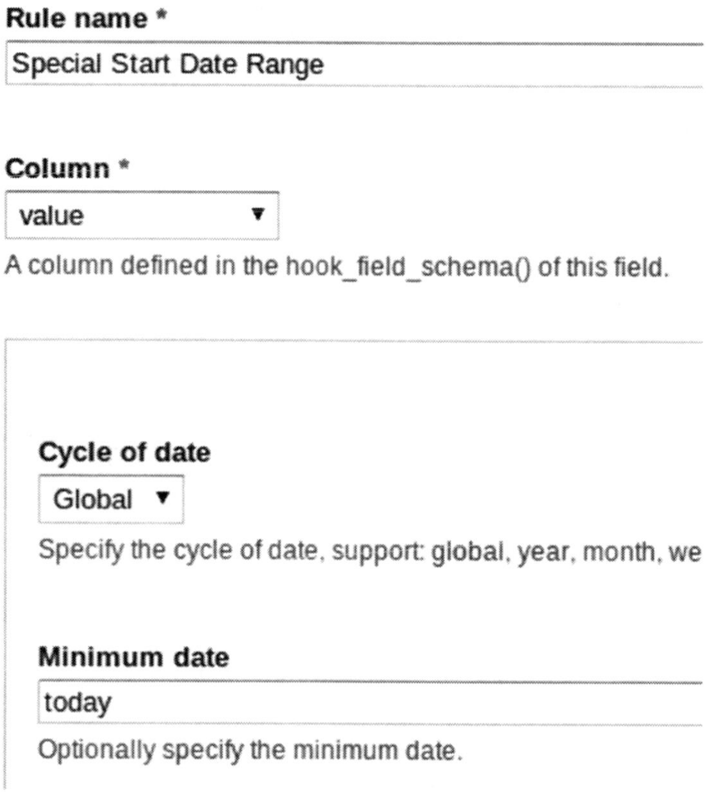

Rule name *

Special Start Date Range

Column *

value ▼

A column defined in the hook_field_schema() of this field.

Cycle of date

Global ▼

Specify the cycle of date, support: global, year, month, we

Minimum date

today

Optionally specify the minimum date.

Figure 6-24. *Validation rule for special's start date*

You will also need to enter a custom validation error message, as shown in Figure 6-25.

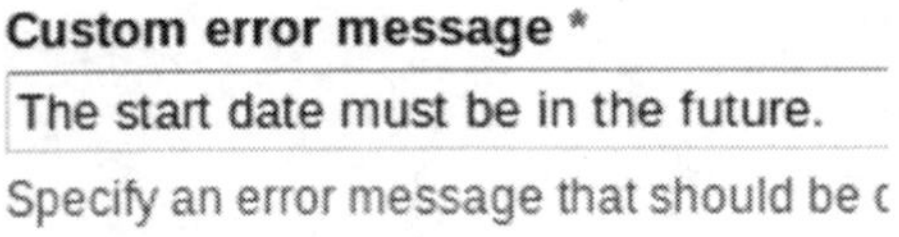

Custom error message *

The start date must be in the future.

Specify an error message that should be c

Figure 6-25. *Custom error message for start date validation rule*

Go ahead and click Save, then use the Add Content link to add a new special. Set its start date to a couple of days ago, and then click Save. You should see your error message displayed in red at the top of the screen. Pretty easy, eh?

Protected Fields

Some fields in Drupal are particularly critical to the application and are not editable from the user interface. For instance, the user entity's username and password fields cannot be removed or edited, and therefore it's impossible to use validation on them from the user interface.

Fortunately, and as you already guessed, there is a module for that. It's called "User restrictions" and you can find it at https://drupal.org/project/user_restrictions. It simply provides you with an additional configuration menu to add validation rules to the user entity's username and password. So, for instance, if you need to prevent a user's email address to be from somepublicemail.com, you go to the "Administration" admin tab, click on "User restrictions," and add a new rule. On the user restriction rule screen, configure as shown on Figure 6-26 to deny validation for email addresses that end with somepublicemail.com.

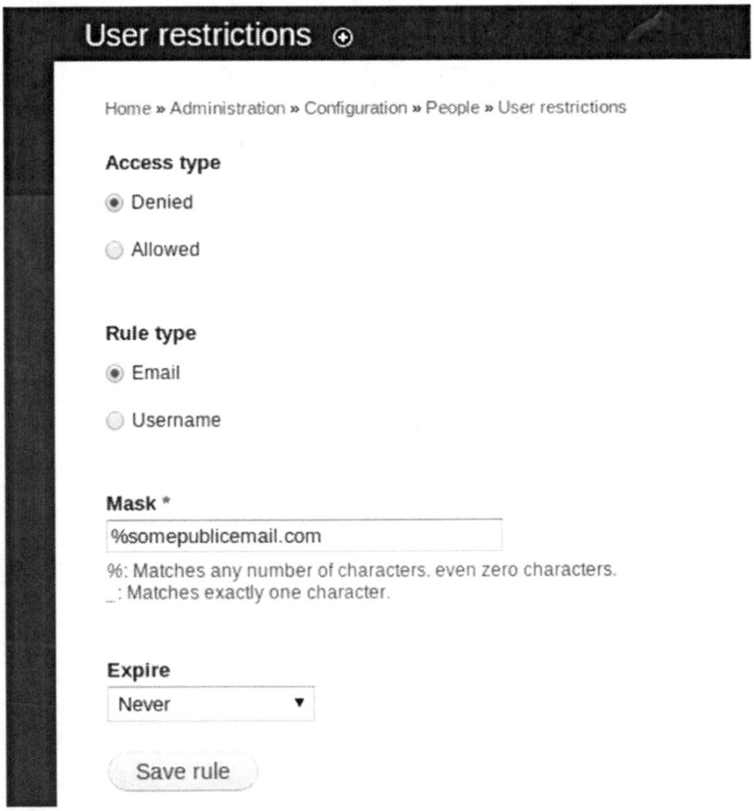

Figure 6-26. *User restrictions rule*

To wrap it up, you can see on the Validation tab of any content type's field settings that there are many field validators to choose from. You can even execute some PHP code, using the various context objects and functions provided to you by Drupal. In fact, from within a PHP code-based validator, you have access to the entire content item and all its fields, in addition to the current user and other Drupal site information. And because it's just PHP code, you can easily call out to other systems for validation when needed.

Revisioning and Content Checkout

Revisioning in Drupal is the concept of tracking all changes to a content item. When editing an item, the author/editor can choose to create a new revision. If so, the changes he makes to the item will be stored in the database, as well as the date and time they were made, and who made them. Additionally, the editor can add a comment explaining what changes were made and why (what and why is a typical best practice).

For those of you who are used to software engineering, this is quite a similar concept to version control for code, where you keep track of changes to the code, who made them, when, and have commit messages to specify what you did and why. In this same way, you can use previous versions to show differences; you can also restore them.

How to Use It?

A good practice is to force revisioning for sensitive content types, so all of their items will be "safe" from human errors. You can set this on the content type itself, and then using permissions prevent individual users from turning it off when creating or editing a piece of content.

When a new revision is made, users with the right to edit the item will see a "revisions" tab on the content item. This will display a list of all the revisions made for the item, with the ability to see what each revision looks like, and more importantly, the ability to revert to a previous revision. So if a content manager has made changes to an item that are undesirable, or break the logic or style of your site, you can easily revert the item to its previous state without spending a lot of time trying to find what went wrong and how.

Our Example

For our example project, we simply want every single content type to force revisioning. The only downside of this is the additional space it will take in the database, but because we don't have millions of items in our site and managed to pass a vote for the extra $12 of budget for additional storage, we should be alright.

Navigate to the Structure administrative tab and select "Content Types" to display a list of all your content types. For all the content types on which you want to force revisioning, click the edit link on the list. That will take you to a simple screen where you can set the name and description of the content type, as well as some default options, including the option to create a new revision on changes.

As shown in Figure 6-27, in the Publishing options, there will be a check box at the bottom to default to creating a new revision each time the item is edited. Just check the box and save. Repeat this operation for all the content types you want.

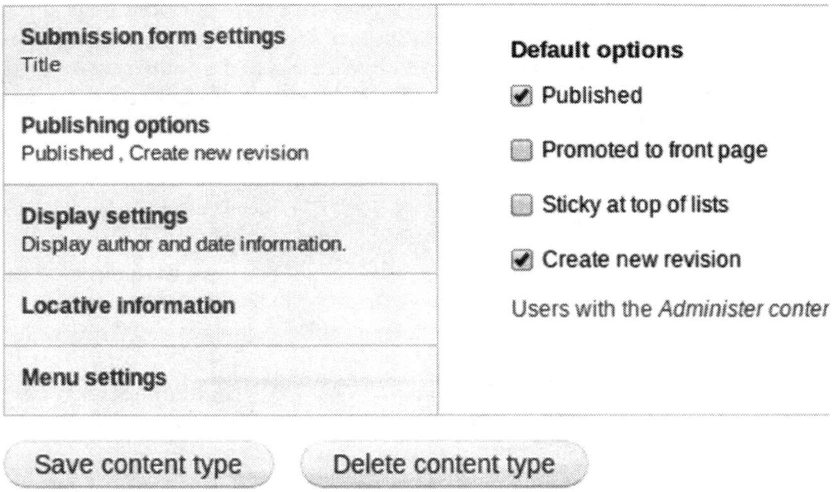

Submission form settings Title	**Default options**
	☑ Published
Publishing options Published , Create new revision	☐ Promoted to front page
	☐ Sticky at top of lists
Display settings Display author and date information.	☑ Create new revision
Locative information	Users with the *Administer conter*
Menu settings	

Save content type   Delete content type

Figure 6-27. *Force revision for content changes*

Now all users without the "Administer content" permission (which only admins should have) will automatically trigger a new revision creation when editing an item. This will make site administration much easier, as well as provide an audit trail of all changes made to the content (of that type).

Checkout

Another module that can come handy at times is the checkout (actual name is "content lock") module. Due to its "Sharepoint-like" behavior, it is often required by customers, who are used to checking out an item in Sharepoint before making changes to it, then checking it back in. It can also be required for sites where many content managers are modifying content concurrently and we want to make sure we don't end up with conflicting changes.

You can find this module here: `https://drupal.org/project/content_lock`. After installing it, you will be able to manage a couple of new permissions, as shown in Figure 6-28:

- Check out/lock documents—With this permission enabled, when a user edits an item, it will put a virtual lock on it so other users can't edit it at the same time until the first user is done editing and releases the item.

- Administer checked out documents—For administrators or highly privileged roles to force the release of a document by breaking the lock on it.

Content locking (edit lock)

Check Out/Lock Documents

Enables users to lock documents and requires them to respect locks others have made.

Administer Checked Out Documents

Enables administrators to view and break locks made by other users. *Warning: Give to trusted roles only; this permission has security implications.*

Figure 6-28. *Content locking permissions*

Once you install the module, the check out/lock permission should be on for each registered user. It is quite transparent when you are editing an item. But if someone else tries to edit it at the same time, they will be denied access and see a warning as shown on Figure 6-29.

Figure 6-29. Editing denied for locked content

Comments, Forums, and Blogs

Although we won't be using any of these in our example project, the following three modules ship with Drupal core and provide ready-to-go content-related features for common content management needs.

Comments

Several types of sites need to be interacting with users on most of their content. Here are some examples:

- E-commerce sites, where people rate and comment on items

- Marketing sites, where potential users ask questions or concerns about products

- New web sites, where the site administrators need feedback from its new users

These are just a few examples of good use-cases for the comments module. It enables for comments to be entered by visitors for a given content item.

Comments Enabling

Just like revisioning, you can enable or disable comments on a per-item basis or for content types in general. Of course, you can disable all comments throughout the entire site by simply disabling the core module called Comment. With the module enabled, you can enable or disable comments per content type the same way as the revisioning options shown in our example in the revisioning section of this chapter: just go to the content type management page in the Structure administrative tab, edit the content type you want to change the setting for, and pick your options to set the default for all items of this type. As shown in Figure 6-30, you can pick default settings for comments, as well as several other options, including managing replies to comments as threads, number of comments per page, previewing options before posting a comment, and so forth. To turn off the ability to comment on a piece of content, simply set the drop-down to Closed. Doing so also hides the Comments HTML elements altogether (that is, the big text box and a Submit button).

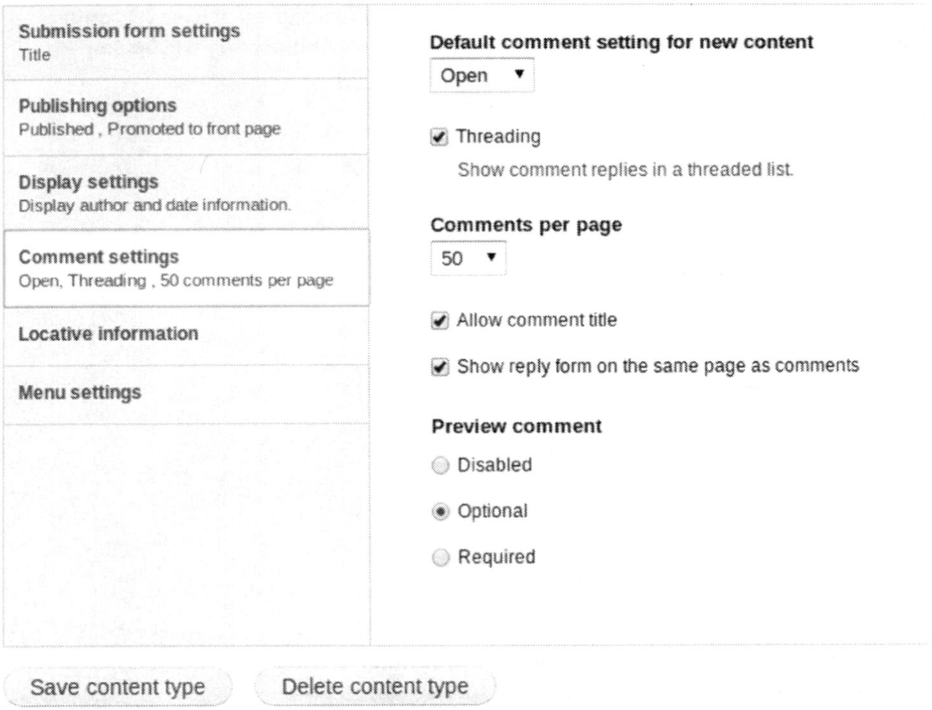

Submission form settings
Title

Publishing options
Published , Promoted to front page

Display settings
Display author and date information.

Comment settings
Open, Threading , 50 comments per page

Locative information

Menu settings

Default comment setting for new content

Open ▼

☑ Threading
   Show comment replies in a threaded list.

Comments per page

50 ▼

☑ Allow comment title

☑ Show reply form on the same page as comments

Preview comment

◯ Disabled

◉ Optional

◯ Required

(Save content type)   (Delete content type)

Figure 6-30. *Comments options*

Permissions

When enabling the Comment module, five self-explanatory new permissions get added to the list, as shown in Figure 6-31.

Comment

   Administer comments and comment settings

   View comments

   Post comments

   Skip comment approval

   Edit own comments

Figure 6-31. *Comment permissions*

Fields per Content Type

Depending on the content type you want people to comment on, you may want the comments themselves to be different. For instance, if a comment is made on a blog post, a simple text field for the commenter's name and text area for what he has to say will do. But for a comment on a product page, you may want to ask for more information: the version of the product the person has, how long they have been a customer, if they are the person who bought it, and so forth. Drupal provides a very convenient way to customise comments' fields per content type. This is very similar to how you added fields to your own content types.

On the content type editing screen, in addition to the "Manage fields" and "Manage display" tabs, there are "Comments fields" and "Comments display" tabs where you can edit comments like their associated content type—that is, for the content type they are attached to. In short, for each content type you have in the site, there is also a matching comment type that you can customize as well, as shown in Figure 6-32.

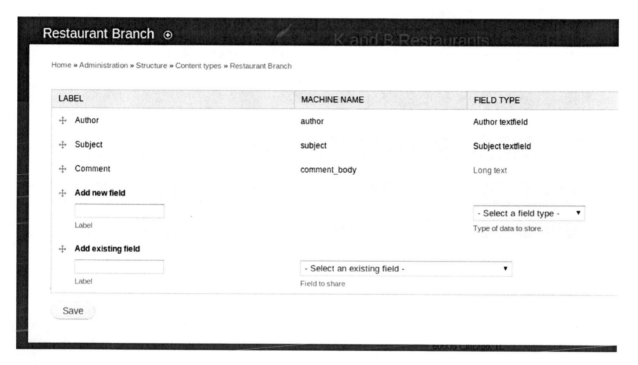

Figure 6-32. *Comment fields*

Blog and Forums

Having a blog as part of a web site is more or less standard business nowadays. Either for marketing purposes, or to showcase your employees' expertise, a blog is a great source of traffic for your site and can help catch the attention of potential clients. Drupal core includes a blog as a module that you can enable, setting everything up to get you blogging right away.

A little bit less common than blogging or comments threads, a forum can still prove useful when you want to take the conversation with your users further. This can allow for discussion thread-style dialogs, or you can use it as a help or FAQ platform attached to your site.

The Blog and Forum modules are part of the core and can be enabled to add two new content types to your site: Blog entry and Forum topic. The blog entry content type will hold its own content, while the Forum topic will leverage the comments module and be a base for a discussion based on comments.

Summary

In this chapter, you learned the ever-important concept of creating, exporting, and importing content. Indeed, no site would be complete without it! Fortunately, Drupal plus some modules provide lots of functionality that enable a multitude of common content-related scenarios you encounter when building, deploying, and maintaining enterprise-level web applications.

You walked through manual out-of-the-box content creation, and then discovered how to use the very powerful Feeds module to import a large CSV file. You then experimented with the Node Export module, which provides super-easy export and import of content—even to the most basic case of copying and pasting some text from one site to another. This module also integrates with the Drush command-line tool, allowing you to create automation scripts that perform mass imports of predefined content.

And, of course, no talk on content is complete without including validation. You learned how to configure a few basic rules with the Field Validation module.

Later in this book, we will dive deep into continuous delivery and other deployment-related topics. At that point, we'll revisit this area of exporting and importing data, as it plays a key role in deploying new sites and updating existing ones. This is especially true within the context of automated deployment tools.

In the next chapter, we're going to take a bit of time to discover the basic site configuration options available in Drupal. Once completed, your site will be nearly functionally complete—minus the attention to user experience.

CHAPTER 7

System Configuration

Whether building a system from scratch, or leveraging the power of Drupal to cut time and reduce bugs, you must have access to adequate configuration throughout the system. By that we mean various settings and options that let you tweak all kinds of functionality. This can include anything ranging from the site name and log, down to the manner in which log entries are created by the underlying PHP code.

In this chapter, you will learn about a variety of configuration options available to you in Drupal. Some of these are very system-oriented, and some are more at the level of the user interface, the home page, and language translations.

As a sneak preview, here are the different configuration-oriented topics we will cover:

- Basic site information

- Setting up a home page

- Caching

- Reporting and reports

- Web analytics

- System jobs

- Logging

- Localization

As is the theme for this entire book, you should see a parallel to this list in the way of concerns for applications you typically build from scratch. That is, all of these areas must be taken care of for any application. Once again, though, we are leaning on the power of the Drupal platform to provide these different features for us. All we need to do is essentially turn them on and fill in the blanks.

You can access most of a Drupal site's configuration from the Configuration administrative menu link. Once there, you will see links for most of the options and settings available in Drupal. This, of course, includes configuration for modules we've added. In other words, many of the Drupal core modules present configuration screens on this page. But so do most non-core modules. So this screen is your go-to screen for most system and module configuration.

Note that some modules don't expose configuration through the Configuration screen. For these, you will need to access their configuration options through the Modules menu.

Let's start off with some basic configuration dealing with site-wide settings.

Site Information

Navigating to the Configuration screen (via the administrative menu), you will see at least a couple dozen different configuration links. If you've been installing the modules mentioned in this book thus far, you should see configuration links for CAPTCHA, Password Policies, Node Export, Twitter, Rules, and many more. Click on the link in the upper right-hand corner titled "Site information." As shown in Figure 7-1, a few basic site settings will appear at the top.

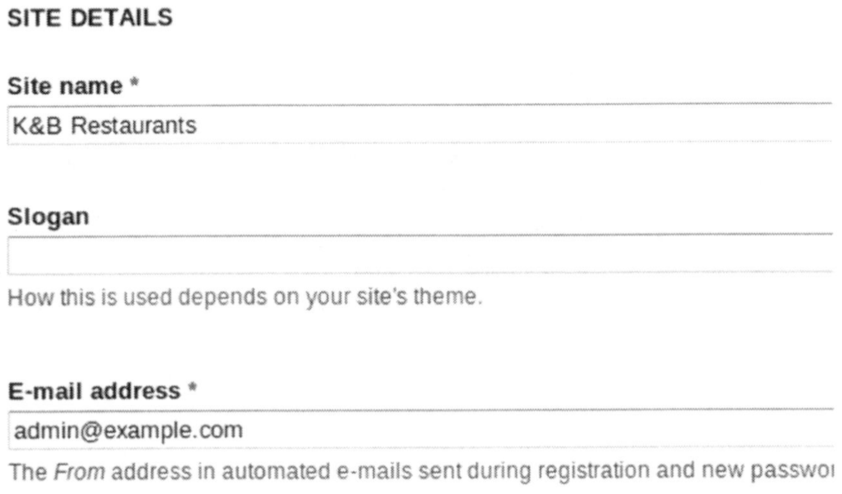

SITE DETAILS

Site name *

K&B Restaurants

Slogan

How this is used depends on your site's theme.

E-mail address *

admin@example.com

The *From* address in automated e-mails sent during registration and new passwoı

Figure 7-1. *Basic site information*

Depending on the theme you are using, the name and slogan are shown on the home page of the Drupal site. Different themes may alter this default behavior, but in general these two values are shown. You can, however, adjust the theme settings to hide the name and/or slogan.

The email address shown on the Site Information page is used as the default From address for all emails out of the system. This includes user registration, password changes, account cancellations, emails sent from rules, and so forth. Most of the time, you can override this address. But it is important to make sure this address is valid and originates from an account representing the web site and its owner.

SMTP MODULE

To make it much easier to configure outbound SMTP emails from your Drupal site, install the SMTP module. With just a few configuration values, your site will be able to send emails through any valid SMTP server.

Figure 7-2 shows this module configured to send email through Gmail.

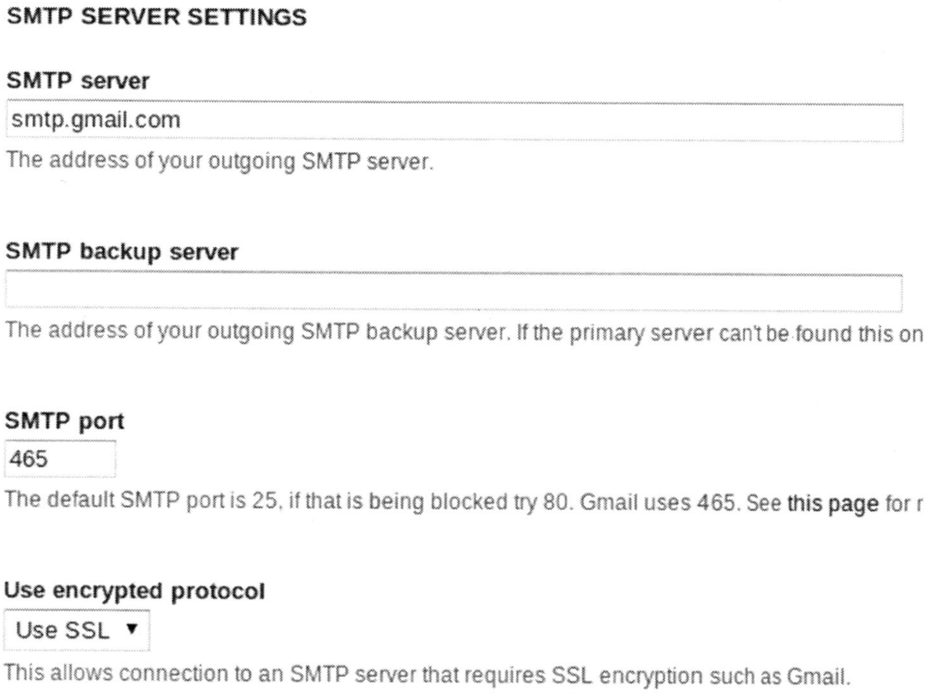

SMTP SERVER SETTINGS

SMTP server

smtp.gmail.com

The address of your outgoing SMTP server.

SMTP backup server

The address of your outgoing SMTP backup server. If the primary server can't be found this on

SMTP port

465

The default SMTP port is 25, if that is being blocked try 80. Gmail uses 465. See **this page** for r

Use encrypted protocol

Use SSL ▼

This allows connection to an SMTP server that requires SSL encryption such as Gmail.

Figure 7-2. *SMTP module configuration for Gmail server*

The name, slogan, and email address are also available throughout the site using Drupal's extensive Data Selectors. We covered these selectors a bit back in Chapter 4 when dealing with Rules. These are the variables that you can use to substitute in for static text in nearly any field in the system. For example, you can see the use of the site's name in the Account Settings configuration page, down at the bottom in any of the three Welcome Email tabs and their text. Figure 7-3 illustrates a few other variables that come from this Site Information screen.

▾DATA SELECTORS

SELECTOR	LABEL		DESCRIPTION
site:name	Name		The name of the site.
site:slogan	Slogan		The slogan of the site.
site:mail	Email		The administrative email address for the site.
site:url	URL		The URL of the site's front page.
site:login-url	Login page		The URL of the site's login page.

Figure 7-3. *Site information-based Data Selectors*

The rest of the settings on the Site Information page allow you to control the pages shown to the user for the home page, the 404 "not found" page, and the 403 "accessed denied" page. You don't have to set these, as Drupal has default content for all three. But many times you will want to control their look or behavior by creating your own custom pages with custom content.

It is worth noting that the default homepage behavior in Drupal is to show the last 10 pieces of content added to the site. Some might see this as an annoyance and not very useful. We find that in most projects, we end up creating a custom "Home" page—using Drupal's Basic Page content typeand then set the "Default front page" to this content item's URL. Let's go ahead and do that now.

Adding a Home Page

To add a dedicated home page, start by adding a new content item, selecting the Basic Page content type. In the Title, just enter "Home". In the content's body, enter "Welcome to K&B Restaurants!"

Click the URL path settings tab at the bottom, and enter the word "home"—sans quotes–in the URL alias box. When finished, the content item should look similar to Figure 7-4.

Title *

Home

Body (Edit summary)

Welcome to K&B Restaurants!

Text format Filtered HTML ▼

- Web page addresses and e-mail addresses turn into links automatically.
- Allowed HTML tags: <a> <em> <strong> <cite> <blockquote> <code> <ul> <ol> <li> <dl
- Lines and paragraphs break automatically.

Menu settings
Not in menu

Revision information
No revision

URL path settings
Alias: home

URL alias

home

Optionally specify an alternative UF
page. Use a relative path and don't

Figure 7-4. *Home page content item*

Click Save, and then navigate back to the Configuration ➤ Site Information page. In the Default Front Page setting, enter "home," as shown in Figure 7-5, then click Save.

Default front page

http://192.168.15.112/kbr/?q= home

Figure 7-5. *Setting the site's home page*

Now click the little Home button in the far-left side of the administrative menu, and you should see your new page as the home page content.

Note that because you are currently logged in as an administrator, you will see the home page content item's View, Edit, and Node Export tabs. This is the default behavior for any account with permissions to edit content items and specifically, in this case, to edit the Basic Page content item. If you now log out of the site, you will see what the normal anonymous user will see. Go ahead and try it now.

Now let's see how to remove the home page's title.

Excluding Page Title

Sometimes you really don't want to show a page's title. Or, for that matter, any content item's title. For a lot of web sites these days, simple and clean rules the day. And thus we want to remove as much clutter as possible. However, out-of-the-box Drupal does not provide a way to remove or hide a content item's title. And so, when viewing the home page we created in the previous section, the word "Home" is shown in big bold letters - as shown in Figure 7-6.

Home

Welcome to K&B Restaurants!

Figure 7-6. Home page showing the big bold "Home"

As you might have guessed it, there's a module for removing the title of a content item. Run the following commands to download and enable it:

```
drush dl exclude_node_title
drush en exclude_node_title -y
```

Once enabled, log back into the site as an administrator, and navigate to the Modules page. Find the Exclude Node Title module, and click on its configuration link. Once there, set the Basic Page option to "user defined nodes," and then select the Full Content check box, as shown in Figure 7-7.

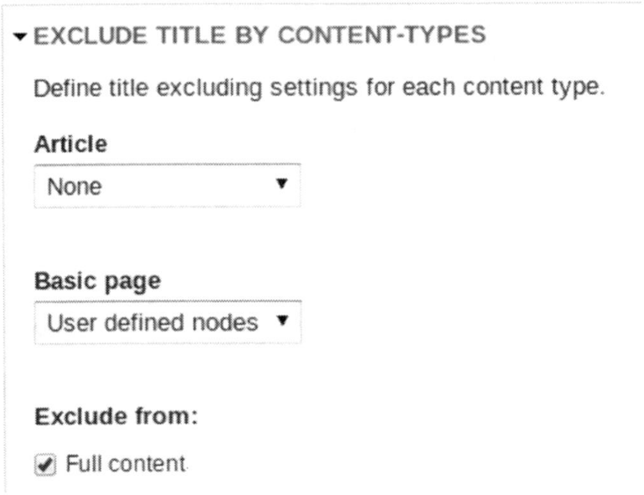

▾ EXCLUDE TITLE BY CONTENT-TYPES

Define title excluding settings for each content type.

Article

None ▾

Basic page

User defined nodes ▾

Exclude from:

☑ Full content

Figure 7-7. Exclude basic page title

Click Save, then navigate to the Home Page content item using the Find Content link in the toolbar. When editing the Home Page item, you should now see a new option directly under the item's title. As shown in Figure 7-8, check the box and hit Save.

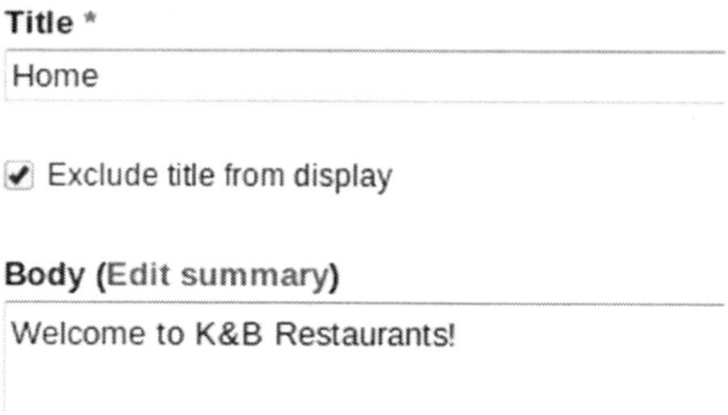

Title *

Home

☑ Exclude title from display

Body (Edit summary)

Welcome to K&B Restaurants!

Figure 7-8. Exclude title option

Log out of the site and you will see the home page again, only this time the big bold title is no longer present. That wraps up our section on basic site configuration. Now let's move onto caching and JavaScript file bundling.

Caching and Bundling

On the Configuration administrative tab, click on the "Performance" link. This will take you to the cache configuration and JavaScript bundling page. Please note that these settings are for Drupal to cache queries and HTML content. They are not a substitute for Apache's HTTP caching features; they are merely meant as a complement.

HTTP caching—by Apache, for instance—consists of memorizing a given page's content and serving its memorized version to users instead of querying Drupal for the page each time. This way users get a page delivered much faster, but the content of it is not guaranteed to be up-to-date. Using HTTP caching, updates to the site may need to wait for the cache (the memorized version of the site's pages) to expire before showing to a user. The expiration period should be set depending on how much traffic the site gets and how long we are ready to wait for changes to propagate to the users.

Drupal's caching works a bit the same way, but happens behind HTTP caching. Every time Apache decides to query Drupal for a page instead of serving a memorized version—which could happen when the HTTP cache expires or for pages that are not cached or even if there is no HTTP caching—the Drupal caching can serve its own memorized version instead of querying its database for the various elements of the page. This can result in substantially faster results, particularly for sites involving heavy querying. For instance, if you have many widgets displaying complex views on a site with a lot of content, the site could benefit a lot from Drupal's caching.As shown in Figure 7-9, the Drupal cache options are:

- *Clear cache button*: Removes all Drupal caching from memory, virtually updating the site for anonymous users. Use this if you just made some changes you want users to be able to see immediately. Most changes that require the cache to be cleared will display a message on the page telling you to clear the cache.

- *Caching pages for anonymous users*: Drupal doesn't allow you to cache for logged in users. A logged in user can still be presented an HTTP-cached version of a page by Apache, but Drupal itself won't serve a cached version unless the user is anonymous. This is a more powerful option than the following one as it caches the whole page, including all of the blocks in it.

- *Caching blocks*: This doesn't mean the blocks on the site are automatically cached. It allows for granular caching on a per-block basis. The option can be found on blog settings, which we will describe in the next chapter. Blocks based on views are also cacheable. Beyond that, there's a module that you can install, described shortly, that allows you to enable or disable cache on any block.

- *Minimum cache lifetime*: How long before a Drupal cached version of an element (block, page) is considered expired and the element will be fully re-queried and rendered by Drupal.

- *Expiration of cached pages*: When using an external cache such as an Apache HTTP cache, this option will set a header on the page that lets the external cache know it needs to refresh a page after so long. This option is not useful if you only use Drupal cache.

- *Bandwidth optimization*: This will aggregate (bundle) your Javascript and CSS files so that a page can load them much quicker, using less bandwidth. Both boxes should always be checked unless you are exceptionally trying to debug a front-end issue that requires you to render Javascript files un-minified. For example, it is much easier to debug un-minified JavaScript in Chrome Developer Tools or Firebug.

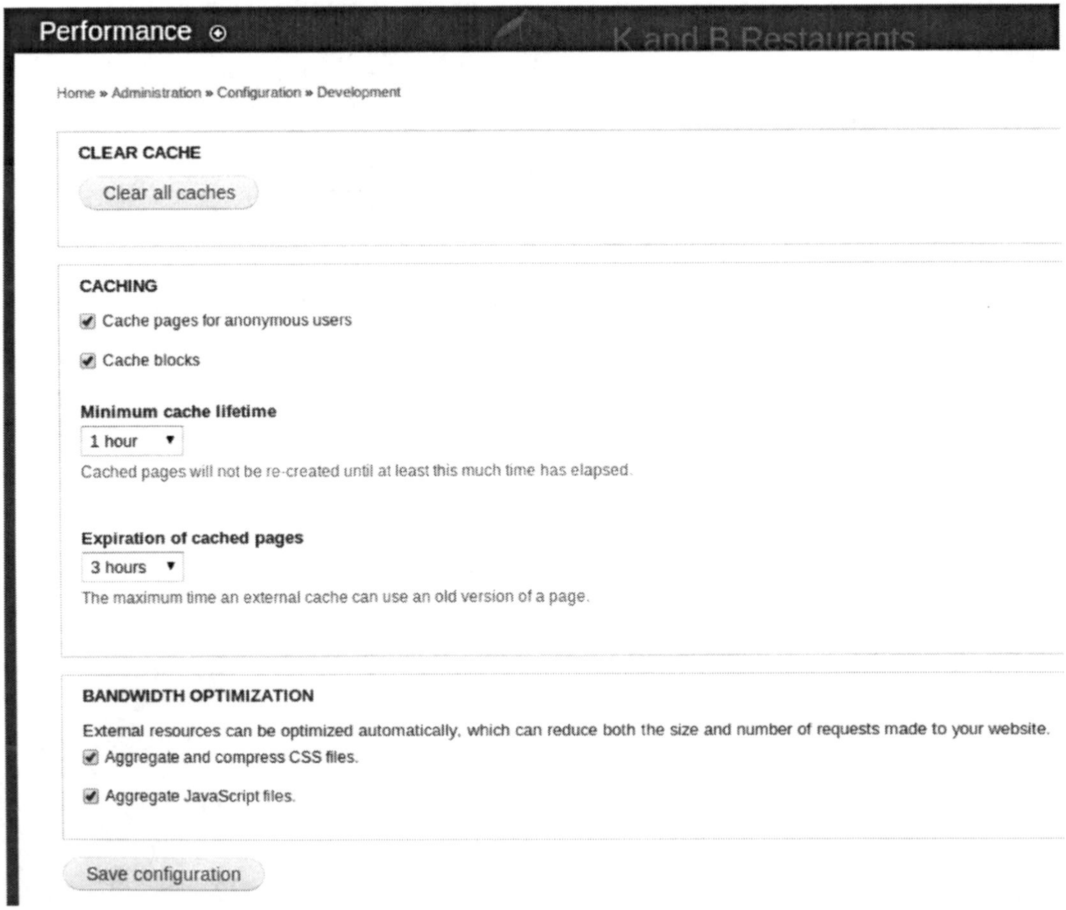

Performance ⊙

Home » Administration » Configuration » Development

CLEAR CACHE

Clear all caches

CACHING

☑ Cache pages for anonymous users

☑ Cache blocks

Minimum cache lifetime

1 hour ▼

Cached pages will not be re-created until at least this much time has elapsed.

Expiration of cached pages

3 hours ▼

The maximum time an external cache can use an old version of a page.

BANDWIDTH OPTIMIZATION

External resources can be optimized automatically, which can reduce both the size and number of requests made to your website.

☑ Aggregate and compress CSS files.

☑ Aggregate JavaScript files.

Save configuration

Figure 7-9. Cache settings

Again, setting the Cache Blocks option does not necessarily cache all blocks. Only those blocks that are pre-programmed to support caching will be cached. However, you can install the blockcache_alter module, which will provide cache settings for every single block on your site. Figure 7-10 illustrates this installed option.

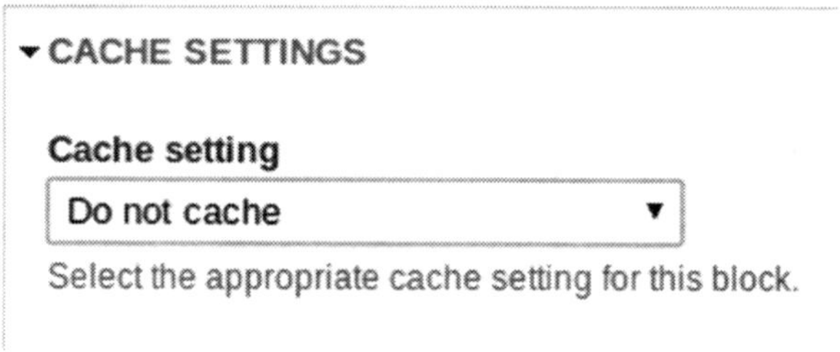

▾ CACHE SETTINGS

Cache setting

Do not cache ▾

Select the appropriate cache setting for this block.

Figure 7-10. *Settings from the Block Cache Alter module*

One of the nice features with this module's settings is that you can fine-tune them down to the role, user, and/or page. The options are:

- Do not cache

- Global (cache the block all the time)

- Per page

- Per role

- Per role per page

- Per user

- Per user per page

These different options mean that you can cache the content on a per-user, per-role, or per-page basis. Remember that a block can present more than a single page, thus the option to cache individual pages separately.

As an example, if a given block is set to cache on a per-user basis, then each of 10 different users will have their own cached copy of the block's contents. When set to the Global option, all 10 users will share the same cached copy.

One last note on caching. There are other non-Drupal options available lower in the stack that can improve Drupal site performance, allowing for massive scale-up well beyond the out-of-the-box Drupal/PHP/Apache/MySQL technology. Tools such as Boost provide additional page-level caching within PHP. And others such as Varnish and Squid sit on top of the entire stack and provide RAM-based caching—completely sidestepping Apache and Drupal cache.

Bottom line: don't underestimate the tremendous power of enabling one or more caching tools on a Drupal site that needs to support thousands and thousands of users. At some point, it really is the only way that a web site can provide speed and scale—Drupal or otherwise.

Reporting and Analytics

When it comes to analytics, we often find that the very popular Google Analytics module for Drupal provides everything we need in terms of usage statistics. If you have another tracking provider of choice, feel free to look at Drupal's modules to see if there is one to adapt to your analytics tools easily.

In addition to web analytics integration, Drupal offers several ways to build your own reports using views and data exporting tools.

Google Analytics Module

The Google Analytics (GA) module (`https://drupal.org/project/google_analytics`) provides a large number of options to intergrate with GA. It really stands out from most CMS analytics plug-ins where all you can do is enter a tracking Javascript snippet that will be rendered on every page. The options in this module allow you to fine-tune the data going into Google, to help you get at the most relevant and important tracking data for your site.

The additional options of this module are:

- Single domain, multiple domains, multiple subdomains tracking.

- Page tracking whitelisting and blacklisting.

- Option to either track or not track based on each role. For instance, if you have a lot of content managers or editors, you may want to turn off tracking for them to not skew your statistics.

- Option for users to opt out of tracking. There is an "opt-in or out of tracking" permission they will need to be given before they can see this choice.

- Options to track outbound links, mailto links, and file downloads. You can specify what extensions you wish to track for files.

- Track site messages: notifications, warnings, and errors, leveraging GA's event tracking. When turned on, GA can actually be used to report on measurements related to numbers and types of messages displayed to users, such as the number of warnings per day, number of errors per month, and so forth.

- Tracking site search and ad data.

- Anonymity options: you can choose to anonymize statistics by telling GA to not track the full IP of users, protecting them from being fully identified. The other option is to respect the "Do not track" header sent by browsers that users have configured to request not to be tracked.

The nice thing about using this module is that it really leans on the power of GA for analytics and other visuals with your site tracking data. All you need to do is configure the collection of the data, and GA takes care of the rest!

Views Reporting

Additional reporting can be made using views and other modules specialized in providing special displays for views, such as CSV and PDF files.

"Views data export" is such a module. You can find it at `https://drupal.org/project/views_data_export` and once installed, it will add a new display option to views that you can use to render the data as files—instead of web pages—for the view. It supports the CSV (comma separated value), DOC (Word), TXT (Plain text file), XLS (Excel), and XML (Extensible markup language) file formats.

For instance if you want to easily see your active users (defined as being users who have logged in within the past week), you can create a view to list all users. Then you can use a Data export display, with parameters as shown in Figure 7-11, to export the view's data as a CSV file. Here are the appropriate view settings:

- *Filter criteria*: Users, last access date greater than or equal seven days ago

- *Sort criteria*: Last access

- *Path*: Any path you want to access the export file from

- *Access*: Bby role, for admin only

- *Pager*: No pager, show all items
- *Format*: Whatever your format of choice is; unless you have a good reason to use a proprietary format, I recommend going for the widely supported CSV format

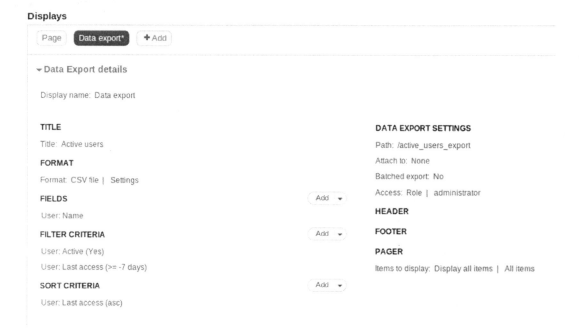

Figure 7-11. *Active users view data export*

The data export display made for this view is accessible at /active_users_export. It will produce and serve a CSV file with all the results. Not only will it do that every time you render the display, the module also comes with a drush command that let's you produce the file and save it from the command line, or better yet, a cron job. This will make it very easy to generate and save periodic versions of the file to your disk.

ARCHIVE REPORTS

In many enterprise-level applications, especially those in the financial industry, it is common practice to run nightly jobs that export "reports" of data to an archive disk. This essentially means that the previous day's (or, in some cases, previous week's or previous month's) system information is exported to a CSV file (or some other format) and then backed up to some archive storage. Doing so allows the system's users to effectively snapshot the important information every day, in a format that can be easily reviewed without any special tools. These file exports (a.k.a. reports) also allow for bulk loading of daily data into other systems—or even reporting and standby copies of the same system.

Whether you need to implement reports in the sense of online views of data, or you need to implement reports as file exports, the Views and Views Data Export modules have you covered.

Statistics

Drupal has a statistics module as part of the core. Once enabled, it will provide you with a few additional options accessible from the Configuration administrative tab, under statistics. There you will be able to configure content access logging and add the ability to track the views of each content item. If enabled, this option will add three variables to every content items, accessible, for instance, from the sort or filter criteria of a view as shown on Figure 7-12:

- *Most recent view*: date of the last view of the item

- *Total views*: number of times the item has been viewed since created

- *Views today*: number of views for the day

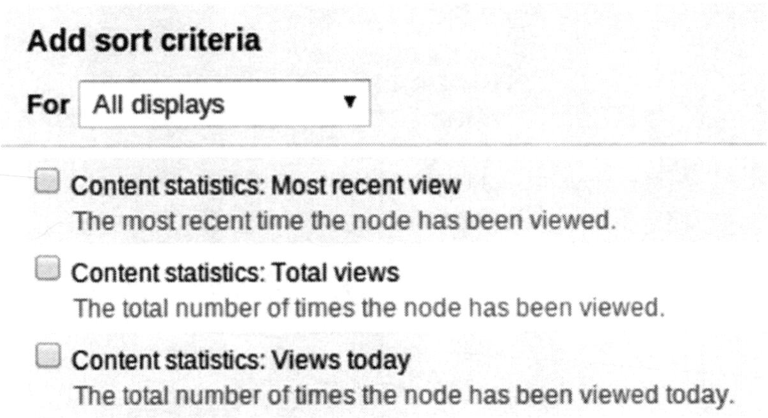

Figure 7-12. Content Statistics

This feature is quite useful when combined with the views reporting, if you want to save regular reports of your most popular content items for instance.

Cron Jobs

Drupal utilizes cron from the underlying operating system (cron on Linux and Mac, and Scheduled Tasks on Windows) to run periodic maintenance and clean-up jobs. Out of the box, you don't really need to do anything. There is a setting you can adjust, if you want to run the jobs more or less often. You can find the setting by going to the Configuration administrative page, and clicking on the Cron link. This will take you to a screen where you can adjust a single option, as shown in Figure 7-13. This setting allows you to tune the frequency of the jobs to the size of your site.

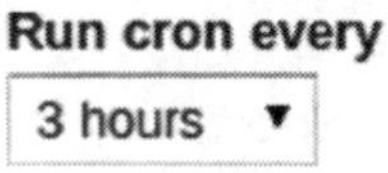

Figure 7-13. Cron scheduling option in Drupal

Various modules and features throughout Drupal utilize cron jobs for their functionality. For example, the search and indexing feature of Drupal is updated whenever the cron jobs are run. And the built-in database logging feature (discussed in the next section) uses cron to periodically clean up the log records, thereby not allowing the log data in the database to grow too large. Drupal itself uses cron jobs, as well, to check for updates to the core and to other modules.

There is no way directly in Drupal to add, edit, or delete the cron jobs themselves. This configuration is left up to the modules, and in general are not exposed through the Drupal web interface. There are, however, a few modules that provide more visibility and fine tuning of the available cron jobs. For example, the Elysia Cron module (available at https://drupal.org/project/elysia_cron) allows you to adjust the frequency of individual jobs, versus the global setting found in the cron Configuration page (shown in Figure 7-13).

To execute all jobs manually, you can use any of the following options:

- Click the "Start cron" button on the cron configuration page

- Navigate in your browser or with wget to the address provided on the cron Configuration page; this will execute the cron.php page, which runs all registered cron jobs

- Use the Drush core-cron command, which runs all cron jobs in Drupal

If you want to add your own jobs to the system, you will have to do that outside of Drupal—in the operating system. On Linux and Mac, this is, of course, through the cron system. In that case, you can use the crontab command-line tool—or many other options. A simple Google search will yield plenty of help in this area. On Windows, you can create a Scheduled Task.

While the cron feature in Drupal is very simple, it is very important for the overall health and performance of your site that job execution is functioning properly. This also helps keep you abreast of important security and other updates to Drupal modules (including the core module) via the regular update checks.

Logging

Like jobs, logging in Drupal is pretty hands-off. The actual decision to log something—that is, create a log entry—and exactly what to log typically happens down in the PHP code. This means that the modules themselves are coded to create log entries appropriate for both their functionality and troubleshooting issues with them. For example, the Rules module, when configured appropriately, creates a plethora of log entries during rule execution to help you see what's going on under the covers.

The underlying log engine in Drupal is called Watchdog. That name is not very relevant to Drupal users, only coming into play if you are writing Drupal module code in PHP. Just know that when you see the name Watchdog in the context of Drupal, it is referring to its logging functionality.

Module Logging

You can tweak various log settings throughout the system. Let's explore a few. To start, let's look at the logging option for the Rules module. Figure 7-14 shows the two options available.

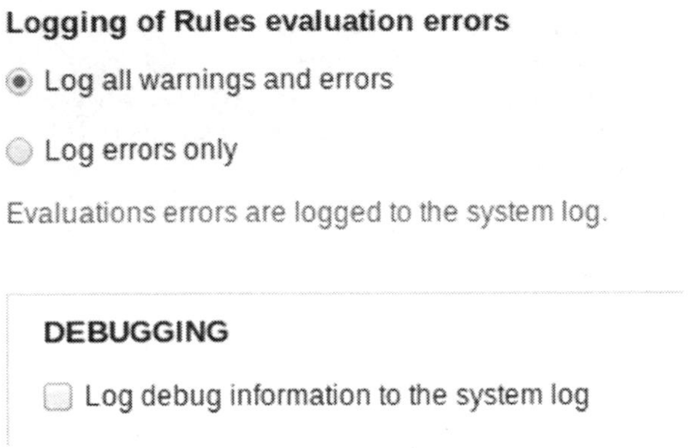

Logging of Rules evaluation errors

◉ Log all warnings and errors

◯ Log errors only

Evaluations errors are logged to the system log.

DEBUGGING

☐ Log debug information to the system log

Figure 7-14. *Logging options for Rules*

Simply put, you can change the level of messages being logged—either just errors, or, warnings and errors. You can also tell Drupal to log all Rules-related debug messages to the log. This is a tremendous help when you are troubleshooting a custom rule.

Once again, we see a parallel to coded-from-scratch enterprise applications. Typically, as developers, you would liberally add debug write statements to your code. This enables you (or some other poor sap!) to more quickly find the source of bugs found in your code. Further, most log libraries these days support run time options for verbosity and log levels. For example, in log4j and log4net, you can filter in or out DEBUG messages at runtime. This allows a system administrator or developer to turn on verbose debug logging to support troubleshooting. As shown in Figure 7-14, this same option applies to Drupal.

Another logging-related setting is found on the Logging and Errors page—navigated to from the Configuration administrative page. In Figure 7-15, we can see the option to limit the number of log records being stored in the database.

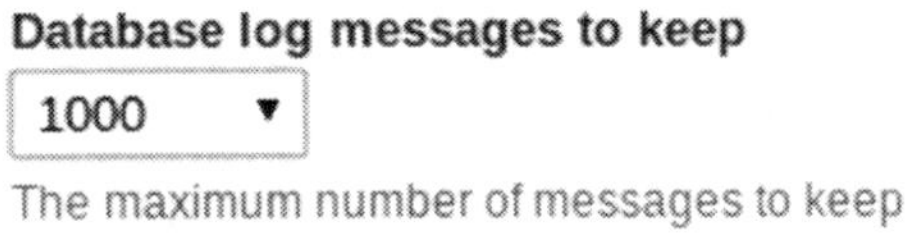

Database log messages to keep

| 1000 ▾ |

The maximum number of messages to keep

Figure 7-15. *Log records to keep option*

As mentioned in the section on cron jobs, Drupal uses a cron job to clean up log records in the database. Whenever the job runs, it will remove any records beyond the option shown in Figure 7-15.

Viewing Log Messages

To view log messages, navigate to the Reports page from the administrative menu. Then click on the Recent Log Messages link. There you will see all messages recently logged by all of the modules in Drupal.

From here, you can easily filter by log message type, as well the message severity. For example, if you only wanted to see messages related to user creation, user updates, and logging on and off, you could select the user type and click the Filter button.

From the Type list, you can see the many modules that offer log messages in Drupal. Each module will no-doubt create many log messages to help you know what's going on within the code. There's even a content message type. Messages of this type show you each and every add, edit, or delete of any content item in the system—including who did it and and when they made the change.

Another message type you might find useful is the System type. This filter will show you messages corresponding to each and every time a module is enabled or disabled. As with any system, built-from-scratch or built on the power of a platform like Drupal, knowing when new libraries or modules are added is one of the first things you look for when troubleshooting.

Localization

It's not uncommon for an enterprise web application to require multilingual support. Having a site maintained in several languages can quickly become an admin's nightmare. Thankfully, Drupal has a simple way of dealing with multilingual sites.

In order to have your site display in several different languages, you will need the Content Translation and Locale modules enabled, both part of the Drupal core. Locale allows you to define additional languages on top of your site's default language. Content Translation will let you import localizations for Drupal as well as create your own localized content. Once those modules are on, you will start by adding languages to your site on top of your default language. On the Configuration administrative tab, you will find a Llanguages link. This will bring you to the language listing where you can add a language to your site's default.

In our case, for the K&B Restaurants web site, we default to English and we are going to add Spanish and French. There are many languages to choose from in Drupal. You can see in Figure 7-16 the three supported languages listed.

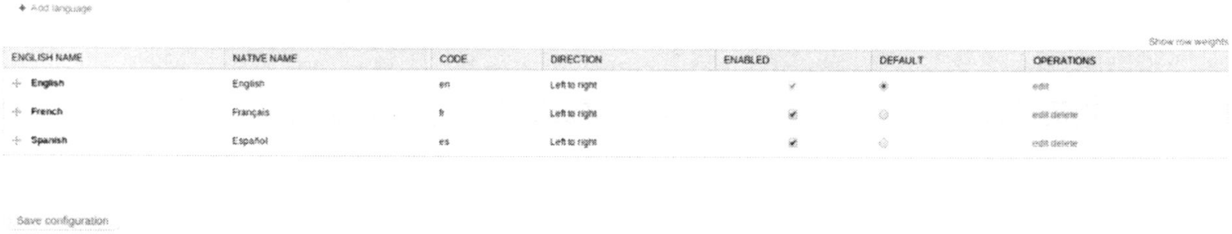

+ Add language

ENGLISH NAME	NATIVE NAME	CODE	DIRECTION	ENABLED	DEFAULT	OPERATIONS
✛ English	English	en	Left to right	✓	⦿	edit
✛ French	Français	fr	Left to right	✓	○	edit delete
✛ Spanish	Español	es	Left to right	✓	○	edit delete

Save configuration

Figure 7-16. *Languages in Drupal*

Once those languages are added, click on the "Detection and selection" tab to decide how you want to detect what localized version of your site a user will see. This tab is shown in Figure 7-17. You can check any method you want to use, and when a user renders the site, it will go through the enabled methods from top to bottom until one of them returns a result (or reach default, which means the user will be shown the default language). A simple way to configure this is to let the user set this as a parameter when creating an account, or default to browser language.

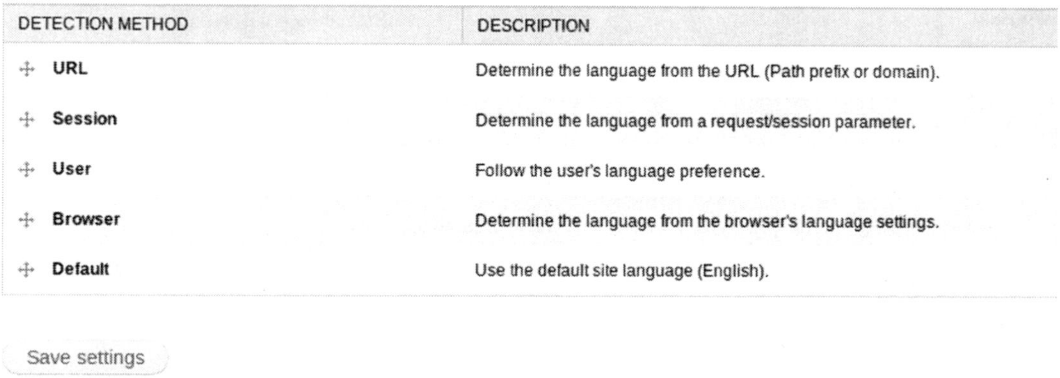

DETECTION METHOD	DESCRIPTION
✛ **URL**	Determine the language from the URL (Path prefix or domain).
✛ **Session**	Determine the language from a request/session parameter.
✛ **User**	Follow the user's language preference.
✛ **Browser**	Determine the language from the browser's language settings.
✛ **Default**	Use the default site language (English).

Save settings

Figure 7-17. *Language detection*

Now that you have several languages, and before you start translating your site's items, let's make good use of the translation talents of the Drupal community. You can download language packs for Drupal at https://localize.drupal.org/, or better yet, let the localization module do it for you: https://drupal.org/project/l10n_update. If you haven't done so already, go ahead and install that module now.

The moment you enable it, "Localization update" will automatically translate itself in all of your enabled languages. Then by going to the "Translate interface" menu from the Configuration tab, you can select the Update tab and see all the modules you could download localized content for, on top of Drupal core. As shown on Figure 7-18, you can batch-localize many modules and also Drupal core, with the option to select only a subset of your enabled languages. You can also provide some overriding options: only new translation strings are added, everything but manually edited strings are added or replaced, or everything is replaced.

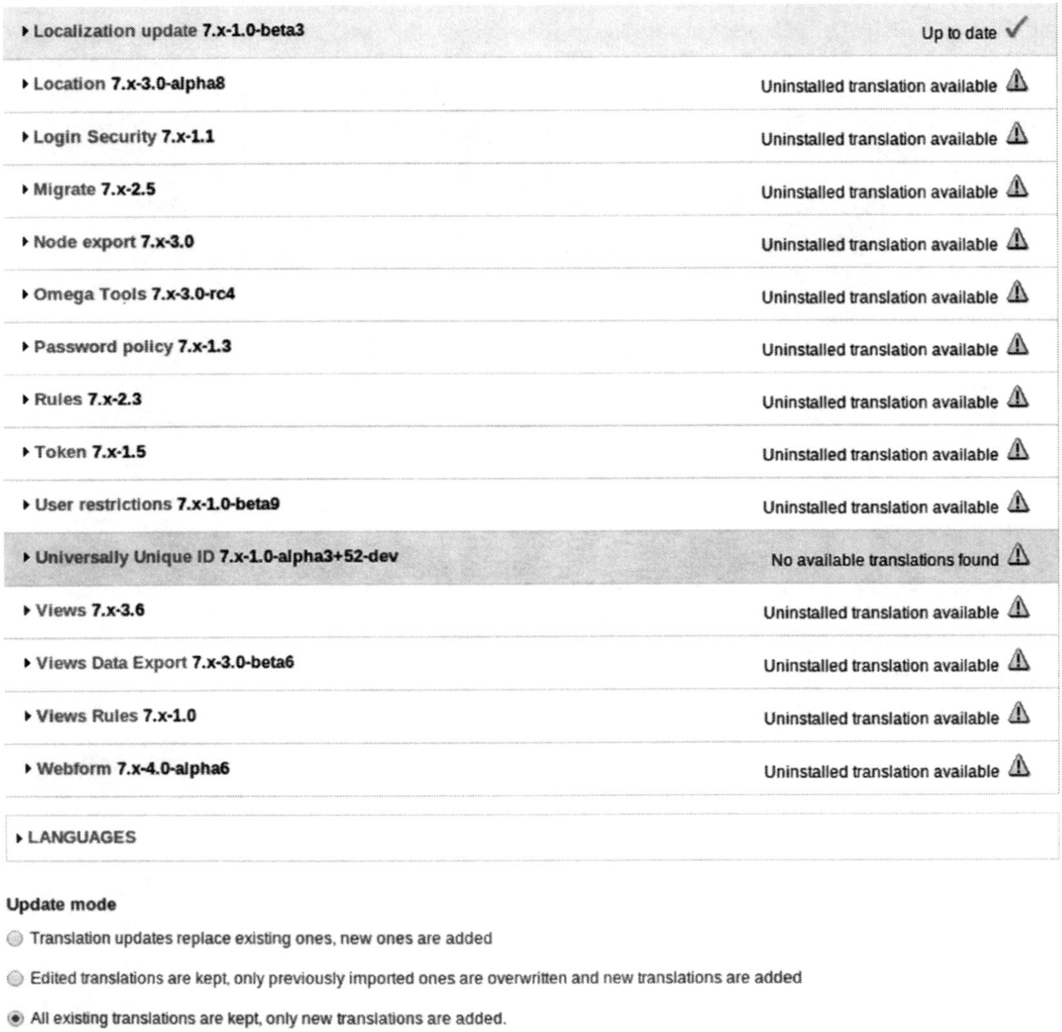

▸ Localization update **7.x-1.0-beta3**	Up to date ✓
▸ Location **7.x-3.0-alpha8**	Uninstalled translation available ⚠
▸ Login Security **7.x-1.1**	Uninstalled translation available ⚠
▸ Migrate **7.x-2.5**	Uninstalled translation available ⚠
▸ Node export **7.x-3.0**	Uninstalled translation available ⚠
▸ Omega Tools **7.x-3.0-rc4**	Uninstalled translation available ⚠
▸ Password policy **7.x-1.3**	Uninstalled translation available ⚠
▸ Rules **7.x-2.3**	Uninstalled translation available ⚠
▸ Token **7.x-1.5**	Uninstalled translation available ⚠
▸ User restrictions **7.x-1.0-beta9**	Uninstalled translation available ⚠
▸ Universally Unique ID **7.x-1.0-alpha3+52-dev**	No available translations found ⚠
▸ Views **7.x-3.6**	Uninstalled translation available ⚠
▸ Views Data Export **7.x-3.0-beta6**	Uninstalled translation available ⚠
▸ Views Rules **7.x-1.0**	Uninstalled translation available ⚠
▸ Webform **7.x-4.0-alpha6**	Uninstalled translation available ⚠

▸ LANGUAGES

Update mode

○ Translation updates replace existing ones, new ones are added

○ Edited translations are kept, only previously imported ones are overwritten and new translations are added

◉ All existing translations are kept, only new translations are added.

Figure 7-18. *Localization auto update*

To download new or update existing languages, simply click on the "Update translations" button at the bottom of the Translate Interface page. This will download and update all enabled languages—for all enabled modules! Granted, this is a community effort and so not necessarily all languages and all modules will be covered. But this is certainly a good head start, if not completed entirely for your selected language(s).

After you click on the "Update translations" button, you should see a screen similar to that shown in Figure 7-19. Note that the status column values have all been updated.

Drupal core

▶ drupal **7.22**	Up to date ✓

Modules

▶ Block Cache Alter **7.x-1.0**	Up to date ✓
▶ CAPTCHA **7.x-1.0-beta2**	Up to date ✓
▶ Chaos tools **7.x-1.3**	Up to date ✓
▶ Date **7.x-2.6**	Up to date ✓
▶ Duo **7.x-1.7**	Up to date ✓

Figure 7-19. *Modules' languages updated*

Now that your site's interface is multilingual, it's time to put your translation team to work on the site's content itself. First, multilingual support needs to be enabled on a per-content type basis. So let's pick a content type and see what it looks like. As shown in Figure 7-20, you will find this under the Publishing options. There will be a multilingual support block, where you can enable the content type for multiple languages and for translation.

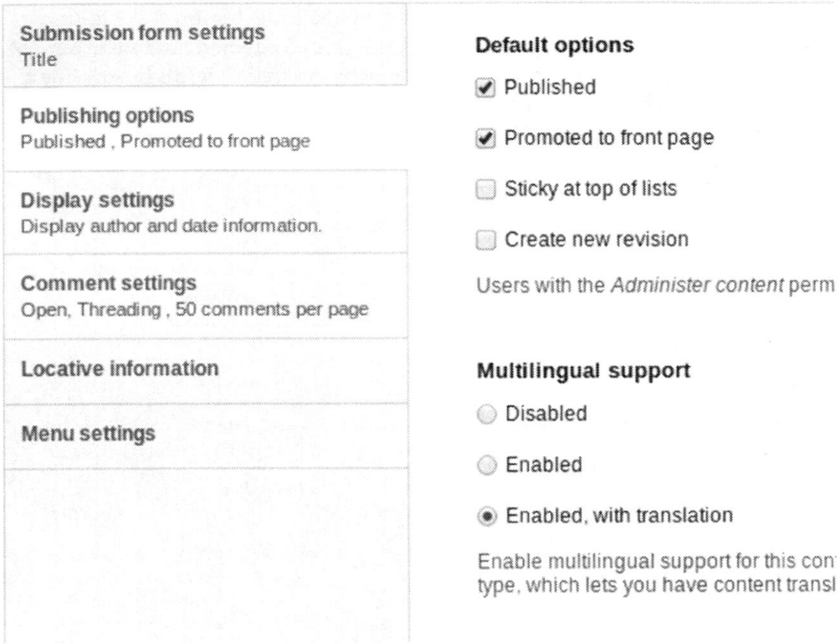

Submission form settings Title	**Default options** ☑ Published
Publishing options Published , Promoted to front page	☑ Promoted to front page
Display settings Display author and date information.	☐ Sticky at top of lists
Comment settings Open, Threading , 50 comments per page	☐ Create new revision Users with the *Administer content* perm
Locative information	**Multilingual support**
Menu settings	○ Disabled
	○ Enabled
	● Enabled, with translation
	Enable multilingual support for this con type, which lets you have content transl

Figure 7-20. Content type translation enabled

In order to have access to the translation interface, a user will need the "Translate content" permission enabled, as shown on Figure 7-21.

Content translation

Translate content ☐ ☑

Figure 7-21. Translate content permission

You are now all set for content translation. Let's say you enabled translation on the Menu Item content type, and created a new menu item in English. After you are done, there will be a "Translate" tab on top of the page that will take you a page similar to that shown in Figure 7-22.

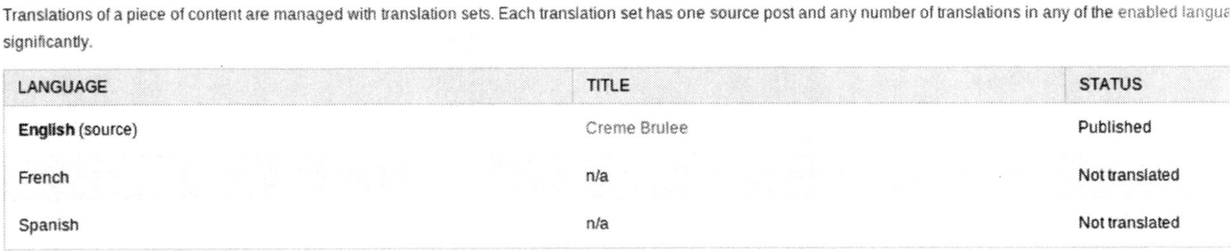

Translations of a piece of content are managed with translation sets. Each translation set has one source post and any number of translations in any of the enabled langua significantly.

LANGUAGE	TITLE	STATUS
English (source)	Creme Brulee	Published
French	n/a	Not translated
Spanish	n/a	Not translated

Figure 7-22. Translate tab for a specific content item

Select a language by clicking its "add translation" link. There you will reach an edit screen, very similar to the normal edit screen, except the selected language is auto-selected and disabled. Every field of the content item will display but be replaceable by its translation. At this point, you would enter the translated text into each field.

Once everything is translated, click Save. It will create a new content item, in the language you selected. Although they are separate items, translations of an item are linked together and there are options to easily access localized versions of a page, using a widget or on the page itself. By default, a language switcher section will be added to a localized page, as shown on the bottom right of Figure 7-23.

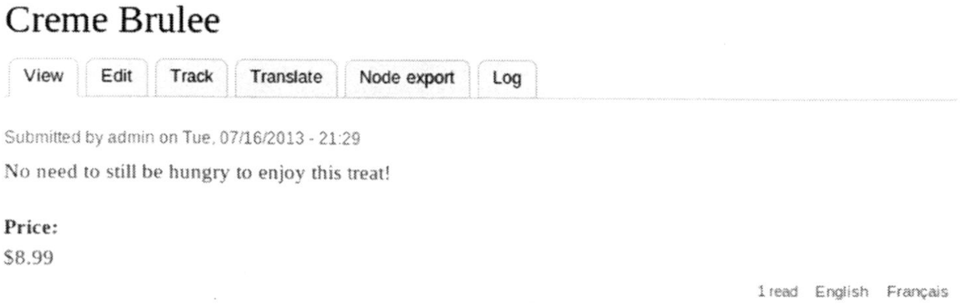

Creme Brulee

| View | Edit | Track | Translate | Node export | Log |

Submitted by admin on Tue, 07/16/2013 - 21:29

No need to still be hungry to enjoy this treat!

Price:
$8.99

1 read   English   Français

Figure 7-23. *Language switcher options*

Like everything else we've seen in Drupal so far, localization has been taken care of for you. All you need to do is translate your own content item values. This is identical to what you'd need to do if you were building an application from scratch, wherein you would typically use resource files or string tables. In this case, we can directly use the Drupal interface.

One last comment on localization. Because the translations are done at the content item level, the Features and Node Export modules fully support exporting and importing content items of different locales. In other words, you can have a team in Mexico create all of the appropriate translations of your K & B Restaurants Menu Items, and then easily export and import them into your target system.

Summary

In this chapter you learned about various configuration options in Drupal. This ranged from basic site information to cron jobs to cache setting to language translations. This is but a handful of options among the many, many more that Drupal provides out of the box, or with a few additional stable modules. And once again, it is clear that leveraging Drupal as our development platform has saved us a lot of time and potential bugs when it comes to configuring our web site.

Next, in Chapter 8, you will learn how to go beyond system configuration, and instead focus on user experience design and implementation in Drupal, covering topics such as menus, navigation, and themes. You will also learn how to customer the CSS for your site within the context of Drupal.

CHAPTER 8

■ ■ ■

User Experience Design

If you've hung in so far, slugging through seven chapters of Drupal concepts, installation, system design, module installation and configuration, security, and system configuration, you've no-doubt noticed that we haven't touched at all on the visual aspects of the user experience. In fact, beyond straight-up content types and some simple site information, we haven't explored anything at all related to the user experience of the K&B Restaurants Drupal web site.

In this chapter, you will learn how to work with menus, layout regions and blocks, forms, and a bit of information about themes. These topics, when stitched all together, provide an extremely powerful set of tools—already at your fingertips—that you can leverage to create a fully customized user experience. Unlike many other content manager systems on the market, the visual architecture in Drupal allows you to customize just a little, or customize everything the user will see and navigate through. In our own experience, we've built sites on both ends of the spectrum, and many somewhere in between.

So let's get started customizing our K&B site. Note that we won't be digging into CSS styles—we're assuming that at this point you are familiar with general standards and techniques of CSS.

Menus, Navigation

As is the same with every other aspect of a web application, Drupal doesn't make any assumptions about menus, allowing for any menu addition or customization. A menu in Drupal is simply a tree of links, and you can add and reorganize links from the menu itself or from the individual content item being linked in the menu. In other words, you can manually add/update menus that point to pieces of content or to views; or, you can have content items and views exposed in menu links when editing the content items and views themselves.

Most themes come with a few pre-configured menus, but you can either disable or remove those any time, as well as create your own menu. In this section, we will create a custom menu to showcase some of the branches for our restaurant. Then in the next section, we will see how to display this menu in its own widget, or block, and how to customize where it displays.

The Administration menu we keep referring to is simply a menu, by the way, and you can edit it and make changes to it anytime to reorganize it in a way that makes more sense to you.

From the Administration menu, select the Structure tab and you will find a Menus link, from which you can see a list of existing menus and create a new one. We will create a new menu named Our branches, as shown on Figure 8-1.

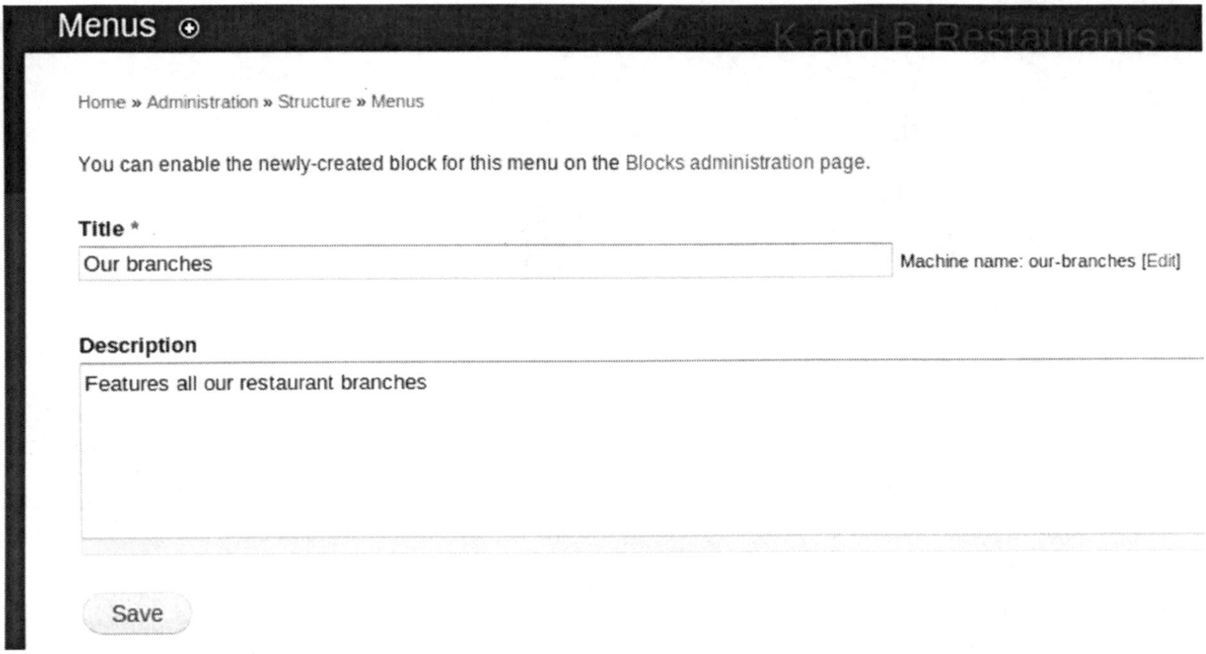

Figure 8-1. *New menu creation*

After you save your new menu, you will be taken to an overview screen where you can see all the links in your menu and edit them or drag and drop them to reorganize your menu. There are no links yet, so let's start by adding one.

The link creation menu is quite similar to the menu setting when creating a content item. As shown in Figure 8-2, you will have to set a menu link title, which is the text that will display on the menu and on which a user will have to click to be redirected to the linked item. The redirection will be based on the path you provide in the link. This path can be an existing content item, a view, a user, or any valid URL in your Drupal site. Note that you won't be able to save an invalid URL as your path, so if you intend to add the item you want to link to later, you should simply create the link on the item itself. You will have the option to disable a menu item, to virtually take it off the menu without having to remove it. This is useful for temporary changes, if you want to make a node unavailable for a little while, for instance.

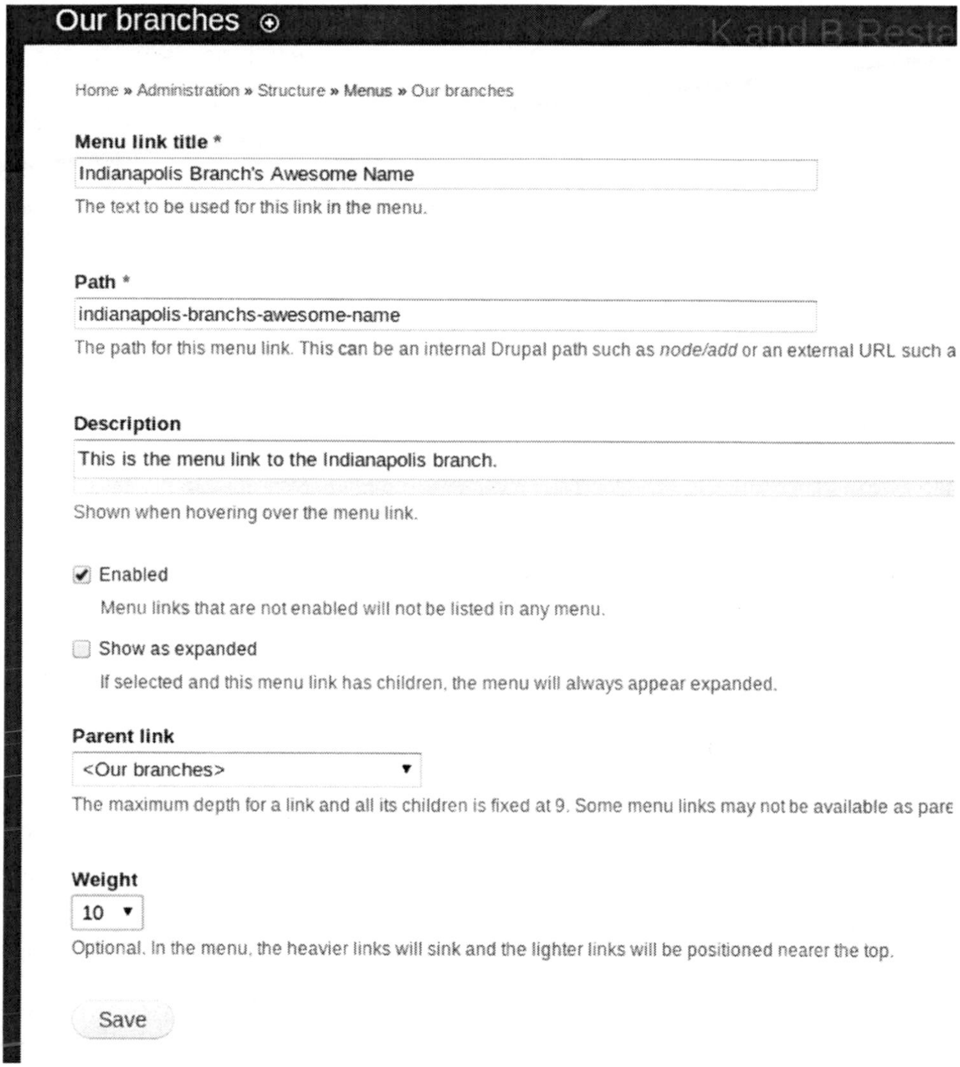

Our branches ⊕

Home » Administration » Structure » **Menus** » Our branches

Menu link title *

Indianapolis Branch's Awesome Name

The text to be used for this link in the menu.

Path *

indianapolis-branchs-awesome-name

The path for this menu link. This can be an internal Drupal path such as *node/add* or an external URL such a

Description

This is the menu link to the Indianapolis branch.

Shown when hovering over the menu link.

☑ Enabled

   Menu links that are not enabled will not be listed in any menu.

☐ Show as expanded

   If selected and this menu link has children, the menu will always appear expanded.

Parent link

<Our branches> ▾

The maximum depth for a link and all its children is fixed at 9. Some menu links may not be available as pare

Weight

10 ▾

Optional. In the menu, the heavier links will sink and the lighter links will be positioned nearer the top.

Save

Figure 8-2. *Menu link options*

The final two options let you define where this link will display on the menu itself. First, you will need to define a parent for the link. Consider a menu to be a tree structure where the root is the menu itself, and every link that displays as a principal menu item is a first-level child of this root. Then every other link is defined as the child of another link. The weight of a link determines in what order it will display compared to its siblings: the lower weight will be displayed earlier and near the top.

It seems a bit lengthy to configure a complex tree by hand like this, but you can just create those links setting the menu itself as the parent, then reorganize them by dragging and dropping them from the menu overview. This will let you rank them quickly and define them as children of another link by dropping them under this link with an indentation, as shown on Figure 8-3 for the Administration menu, as an example. When saving your changes, Drupal will edit the links automatically to assign the right parent and weight.

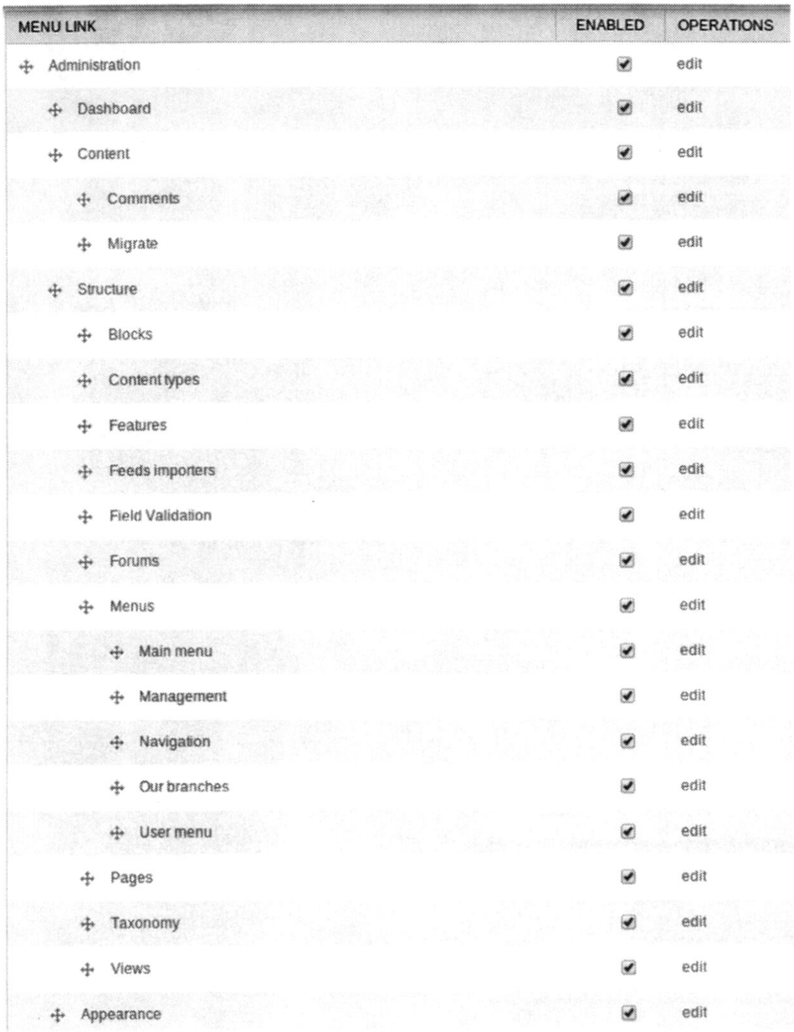

MENU LINK	ENABLED	OPERATIONS
⊹ Administration	☑	edit
⊹ Dashboard	☑	edit
⊹ Content	☑	edit
⊹ Comments	☑	edit
⊹ Migrate	☑	edit
⊹ Structure	☑	edit
⊹ Blocks	☑	edit
⊹ Content types	☑	edit
⊹ Features	☑	edit
⊹ Feeds importers	☑	edit
⊹ Field Validation	☑	edit
⊹ Forums	☑	edit
⊹ Menus	☑	edit
⊹ Main menu	☑	edit
⊹ Management	☑	edit
⊹ Navigation	☑	edit
⊹ Our branches	☑	edit
⊹ User menu	☑	edit
⊹ Pages	☑	edit
⊹ Taxonomy	☑	edit
⊹ Views	☑	edit
⊹ Appearance	☑	edit

Figure 8-3. *Administration menu links*

For our example, we will just have to add all our restaurant branches to this menu. This new menu won't be displayed anywhere until we display it as a block, as discussed in the next section.

Regions and Blocks

An important and central concept in content management is the separation of style and content. Part of Drupal's approach to this is to separate the different spatial sections of a page and the content that goes in them, called regions and blocks, respectively.

The different sections of a page (that is, the regions) are defined in the template files as part of the site's theme. Typical examples of regions are the page header, footer, sidebars, and main content. To reveal those regions, go to the Structure administrative tab, then select the Blocks link and use the Demonstrate block regions option to display a visual representation of the theme's regions, as shown in Figure 8-4.

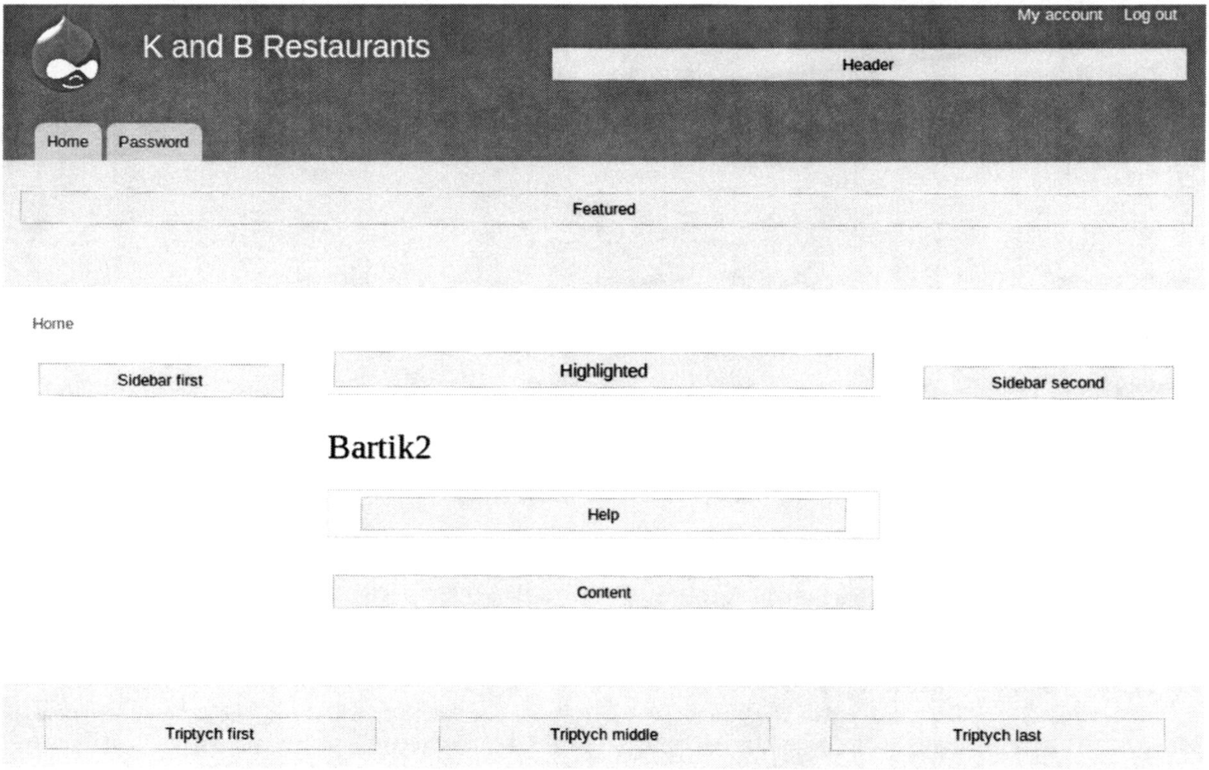

Figure 8-4. *Regions highlight*

An important step when choosing the right theme for your site, or the right theme from which to build a sub theme, is to figure out whether or not its regions will allow for the layout you are looking for. For instance, if you plan on having more regions than a candidate theme contains, or regions with a completely different layout, then it's probably not the right theme for you. A theme with the same overall structure with what you have in mind, or with a few more regions that you can simply leave empty, will be a better choice.

Inside those regions, you will be able to insert blocks of content. Those blocks are managed by Drupal and can easily be added, edited, removed, or switched to another region. Modules often define their own type of block with preconfigured content in it. A good example of this is the Views module that will let you display a view in a block that you can then display wherever you want (that is, in whatever region you want) using the blocks interface. The menu we created in the previous section will also be available as a block automatically. You can also create your own blocks with a body field where you can enter static HTML or PHP, with access to the Drupal API, for virtually unlimited customization.

The blocks management page is shown in Figure 8-5, illustrating the block names on the left – e.g., "Search form," "Our branches" – and the region names listed in the dropdowns.

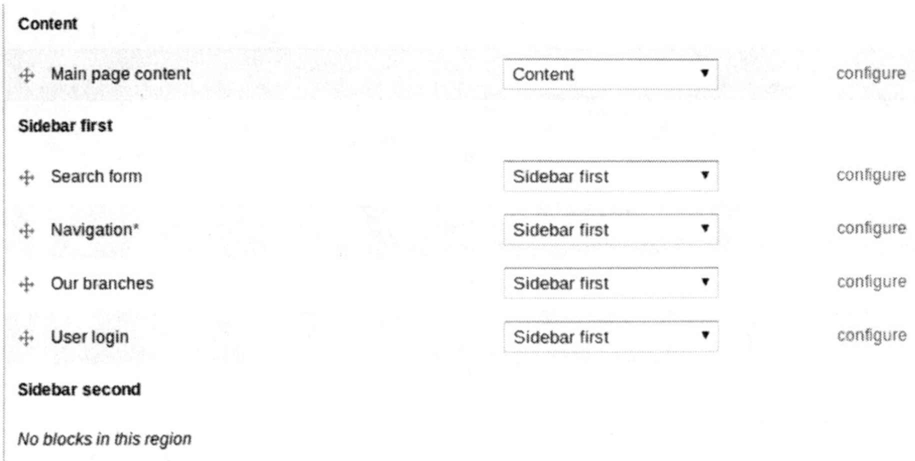

Content

+ Main page content

Content ▼

configure

Sidebar first

+ Search form

Sidebar first ▼

configure

+ Navigation*

Sidebar first ▼

configure

+ Our branches

Sidebar first ▼

configure

+ User login

Sidebar first ▼

configure

Sidebar second

No blocks in this region

Figure 8-5. *Manage blocks*

From the blocks management interface, let's go down to the disabled blocks and find our newly created "Our branches" menu. The region we want to add the block to is the "Sidebar first" region. You can see this region defined in Figure 8-4, right under the Home link. To do this, either select the region from the block row on the drop-down, or drag and drop the block row itself directly into the right region, using the arrow icon on the left. Using the same icon, you can order the blocks within a given region.

After adding your block to a region, you can define where in the site the block will show. The region it is in defines where it will display spatially on the page, but you can also limit its display to certain pages, content types, or roles. In order to define this, click the configure link on a block row on the block management interface. There, you can also allow users to decide whether to see this block or not as an option in their account settings. When going to a page that elects to render the block, you will see it appear in its assigned region, as shown on Figure 8-6. Note how the Chicago and Indianapolis branch menus appear in the branches block - in the "Sidebar first" region. As previously mentioned, the block's content appears directly under the "Home" link.

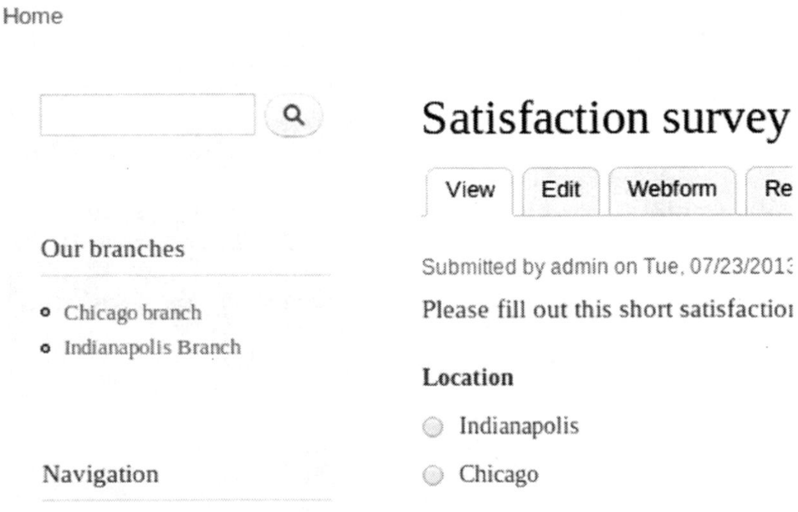

Home

Q

Satisfaction survey

| View | Edit | Webform | Re |

Submitted by admin on Tue, 07/23/201:

Please fill out this short satisfactio

Our branches

o Chicago branch
o Indianapolis Branch

Location

○ Indianapolis

○ Chicago

Navigation

Figure 8-6. *Menu shown in block*

The manner in which Drupal separates regions from blocks is incredibly powerful, effectively decoupling content from the content's display location. Further, each block includes with it various configuration settings, allowing you to customize displayed content by user, role, page, and so forth. And all of this without actually updating the content itself.

Themes

You've probably heard the speech about separation of content and presentation a million times throughout your web development career, but now that you're using Drupal, this is being taken care of for you. Drupal defines the whole presentation and style of your site within a separate package called a theme. It is much like a module in that you add the theme's code at a given location and it is then made available to your site and can be enabled and set as your theme. In fact, much of the way Drupal deals with themes is identical to the way Drupal deals with modules. You can even use the same Drush commands we've used for modules to download and enable themes.

To talk about everything there is to know about themes in Drupal would take a whole new book (or two). In this section, we'll simply give an overview of Drupal's themes from a site admin prospective, and then provide starting points to get started with your own theming in Drupal.

What's in a Theme and What Does It Do?

A theme consists of three main types of artifacts:

- *Templates*: These define the different regions available, drawing the overall layout of your site's pages (see Figure 8-4 for an example).

- *Images*: Some themes require custom images. Not necessarily huge images for headers and slideshows (those should be considered content and live in the public files), but small images like button backgrounds, icons, and custom bullets.

- *CSS files*: These define the look and feel of the site. After one defines the layout of the theme using templates, the whole theming process happens within CSS.

Sub Themes

By now you're most likely wondering: Drupal is so uncompromising in terms of pluggability and extensibility, shouldn't there be a way for a theme to be built on top of another theme so as to avoid redesigning and rebuilding an existing theme every time there is a similar look and feel?

Good thing you ask! There is indeed a way to create a sub theme that inherits everything from a parent theme, with the ability to override whatever you want changed. A sub theme, being a theme itself, can also be used as a parent for another sub theme, and so on. Think of this as being similar to class inheritance in object-oriented programming. The sub theme need only provide overrides for behavior it needs different from the parent theme.

For instance, if you are a design company that provides fully custom themed Drupal sites to your customers, you will most likely have realized that there is a large chunk of each design that is repeated from site to site, due to your branding, the way your designers work, and so forth. This is a good case for two layers of sub theming.

First, you'd have to find a parent theme that is easy to customize, responsive (yes, many themes available from the Drupal site already focus on mobile responsive design so you don't have to), and doesn't make any specific assumptions on the design so you don't have to fight it for you custom themes.

Then, you will create your own company's sub theme that will hold the common aspects of all your themes: layout, some images and styles, branding, and so forth.

Finally, for each project you do, you will sub theme your company's sub theme, which will only require you to code the actual specifics and differentiators of the design you're implementing.

Of course, following this convention of sub theming allows downloaded themes to be updated without undoing your specific changes and overrides. To say it another way, if you alter a downloaded theme by modifying its source files, you are setting yourself up for quite a bit of unnecessary (and risky) work should the theme ever get updated. By utilizing a sub theme, your code is kept completely separate from the downloaded theme's code.

Theme Settings

When it comes to your enterprise line of business customers, one of the coolest aspects of Drupal themes is the fact that you can provide options or settings to your theme. This is a feature built deep into the Drupal theme architecture that allows you to expose one or more options to be configured by your customers.

For example, maybe your customer wants control over the site's background color, or title font. Or maybe your customer is creating multiple sub-sites to be used by different departments within their organization, and each department needs to the freedom to customize various aspects of the overall theme. By using the capabilities built into the theme architecture, you can purposefully expose only the theme setting that your customers need to be able to update.

The theme options available in the Bartik theme are shown in Figure 8-7. These options are defined within the theme's files, and are also provided default values.

COLOR SCHEME

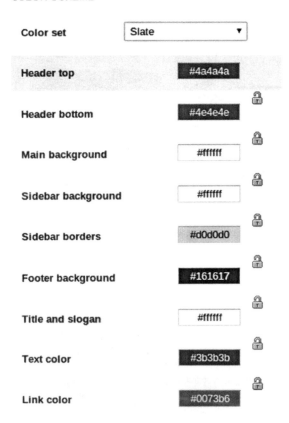

Figure 8-7. *Theme options*

So as you're designing and building out web sites for your customers, remember to identify any visual design options they may want control over.

Getting a theme

There are two ways for you to find a theme for your site:

- From the Drupal site: `https://drupal.org/project/themes`, where you want to sort by most installed and start there. This is your place of choice for excellent base themes that are easy to sub theme, stable, and often responsive.

- Buying them from reputable companies. If you are looking for a fully polished stunning theme, you may find the themes on the Drupal site a bit too basic (which is normal, as they are mostly meant to be used as a parent theme for your custom sub themes). You can find several reputable sites offering themes for a price.

Either approach to finding a theme works very well, and will indeed save you a significant amount of time and money in building out your site's overall user experience. That said, in the spirit of open source community support and involvement, we generally recommend to first try to find a suitable theme on the `Drupal.org` site. If nothing fits the bill, then you may need to fork over a few dollars for a professional and commercially built and maintained theme.

Finally, if you are a designer and plan on developing your own theme, there is a little bit of reading and understanding of best practices to do before you get started. We suggest Drupal's public documentation as a starting point: `https://drupal.org/documentation/theme`. There is also a great book called *The Definitive Guide to Drupal 7*, by Benjamin Melançon, etal (Apress, 2011). It is essentially a collection of many different Drupal-related topics, among which are some chapters on theming.

To recap, the main idea we want you to remember from this section is that Drupal provides themes as a way to help you separate content from presentation, and to support overriding and tweaking downloaded themes. The more you follow the rules and work within the intended toolset and way of designing the visual experience of your site, the richer and more pleasant your own development experience will be.

Forms

Most user-originated interaction and feedback on a web site can be handled by the right content type or comment configuration. For instance, if you want users to be able to make tickets for issues with a product, you will make a ticket content type that your users can creat. If you want your users to react to a product, you can configure comments for the product type you are using.

Sometimes however, you need to collect user input without creating content from it, for a survey or a contact form, for instance. This is when the Webform module comes in handy: `http://drupal.org/project/webform`. Some people refer to this module as something used to implement surveys. However, don't be fooled into thinking it's ONLY for surveys, as you can use this module for much more. Many Drupal sites use the Webform module to implement a Contact Us page, or a subscription sign-up page—in addition to surveys.

After installing the module, a Webform content type will be added to your site and you will be able to create Webforms like any other item from the Content administrative tab. Let's make a Webform for our example project, to collect customer's impressions about the various restaurants (see Figure 8-8).

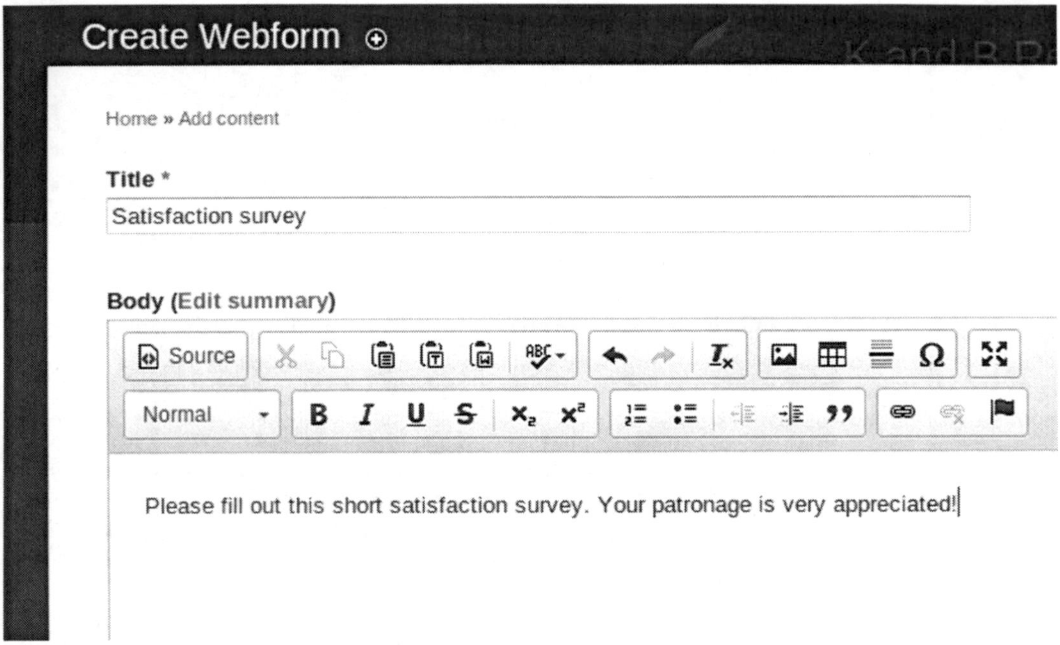

Figure 8-8. Webform creation

As shown on Figure 8-8, the content item itself has very few fields: a title and a body that will be displayed as an introduction to the form. Use the body to request feedback from the customer, or thank them for their time. Once you have saved the Webform, you will see a Webform"tab for it, where you can add and configure form components. The following component types are available:

- *Date, Email, File, Number, Select options, Textarea, Textfield, and Time*: Simple inputs that you are already familiar with from content types.

- *Fieldset*: It is not really a field but a group of fields bound together for easy visual association or group toggle.

- *Grid*: A matrix field where you define rows headers (options) and column headers (questions) to generate a matrix of radio input (detailed in the Grid section).

- *Hidden*: A field that will not be shown to the user, but will display in the results.

- *Markup*: Used to insert custom html or php elements, useful for custom visual demarcation between fields, additional instructions, or dirty php hacks.

- *Page break*: Spreads the form over several pages, inserts a navigation to easily move from a page to the previous/next one. All results are saved on the last page.

Our example satisfaction survey will be making use of key Webform elements: fieldsets, grids, and page breaks.

Fieldset

Let's start by adding as many fieldsets as we need sections in our survey. For instance, a decor, a service, a food, and an overall fieldset. When adding a new fieldset, you will be redirected to a component edit page where you will be able to customize your fieldset, allowing it to be collapsible by the user, for instance, or hiding its label, as shown on Figure 8-9. Once you are done, save the component to be redirected to the Webform tab.

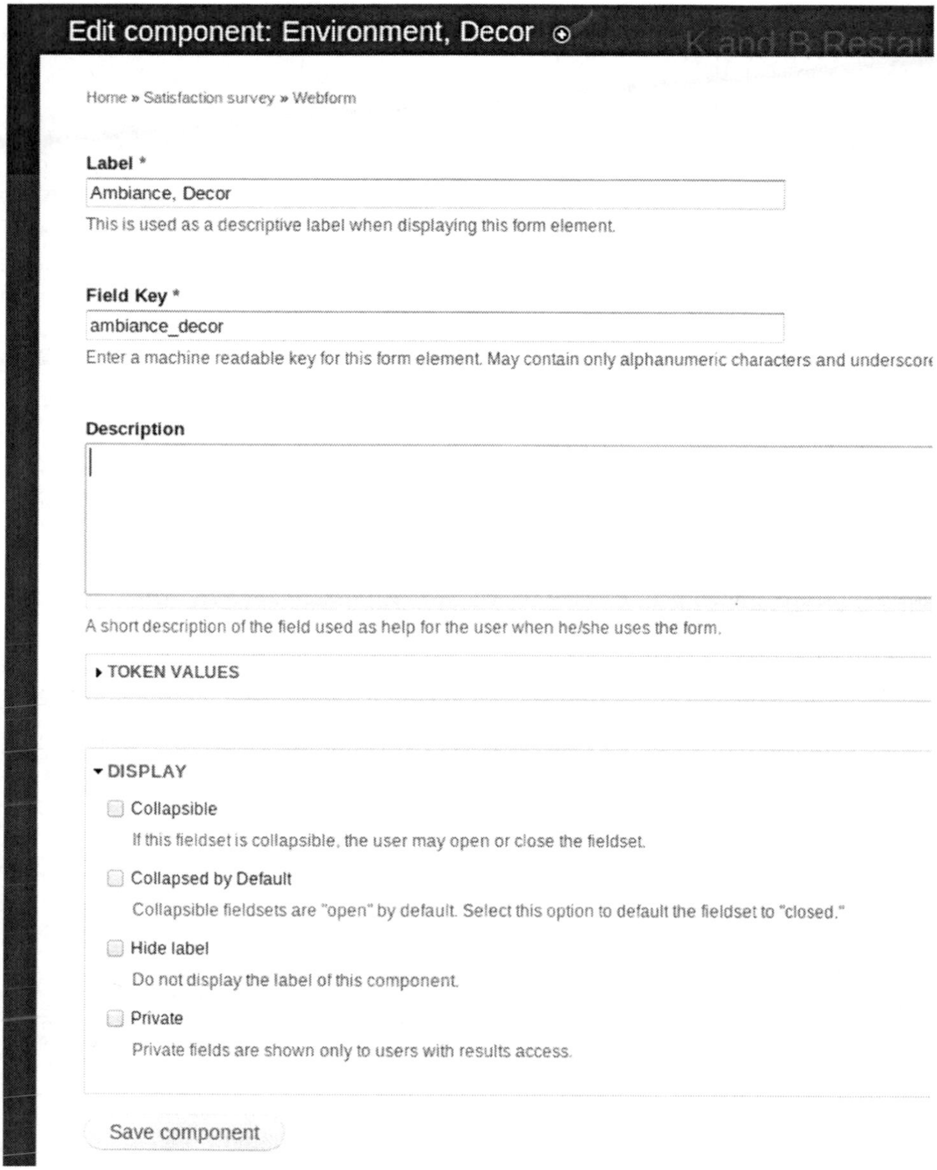

Figure 8-9. *Fieldset options*

Grid

The grid is a bit more complex. It has an Options field where you define the possible answers a user can select for each question, and a Questions field that lists those questions. Example options might be: 1 through 5, Poor-Fair-Good-Excellent, and so forth. For each of those fields, you will specify a key and the display text on the same line, separated by a vertical bar, aka pipe (ASCII 124). It is important to note that the option key must be unique throughout the whole form, not just the grid. Thus for a form that uses a lot of grids with the same options, we must add a prefix to the key for each grid. For the ambiance grid as shown on Figure 8-10, we prefix each option key with "ambiance_".

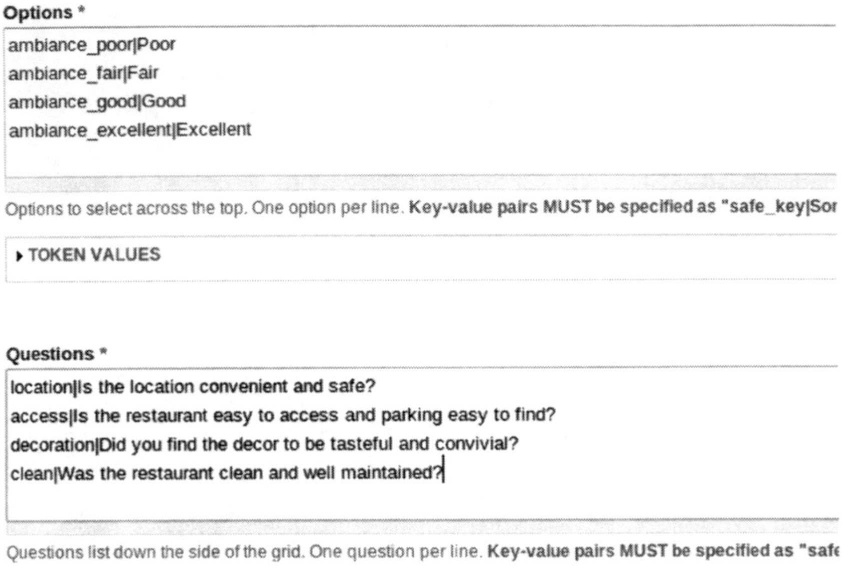

Options *

ambiance_poor|Poor
ambiance_fair|Fair
ambiance_good|Good
ambiance_excellent|Excellent

Options to select across the top. One option per line. **Key-value pairs MUST be specified as "safe_key|So**

▸ TOKEN VALUES

Questions *

location|Is the location convenient and safe?
access|Is the restaurant easy to access and parking easy to find?
decoration|Did you find the decor to be tasteful and convivial?
clean|Was the restaurant clean and well maintained?

Questions list down the side of the grid. One question per line. **Key-value pairs MUST be specified as "safe**

Figure 8-10. *Grid values*

There are even more configuration options for grids. They can be made mandatory, which means each row must be answered in order for the form's submission to be validated. In this case, it is usually recommended to have a "not applicable" or "decline to answer" option on the grid to allow for people to skip questions they don't want or can't answer while forcing a full grid completion; otherwise, users might find themselves blocked and drop your form altogether. You can also randomize options and questions, when their order doesn't matter, which can be useful for more unbiased statistics. Some of these options are shown in Figure 8-11.

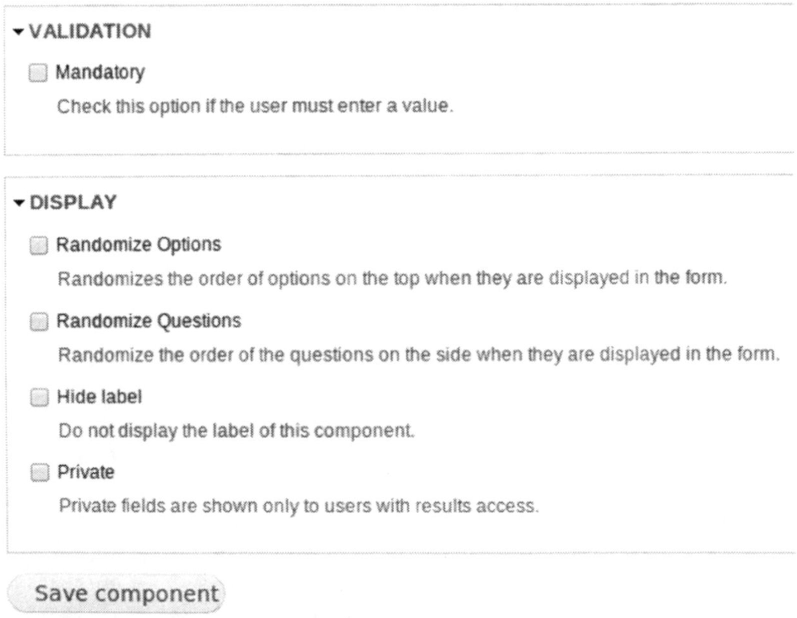

▾ VALIDATION

☐ Mandatory

Check this option if the user must enter a value.

▾ DISPLAY

☐ Randomize Options

Randomizes the order of options on the top when they are displayed in the form.

☐ Randomize Questions

Randomize the order of the questions on the side when they are displayed in the form.

☐ Hide label

Do not display the label of this component.

☐ Private

Private fields are shown only to users with results access.

(Save component)

Figure 8-11. *Grid display options*

Page Break

The page break is a very simple component that will split your form across several pages. The only options you provide on a page break are what the page before it will name the "next" link, and what the page after it will name the "previous" link, as shown in Figure 8-12.

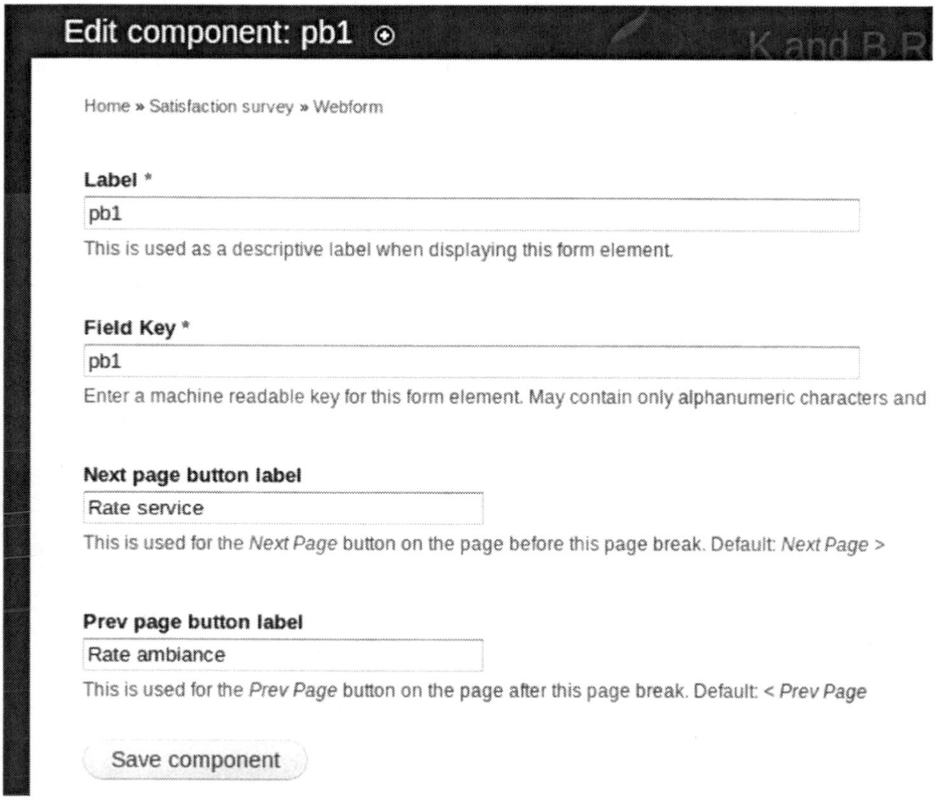

Figure 8-12. *Form page break*

Note that Next and Previous buttons in our survey actually reference the next/previous sections—not simply "Next" and "Previous."

Indentation

In order to group fields together in a fieldset, we will use the now-familiar Drupal indentation technique. On the Webform tab, you can drag and drop components to reorder them or to indent them under a fieldset. Figure 8-13 shows our completed Webform with proper indentation.

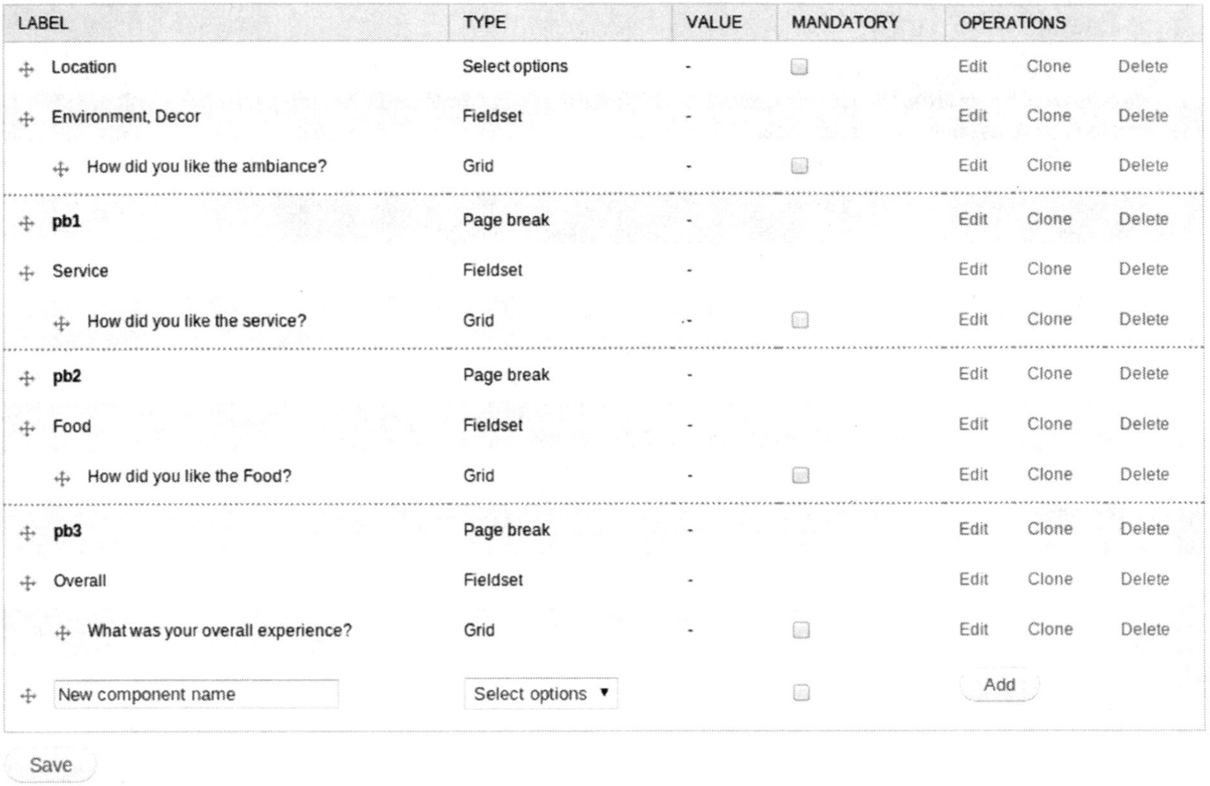

LABEL	TYPE	VALUE	MANDATORY	OPERATIONS		
⊹ Location	Select options	-	☐	Edit	Clone	Delete
⊹ Environment, Decor	Fieldset	-		Edit	Clone	Delete
⊹ How did you like the ambiance?	Grid	-	☐	Edit	Clone	Delete
⊹ **pb1**	Page break	-		Edit	Clone	Delete
⊹ Service	Fieldset	-		Edit	Clone	Delete
⊹ How did you like the service?	Grid	.-	☐	Edit	Clone	Delete
⊹ **pb2**	Page break	-		Edit	Clone	Delete
⊹ Food	Fieldset	-		Edit	Clone	Delete
⊹ How did you like the Food?	Grid	-	☐	Edit	Clone	Delete
⊹ **pb3**	Page break	-		Edit	Clone	Delete
⊹ Overall	Fieldset	-		Edit	Clone	Delete
⊹ What was your overall experience?	Grid	-	☐	Edit	Clone	Delete
⊹ New component name	Select options ▼		☐	Add		

Save

Figure 8-13. *Webform fields UI*

After the Webform is completed, it can be used and viewed like any other content item. This means you can place it in a region using the Blocks configuration page. Figure 8-14 shows a page on our example satisfaction survey. Note that even though you see the tabs in the figure, non-administrators will only see the form contents.

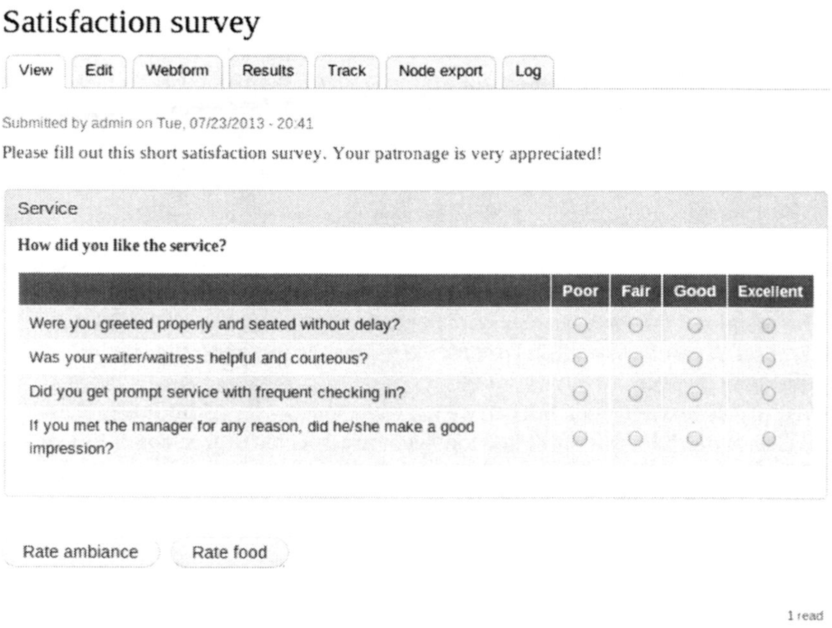

Satisfaction survey

| View | Edit | Webform | Results | Track | Node export | Log |

Submitted by admin on Tue, 07/23/2013 - 20:41

Please fill out this short satisfaction survey. Your patronage is very appreciated!

Service

How did you like the service?

	Poor	Fair	Good	Excellent
Were you greeted properly and seated without delay?	○	○	○	○
Was your waiter/waitress helpful and courteous?	○	○	○	○
Did you get prompt service with frequent checking in?	○	○	○	○
If you met the manager for any reason, did he/she make a good impression?	○	○	○	○

(Rate ambiance)   (Rate food)

1 read

Figure 8-14. *Form view*

In addition to the component management, on the Webform tab, you will find a way to manipulate some components based on other components' answers. It works a bit like mini rules in real time: based on a condition on a field's value, another field can be either displayed or hidden. Figure 8-15 shows an example where we want to hide the Decor question if the selected location is Indianapolis.

Home » Satisfaction survey » Webform

Conditionals may be used to hide or show certain components (or entire pages!) bas

⊕ If [Location ▼] [is ▼] [Indianapolis ▼]

then [hide ▼] [Environment, Decor   ▼]

(Save conditions)

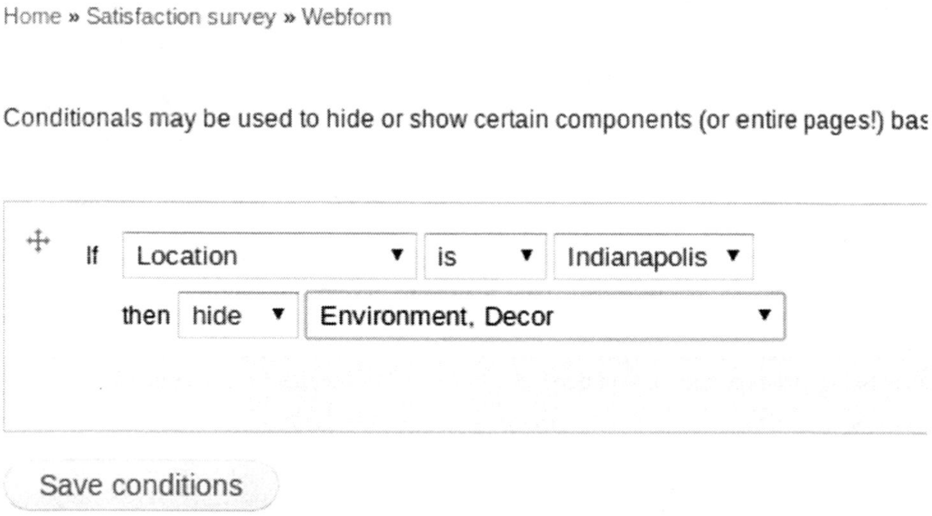

Figure 8-15. *Webform conditionals*

The other tabs, Emails and Form settings, will let you specify email recipients to be emailed form results as they are submitted, and configure a lot of additional options for the form, such as a confirmation message, a custom redirect url after form completion, submission limits per user or total, the ability to save a from as a draft before completion, and to do so automatically on each page change, and much more. There is even an option to make a block out of your Webform! As discussed in the previous section, this lets you place your form anywhere on the site within a region, and associate display rules to enable/disable when the form is shown and for whom it appears.

Results

Of course, the whole point of a Webform is to gather data. Thus, there exists a Results tab that will list the submissions, including the user and IP address of who submitted the form, display statistics for every field or list, all results per submission in a large table, and let you export all results as an Excel or CSV file for any custom statistics you would want to run. You can also clear the results using this tab.

By now you are certainly wondering: "Webforms are great, but can we use them in rules for additional processing and automation?" After installing the Webform module, you won't find any Webform-specific trigger, condition, or action in rules. Remember that a Webform is a content type like any other though, so you can use any node trigger and set a condition that tells the rule to only run if the node type is a Webform.

However, as you would expect, there is a module for additional integration with rules: Webform rules, `https://drupal.org/project/webform_rules`. Check it out.

Customizing Styles

As a matter of standard practice, you should always create a sub theme when building a new Drupal web site. That way, if you want to change anything with the theme—even a minor CSS modification—you will already have an empty CSS file in which to make your changes.

Drupal inserts many class names into the nearly all HTML elements it generates. This allows you to easily override default styles by using your own style sheet. For example, the list of classes on a simple text box for the body of a basic page looks like Figure 8-16, as seen in the Chrome developer tools.

```
<div class="field field-name-body field-type-text-with-summary field-label-hidden">
```

Figure 8-16. *Text box class names*

Note that there is a class name with the name of the field—that is, `field-name-body`. So not only is Drupal associating the general "field" class to the control, but also a class with a name that corresponds to the actual field name in the content type. Further, the field's type is associated with the class names. These very specific classes make it extremely easy to override default behavior in your own style sheet, as defined in your sub theme.

In fact, your sub theme could simply be ONLY a style sheet. It is not unusual to create a theme with only one file (other than the theme's `.info` file): a style sheet with only one or two simple style overrides. The entire Drupal site gets added to your Git or Subversion repository, and your sub theme's folder will be included along with the rest of the site's files and folders.

Styles and Views

The Views module offers even more customization with regards to CSS styles. First, the display's format settings include various CSS settings—depending on the type of display selected. For example, if an unformatted list is selected, you will be able to set a few different class options, as shown in Figure 8-17.

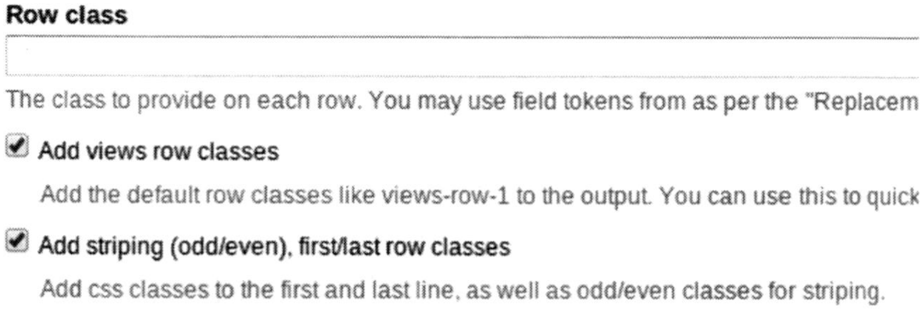

Row class

The class to provide on each row. You may use field tokens from as per the "Replacem

☑ **Add views row classes**

Add the default row classes like views-row-1 to the output. You can use this to quick

☑ **Add striping (odd/even), first/last row classes**

Add css classes to the first and last line, as well as odd/even classes for striping.

Figure 8-17. *Class settings for an unformatted list*

The option titled "Add views row classes" results in style classes similar to those shown in Figure 8-18. This example is from a table that contained 10 rows.

```
▶ <div class="views-row views-row-1 views-row-odd views-row-first">…</div>
▶ <div class="views-row views-row-2 views-row-even">…</div>
▶ <div class="views-row views-row-3 views-row-odd">…</div>
▶ <div class="views-row views-row-4 views-row-even">…</div>
▶ <div class="views-row views-row-5 views-row-odd">…</div>
▶ <div class="views-row views-row-6 views-row-even">…</div>
▶ <div class="views-row views-row-7 views-row-odd">…</div>
▶ <div class="views-row views-row-8 views-row-even">…</div>
▶ <div class="views-row views-row-9 views-row-odd">…</div>
▶ <div class="views-row views-row-10 views-row-even views-row-last">…</div>
```

Figure 8-18. *Class names for a table in a view*

These classes allow you to style very specific elements of a view, all from your sub theme's one style sheet.

And second, each and every field in a view includes several class options that you can use in order to provide custom styles in your sub theme's CSS file. Figure 8-19 illustrates a simple example:

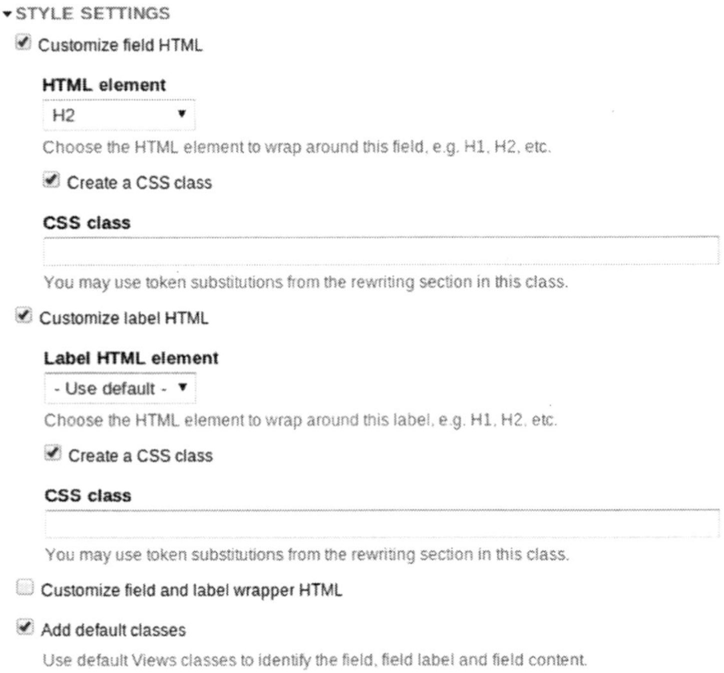

▾ STYLE SETTINGS

☑ Customize field HTML

HTML element

| H2 ▾ |

Choose the HTML element to wrap around this field, e.g. H1, H2, etc.

☑ Create a CSS class

CSS class

| |

You may use token substitutions from the rewriting section in this class.

☑ Customize label HTML

Label HTML element

| - Use default - ▾ |

Choose the HTML element to wrap around this label, e.g. H1, H2, etc.

☑ Create a CSS class

CSS class

| |

You may use token substitutions from the rewriting section in this class.

☐ Customize field and label wrapper HTML

☑ Add default classes

Use default Views classes to identify the field, field label and field content.

Figure 8-19. *CSS options for a specific view field*

Note that you can associate separate class names with the field's label—versus the field's value. You can also turn on and off the default classes, similar to the ones shown back in Figure 8-16.

Summary

In this chapter, we finally covered the basics of building a customized user experience in Drupal. Starting with menus and navigation, you learned that you can create a customized navigational experience either manually, through the menu editor, or through the individual content items and their menu options.

We then walked through the incredible power of Drupal's regions and blocks, and how you can leverage them to build a custom layout for your sites. The idea of themes was explored, specifically how each theme includes three main types of files:

- Templates
- CSS files
- Images

The theme defines the regions available to site, which you can use on the Blocks administration page. And you can specify the styles used by your site in a sub theme—which every Drupal site should have. Indeed, Drupal was built to deal with styles and themes in a way that provides ultimate flexibility and customizability, without having to cross the line between a downloaded theme's files and your own. Again, we strongly encourage you to invest the time it takes to leverage Drupal themes the way they were intended.

Next up in our exploration of Drupal in the enterprise: REST services.

▨ ▨ ▨

CHAPTER 9

REST Services with Drupal

Representational State Transfer (REST). It's all the rage these days. And, actually, has been for the last few years (at least). Even so, many developers are still trying to wrap their heads around what it actually means to build a RESTful service. No doubt if you're developer, or anyway near development activities, you've had a run-in with designing, building, or fixing a REST service. It's become one of those things that everyone wants to do, but not many know exactly why they should or shouldn't. On top of that, there's a wide variety of technologies out there for building RESTful services, many of which actually get in the way of understanding what REST is really about.

In this chapter, we hope to quickly dispel some of the mystery and misunderstandings with REST, building on our clearer understanding as we explore REST in Drupal. As has been talked about throughout this book, Drupal offers yet another module (really, a set of modules) to help you get a REST service up and running in no time—without writing any code. You will find that some of the mechanisms used are at this point already familiar. For example, the Views module will be used to define some of the data available in our service, and the Rules module will be used to define activities in our K&B Restaurants REST application programming interface (API).

A word of warning . . . as easy and fast as it is to enable REST in Drupal, we need to understand that in Drupal 7, REST support is still evolving. That is, you will be able to technically turn on a REST endpoint, and interact with it using JSON or XML, and it surely won't be a SOAP-based interaction; but it won't strictly follow the constraints and guidelines of the REST architecture. The services infrastructure in the nearly complete Drupal 8 is being overhauled to include REST "as a first-class citizen"—which you will learn about in more detail later in this chapter.

Bottom line: even though we won't be able to honor the full breadth of the REST architecture in Drupal 7, the resulting services and their implementations are nonetheless well worth the investment as compared to writing all of this stuff from scratch. But given that the industry as a whole is still very much trying to grok RESTful services and RESTful clients, you're not missing anything. In reality, most people simply want to be able to use HTTP and AJAX calls from JavaScript or iOS code, and be able to use JSON instead of XML and SOAP envelopes. The Services module in Drupal 7 makes this task absolutely drop-dead simple.

To make sure we're all on the same page, let's start with a brief architectural discussion on REST, as it was intended. Then we'll move on to a practical implementation in Drupal.

REST Basics

REST is quite simply an architecture style meant to define the ideal distributed application. Nearly every day you are online using web sites that implement the REST style of architecture—likely without even realizing it. Only recently has REST emerged as a design approach for web-oriented APIs. In short, we can think of REST with the following statements:

- Use one or more representations (HTML, XML, JSON, FORMS) to view the state of a thing
- Use similar representations to alter the state of the thing

In his doctoral dissertation back in 2000, Roy Fielding created the REST architecture to embody a set of constraints and principles to help engineers "see" what a well-architected web application looks like. It is a reference architecture for web sites and web APIs. Even though HTTP and other web protocols have been around since about 1990, the additional REST constraints and principles aid us in understanding the true intent of these protocols as they provide additional guidance and clarification in building distributed applications on the web.

The REST Constraints

The ideal application defined by REST must adhere to a set of six constraints, the first of which says that the client (that is, the caller) and the server in a distributed web application must be completely decoupled. They must not be constrained by any sort of hard-wired contract or pre-arranged knowledge of each other. Further, the client and the server must not share binary-compiled code, instead only relying on message formats such as XML or JSON to contain all required information.

Second, the server must be stateless. That's right, the server in a web application must not store state between calls. This constraint is intended to promote scalability and performance, as well as allow applications to leverage intermediate network tools such as load balancers and cache layers. State may indeed be stored on the client, but the server should be completely stateless.

Third, information retrieved from a RESTful web application must include an indication of whether or not the information itself is cachable. Ideally, all data would be cachable. But that is not always possible. But this constraint is meant to promote the use of intermediary caches to increase performance and scalability.

The fourth constraint requires that web applications implement a common interface. This is not an interface as in object-oriented programming, but rather all web applications should look and behave essentially the same way. Fielding expanded on this interface constraint with four interface-oriented principles, which we'll define shortly.

The fifth constraint to the REST architecture is that the distributed system must be able to exist within the context of a layered system. For example, a web application must continue to function properly even if routers and caches and load balancers are introduced between the client and the server. This, again, is to promote application designs that leverage the scalability infrastructure of the Internet. The constraint also says that the client must typically not be able to tell if additional network layers are inserted between it and the server.

The final constraint says that servers must be able to extend or update client functionality by distributing executable code to those clients. One very obvious example of this constraint as seen in many of today's web applications is JavaScript. JavaScript libraries are typically served up by the application's server, thus making it possible for the server to update the libraries at any time. As long as the client in the application is built to fetch JavaScript libraries on every call, the server can successfully update client functionality.

Now let's explore the uniform interface principles, further defining one of the more visible REST constraints.

The Uniform Interface Principles

When it comes to how clients interact with the server in a RESTful web application, Fielding defined four principles in addition to the six constraints discussed previously. These principles help promote a common interaction model for all web-based applications, making it possible for clients of one application to easily communicate with servers of other applications.

First, a resource must be uniquely identifiable via a web address—that is, a URL. This means that any resource or object available to clients must be discoverable and addressable via a unique URL. Rather than relying on a single SOAP-style web method, with one or more parameters, to retrieve different resources, REST requires that every publically available resource be addressable by a unique URL. For example, instead of calling a method called GetRestaurant with an ID value of 123, a RESTful resource address might look like /api/restaurants/123. And a restaurant's menus might be available from a URL of /api/restaurants/123/menus, with a single menu available at /api/restaurants/123/menus/678. As you can see, these URLs are markedly different from an RPC address of /api/service with a SOAP method of GetRestaurantMenu().

Once we've established our resource URLs, the next principle dictates that a resource's state be modified only with the data available in a representation. To say it another way, if a client has a resource's data—that is, a representation of a resource's data—then it necessarily has sufficient information to modify the resource. No other bit of information is required in order to update the resource. This supports the constraint that the client not be coupled to the server with so-called out-of-band or assumed knowledge.

Third, and less visible, a resource's representation must include everything needed in order for the client to process the message. Think, for example, of an image file. The PNG media type, along with the contents of the image itself, are all that is needed for the client to know what to do with the resource—that is, display it for the user to see. This again supports the constraint that the client and server utilize only agreed-upon standards for sharing information, not relying other contract or hard-wired information.

Last, and possibly most difficult to implement in a web API, is what Fielding called Hypermedia As The Engine of Application State—or, HATEOAS. The most straightforward way to think of HATEOAS is to think of your typical web site. All a user or client needs to explore all of the data on a well-architected web site is the root URL. Once the user is viewing data obtained from the site's entry point, he or she can navigate through the entire site using various menus, links, and forms. No pre-arranged knowledge is required for the user to access all resources in the system. As long as the site's pages are well designed, all of the site's pages (that is, resources) are accessible via links and forms that reference unique URLs.

HATEOAS defines a system that is truly discoverable. All the client needs is the entry point address, and then all responses include sufficient link information to let the user access any other page or bit of information.

In the end, these constraints and principles are meant to promote performance, scalability, security, reuse, and interoperability across all web applications. They also lessen the burden on developers to figure out and implement already-established patterns and practices, instead letting them lean into standard implementations of these constraints and principals. For example, the HTTP protocol defines standard and well-understood response codes (for example, 200, 400, 401, 403, 404). Therefore, developers don't need to individually create response message types for resources not found, unauthorized access, and so forth.

The REST Maturity Model

To summarize what makes a service a RESTful service, we can look to Leonard Richardson's REST Maturity Model, shown in Figure 9-1.

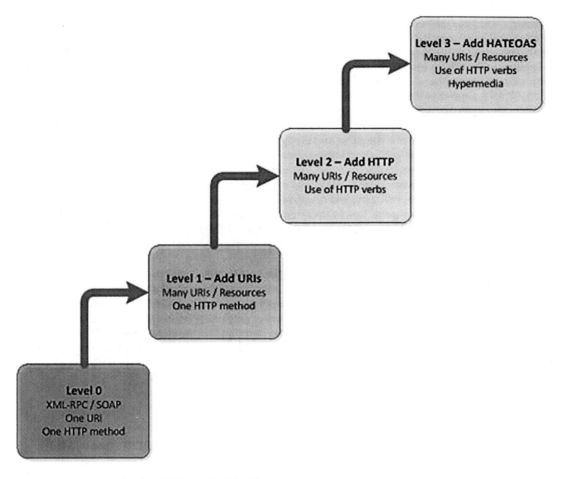

Figure 9-1. *Leonardson's REST Maturity Model*

The REST Maturity Model (RMM) defines an evolution of-sorts in moving from an RPC/SOAP-style service to one that adheres to the REST architecture. As you can see in its final level, the model provides a succinct list of characteristics most relevant for a RESTful service:

- Resource-centric. . . not method-centric

- Use of HTTP verbs. . . not arbitrary methods

- Hypermedia discoverability. . . not WSDL+knowledge

That is, the ideal RESTful web service would make its resources the focal point, not SOAP methods. It would also only utilize the known HTTP verbs for its "methods"—not arbitrary RPC-style method names. And lastly, the entire service and all of its resources should be discoverable via hypermedia links and forms, not be bound to a static published contract.

As mentioned in the opening section of this chapter, Drupal 7 doesn't provide great support for the constraints and principles of the REST architecture. That said, you can indeed leverage the Services module to expose a mostly RESTful service from your Drupal web site. Throughout the rest of this chapter, you will learn how to implement services in Drupal 7 that mostly look and act like RESTful services. We will also briefly discuss the REST and service-orientee changes expcted in Drupal 8—which, coincidentally, will much better support for REST.

Drupal Services and Views

Now that we've covered the basics of the REST architecture, let's dig into some implementation on Drupal. To start, let's make sure we have a few of modules installed and enabled:

```
drush dl services services_views -y
drush en services rest_server services_views -y
```

The Services module is what gives us all of the functionality we need in order to interact with Drupal in a RESTful way. The module includes a submodule called REST Server. The previous commands also installed the Services Views module, which allows views to be exposed through the REST interface.

Creating the REST Service

To create your first REST service, click on the Structure administrative menu, and then click on the Services link. You should see a screen similar to Figure 9-2—an empty list of services.

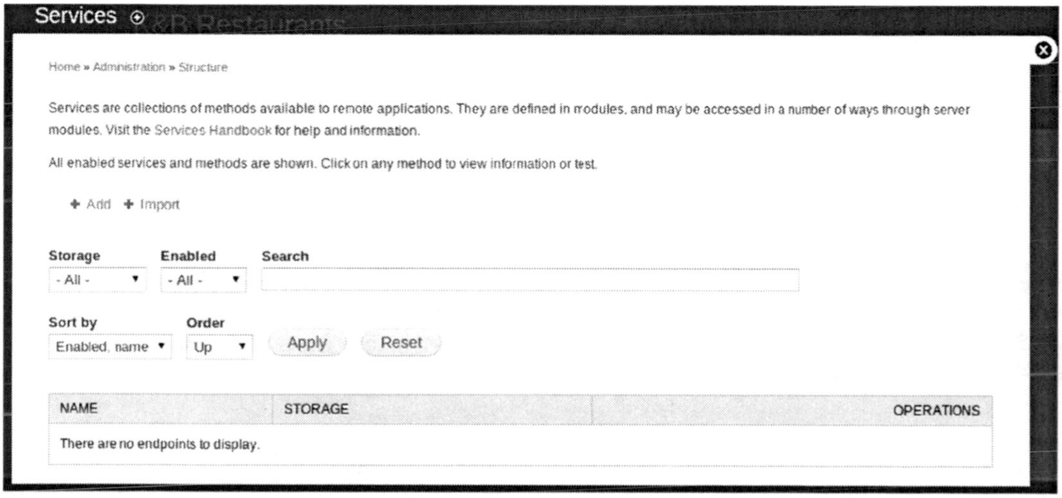

Figure 9-2. *Services page*

To create the service, click on the Add link. For the service's machine-readable name, go ahead and enter rest_api. Then select the REST option from the Server drop-down. Then, in the "Path to endpoint" property, enter api. This value is completely arbitrary, but we want to keep it simple yet also pick a path that distinguishes the service from the rest of the Drupal site. Using a path such as /api is a bit of a de facto standard in the community, so we suggest using it—for now, at least. Further, the service examples in this chapter and remainder of the book will use this path.

Finally, enable the Authentication option for "Session authentication". This will allow users to access your REST service if they have a valid Drupal session in their HTTP cookies. Of course, this happens automatically when a user logs into the site. How this works from a non-browser client will be discussed a bit later. For now, make sure to log into the K & B Restaurants site BEFORE trying to access the REST interface—all within the same browser window. It can be a different tab, as long as at least one tab within the window has been used to log in to the site. This will ensure a Drupal session cookie is sent to the REST service for authentication.

Once complete, your screen should look similar to Figure 9-3.

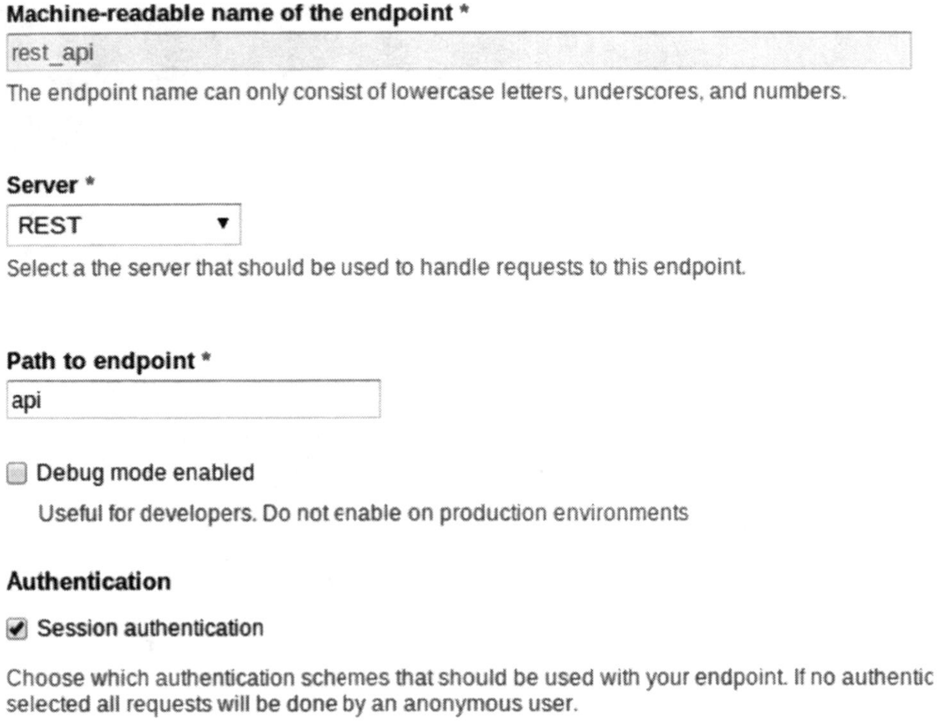

Machine-readable name of the endpoint *

rest_api

The endpoint name can only consist of lowercase letters, underscores, and numbers.

Server *

REST   ▼

Select a the server that should be used to handle requests to this endpoint.

Path to endpoint *

api

☐ Debug mode enabled

Useful for developers. Do not enable on production environments

Authentication

☑ Session authentication

Choose which authentication schemes that should be used with your endpoint. If no authentic
selected all requests will be done by an anonymous user.

Figure 9-3. REST service properties

Upon clicking Save, you will be returned to the list of services page. Before moving on, we need to make one last adjustment. In order to get JSON back from our service by default, we need to disable the other response formatters. Click on the Edit Server link option in the drop-down under Operations. Then simply deselect all response formatter options except JSON, as shown in Figure 9-4.

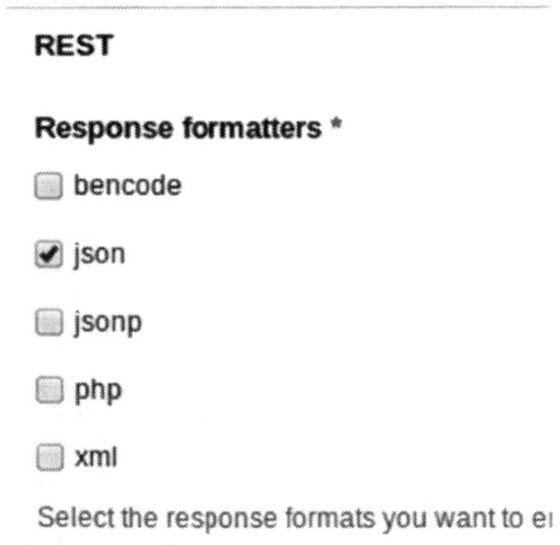

REST

Response formatters *

☐ bencode

☑ json

☐ jsonp

☐ php

☐ xml

Select the response formats you want to er

Figure 9-4. Enabling only JSON responses

Click Save, and then click on the Resources tab to edit the resources for your new rest_api service. You will be presented with a table showing the resources automatically available in your new service. By default, none of them are enabled, as shown in Figure 9-5.

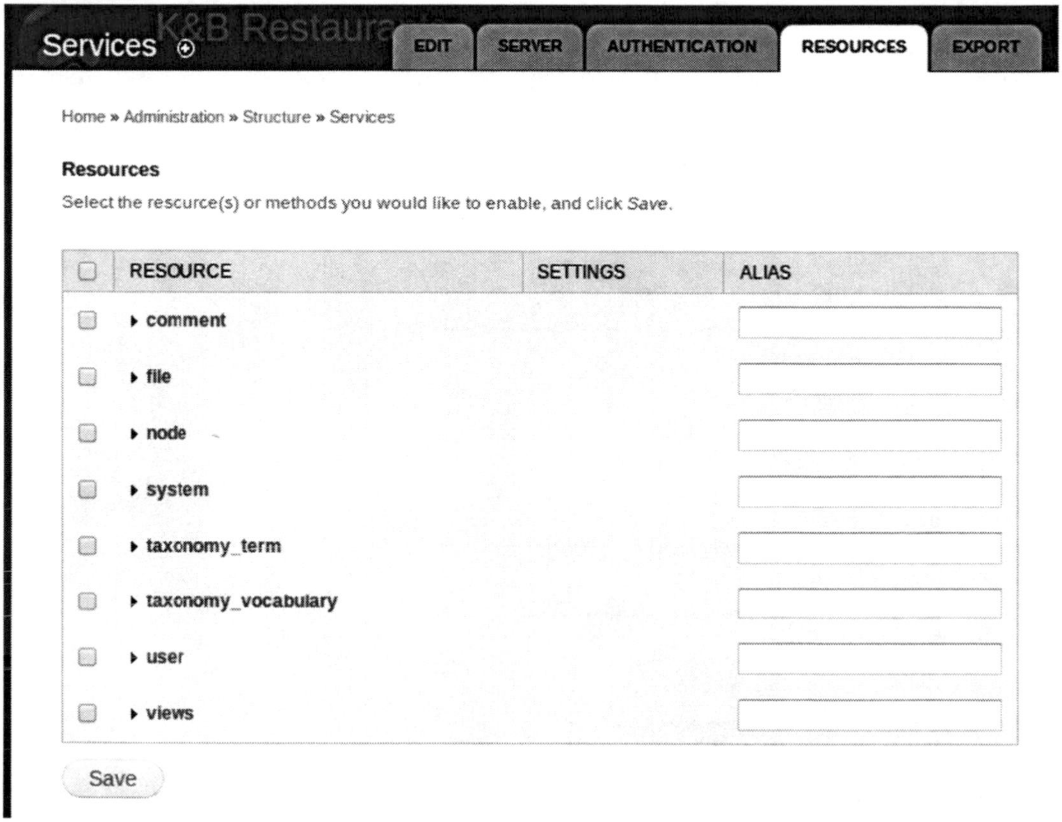

Figure 9-5. *Built-in REST service resources*

For the purpose of this book, let's just enable the node resource. This will allow us to perform all necessary operations against the system: Create, Read, Update, and Delete (CRUD). Simply click on the check box next to the node resource, and all operations will be enabled. Expand the section, and you will see the resource's operations, as shown in Figure 9-6.

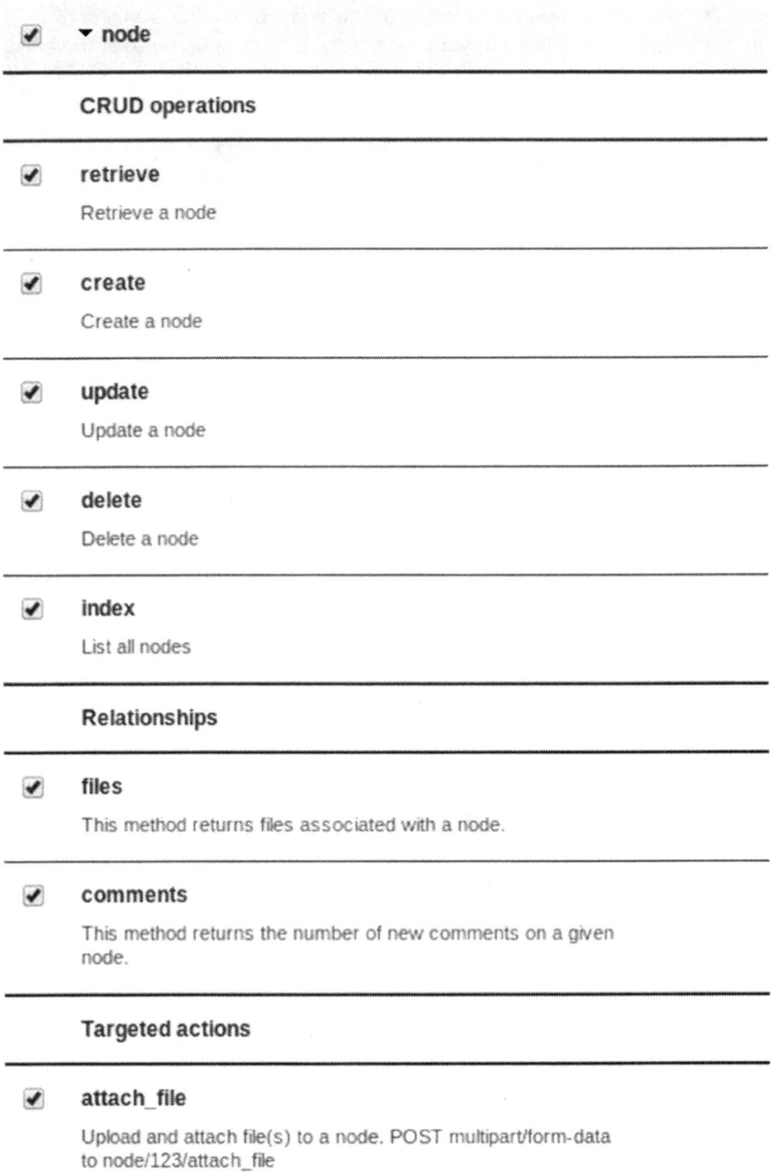

☑ ▼ **node**

CRUD operations

☑ **retrieve**

Retrieve a node

☑ **create**

Create a node

☑ **update**

Update a node

☑ **delete**

Delete a node

☑ **index**

List all nodes

Relationships

☑ **files**

This method returns files associated with a node.

☑ **comments**

This method returns the number of new comments on a given node.

Targeted actions

☑ **attach_file**

Upload and attach file(s) to a node. POST multipart/form-data to node/123/attach_file

Figure 9-6. *Node resource operations*

If we wanted to limit the operations available to the service's consumers, we could simply uncheck some of them. For example, to make the node resource read-only, you would uncheck the create, update, delete, and attach_file operations.

Getting Data

By this point in the book, you should have some content available for us to retrieve from the REST service. But if not, do so now. The sample code for this book includes a `.export` file that you can use to import all of our custom content.

Let's try a simple GET request. With your browser open, make sure you are logged into the K & B site, then open a new tab using the same browser window. Assuming you are running the site on your local machine (and if not, substitute the correct machine name for localhost), navigate to the following address:

```
http://localhost/kbr/?q=api/node
```

Likely the first thought in your mind, especially if you know a bit about RESTful services, is that this URL uses a query parameter for the path, as opposed to a "proper" URL. By default, Drupal is configured to not use "clean URLs"—which would make this URL more like: `http://localhost/kbr/api/node`. In order to use clean URLs, specific settings must be enabled on the machine ,whether Apache or IIS. As this feature doesn't directly affect the API nor the examples in this book, we're going to keep it simple and keep using the q query parameter. Just know that you can simply remove the `?q=` part of the URL if you want to use clean URLs instead.

The request to `/api/node` will return all nodes in the system, in a paged response. By default, Drupal's REST service will return 20 nodes per page, with page 0 being the default page returned. As we might expect, though, the Services module provides some built-in query parameters you can use to modify the page and page size. For example, the following request will return the 3rd page in the set of 5-node pages:

```
http://localhost/kbr/?q=api/node&pagesize=5&page=2
```

If pagesize is not given, Drupal will default to 20. If the page parameter is not given, Drupal will default to page 0, which is the first page.

Figure 9-7 shows part of the results of the request on the K & B Restaurants site. Of course, the data you get will be a little different, but the structure should be the same.

```
{
    nid: "2",
    vid: "2",
    type: "restaurant_branch",
    language: "und",
    title: "Upstate New York",
    uid: "1",
    status: "1",
    created: "1376415718",
    changed: "1376422585",
    comment: "2",
    promote: "1",
    sticky: "0",
    tnid: "0",
    translate: "0",
    uuid: "bdf1a0ce-d027-4763-8196-f3c3c4854b44",
    uri: "https://usrv01/kbr/?q=api/node/2"
},
```

Figure 9-7. *Results from REST node request*

Take note of the fields returned. These fields are, more or less, hard-coded by the Services module. They only include the basic content type fields; there's no body, and no custom fields. If needed, you can reduce the fields returned by using the `fields` query parameter. For example, if you know you only need the node's ID and title, then you can greatly reduce the size of the data returned by running the following query:

```
http://localhost/kbr/?q=api/node&fields=nid,title
```

These results are shown in Figure 9-8.

```
{
    nid: "13",
    title: "Chocolate milk",
    uri: "https://usrv01/kbr/?q=api/node/13"
},
{
    nid: "12",
    title: "Raspberry Lemonade",
    uri: "https://usrv01/kbr/?q=api/node/12"
},
{
    nid: "11",
    title: "Pepsi, Mountain Dew, Sierra Mist, Root Beer",
    uri: "https://usrv01/kbr/?q=api/node/11"
},
{
    nid: "10",
    title: "Three-layer chocolate lava cake",
    uri: "https://usrv01/kbr/?q=api/node/10"
},
```

Figure 9-8. Including fields specification in REST GET request

Now, what if we want to return content items of a specific type? This can be accomplished with the "parameters" parameter. Figure 9-9 illustrates some of the data returned when we filter by the Menu Item content type with the following query:

```
http://localhost/kbr/?q=api/node&fields=nid,title,type&parameters[type]=menu_item
```

```
{
    nid: "13",
    title: "Chocolate milk",
    type: "menu_item",
    changed: "1376422545",
    uri: "https://usrv01/kbr/?q=api/node/13"
},
{
    nid: "12",
    title: "Raspberry Lemonade",
    type: "menu_item",
    changed: "1376422516",
    uri: "https://usrv01/kbr/?q=api/node/12"
},
{
    nid: "11",
    title: "Pepsi, Mountain Dew, Sierra Mist, Root Beer",
    type: "menu_item",
    changed: "1376422449",
    uri: "https://usrv01/kbr/?q=api/node/11"
},
{
    nid: "10",
    title: "Three-layer chocolate lava cake",
    type: "menu_item",
    changed: "1376422376",
    uri: "https://usrv01/kbr/?q=api/node/10"
},
```

Figure 9-9. *Filtering REST request by content type*

That's about the extent to which you can use the query parameters in the REST endpoint to customize your requests. For further customization, we turn now to the Services Views module.

Services Views

When it comes to fetching data from Drupal via the Service module's REST service, you may need to mold the data beyond what is possible with just the module itself. In this section, you will learn how to leverage the Services Views module to gain more control of REST resources, filters, paging, and so forth. To start, make sure you've installed and enabled the module: drush dl views views_ui services_views -ydrush en views views_ui services_views -y.

Then navigate to the Views page using the Administrative menu's Structure link. Click the link to add a new view. Let's call it Value Menu Items. As shown in Figure 9-10, we want to filter by the Menu Item content type.

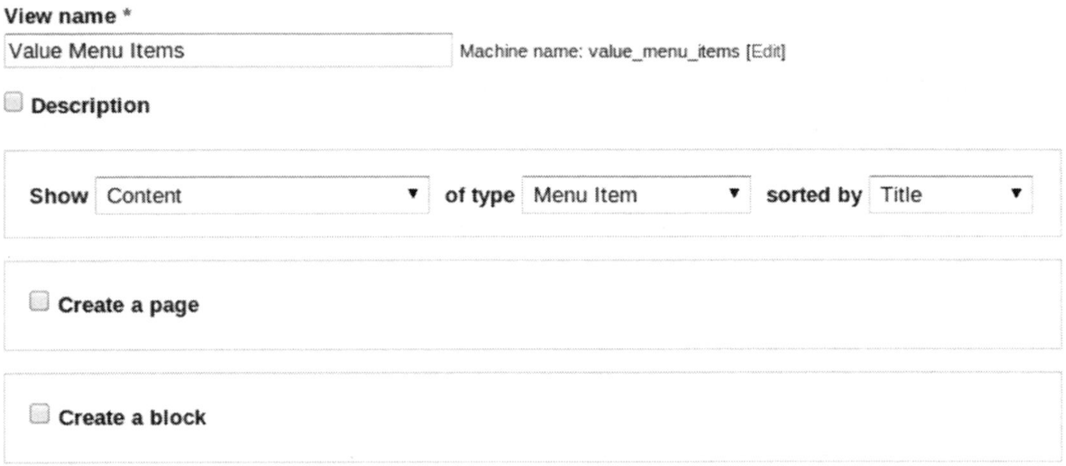

View name *

| Value Menu Items | Machine name: value_menu_items [Edit]

☐ **Description**

> Show [Content ▼] of type [Menu Item ▼] sorted by [Title ▼]

☐ **Create a page**

☐ **Create a block**

Figure 9-10. *View definition for REST service.*

Also, we don't need to create a page, so uncheck that option. When building views for services, we don't need a UI page, since the data will only be accessed via the REST interface. When finished, click on the Continue and Edit button to define the rest of the view's attributes.

The first thing you need to do once on the Displays page is click the Add button and select the Services option. This is the link between views and services—that is, creating a display for a view that will be exposed via the REST service we've already created.

Back in Chapter 4, you learned the basics of defining a view in Drupal (using the Views module). Much of that will apply here, in the way of fields, filters, sort orders, and so forth. So let's quickly move through these particular attributes for our Value Menu Items view. We will add a couple fields—the Body and the Price. For the Price field, select the unformatted Formatter option, which will be more appropriate for REST service consumers.

Back on the main view Displays page, click on the path value, which at this point should just be a single forward slash, as shown in Figure 9-11.

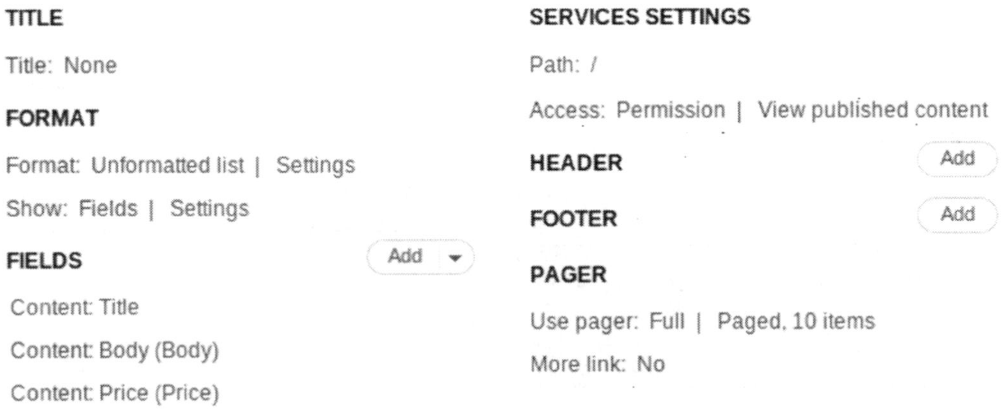

TITLE

Title: None

FORMAT

Format: Unformatted list | Settings

Show: Fields | Settings

FIELDS   Add ▼

Content: Title

Content: Body (Body)

Content: Price (Price)

SERVICES SETTINGS

Path: /

Access: Permission | View published content

HEADER   Add

FOOTER   Add

PAGER

Use pager: Full | Paged, 10 items

More link: No

Figure 9-11. *Service view display properties*

When the dialog box appears to enter a new path for the resource, let's enter `value-menu-items`, as shown in Figure 9-12. Click Apply to save and close the dialog box.

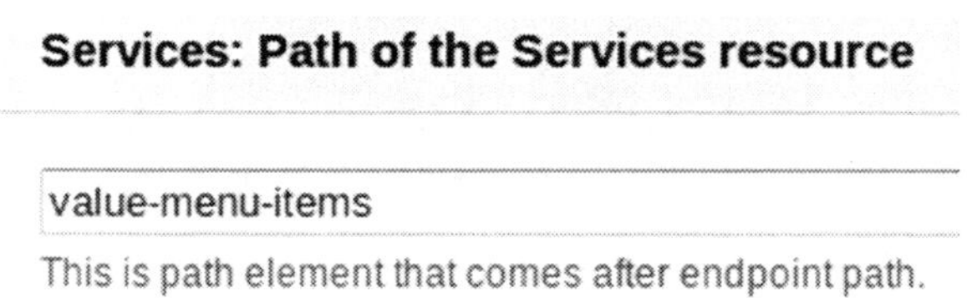

Services: Path of the Services resource

value-menu-items

This is path element that comes after endpoint path.

Figure 9-12. *Path for new service view*

One last change (for now) before we enable the view as a REST resource. Where you see the "Paged, 10 items" link, under the Pager section, click on it and change the page size to 5. This is just to show that paging works for views just as it did previously against the node resource endpoint. You simply change the "Items to display" field to 5, and click Apply. Then click Save to save the entire view.

Head back over to the REST resources page, using the Structure administrative menu and the Services link. Then click the Edit Resources link for our rest_api service, and scroll to the bottom of the resource list. You should now see our value-menu-items view available as a resource we can enable. Go ahead and check the box to enable the view, and click Save.

Now, in another browser tab (remember, it must be in the same browser window so as to inherit the same Drupal session cookie as is being used by the site itself), navigate to the following URL:

```
http://localhost/kbr/?q=api/value-menu-items
```

You should see something similar to the menu items shown in Figure 9-13 (with your own menu item data, of course).

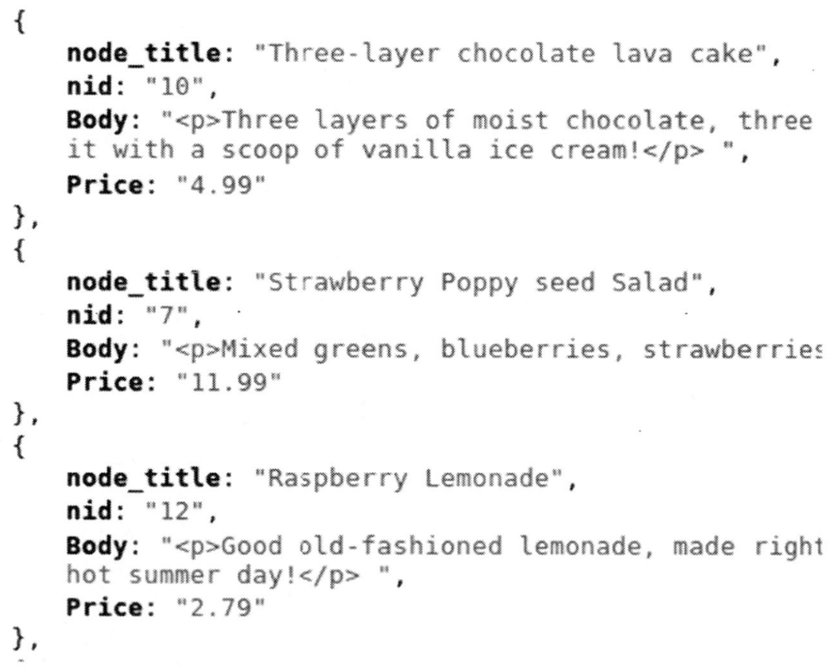

```
{
    node_title: "Three-layer chocolate lava cake",
    nid: "10",
    Body: "<p>Three layers of moist chocolate, three
    it with a scoop of vanilla ice cream!</p> ",
    Price: "4.99"
},
{
    node_title: "Strawberry Poppy seed Salad",
    nid: "7",
    Body: "<p>Mixed greens, blueberries, strawberries
    Price: "11.99"
},
{
    node_title: "Raspberry Lemonade",
    nid: "12",
    Body: "<p>Good old-fashioned lemonade, made right
    hot summer day!</p> ",
    Price: "2.79"
},
```

Figure 9-13. *Value menu items results*

To see the paging in action again, go ahead and append the page number to the query parameters to show, for example, page number 2:

```
http://localhost/kbr/?q=api/value-menu-items&page=1
```

Because the page numbers are zero-index based, you need to specify the page number value as one less than the page you actually want. Also, as was the case when querying the node resource, if you provide a page number that is beyond the number of pages available, you simply get an empty result.

Filtering with Service Views

We suppose you've realized by now that the view is called Value Menu Items, but we're not filtering the menu items in any way. It might be appropriate to remove all items from the view results that are greater than $10. To do this, we're going to leverage the filtering capability of views, and then expose the filter criteria as an optional parameter via the REST service.

Let's start by defining the filter itself. Navigate back to the Value Menu Items view, and click the Add button next to the Filter section. In the search box, type `price`, and then select the Price field (should belong to the menu_item content type). After you click Apply, you will be presented with another screen allowing you to define the filter. Because we want to only return those menu items that are less than or equal to $10, select the appropriate operator and enter 10 in the value text box, as shown in Figure 9-14.

Operator	Value
Is less than or equal to ▼	10

Figure 9-14. *Defining menu items of less than or equal to $10*

Click Apply, and then back on the main view page, click the Save button. In your other browser tab, navigate again to the view's REST URL:

```
http://localhost/kbr/?q=api/value-menu-items
```

This time, you should only see those menu items that are $10 or less in price.

But what if you have a scenario where you want the callers of your service to be able to specify the filter value? For example, maybe someone wants to build a mobile app that retrieves all menu items from your restaurant where the price is $5 or less? Fortunately, the services_views module has got you covered!

Navigate back to the view's edit page, and click on the Price filter criteria field. When the dialog pops up, check the box next to "Expose this filter to visitors, to allow them to change it". This will open a new set of options that you can use to specify what the filter will look like to the user. Most of the options are only relevant if you are building a UI-based view, not a REST service view. Nonetheless, the new option we are looking for here is actually under the More link. So click More to expand a few more options, one of which is the option called "Filter identifier." The value you enter in that field will be used in the query string as a new optional query parameter. Let's call it `max_price`, as shown in Figure 9-15.

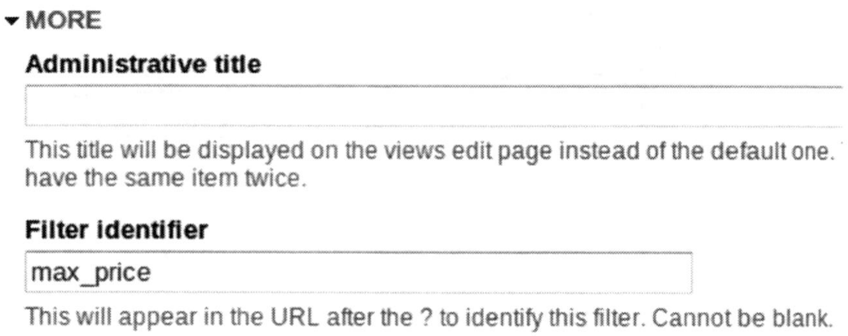

▼ MORE

Administrative title

This title will be displayed on the views edit page instead of the default one. have the same item twice.

Filter identifier

max_price

This will appear in the URL after the ? to identify this filter. Cannot be blank.

Figure 9-15. Field name for new filter criteria

Click Apply, and then save the view (from the main view edit page). Then back on your other browser tab, navigate to the following URL:

```
http://localhost/kbr/?q=api/value-menu-items&max_price=5
```

This time, only those menu items with a price no greater than $5 will be returned.

Permissions

The last thing we want to cover with services_views is related to security. Navigating back to the Value Menu Items view, you see a pair of Access settings under the Services Settings section. By default, the view is security by a specific permission—"View published content." This means that the user being used to make the HTTP request for the view (that is, the GET request) will need to have the "View published content" permission in order to access the view resource.

To tighten down the permissions, and make them more specific for services-related access, we can utilize a specific role created to represent a service client. Click on the Permission link next to Access, select Role, and click Apply. In the next screen that appears, select the role appropriate for granting access to the view. In Figure 9-16, you can see that we've selected "service user" for the role that can access the view. Click Apply, and then save the view.

Role

☐ administrator

☐ anonymous user

☐ authenticated user

☑ service user

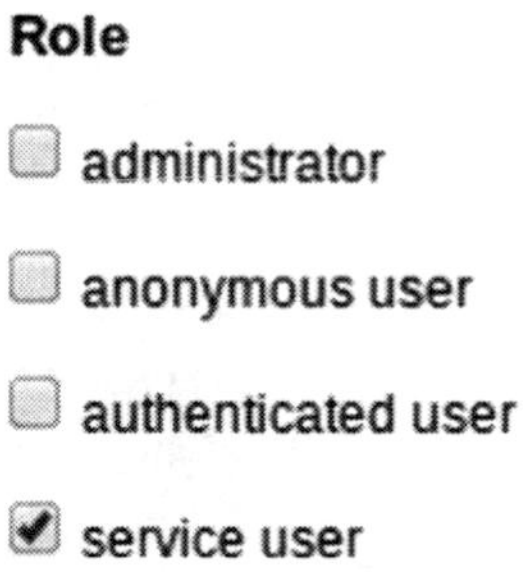

Figure 9-16. Roles for service view

That's about it for services_views. Let's quickly look at content negotiation before we dive into making updates to the system via the REST service.

Content Negotiation

Inherent in a RESTful service is the ability for the caller to specify the desired format of the returned content. Back on Figure 9-4, we modified our rest_api service to only support JSON. Now we want to support XML, as well.

Navigate back to the Services page, via the Structure menu on the administrative menu. Click on the Edit Server link under the Operations column. Add XML to the list of supported Response Formatters, as shown in Figure 9-17. Then click Save.

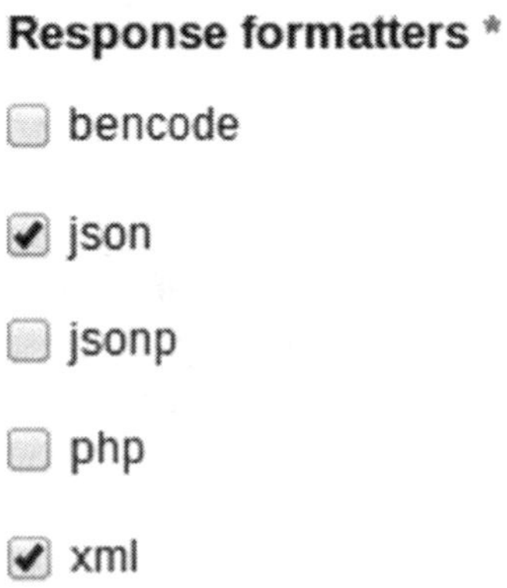

Response formatters *

☐ bencode

☑ json

☐ jsonp

☐ php

☑ xml

Figure 9-17. Supporting both JSON and XML

Back in the browser tab you were using to call the service, refresh the page (`http://localhost/kbr/?q=api/value-menu-items`). The response format should now be XML, instead of JSON. This is because the default format for the service, per the Drupal Services module, is XML.

In order to demonstrate content negotiation, we are going to use a Chrome browser extension called Postman. Do this in a new tab. Once installed, paste the URL for the Value Menu Items service into the appropriate address box in Postman, as shown in Figure 9-18.

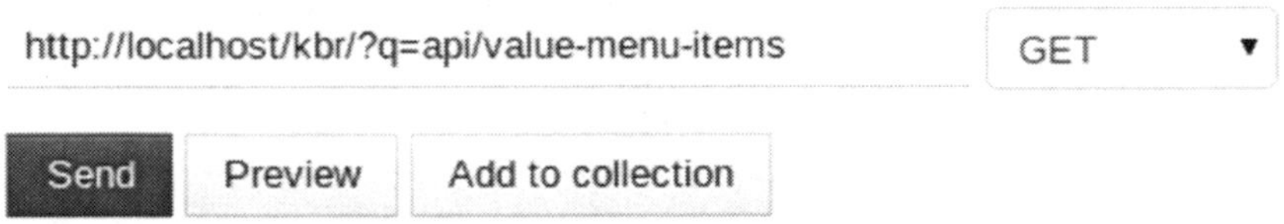

http://localhost/kbr/?q=api/value-menu-items   GET ▼

Send   Preview   Add to collection

Figure 9-18. Postman GET request for Value Menu Items

Click the Send button, and you should see the same XML response for menu items as we did previously in the browser. To request that the response be formatted with JSON, add the following header to the HTTP request by clicking the Headers button:

`Accept: application/json`

In Postman, this will look like Figure 9-19.

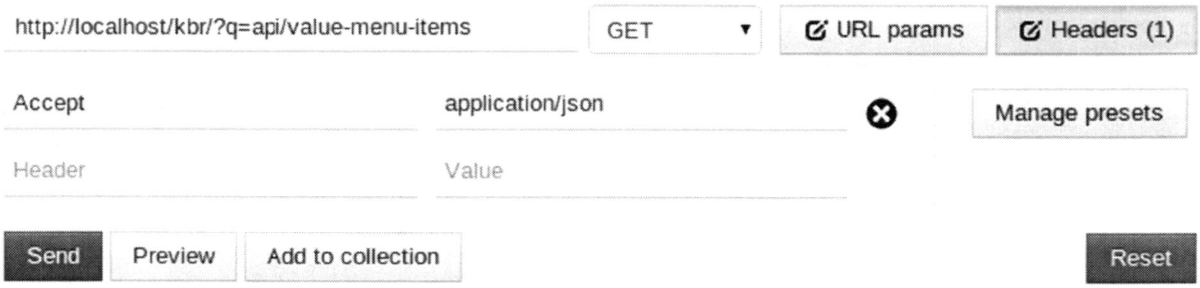

| http://localhost/kbr/?q=api/value-menu-items | GET ▾ | ☑ URL params | ☑ Headers (1) |

| Accept | application/json | ✖ | Manage presets |

| Header | Value | | |

| Send | Preview | Add to collection | | Reset |

Figure 9-19. JSON content request in Postman

Clicking the Send button, you will see that the response is again JSON.

Content negotiation allows consumers of your service—whether JavaScript code, mobile apps, or Java or .NET applications—to specify the content type that works best for them. All of this is done transparent to the features and abilities of your service's resources.

Creating, Updating, and Deleting Data

By this point, you should be fairly comfortable with configuring the Services and Services_Views module in Drupal. You should also have a decent understanding of how to fetch data out of Drupal using RESTful HTTP GET requests, including the ins and outs of query parameters, paging, and content negotiation. While the interaction with the service isn't the ideal picture of true REST, it is indeed not SOAP, and will be much more portable across various client platforms than would a SOAP-based API.

Let's now look at what it takes to update some data in Drupal using the REST service we've built. If you haven't yet installed the Postman Chrome browser extension, do so now. We will be using it to explore the data modification-related operations in our rest_api service.

Just as a heads-up, some of the JSON used to create and modify content in a Drupal REST service can, at first, seem a bit ugly and complex. We'll get to that in a minute, but just know there are reasons for the seemingly over-engineered JSON formats.

For now, though, we're going to start simple. Let's create a new menu item using Postman by making an HTTP POST request to our rest_api service. Enter the following information into a new Postman request, making sure to select POST instead of GET:

```
URL: http://localhost/kbr/?q=api/node
Content-Type header: application/json
Accept header: application/json
Body: { "title":"Iced Tea", "type":"menu_item" }
```

The request should look similar to Figure 9-20 (note that the server name in the URL shown is not localhost).

https://usrv01/kbr/?q=api/node   POST ▾

Content-Type   application/json

Accept   application/json

Header   Value

| form-data | x-www-form-urlencoded | raw | JSON ▾ |

```
1 { "title":"Iced Tea", "type":"menu_item" }
```

Figure 9-20. *POST request to create a new menu item*

Click the Send button to submit the request. If all goes okay, the call should actually fail with a response of "CSRF validation failed." This is the result of a security enhancement added to the Services module in the summer of 2013, in response to a discovered cross-site request forgery vulnerability in the module. As such, we need to first obtain a CSRF token from Drupal, and then include it for all subsequent calls.

Make the GET request shown in Figure 9-21 to obtain a valid CSRF token. Note that the address is /services/session/token—which is not directly part of our rest_api service.

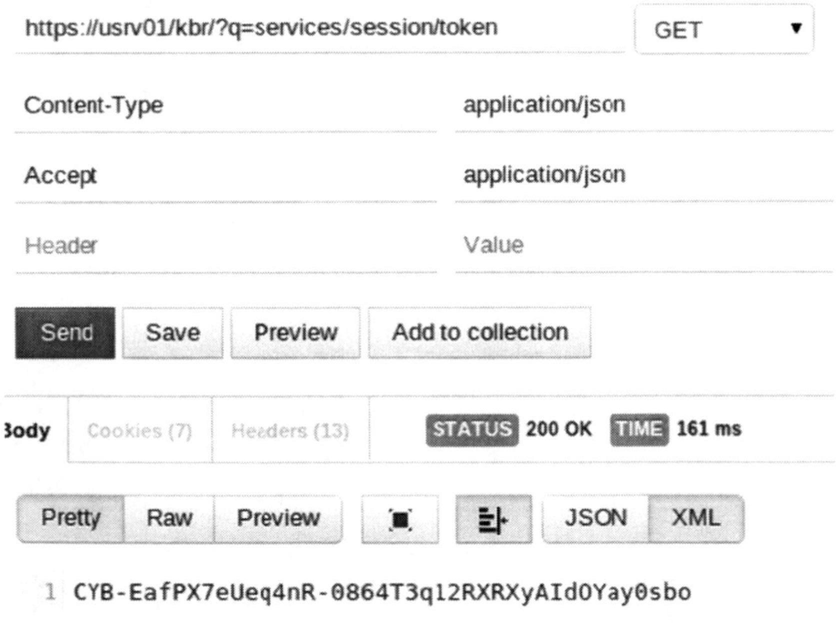

https://usrv01/kbr/?q=services/session/token   GET ▾

Content-Type   application/json

Accept   application/json

Header   Value

| Send | Save | Preview | Add to collection |

Body   Cookies (7)   Headers (13)   STATUS 200 OK   TIME 161 ms

| Pretty | Raw | Preview | ▣ | ☰ | JSON | XML |

```
1 CYB-EafPX7eUeq4nR-0864T3ql2RXRXyAId0Yay0sbo
```

Figure 9-21. *GET request to obtain CSRF token*

The text you receive back needs to be copied into a new header—for use on subsequent requests. The header is called X-CSRF-TOKEN. The complete request to create a new menu item is shown in Figure 9-22.

Figure 9-22. *POST request to create a new menu item*

The response you get back from a successful request contains just a couple of fields: the new node's ID, and a URL you can use to fetch the new content item.

Now let's do a PUT request to update the new menu item's price. The request will be similar to the POST used previously, only we just want to include the price value. So let's try something similar to the request in Figure 9-23, being sure to use a URL that points directly to the content item—for example, /api/node/15.

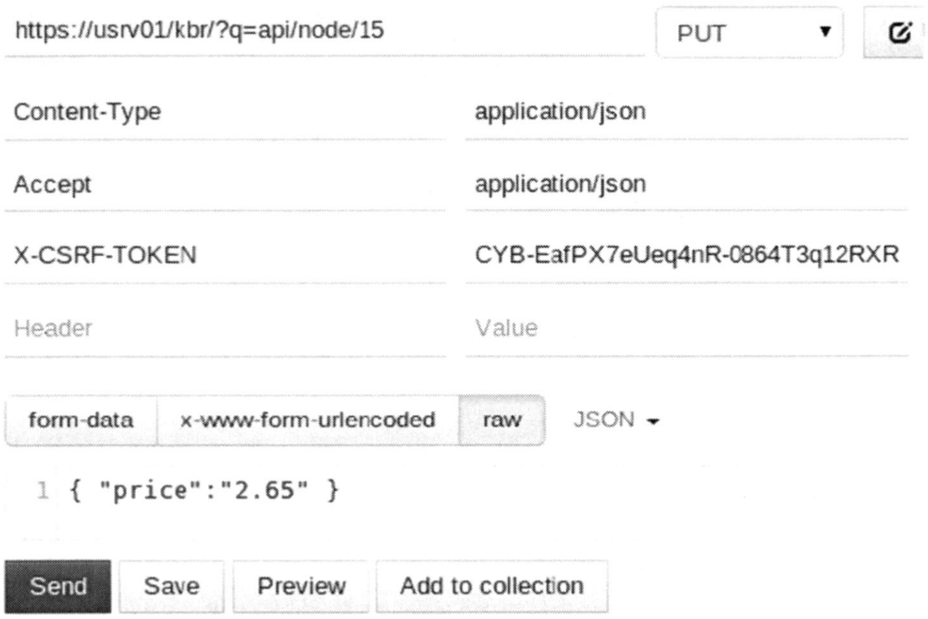

| https://usrv01/kbr/?q=api/node/15 | PUT ▾ | ☑ |

Content-Type	application/json
Accept	application/json
X-CSRF-TOKEN	CYB-EafPX7eUeq4nR-0864T3q12RXR
Header	Value

| form-data | x-www-form-urlencoded | raw | JSON ▾ |

```
1 { "price":"2.65" }
```

Send   Save   Preview   Add to collection

Figure 9-23. *PUT request to update the price of a menu item*

The call will succeed, but unfortunately the price won't be updated. This is where we get into some of the uglier parts of the REST interface in Drupal. That is, the format of the JSON used to update a custom field is not as straightforward as that of built-in fields. For example, updating the price of an item will use more complex JSON as compared to updating the menu item's title. To see the format we need to supply, let's execute a GET against a menu item known to have a valid price. What you'll see is something similar this:

```
"field_price": {
        "und": [
            {
                "value": "2.79"
            }
        ]
}
```

Yuck! Well, fear not, there is a reason. If you recall back when we were building our content types, every custom field in Drupal has the option of specifying one or more values for a given field—thus the need in the REST interface for the array. Further, since Drupal supports localization, the interface needs to account for multiple languages being submitted—thus the need for the "und" part of the field. This tells Drupal that the supplied language is "undefined"—or, to use the default language of the system. Bottom line, whenever you are submitting JSON content for custom fields, you must supply the language, which can be "und", and you must supply the value(s) as an array.

So let's try again. Just copy the preceding JSON into your PUT request for the newly created menu item. The request should look similar to Figure 9-24.

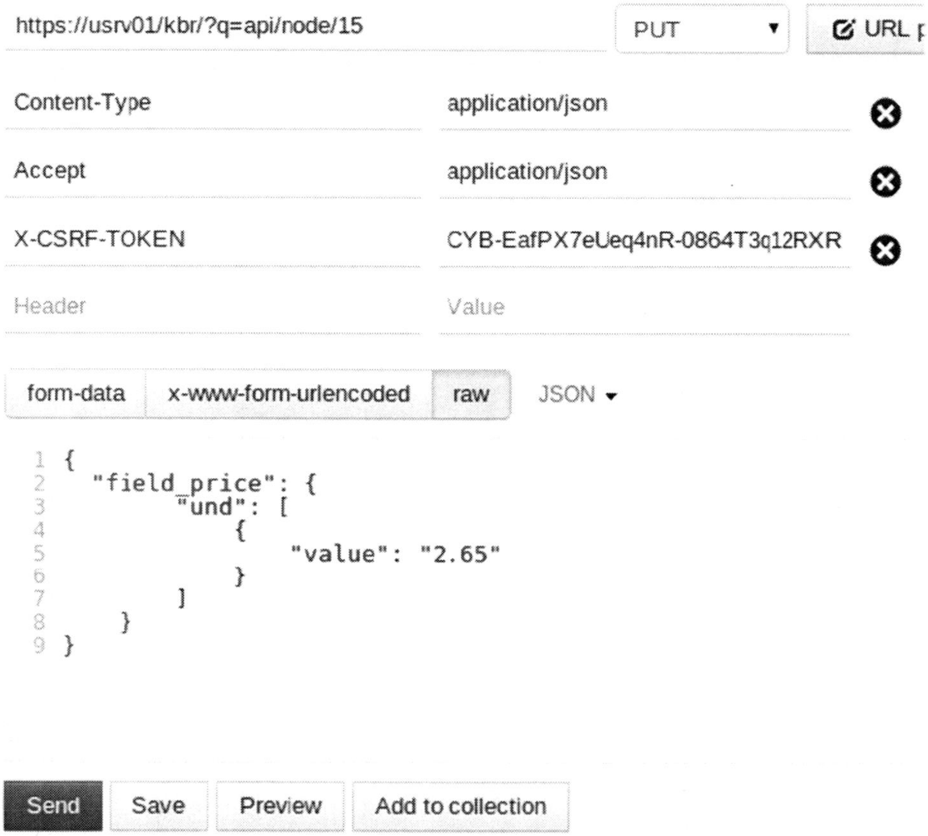

https://usrv01/kbr/?q=api/node/15   PUT ▼   ☑ URL

Content-Type	application/json	✖
Accept	application/json	✖
X-CSRF-TOKEN	CYB-EafPX7eUeq4nR-0864T3q12RXR	✖
Header	Value	

form-data   x-www-form-urlencoded   raw   JSON ▾

```
1 {
2     "field_price": {
3         "und": [
4             {
5                 "value": "2.65"
6             }
7         ]
8     }
9 }
```

Send   Save   Preview   Add to collection

Figure 9-24. *PUT request to (successfully) update a menu item's price*

Now that we've created and then modified a content item via our REST service, let's now delete it! Simply submit an HTTP DELETE request to the same URL (for example, /api/node/15) to delete the content item from the system. The complete request and response is shown in Figure 9-25.

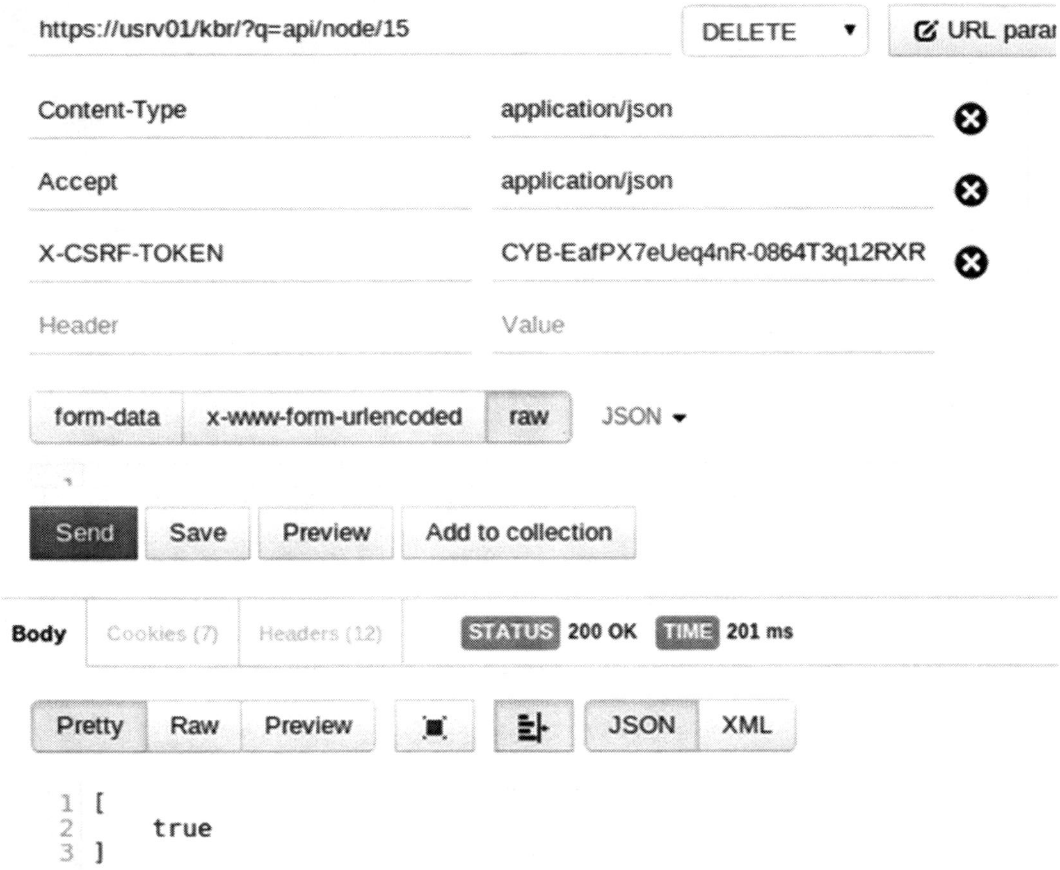

https://usrv01/kbr/?q=api/node/15   DELETE   ▼   ☑ URL para

Content-Type   application/json   ✕

Accept   application/json   ✕

X-CSRF-TOKEN   CYB-EafPX7eUeq4nR-0864T3q12RXR   ✕

Header   Value

| form-data | x-www-form-urlencoded | raw | JSON ▼

Send   Save   Preview   Add to collection

Body   Cookies (7)   Headers (12)   **STATUS** 200 OK   **TIME** 201 ms

| Pretty | Raw | Preview | ▣   ≣↓ | JSON | XML |

```
1 [
2     true
3 ]
```

Figure 9-25. *DELETE request for a content item*

The service should, upon successful deletion, return an HTTP "200 OK", with a value of true in the JSON response.

Data Validation

Let's now look at how field and content item validation works in conjunction with the REST service we've built. To start with something easy, let's modify the Menu Item content type to make the price required. In case Chapter 3 was a while ago for you, navigate to the Menu Item fields via the Structure→Content Types administrative menu, clicking on the Manage Fields link in the Menu Item row. Once there, click the Edit link for the Price field, then check the box to make the field required, as shown in Figure 9-26.

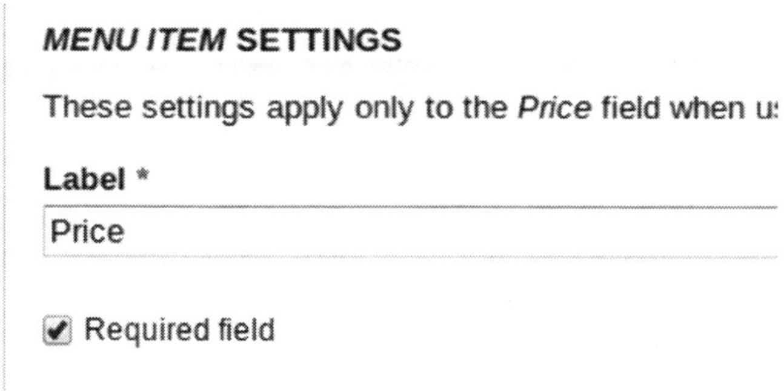

MENU ITEM SETTINGS

These settings apply only to the *Price* field when u:

Label *

Price

☑ Required field

Figure 9-26. Making the Price field required

Click Save, and then return to your Postman browser tab. Submit the same request as in Figure 9-22, leaving off the price value just like last time. Submit the request, and this time we should get a response back in the form of an HTTP 406 error:

```
{
    "form_errors": {
        "field_price][und][0][value": "Price field is required."
    }
}
```

Again, the JSON looks kind of ugly, and in fact, doesn't even look to be valid—there are some square brackets missing! Regardless, you can see that validation is working so far.

Now let's add some slightly more complex validation to the Menu Item content, using the Field Validation module. If not already installed, install the module using the following commands:

```
drush dl field_validation
drush en field_validation field_validation_ui -y
```

Once installed, navigate your way back the Manage Fields page of the Menu Item content type. Click on the Validate link for the Price field. Let's add a RegEx validator that verifies the price ends with a 9. The validator is called "Regular expression (POSIX multibyte)," and in it we want to enter the RegEx string **.*9$**. This will only match if the value entered ends with a 9. The complete validation rule is shown in Figure 9-27. Note the use of a custom error message, which is required to create a validation rule.

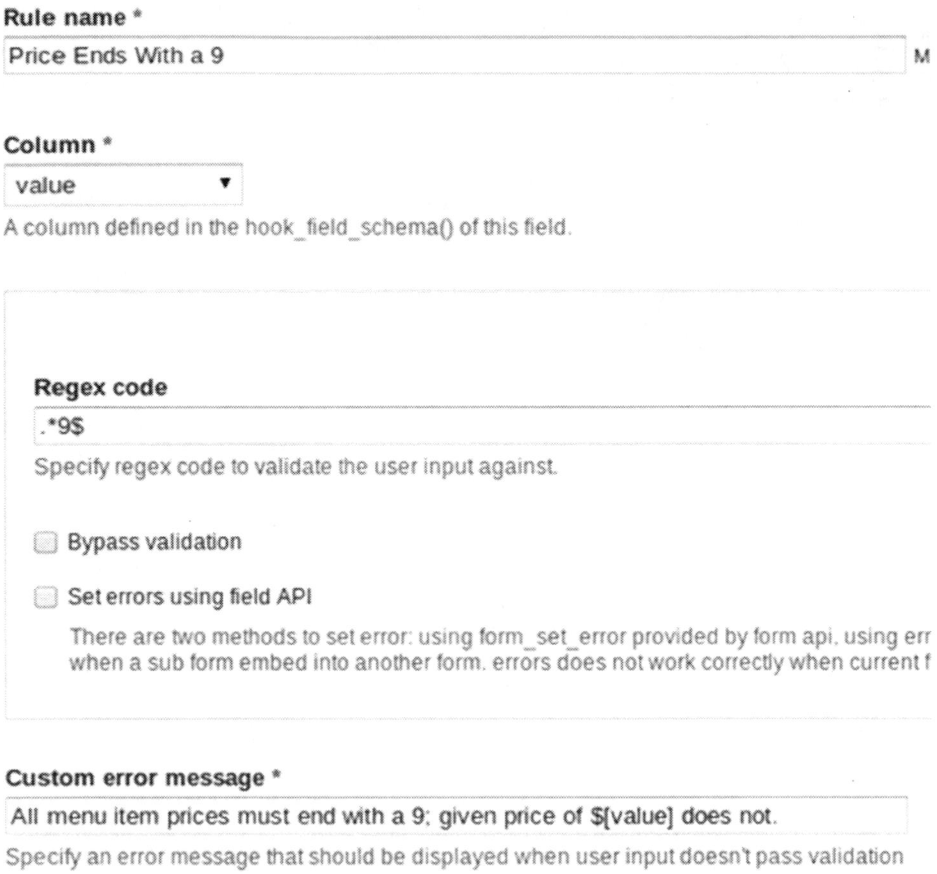

Rule name *

Price Ends With a 9   M

Column *

value   ▼

A column defined in the hook_field_schema() of this field.

Regex code

.*9$

Specify regex code to validate the user input against.

☐ Bypass validation

☐ Set errors using field API

There are two methods to set error: using form_set_error provided by form api. using err
when a sub form embed into another form. errors does not work correctly when current f

Custom error message *

All menu item prices must end with a 9: given price of ${value] does not.

Specify an error message that should be displayed when user input doesn't pass validation

Figure 9-27. *RegEx validation rule for Menu Item Price*

Click Save, and return back to your Postman browser tab. Let's submit a request to create a new menu item, only this time include a price that does not end with a 9. For example, Iced Tea for a cost of $2.65. Upon hitting the Send button, you should get a validation error back—in the form of another HTTP 406 error. The complete request and response is shown in Figure 9-28.

Figure 9-28. *Invalid request and response for a new menu item*

As you can see, field validation works within a REST service just as it did for a user creating a new content item from the web interface. Thus you can create your rules once, and know that invalid data will not be allowed into the system.

Rule-Based Services

So far we've covered how to do basic CRUD against a Drupal-based application using the features of a REST service. While this should handle most of what you need to offer your service consumers, there may be cases where you need to "run some code." For those cases, we turn to another module called Services Rules. This module allows you to write Rules, like we talked about in Chapter 4, but also expose them as REST resources. Rules are typically activated with some system event, such as saving a piece of content or creating a user. But in this scenario, we want to activate a rule when a POST request is made against one of our REST resources.

In order to begin, install and enable the services_rules module:

```
drush dl services_rules
drush en services_rules -y
```

We are also going to use the views_rules module for this example, so let's make sure that module is installed:

```
drush dl views_rules
drush en views_rules -y
```

Since we covered the details of views_rules in Chapter 4, the following instructions will be mostly high-level, just making sure the important parts are consistent with our example code.

The feature we're going to build is going to leverage the capabilities of the Views, Services, Rules, Views Rules, and Services Rules modules. Essentially, we want to offer a REST method call that adjusts the prices all of the menu items in the system according to a given multiplier. For example, an app can call the service, passing in 0.9 to reduce all prices by 10%.

One more thing: we can implement this scenario in one of two different ways, both of which use Rules—but use them in a slightly different way. The first approach leverages the services_rules module to expose a rule as a REST endpoint. As described previously, the rule is executed when a caller submits a POST request to the endpoint. In this approach, there is no specific content type of content item involved—that is, the HTTP POST request results in a rule execution.

The second approach is to create a new content type called "Price Adjustment Request"—or something similar. We would use the new content type to define our fields, configure needed validation, and then create a rule that triggers when a new item of this type is created. This approach offers a few benefits:

- All requests are "logged" as actual content in the system, allowing further workflow to occur on the requests, and for them to be available to views, reports, exports, and so forth.

- All of the content type validation we've discussed in this book is readily available for the service requests (since the requests are actually just new content items).

- Triggering multiple rules off of a new request becomes a matter of creating multiple rules that aren't related or tied to each other. This is more true to an event-based system, versus having to add more and more logic to a single synchronous rule.

The only real drawback for the second approach is that you could end up with lots of useless content items—that ultimately just need to be deleted.

Bottom line is that either of these approaches works great. It boils down to whether or not you want to leverage content types and their items to track and report on requests, and if you need to leverage the inherent field validation available with content types. If not, then the first approach, that of using the services_rules module, will suffice.

Since we covered rules, and triggering them off of content item creation, back in Chapter 4, we won't do that again here. Just know that in order to use that approach, you just need to:

- Define your "request" content type, including field validation

- Define the necessary triggers for the request

- Execute POST requests against the /api/node resource to create instances of those content types

Ok, so let's get started on the services_rules approach. Since we know we need to loop through all of the menu items in order to set their prices, let's create a new views to be used in a rule (just like we did back in Chapter 4). Using the Views menu under Structure, create a new view called All Menu Items. Uncheck the option to create a Page for the view. Instead, once the view page is displayed, add a new Rules display type. Of course, make sure the new view is only fetching content of type Menu Item. As shown in Figure 9-29, ensure that the Title, Nid, and Price fields are defined. You also need to turn off paging, and instead tell the view to display all items. If you don't, then the view will only return the first 10 menu items to the rule we're going to build.

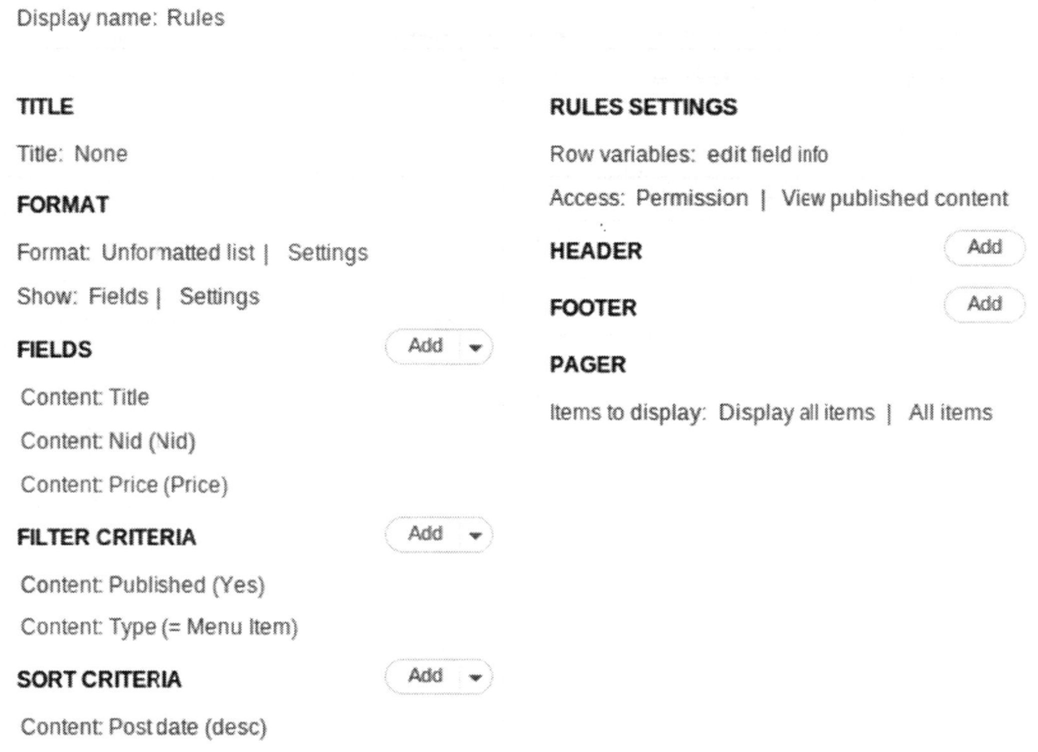

Display name: Rules

TITLE

Title: None

FORMAT

Format: Unformatted list | Settings

Show: Fields | Settings

FIELDS   Add ▼

Content: Title

Content: Nid (Nid)

Content: Price (Price)

FILTER CRITERIA   Add ▼

Content: Published (Yes)

Content: Type (= Menu Item)

SORT CRITERIA   Add ▼

Content: Post date (desc)

RULES SETTINGS

Row variables: edit field info

Access: Permission | View published content

HEADER   Add

FOOTER   Add

PAGER

Items to display: Display all items | All items

Figure 9-29. *View used for price update rule*

Next, click on the "edit field info" link under RULES SETTINGS. In it, we need to define the fields that will be returned to the rule as it loops through all menu items. Ensure that the data types are correct, and make sure you like the field names.

One very important note with these field info options: any custom fields MUST have the "Use rendered result" option checked. If this option is unchecked, then the rule won't be able to use the data returned from the view, as the data will be presented as an array of values for each language in the system. Instead, we want Drupal to actually "render" the value—that is, just give the rule the current single value per the current language. You can see this option in Figure 9-30, used for the price field.

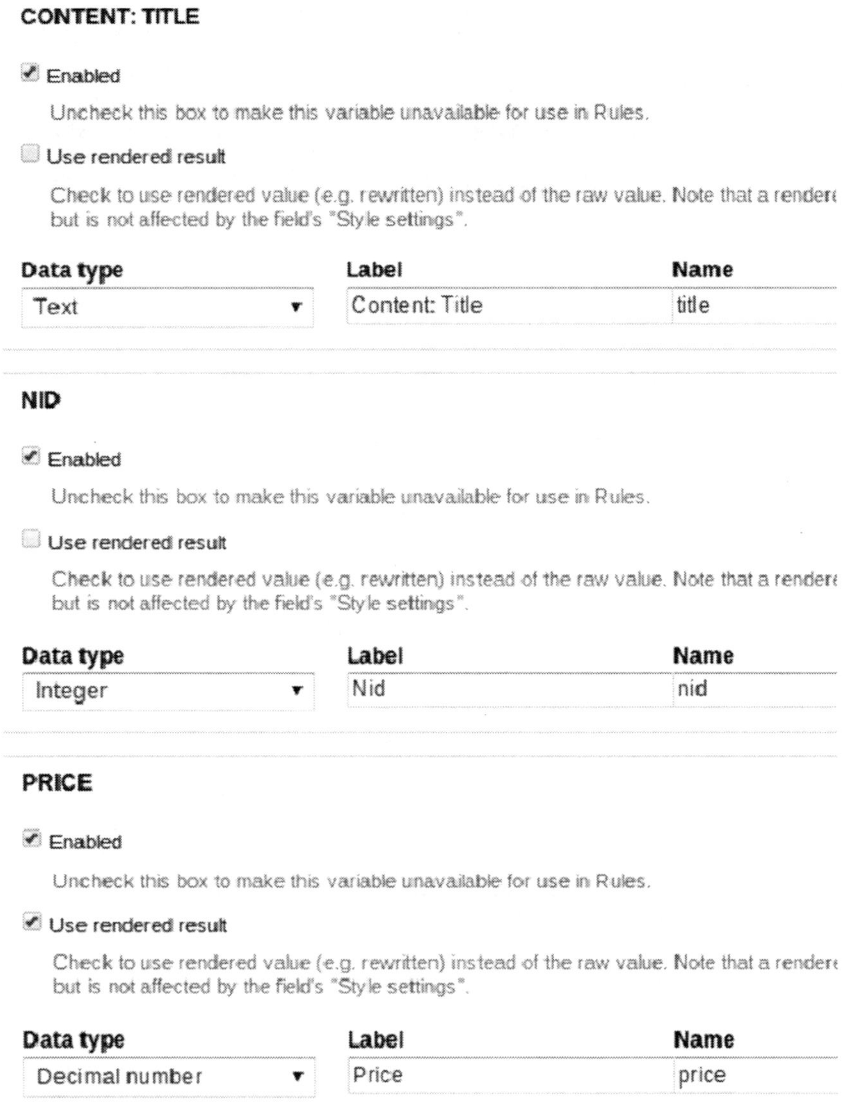

CONTENT: TITLE

☑ Enabled

Uncheck this box to make this variable unavailable for use in Rules.

☐ Use rendered result

Check to use rendered value (e.g. rewritten) instead of the raw value. Note that a rendere
but is not affected by the field's "Style settings".

Data type	Label	Name
Text ▾	Content: Title	title

NID

☑ Enabled

Uncheck this box to make this variable unavailable for use in Rules.

☐ Use rendered result

Check to use rendered value (e.g. rewritten) instead of the raw value. Note that a rendere
but is not affected by the field's "Style settings".

Data type	Label	Name
Integer ▾	Nid	nid

PRICE

☑ Enabled

Uncheck this box to make this variable unavailable for use in Rules.

☑ Use rendered result

Check to use rendered value (e.g. rewritten) instead of the raw value. Note that a rendere
but is not affected by the field's "Style settings".

Data type	Label	Name
Decimal number ▾	Price	price

Figure 9-30. *Views rules fields definition*

When done, click Apply, and then save the view.

Navigate over to the Rules page. In order for a rule to be exposed as a REST service resource, it must be a rule Component. So click on the Components tab, and click the link to create a new component. Select Rule from the Component Plugin drop-down, and then click Continue. Give the new component a name—for example, "Update All Menu Item Prices", and then create a single variable called Price Multiplier, of type Decimal, shown in Figure 9-31.

Component plugin

Rule ▼

Choose which kind of component to create. Each component type is described in the online documentation.

Name *

Update All Menu Item Prices	Machine name: update_all_menu_item_prices [Edit]

Tags

◯

Tags associated with this configuration, used for filtering in the admin interface. Separate multiple tags with commas.

Variables

Variables are normally input *parameters* for the component – data that should be available for the component to act on. Additionaly, action comp have a specified data type, a label and a unique machine readable name containing only lowercase alphanumeric characters and underscores

	DATA TYPE	LABEL	MACHINE NAME
⊹	Decimal number ▼	Price Multiplier	price_multiplier
⊹	-- ▼		
⊹	-- ▼		

Figure 9-31. Rule definition

Click Save, which will return you to the main component edit page. Add a new view loop under the Actions section, and select the All Menu Items rule we created a bit ago as the "Views iterator display." At this point, we recommend changing the variable names to make them distinctly reflect the fact that they are coming from a menu item. For example, change title to `item_title`, nid to `item_nid`, and price to `item_price`. Then click Save.

At this point, we have a rule fully ready to loop through all menu items in the system and do something with them. Let's start by calculating the new price (for each item). Next to the new action, click on Add Action, to add a new action under the views loop. Select "calculate a value," and then fill in the details as follows:

```
Input value 1:  item-price
Operator:  ( * )
Input value 2:  price-multiplier
Result label: New Price
Result variable name: new_price
```

Click Save. At this point, the rule actions section should look similar to Figure 9-32, with the newly added calculation step being indented under the main views loop.

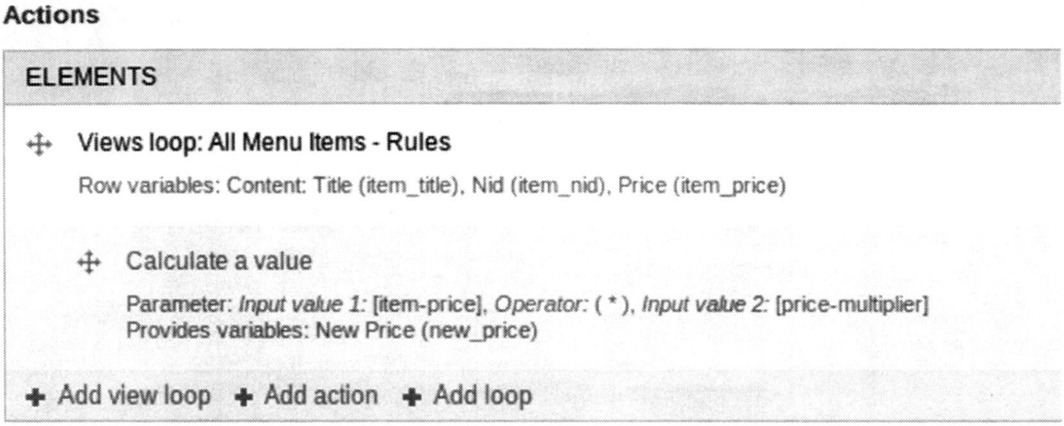

Actions

ELEMENTS
✥ **Views loop: All Menu Items - Rules**
Row variables: Content: Title (item_title), Nid (item_nid), Price (item_price)
✥ Calculate a value
Parameter: *Input value 1:* [item-price], *Operator:* (*), *Input value 2:* [price-multiplier] Provides variables: New Price (new_price)
✚ Add view loop ✚ Add action ✚ Add loop

Figure 9-32. Update price rules component actions

Now that we have our new price, we need to actually fetch the entity represented by the item_nid value. We can't directly update the item_price, as that is coming from a read-only view and can't be saved back to the database. So we need to fetch the actual entity, update its price, and then save it again.

To fetch an entity, add a new action and select the "fetch entity by ID" option. Make sure you are using the "Add action" link that belongs to the views loop action—NOT the main "add action" link for the entire rule component!

Select "node" for the entity type. Then enter item-nid for the Identifier, followed by a new name for the entity variable returned—that is, fetched_menu_item. This is shown in Figure 9-33.

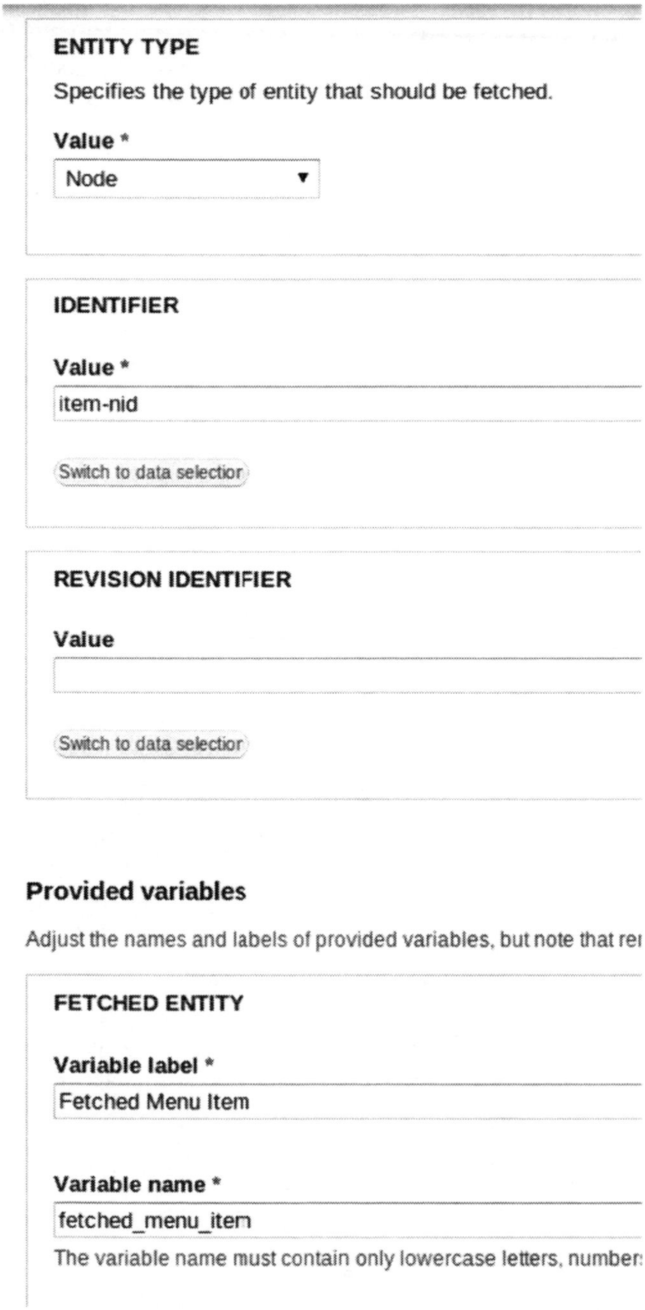

ENTITY TYPE

Specifies the type of entity that should be fetched.

Value *

| Node ▼ |

IDENTIFIER

Value *

| item-nid |

(Switch to data selection)

REVISION IDENTIFIER

Value

| |

(Switch to data selection)

Provided variables

Adjust the names and labels of provided variables, but note that rer

FETCHED ENTITY

Variable label *

| Fetched Menu Item |

Variable name *

| fetched_menu_item |

The variable name must contain only lowercase letters, number:

Figure 9-33. *Fetching an entity within a rule*

Click Save. You should now have two actions indented under the main views loop action.

The next action we are going to add is going to be another component. We really just want to update the price on the fetched_menu_item object but, if you recall from Chapter 4, a little nuance of the Rules module is that custom fields aren't available for use in actions unless you specifically check the entity for that field. In other words, we need a condition for "entity has field" prior to being able to use the field in an action. However, because we're already in an action with a views loop result, we can't utilize a condition on the existing rule component. The fetched_menu_item object isn't even available. Thus, we need to create a component to do two things:

- Check that the entity has the Price field
- Update its price to the newly calculate value

So let's create a new component with a condition that checks that the passed in node has the Price field. The new component should have settings similar to Figure 9-34—specifically the input variables.

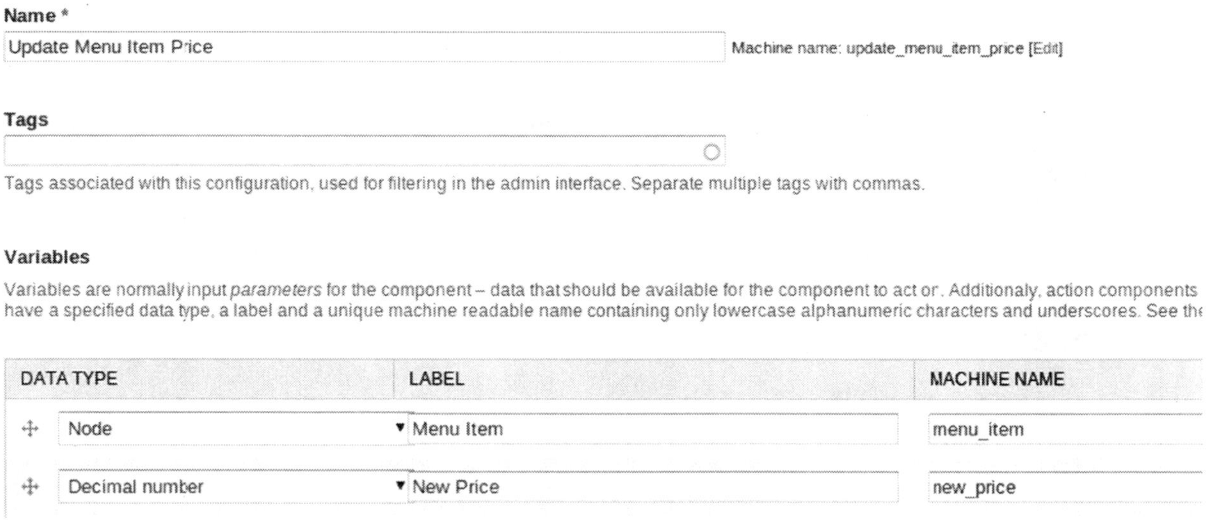

Name *

| Update Menu Item Price | Machine name: update_menu_item_price [Edit] |

Tags

| ⭘ |

Tags associated with this configuration, used for filtering in the admin interface. Separate multiple tags with commas.

Variables

Variables are normally input *parameters* for the component – data that should be available for the component to act or. Additionaly, action components have a specified data type, a label and a unique machine readable name containing only lowercase alphanumeric characters and underscores. See the

DATA TYPE	LABEL	MACHINE NAME
✛ Node	▼ Menu Item	menu_item
✛ Decimal number	▼ New Price	new_price

Figure 9-34. *Rules component settings for updating a single menu item's price*

Then add a condition to the component for "entity has field," which should be checking the incoming menu_item object to make sure it has the field_price field (that is, the field's machine name). Figure 9-35 shows the resulting settings.

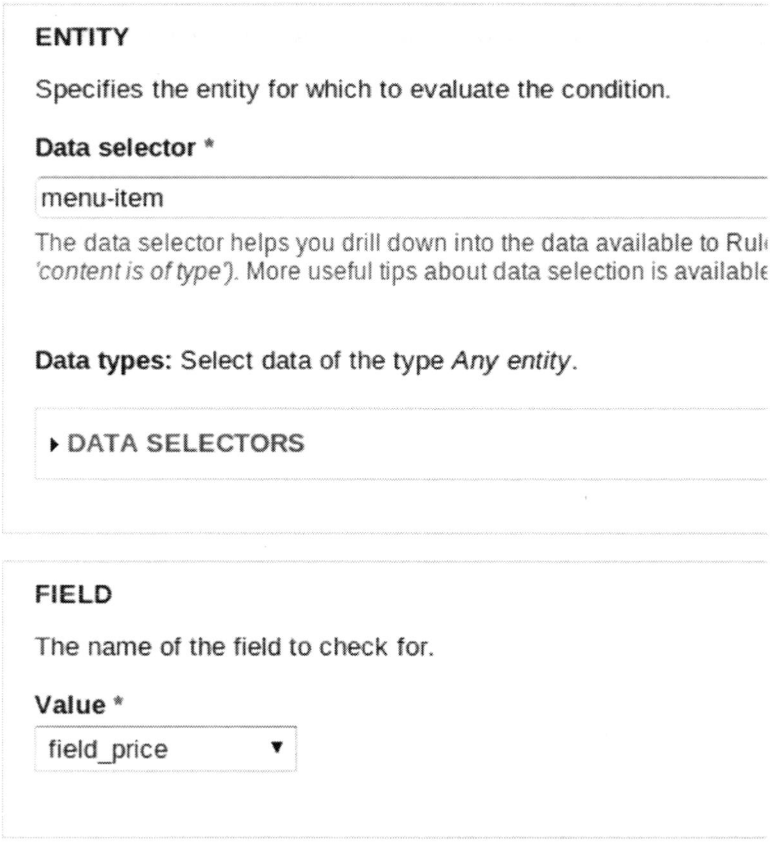

ENTITY

Specifies the entity for which to evaluate the condition.

Data selector *

menu-item

The data selector helps you drill down into the data available to Rul(
'content is of type'). More useful tips about data selection is available

Data types: Select data of the type *Any entity*.

▸ DATA SELECTORS

FIELD

The name of the field to check for.

Value *

field_price ▼

Figure 9-35. *Entity has field settings for menu item price field*

Finally, add an action for "set a data value." Enter menu-item:field-price for the Data Selector—that is, the data that will have its value set. Then click Continue. In the Value text box, use the data selector to enter new-price. In short, this action means we will be using the new-price value to set the menu_item's price field.

That's it for the component. Make sure your changes are saved. Then return back to the Rules Components tab. You should now see two separate components—one for updating a single menu item's price, and another to loop through and update all menu items' prices. Let's go back into the edit screen for the "Update All Menu Item Prices" component. Add the new component we just created by clicking Add Action (on the views loop row). Scroll to the bottom of the actions drop-down and select the "Rule: Update Menu Item Price" component. This, as discussed in Chapter 4, will allow us to call that component from this one, passing in the necessary values.

We just need to pass in two arguments: the menu item itself, and the new price we already calculated. Use the fetched_menu_item and new_price variables, respectively. The screen should look similar to Figure 9-36 when filled in.

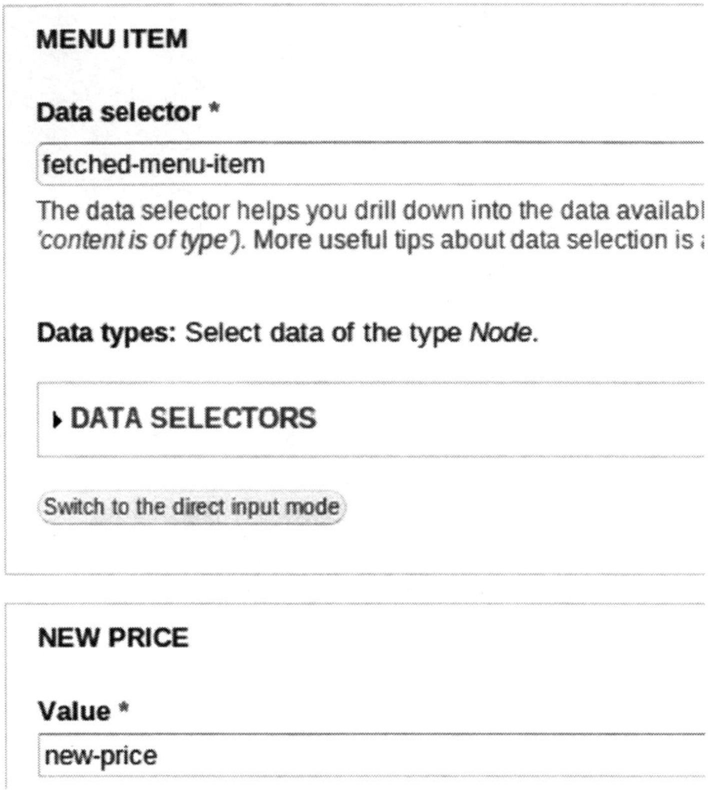

MENU ITEM

Data selector *

fetched-menu-item

The data selector helps you drill down into the data availabl
'content is of type'). More useful tips about data selection is ;

Data types: Select data of the type *Node*.

▸ DATA SELECTORS

Switch to the direct input mode

NEW PRICE

Value *

new-price

Figure 9-36. *Passing arguments into component to update menu item price*

Click Save to return to the main rule edit page. You should now have three actions under the main views loops action.

Lastly, we need to add an action to save the updated menu item entity. Click the Add Action link again, and select the action type of "save entity." We just need to pass in the entity we already fetched, called fetched_menu_item. And then click Save.

At this point, the rule is complete, and should look similar to Figure 9-37.

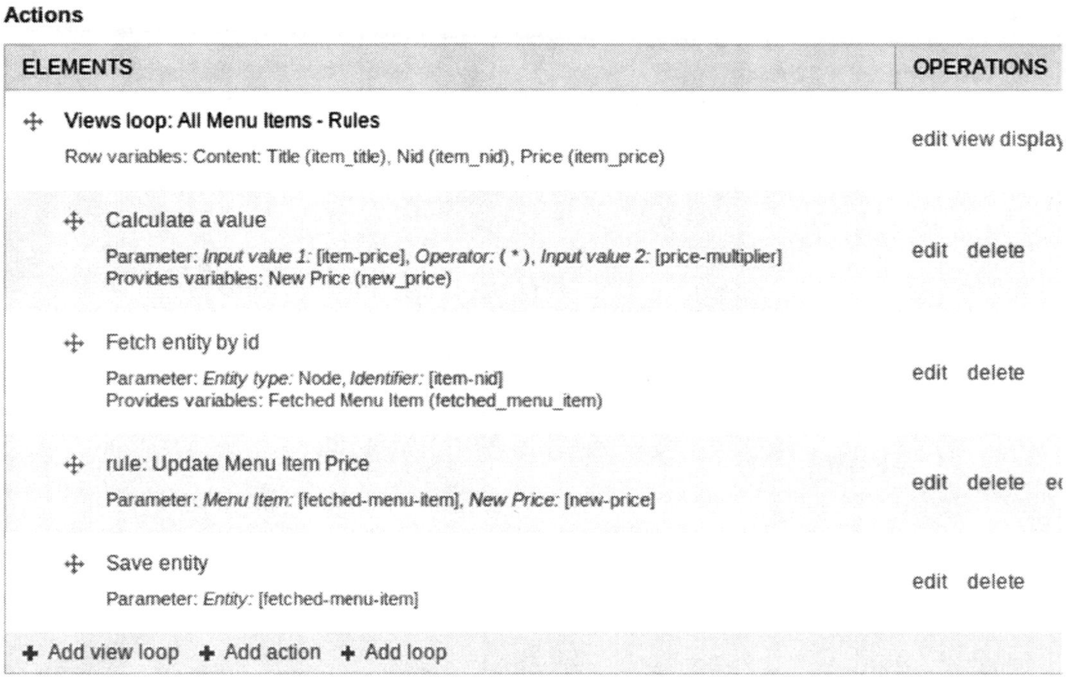

Actions

ELEMENTS	OPERATIONS
⊹ **Views loop: All Menu Items - Rules** Row variables: Content: Title (item_title), Nid (item_nid), Price (item_price)	edit view display
⊹ Calculate a value Parameter: *Input value 1:* [item-price], *Operator:* (*), *Input value 2:* [price-multiplier] Provides variables: New Price (new_price)	edit delete
⊹ Fetch entity by id Parameter: *Entity type:* Node, *Identifier:* [item-nid] Provides variables: Fetched Menu Item (fetched_menu_item)	edit delete
⊹ rule: Update Menu Item Price Parameter: *Menu Item:* [fetched-menu-item], *New Price:* [new-price]	edit delete e(
⊹ Save entity Parameter: *Entity:* [fetched-menu-item]	edit delete
✚ Add view loop **✚** Add action **✚** Add loop	

Figure 9-37. Rule to update all menu item prices in the system

The rule is complete! Now all we need to do is enable it as a REST resource. To do this, navigate to the Services page, and click on the Edit Resources link associated with the rest_api service. Scroll down to and expand the rules item. You should see two components that are disabled. We want to enable the one called "rules_update_all_menu_item_prices"—as that corresponds to the rule we created for the purpose of exposing as a REST resource. This is shown in Figure 9-38. Note that the name for the input parameter is displayed—that is, price_multiplier.

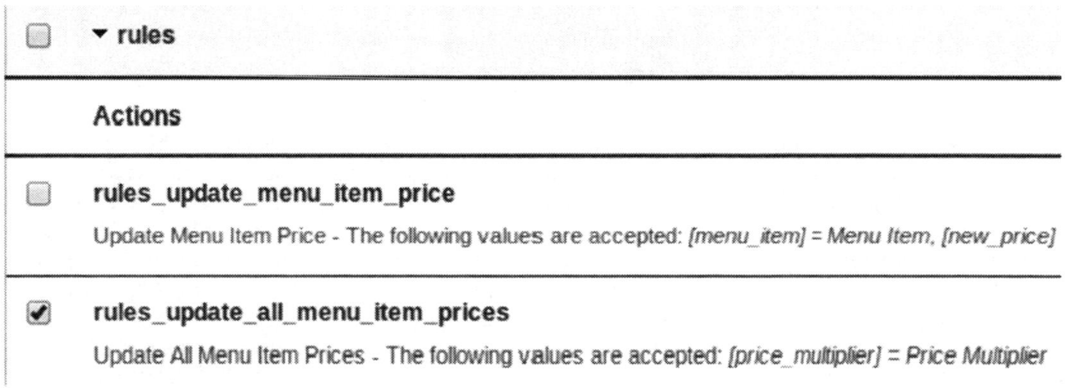

☐ ▾ **rules**
Actions
☐ **rules_update_menu_item_price** Update Menu Item Price - The following values are accepted: *[menu_item]* = Menu Item, *[new_price]*
☑ **rules_update_all_menu_item_prices** Update All Menu Item Prices - The following values are accepted: *[price_multiplier]* = Price Multiplier

Figure 9-38. Enabled rules service

Click Save, and then hop over to your Postman browser tab. Configure a new POST request to the `http://localhost/kbr/?q=api/rules/rules_update_all_menu_item_prices` URL, making sure to include the appropriate Accept, Content-Type, and X-CSRF-TOKEN headers. Then, in the body, enter JSON that specifies the price_multiplier field. Your request should look like Figure 9-39.

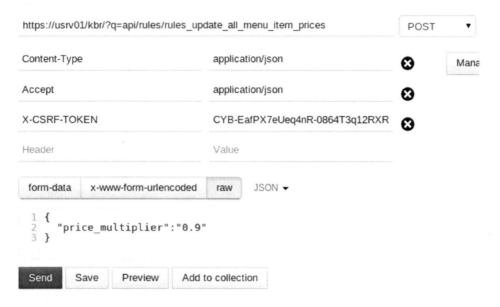

Figure 9-39. *HTP request to adjust all menu item prices*

Click the Send button, and watch the magic happen! Actually, if it's successful, all you'll see is an HTTP 200 status returned. But you can then go back into your other browser tab, and click on the Find Content link to show all of your menu items. All of them should show an Updated date/time that reflects the service call you just made. And all of their prices should now be 10% reduced.

So with most of the chapter behind us, and having discovered how to build and interact with REST services in Drupal, we need to cover one more topic.

Backend as a Service for Mobile Applications

As we've discussed throughout this chapter, one major type of consumer of your REST services will likely be mobile applications. These apps will not already have the proper Drupal session token needed to log in to your service, as the calling code is not being executed within a browser window that has already logged in to the main Drupal site. As such, we'd like to show you how to set up a mobile client application to be able to successfully call your service.

Mobile applications have recently taken the world by storm, mostly following the introduction of the iPhone in mid-2007. No doubt, if you haven't already, you will need to support mobile applications by way of a REST service. Naturally, we strongly recommend using Drupal as the backend technology on which you build these services, especially given that most small mobile teams don't necessarily have engineering around non-mobile backend technologies. Being able to quickly spin up an enterprise-level REST backend for you mobile app, complete with an entire administrative web site, content management system, eCommerce, on and on. . . all without having to write any code. . . it's simply priceless!

Drupal Access Token

The main thing we want to cover is the login sequence as required by a non-browser application. It's quite simple, really. Just two steps to make before you can successfully make HTTP REST calls. But before we cover those two steps, we first need to enable the appropriate user REST resources in the service. To do so, as covered previously, navigate to the Edit Resources page for the rest_api service. Scroll down to and expand the user resource. Enable the login, logout, and token actions, then click Save.

Once those resource actions are enabled, you need to first perform an HTTP request for a CSRF token. You can either use the URL we covered previously:

```
http://localhost/kbr/?q=services/session/token
```

Or, you can use the newly enabled user resource's token action:

```
http://localhost/kbr/?q=api/user/token
```

We prefer to use the second one, which goes with the user resource, as that is more consistent with the login and logoff actions. But either URL will work fine. The main difference is that the /services/session/token URL supports either GET or POST, whereas the the /api/user/token URL supports only POST requests.

Once you have the CSRF token, add it to the request object's header, using a header key of X-CSRF-TOKEN. This is identical to what we did with Postman in the browser.

The second step is now to submit a POST request to the login resource action. The request must include a body that contains two fields: username and password. Since most of the time from a mobile application you will be using JSON, make sure to add the appropriate Accept and Content Type headers to the request, in addition to the CSRF token. While we aren't going to show you how to make an HTTP request from an Android, iOS, or Windows Phone app, we can show you the raw request itself, and you can use it to create your platform-specific request objects.

The URL to use to post the login request is:

```
http://localhost/kbr/?q=api/user/login
```

The complete raw HTTP POST using JSON looks like this:

```
POST /kbr/?q=api/user/login HTTP/1.1
Host: usrv01
Content-Type: application/json
Accept: application/json
x-csrf-token: p_QXow48y4XNL2KAloE-m9o8At-rhcz6hHy18gwrp5c
Cache-Control: no-cache

{ "username":"admin", "password":"password123" }
```

Upon successful login, you will receive two values (in the JSON response) that you will need for all subsequent calls to the service. The first two values in the response are:

```
"sessid": "G5u-dkN9l80aOxROaWUGcOeG2P57W8Cw3dZclOYSOuE",
"session_name": "SSESS300613192f9122d96961dcf417a86663",
```

Add a cookie to all subsequent HTTP requests, using the value of session_name for the cookie's key, and the value of sessid as the cookie value. Of course, this new cookie header is in addition to the Accept, Content Type, and X-CSRF-TOKEN headers. The complete request header content, which will be used on all service calls following login, should look like:

```
Content-Type: application/json
Accept: application/json
x-csrf-token: p_QXow48y4XNL2KAloE-m908At-rhcz6hHy18gwrp5c
Cache-Control: no-cache
Cookie: SSESS300613192f9122d96961dcf417a86663=G5u-dkN9l8OaOxROaWUGcOeG2P57W8Cw3dZclOYSOuE
```

To be clear, Drupal relies on session cookies to maintain the logged-in state of a user. Unlike using HTTP Basic or Digest authentication, you can't just add a username and password to the request header. Drupal authentication is indeed stateful—as opposed to stateless. So while a REST service is ideally stateless, Drupal forces us to establish a session by first submitting a login request, and then maintaining proof of that login on all calls by way of the cookie. It's not ideal, but it does work.

Lastly, at some point, the session cookie you retrieved will time out. By default, Drupal expires a session token after 14 days. So your mobile code must be ready to catch an exception when that happens. Then you can simply resubmit the login request, obtain a new session cookie value, and continue on your way.

HTTP Response Codes

Unlike a SOAP service, which is typically defined with a plethora of proprietary response codes, errors, and other such values, REST-style services utilize standard HTTP response codes in responses. This means your mobile application will need to handle responses from the Drupal REST service that look like any other HTTP response. That is, a 404 means that the resource you are looking for doesn't exist. A 403 means the request isn't authorized for the given user. A 200 means the validation was successful. And a 406 means that validation has failed.

The real benefit here is that your mobile application code can, in theory, expect similar responses from any REST service to and from any platform. Further, per the consistency and standards that the REST architecture was created to promote, the definitions of these HTTP response codes are widely accepted and used by every HTTP-based service.

Drupal 8

Throughout this chapter, we've been making note of some of the REST-related shortcomings of services in Drupal 7. So in this final section, we want to draw attention to some of the potential improvements being made in Drupal 8. At the time of this writing, nothing is set in stone. But these are a few of the things being discussed and worked on.

First, as mentioned in the previous section, Drupal 7 utilizes stateful sessions for user authentication. This makes service-oriented interfaces stateful, which is not only more complex to deal with, but also goes against one of the constraints of the REST architecture. Drupal 8 promises to offer stateless authentication, in the way of Basic authentication and other HTTP-based standards.

Drupal 8 is also on track to making sure REST is a first-class citizen within the architecture, baked deep into the core—as opposed to an after thought in a non-core module. This means that the underlying API will be more reflective of a REST interface, as opposed to the current page view-based model.

Finally, when it comes to a REST API, Drupal 8 is to support more REST-like routes and URLs. This should make it possible to create arbitrary resource-based routes for content, as opposed to being forced to use the /api/node resource for everything.

To read more about REST in Drupal 8, Google the terms Drupal 8 wscci.

Summary

This chapter was all about doing REST in Drupal. You learned how to configure a RESTful service with the Services module, and how to enable service resources so that they can be consumed by external clients. There are a couple of approaches that you can use to get data out of a Drupal REST service: using the node resource for straight-up CRUD operations, and then using the services_views module to create a fully customized view of any data in the system. Then the view can be exposed as a read-only resource on the REST service.

When it comes to updating data via a Drupal REST service, the primary mechanism is to use the node resource, utilizing different HTTP request types (that is, PUT, POST, DELETE) to modify content in Drupal. But when a basic create, update, or delete isn't sufficient, you can leverage the services_rules module to build custom service actions. These actions take a set of custom defined arguments, and then execute a rule (the same rules you learned about in Chapter 4).

Lastly in this chapter we discussed authentication with a Drupal REST service. Because it simply piggy-backs on the main Drupal authentication system, you essentially need to establish a session from any client code, and then pass the session token into all subsequent calls, adding the token to the HTTP request header as a cookie.

In the next chapter, as we begin to wrap up our exploration of Drupal as an Enterprise development platform, we will discuss various best practices when building software on Drupal.

CHAPTER 10

Software Development Best Practices with Drupal

One of the main reasons we mentioned earlier for why one should consider using Drupal to build enterprise applications is that the consistency of using the same platform for different projects makes it easy to establish best practices, write down processes, and otherwise automate tasks. This chapter is all about that—best practices with Drupal.

We will be exploring multi-customer architecture options, using deployment profiles, developers working with artists and designers, version control, continuous integration, release packaging, install scripts, and business continuity. Some of the topics will be covered in detail, and some will simply be mentioned, saving the research for you to do on your own.

Design and Architecture

When facing the raw requirements of a project, you will be in this exciting position when the Drupal pieces of the puzzle slowly start to match and you see how you can architect it with Drupal and a set of modules. Hopefully by now, you're making good use of Drupal's content types, views, rules, and so forth. Here are a few more tips that can help you assemble the various pieces of your Drupal web application architecture.

Profiles and Distributions

In order to minimize your time to deployment and hit the floor running on every project you do, you will need to take a close look at profiles and distributions. Let's start by defining those two.

Profile

A Drupal profile is a code package, much like a module, that lives in the profiles directory of your Drupal site. There are already three profiles there by default: minimal, standard, and testing. When making a new site install, from the web GUI or from drush, you have to choose between one of those. Profiles hold information about modules that need to be enabled when the site installs, the theme that gets enabled and its settings, as well as a series of settings and actions that need to be performed once.

Distribution

A distribution is "the whole package." It designates the Drupal core code, with a set of additional modules, themes, configurations, and even sometimes files (images, videos, CSV import files), libraries, and additional applications. It also has a special profile, usually named after the distribution, that you will select during install in order to get a fully functional and ready-to-go site after installation completes. You can still customize everything as with a regular Drupal install, but many settings are preconfigured, and content is pre-entered to enable for a substantial jump start in achieving what the distribution is released for: an e-commerce site, a news publication site, or even a local businesses deals site.

We strongly encourage you to take a look at the current distributions available on Drupal.org at https://drupal.org/project/distributions and try out a couple of them to see how advanced a site they can deliver out of the box.

So why should you care about distributions if you don't plan on using one of the ones from the Drupal site? Because you can make your own! Put together the Drupal core code, all the modules you already know you will use or want available (for instance, views, rules, tokens, entityreference, and so forth), the themes you plan on using, and create a profile to have the site preconfigured for you with the settings you tend to use all the time. At the very least, have the profile enable some modules for you. The following documentation can get you started with a custom profile that does exactly what the default profile does, plus enables the modules you need so you don't have to go do that first thing: https://drupal.org/node/1022020.

Migration

A recurrent dilemma in solution architecture is the choice between fixing a platform or creating a better one from scratch and migrating the content. Having a CMS like Drupal often solves this dilemma for you: you can build a new platform using Drupal, then migrate the content from the old site to the new Drupal site. As discussed earlier, the Feeds module is an excellent tool for migrating data from other systems.

Not only will migration almost always be quicker than messing around with some custom code that is misbehaving, but you will also make it much easier on yourself next time additional changes have to be made, or new features implemented. For the same reason this entire book recommends using Drupal as an enterprise development platform, moving away from a custom built-from-scratch application often results in a relatively quick payback for the time and money invested in the new system and data migration.

Development vs. Styling Timeline

In order to maximize efficiency and minimize delivery time, site developers and designers need to work things in a certain order and will each be blocked at some point pending the others' work. We couldn't find an ideal situation where at least one of the two could just keep working without having to adjust pending on the other's work. The simplified timeline shown in Table 10-1 is our best shot at the order in which to execute your tasks between your developers and designers.

Table 10-1. *Development vs. Styling Timeline*

Timeline	Development	Styling
Step 1	Design (modules, content types, rules, views base, roles, permissions)	Design (comprehensive layout)
Step 2	BLOCKED by templating	Templating
Step 3	Menus, blocks, view displays	BLOCKED by menus, blocks, view displays
Step 4	Additional configuration, feature sets, content	Styling

After developers figure out and implement the architecture of the project, they will need for the designers to be done templating their theme before they can complete work on template-specific items such as menus (they can prepare the menu but it can hardly be placed in a block in a region that doesn't exist yet). While they place those elements, the styling folks will also be blocked (it's significantly faster to produce CSS based on existing menus, views, and so forth).

Multi-Customer Scenarios

The subject of supporting multiple customers or clients is sure to come up during the requirements and design process of nearly any enterprise-level web application. These days, it is fairly common to have to support varying levels of customer isolation within an application. Reasons range from needing isolation and autonomy at the theme or styling level, all the way to regulatory constraints around medical or other sensitive and personal information.

You also have to deal with scale out strategies—that is, do you expect the web application to grow to 1,000 different clients? 10,000? Ten million? If so, what does each client require in the way of separated data? Does each client need a separated list of users? Configuration options? Or is it merely the need to separate content (for example, pages, blog posts, articles)?

Will one client want to support OAuth integration with Twitter and Facebook, while another customer chooses to only provide username/password authentication? Will each customer want or need to specify different configuration values for Google Analytics integration? Or will customers be making heavy use of views and rules, and therefore need isolation—that is, so each customer isn't seeing and potentially editing each other's views?

These are the kinds of questions that need to be answered before you decide on an approach to support multiple customers with your Drupal-based web application. And really, these same questions need to be answered for *any* enterprise-level web application.

Multi-Customer Options

Drupal is architected to deal with the support of multiple customers in three distinct ways:

- Single code-base, single database
- Single code-base, separate databases
- Separate code-bases, separate databases

Each of these options offers various advantages and disadvantages in terms of trying to balance between maintenance and upkeep and data isolation. In the following sections, we will explore these advantages and disadvantages, covering example scenarios where each applies best. Note that we aren't going to dive deep into implementation details, but will instead stick with the various aspects involved in deciding on which approach to take.

If you recall from earlier in this book, the Drupal platform consists of code and a database. The code holds the definition of the version of Drupal you're on, the modules downloaded and available to be enabled and configured, as well as themes available to the site. The database, then, contains users and roles, permissions, content types, content, and various system-level settings. It also contains data for all modules, such as: the core module, views, rules, services, password policies, OAuth configuration, feature sets, feeds, and any other data stored by modules.

We can therefore make the following claim: the code defines what is *available* to be enabled and configured (including the specific version available), and the database contains all site-specific data related to that which is enabled. Of course, this is identical to any other software application, where the code or compiled binaries are built and released by a team of software engineers. And then, upon installation, various pieces of customer data are added to the system—typically stored in a database of some flavorfor example, config files, Windows registry, RDBMS).

Table 10-2 attempts to illustrate the information stored in code versus the database.

Table 10-2. *Drupal Code and Data Definitions*

Defined in Code	Defined in the Database
Version of Drupal core	Enabled modules
Available modules	Enabled and default themes
Patches and updates applied	Module configuration
Available themes	Theme configuration
Available permissions	Users
PHP and physical site configuration	Roles
	Permissions
	Content types
	Content items
	Module data:
	Views
	Rules
	Services
	And so on

So when designing a multi-customer system, you need to know whether the items listed in either one of or both columns needs to be separated by customer.

Let's examine each of the three options. We'll look at the option with the most isolation first.

Separate Code, Separate Database

Looking again at Table 10-2, if each customer needs their own version of Drupal, then you must go with the option where each customer has their own code-base and database. This might be the case when security updates can't simply be applied to all customers at once. Maybe your customers want to schedule downtime and regression testing for any update to the system.

As another example, if each customer must have control over the themes available to its users, then you have no choice but to give each customer their own code and database. Of course, this option is the most complex to deploy and most time consuming to maintain. Fortunately, as we've seen thus far in this book, all of Drupal can be configured at the command line using Drush. It is therefore quite possible to fully automate site creation and updates, even when every customer has their own code and database. In fact, there are tools such as Pantheon Zeus and Aegir that provide really good enterprise-level dashboards and automation around deploying, updating, maintaining, backing up, cloning, renaming, and dropping large networks of Drupal sites. These tools can even manage Drupal sites across multiple servers and server clusters.

Figure 10-1 shows a screenshot of the Create Site screen in Aegir (as seen on the Aegir project site's user manual, http://community.aegirproject.org/using).

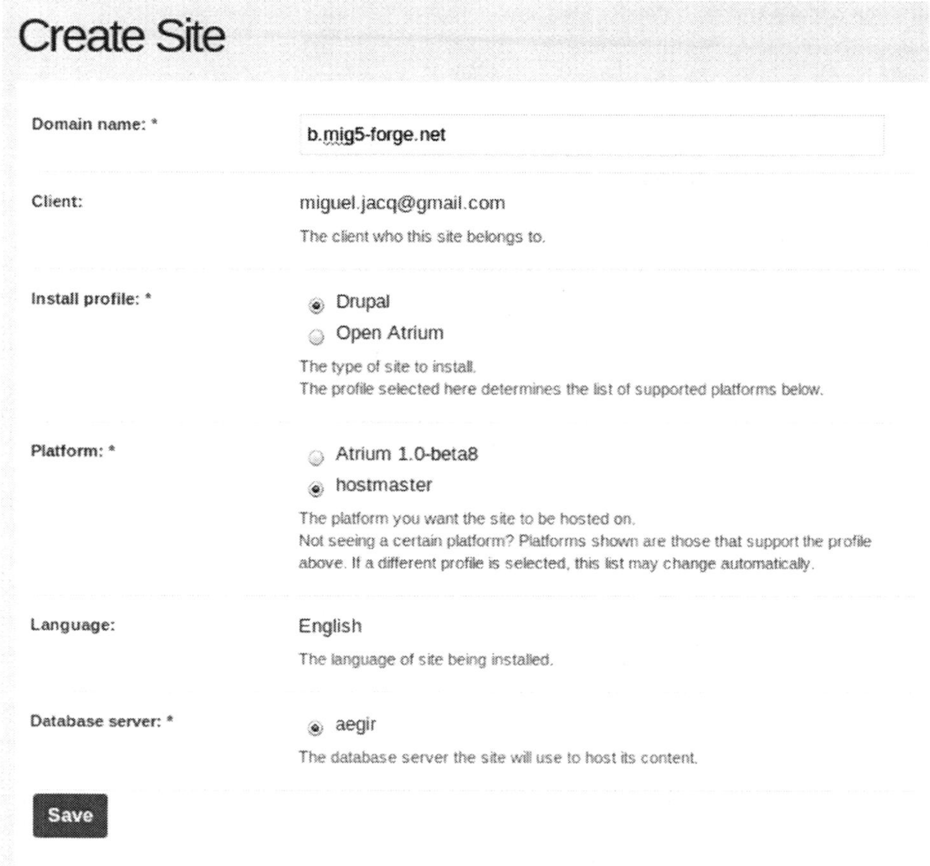

Create Site

Domain name: *

b.mig5-forge.net

Client:

miguel.jacq@gmail.com

The client who this site belongs to.

Install profile: *

◉ Drupal
○ Open Atrium

The type of site to install.
The profile selected here determines the list of supported platforms below.

Platform: *

○ Atrium 1.0-beta8
◉ hostmaster

The platform you want the site to be hosted on.
Not seeing a certain platform? Platforms shown are those that support the profile
above. If a different profile is selected, this list may change automatically.

Language:

English

The language of site being installed.

Database server: *

◉ aegir

The database server the site will use to host its content.

[Save]

Figure 10-1. *Aegir Create Site page*

A word of caution with this approach: even though each site can technically have its own version of Drupal core and modules installed, it is much simpler and less risky to, as much as possible, maintain consistency across all the sites. Most teams that implement this approach, of a separate code-base and database for each customer, use a single version control repository from which all sites are created. Not doing so makes it very complicated (and risky) to maintain all of your sites, as they will invariably diverge in their modules and versions.

One of the main benefits of this option is in scalability. Because each customer's code and database can reside on a separate server, or at least have their own web site, PHP process, and database instance, it is trivial to scale out forever. In other words, the size and performance of each site can be controlled completely independently of all other customer sites. This is very important for not only pure performance, but also for reliability, as each site can go up, down, crash, or go offline all on its own.

Separate databases per customer also create a much safer and more secure environment for HIPAA and PCI concerns, as well as backups and moving production data into test environments. For example, if a specific customer has an issue that needs to be replicated in a test or development environment, then only that one customer's database (possibly obfuscated first) need be copied. Backup files are also separated by customer. Dropping a specific customer from the system is as easy as removing that one customer's database—as opposed to archiving and removing complex slices of relational data from a single database.

After we've looked at all three options and their details, pros, and cons, we'll summarize their associated strengths and weaknesses.

Same Code, Separate Databases

The next approach, of using a single code-base but separate database for each customer, provides many of the same benefits of the previous option, but with less complexity and risk in terms of maintaining and updating the system. With this approach, every customer shares the same items listed in the first column of Table 10-2. That is, every customer is running the same physical site code, which means the same version of Drupal, the same available modules, and the same available themes. And it's not just that each customer is using the same versions; the reality is that every customer is running the same exact instance of code—in the same directory on the web server. Thus, every customer's site will be running in the same server and PHP process and memory space, and a crash will take down all customers' sites.

However, because each customer will still have its own database, all of the items in the second column of Table 10-2 will be separated and isolated per customer. This means anything dealing with content, content types, users, enabled modules and themes, and all module configuration will be unique per customer. This approach is similar in concept to systems that utilize a single multi-tenant database, except that instead of relying on a CustomerId field on every table, view, procedure, query, data access class, and domain class, we partition customer data by way of different databases. In short, everything that defines the web application itselfthat is, the first column in Table 10-2 is shared across all sites. But everything that needs to be defined unique for each customer—that is, the second column of Table 10-2—are kept separate.

Just remember that with this option, all customers will be upgraded and updated at once. Sometimes this is desirable, sometimes it's not.

In terms of security, one big thing to consider is PHP code execution. Because Drupal can be configured to allow storage and execution of arbitrary blocks of PHP code (by administrators), and that code would have access to not just one site but potentially all sites, administrators in all sites with this approach, from different customers, need to share a mutual trust. Or, if this trust doesn't, can't, or shouldn't exist, then the first option of separate code-bases might be more appropriate.

For guidance on configuring a multi-site Drupal system, you can follow the instructions on the multi site Drupal documentation page at https://drupal.org/documentation/install/multi-site. One key aspect of this configuration is that you use subfolders of the site's folder to create code that is specific to each customer's site. Everything else is inherited from the main code folders. So for a clean multi-site install, where all customer sites share all code and all modules, but each has its own database, you only need to have a settings.php file in the site's subfolder.

So far we've been using the /sites/all folder for modules and such. But with the multi-site approach, each domain or subdomain gets its own folder under the sites folder for any overrides or additional themes or modules. The only file absolutely needed is the settings.php file, which contains the database connection information. Table 10-3 shows some examples.

Table 10-3. *Mapping of Sites to Physical Folders*

Domain / URL / port	Site folder / files
www.example.com	sites/example.com sites/example.com/settings.php sites/example.com/modules/ sites/example.com/themes/
bob.example.com	sites/bob.example.com sites/bob.example.com/settings.php sites/bob.example.com/modules/ sites/bob.example.com/themes/
kbr.example.com:3000	sites/3000.kbr.example.com sites/3000.kbr.example.com/settings.php sites/3000.kbr.example.com/modules/ sites/3000.kbr.example.com/themes/

Like the warning in the previous section, we strongly recommend that even though Drupal supports it, you try to avoid configuring different modules and themes for each customer's site. When a single PHP site is serving sites that are configured differently, you can quickly get into trouble with updates and security patches needing to be applied. Especially given that updates to one module may require updates to another, and those modules that need to be updated may impact other customers. As such, try as much as possible to only have a settings.php file in the site's subfolder.

Again, this option can be thought of as being nearly identical to multi-tenant systems that use a single database and a customer-related partitioning key. Only with Drupal, each customer has a separate physical database.

Same Code, Same Database

In our final option, we keep things very simple and use a single code-base and single database. In this approach, you essentially acknowledge that neither the items in the first column of Table 10-2, nor the items in the second column, need to be separate or unique per customer. This option simply uses menus, folders, and permissions to control access to content. But essentially all customer sites share their data. This option works well when each customer needs only to post a page or two, such as those found on university faculty pages or department subsites on a corporate intranet.

There are a couple modules that can help provide basic content isolation when implementing this multi-customer option. The first is called Domain Access. It provides functionality that determines a user's access to content based on the URL or domain name currently being browsed. For example, users coming in through siteA.example.com can be granted access to different content than those coming in through siteB.example.com.

The second module, called Organic Groups, provides the functionality common in sites like Google Groups or Drupal Groups. That is, each group has a home page, and can grant access to subscription requests, and maintain the group's users. Then posts to blogs and articles made within a group are kept within that group's site.

Just remember that even with these modules, all of their data is stored together in a single database.

Summary of Multi-Customer Options

Table 10-4 illustrates the primary advantages, disadvantages, and best scenarios for each of the three multi-customer options we've discussed.

Table 10-4. *Summary of Three Multi-Customer Options*

Option	Advantages	Disadvantages	Scenarios
Single code, single database	Simple to configure and maintain One database to back up and keep running	No real isolation of data between customers No isolation of sites (for example, performance, crashes) Must scale up by buying bigger database hardware All sites must be backed up and restored at once; cannot restore individual customers	Groups and forums All sites are essentially identical, with only some basic pages or posts being different Corporate intranet subsites Charity organization bio pages
Single code, separate databases	Customer data completely isolated; great for regulatory restrictions and testing and troubleshooting specific customer issues Can scale out, since each customer has its own database and potentially database server Ability to independently restore customer database backups	Potential security risk with PHP code All customer sites running in single PHP process; all customer sites affected by issues Must upgrade and apply updates to all customer sites at once	Hosting scenarios such as Wordpress or Drupal Gardense Commerce platforms, where each customer must have separate products, catalogs, and users Corporate customers that need separate access to database backups for testing purposes
Separate code, separate databases	Supports running separate sites on separate servers Each site can potentially be updated/upgraded separately Each customer site runs in separate server/PHP process	Complexity in configuring and managing all instances If and when site code diverges, versions and dependencies must be carefully managed to avoid problems	Premier or top-tier customers needing complete isolation

In most enterprise environments that need to support multiple customers, where multi-tenant databases are typically used, we recommend giving the single-code-separate-database option a serious try. We believe this is a great option, that in many ways scales and meets the typical multi-tenant needs much better than the typical single multi-tenant database.

Development

Now that you have your implementation strategy figured out, it's time to get started with the development of your web application. But before you run into the fun part, make sure you're not setting yourself up for failure. This section contains a few best practices you should consider each time you start a project's implementation, or even once and for all to apply to all of your projects.

Development Environment

In order to get started with development work, or even simple tests or administrative tasks locally, your developers will need a properly configured AMP stack, as explained in Chapter 3.

A nice way to do this is to make a VM and configure it exactly the way you want it for Drupal development (AMP stack, PHP settings, version control, and so forth), then save the VM image and make it available to all your developers and designers.

All they will have to do to get started is install a VM software and mount the image. Using shared folders, they will still be able to edit the project's files from their host OS using their editor of choice, as well as access the site using their host OS browser. For example, Oracle's free VirtualBox software includes the Shared Folders feature, which allows a guest VM to create a folder on the host computer as if it existed directly in the VM. This allows Apache on your VM to serve up files from a shared folder that can be edited and managed from the host machine. In this way, the host computer is configured with all necessary development and designer tools, but runtime configuration and execution is reserved for an isolated VM.

Version Control

If your Drupal site's code is not under version control, it doesn't exist! There is no way around it, you need to decide on a version control solution of choice (we recommend Git) and use it from the very beginning. We found it better to have your whole code base under a single repository. This includes Drupal core, added modules and themes, custom modules and themes, feature sets, installation profiles, and import reference and test data files. We even like to add Drush and all our automation scripts to the repository.

The reason why we prefer to have everything under one single repository, when you could find it useful to get the core and modules from the drupal.org repos directly or using a script to get all the pieces with Drush, is so that we can easily check the status of this one project on testing and prod environment to see if anything has been changed. The general rule that no one should make a change directly on production code doesn't mean no one does. So having even your production server's Drupal site linked with a version control repository means you can not only easily pull the latest code, but can also use all of the power of a version control tool to track changes being made.

The same level of control could be obtained by using Git submodule ability, which allows you to control external projects (like modules) from your main project without them being part of its repository. This gets a bit complicated when releasing though, as you need to keep a list of versions for those submodules to know which one of them (if any) is being updated, and to which version.

Bottom line: we recommend keeping it simple and just put the entire site—Drupal core, all modules, themes, and so forth—into a single repository that you use to deploy to different servers.

Extensibility and Updates

Drupal's approach to extensibility is less compromising than most other CMSs and code frameworks, and you should likewise adjust your development style to be uncompromising. When people need a new feature in Drupal, they don't hack it into the code and release a new core; they make a module for it that can easily be added to a site to provide said feature.

This looks like a basic best practice, but let's take this a bit further. When a feature provided by a module is not working exactly the way you expect, don't change the module to fit your needs; make a different module that will depend on the first one and add the feature you need. When a theme is almost the way you want it to look, don't make a few CSS tweaks in the theme directly. Instead, create a sub-theme and make your changes there.

There is a good reason why you should do this instead of modifying the code of the module itself or the core: extensibility and updates! If you need a new feature implemented, and there is a module for it, you want to be able to add the module to your site and have it work the way it is expected to. But if you've made changes to the core or to a module that this new module depends on, it might not work. If there is a security update to a module you have modified, your changes will be lost when you replace it with the newer module. Or, if using version control, you will have to merge your changes with the ones of the newer version; and good luck with that!

So as a rule of thumb, if you are writing code for a Drupal site that is not for a custom module you created or a module your are a maintainer of, you are probably doing something wrong. And if you end up finding a good reason to make a change on a module itself (obvious bug, security issue), you should make sure to let the maintainers know about it. If you're right, those changes will be implemented and released shortly, and your temporary changes can be overridden. This is, of course, the beauty of open source software.

Feature Sets

As much as possible, we like to leverage feature sets via the Features module. They allow you to put many things that otherwise have to live in the database into the code, which makes it very easy to release seamlessly.

For instance, if you need to add a new content type and a couple more views to your site, but want to make sure you can test it before you do it, you could just do it on your QA server first, then do it on prod, which is twice the work and hardly a best practice. Instead, make a feature set for those changes from a development environment, then follow the normal release process, using Drush to migrate the exported feature set(s) to all target environments—including production. And since the Features module exports feature sets as code (in the modules folder), you can easily push all feature sets into the site's repository—and subsequently pull them down onto test and production servers.

Database

One of the reasons why you want to use Drupal for application development is that you don't have to deal with the database anymore. That is, the details of physical database design are no longer a concern. You still have a database on your server, but it's Drupal's and Drupal manages it. If you find yourself running DB queries on your server to modify some setting or add/remove some kind of content, hold it right there! There's certainly a better way to do it. It could be a feature set, or a Drush command, but it is quite unlikely that you would ever do it best by changing database data directly.

Continuous Integration

You may have found yourselves in the past with a project that just can't seem to move past QA because of the number of participants and people breaking other people's work, and more generally because you wait for a "wave" of testing to happen on QA instead of continuously testing the code every time a commit is made.

With a platform of choice like Drupal, it is quite easy to configure a continuous integration (CI) tool, such as Jenkins, to monitor your every change in all of your projects. It would take a full book to go through the whole benefit of using a CI tool like Jenkins, or to go through the full extent of what Jenkins can do for you. We'll simply list the steps you'll have to follow for a simple integration of your Drupal project with Jenkins.

1. Install Jenkins `https://wiki.jenkins-ci.org/display/JENKINS/Installing+Jenkins`

2. At the end of the install process, the documentation will tell you what port to go to (most likely 8080) to access the web interface. From the Jenkins web GUI, go to Manage Jenkins then Manage Plugins, and install the Jenkins GIT Plugin if you use git. Jenkins will support SVN and CVS.

3. Back to the dashboard, select New Job to get started with creating a job for your project. A job is a set of automated tasks managed by Jenkins that determine if your project is doing well. It usually consists of getting the latest changes from your project, then running a series of scripts and commands, and reporting the result to you. Jobs can be triggered when you make a change to the project's code or on a schedule.

4. Fill in the repository address, as shown on Figure 10-2. Jenkins will complain immediately if it can't access it. Make sure your repo knows Jenkins' ssh authentication keys.

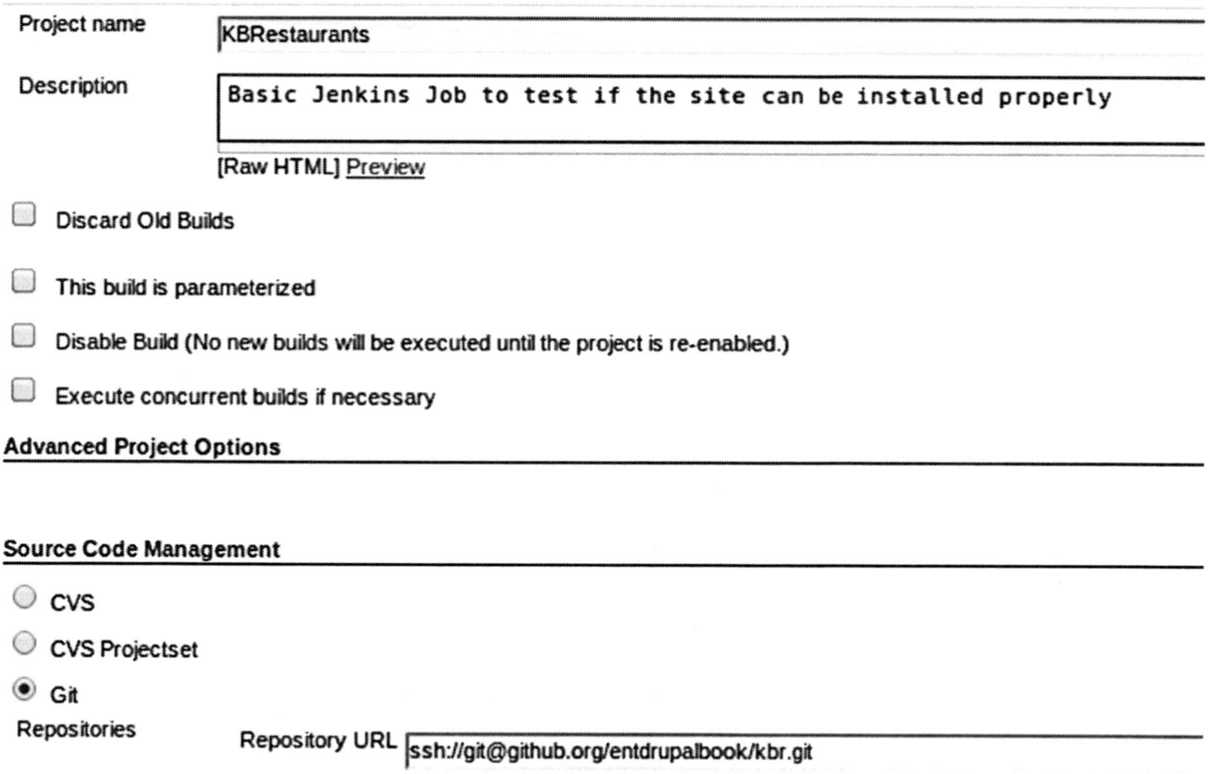

Project name   KBRestaurants

Description   `Basic Jenkins Job to test if the site can be installed properly`

[Raw HTML] Preview

☐ Discard Old Builds

☐ This build is parameterized

☐ Disable Build (No new builds will be executed until the project is re-enabled.)

☐ Execute concurrent builds if necessary

Advanced Project Options

Source Code Management

○ CVS

○ CVS Projectset

◉ Git

Repositories   Repository URL   `ssh://git@github.org/entdrupalbook/kbr.git`

Figure 10-2. New Jenkins job parameters

5.   This is the fun part. Now you can tell Jenkins what to do with the code it grabbed. In our case, because we like to include site install scripts in our distributions, we'll simply run the site install script, after copying and renaming its config file, and see if it completes successfully, as shown on Figure 10-3.

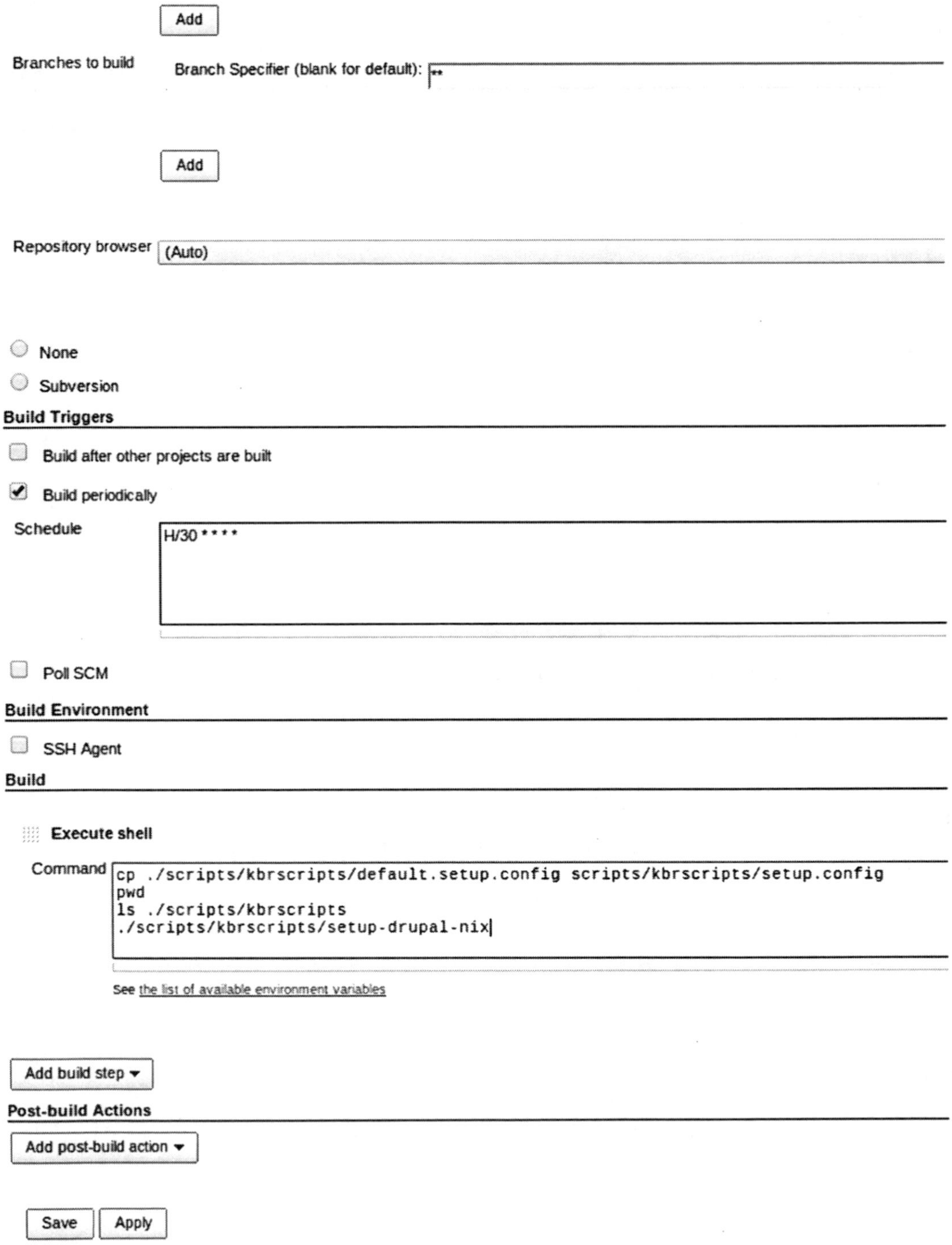

Add

Branches to build   Branch Specifier (blank for default): **

Add

Repository browser   (Auto)

○ None
○ Subversion

Build Triggers

☐ Build after other projects are built

☑ Build periodically

Schedule

```
H/30 * * * *
```

☐ Poll SCM

Build Environment

☐ SSH Agent

Build

Execute shell

Command
```
cp ./scripts/kbrscripts/default.setup.config scripts/kbrscripts/setup.config
pwd
ls ./scripts/kbrscripts
./scripts/kbrscripts/setup-drupal-nix
```

See the list of available environment variables

Add build step ▼

Post-build Actions

Add post-build action ▼

Save   Apply

Figure 10-3. *New Jenkins job actions*

6. Now that your job is created, you can decide when it runs. If your Jenkins interface is accessible from your repository server, you can configure commit/push hooks from your repo. For instance, in github: `https://help.github.com/articles/post-receive-hooks`. If not, you can just schedule Jenkins to repeat the job regularly using a cron-like syntax, as shown on Figure 10-3, for instance, to run every half-hour.

Note that you can also run a job manually. When it runs, it will either pass or fail, and can report those through several means. It has a dashboard on which you can observe how well your application is doing and when it breaks, as shown on Figure 10-4. Jenkins also provides RSS feeds with build results and build errors only. You can also have Jenkins send you an email when a build succeeds and/or fails. So if you're using email notifications and commit hooks, Jenkins can test the project every time a commit is made, and send an email if the commit broke something (install script, tests, anything you can script).

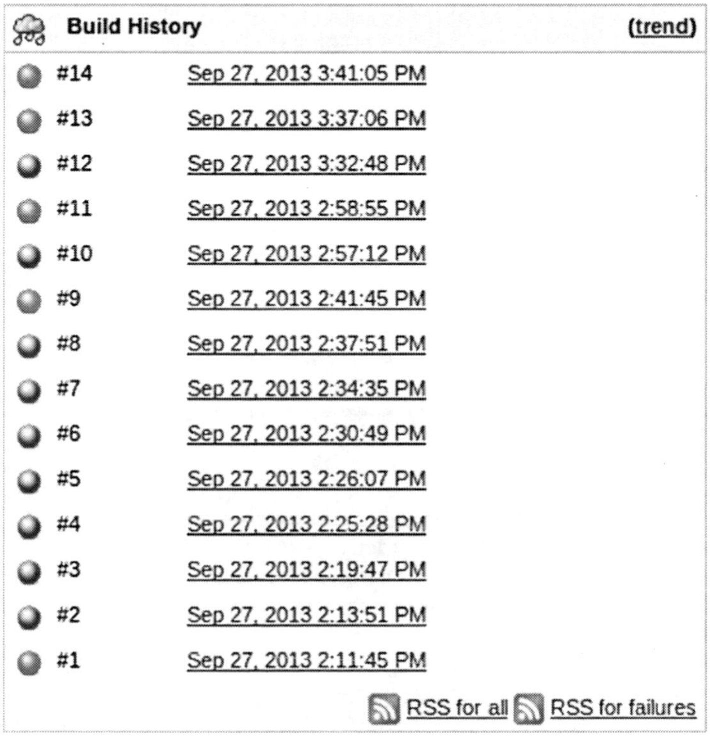

Build History		(trend)
● #14	Sep 27, 2013 3:41:05 PM	
● #13	Sep 27, 2013 3:37:06 PM	
● #12	Sep 27, 2013 3:32:48 PM	
● #11	Sep 27, 2013 2:58:55 PM	
● #10	Sep 27, 2013 2:57:12 PM	
● #9	Sep 27, 2013 2:41:45 PM	
● #8	Sep 27, 2013 2:37:51 PM	
● #7	Sep 27, 2013 2:34:35 PM	
● #6	Sep 27, 2013 2:30:49 PM	
● #5	Sep 27, 2013 2:26:07 PM	
● #4	Sep 27, 2013 2:25:28 PM	
● #3	Sep 27, 2013 2:19:47 PM	
● #2	Sep 27, 2013 2:13:51 PM	
● #1	Sep 27, 2013 2:11:45 PM	
	RSS for all ⓝ RSS for failures	

Figure 10-4. Jenkins job build history

Releases

In this section, we're going to explore best practices as they relate to the integration and deployment process with a Drupal-based web application. Such a release isn't a whole lot different from deploying any other application, in that most web applications are comprised of at least the following:

- HTML, CSS, JavaScript code
- Server-side interpreted code
- Server-side compiled binaries

- Database schema

- Database data

- Database code

- Configuration data

- Web server configuration (e.g. Apache, IIS)

- Permissions

And so we need to make sure all items in this list are packaged and deployed in a way that supports downloads and automation. Your applications, even when built on top of Drupal, must include the ability to quickly and easily deploy into nearly any test or production environment. As has been briefly discussed earlier in this book, there are various modules and features available for Drupal that greatly simplify and support rapid and continuous integration and deployment.

CONTINUOUS DELIVERY

Throughout this chapter on releases and best practices, we will be covering various concepts and techniques associated with the relatively recent emergence of Continuous Delivery. Loosely defined, Continuous Delivery describes the idea of being able to deploy into a test or production environment at any time. Not that we actually DO deploy continuously, but we allow the potential to deploy at any moment to be a governing force throughout the practice of software development. This includes the design process, application architecture, the way we write and test code, the way we package and release versions of our software, and the tools we use to manage the entire effort. For more information, we encourage you to read "Continuous Delivery: Reliable Software Releases through Build, Test, and Deployment Automation" by Jez Humble and David Farley (Addison-Wesley Professional, 2010).

What's in a Release?

The first thing we want to define is the release itself. That is, exactly what is included in a release of a Drupal-based web application? To start, we need all of the PHP code. This includes the Drupal code, all modules, and theme files. For those of you with a background in .NET or Java applications, you would typically have to compile your code into binary executables before deploying to a server. However, with a PHP application like Drupal, all we need is the codethat is, there's nothing to compile. Technically speaking, the code you need to deploy is the exact same code you store in your version control repository. You can, of course, zip the files before releasing them, but that's not required. In fact, many deployments are configured by simply using Git or Subversion to check out or pull the code directly from a version control system onto the server. And as described in the Version Control section of this chapter, this approach has the further benefit of providing full change tracking for the entire site's directory tree.

Beyond PHP files, the site's code also includes associated files for CSS, themes, JavaScript files and libraries, images, fonts, and any other file needed to support the site's look and feel.

Next, we want to include various pieces of configuration for the site. This includes things like:

- Blocks

- Content types (and their fields)

- Enabling all dependent modules

- Menus and menu links

- Permissions and roles

- Rules

- Field validators
- Services
- Views

Fortunately, all of these can be packaged up using the Features module. You simply need to create a new Feature (a.k.a. Feature Set) that includes these particular items. The mechanics of doing so were covered to some degree in Chapter 3. Figure 10-5 shows what the Features screen might look like when configured for packaging these various items within the K & B Restaurants site.

▶ CONTENT TYPES (node)

☑ Menu ☑ Menu Item ☑ Restaurant Branch ☑ Special

▶ DEPENDENCIES (dependencies)

☑ Date ☑ Entity Reference ☑ Features ☑ Image ☑ Number ☑ Options ☑ Services ☑ Service
☑ Views Rules

▶ FIELD BASES (field_base)

☑ body ☑ field_picture ☑ field_price ☑ field_appetizers ☑ field_deserts ☑ field_drinks ☑ field_e
☑ field_menu ☑ field_menu_items ☑ field_owner ☑ field_restaurants ☑ field_start_date ☑ field_sala

▶ FIELD INSTANCES (field_instance)

☑ node-menu_item-body ☑ node-menu_item-field_picture ☑ node-menu_item-field_price ☑ node-menu-body
☑ node-menu-field_appetizers ☑ node-menu-field_deserts ☑ node-menu-field_drinks ☑ node-menu-field_en
☑ node-menu-field_salads ☑ node-restaurant_branch-body ☑ node-restaurant_branch-field_hours
☑ node-restaurant_branch-field_menu ☑ node-restaurant_branch-field_owner ☑ node-special-body ☑ node-s
☑ node-special-field_restaurants ☑ node-special-field_start_date

▶ FIELD VALIDATION (field_validation_rule)

▶ MENU LINKS (menu_links)

▶ MENUS (menu_custom)

▶ PERMISSIONS (user_permission)

▶ ROLES (user_role)

▶ RULES CONFIGURATION (rules_config)

▼ SERVICES (services_endpoint)

☑ rest_api

▶ TAXONOMY (taxonomy)

▶ TEXT FORMATS (filter)

▼ VIEWS (views_view)

☑ All Menu Items (all_menu_items) ☑ Menus (menus) ☑ Value Menu Items (value_menu_items)

Figure 10-5. Feature set for Drupal site configuration items

Since creating a feature set results (by default) in a new module in the /sites/all/modules folder, you can add all exported feature files/folders to the version control repository alongside the rest of the site's code. In other words, generating the feature itself simply creates some PHP and related code in the site's modules folder. So not only does the feature's content get full change and version tracking, it also means these items (that is, content types, rules, views, and so forth) are included with the rest of the site's code when either pulled directly from source control or when distributed as a ZIP file. That's because the Features module works by exporting database content as PHP module code. Of course, having content types and views and such stored as PHP files is all part of the Drupal architecture—these items don't have to only reside in the site's database.

Next, we want to export and include reference or default data needed by the site. This might include status codes, drop-down options, states or cities, and the like. We don't really have any data of this type in the K&B Restaurants site. But you can use the node_export module, combined with its integration with the Features module, to export all required content items. You may also choose to use the node_export module separate from the Features module, as discussed in Chapter 6. That is, you can selectively export data into text files, and then use a simple Drush command to import those files into a target Drupal instance during deployment.

You can even use the Feeds module to bulk import data, which works particularly well for externally sourced data such as a spreadsheet or XML file of all cities and states in the country. The main point here being that the data you include in your Drupal site's deployment might not all be based on site content. Some might be content items, and some might not. But between the Features, Feeds, and node_export modules, you have plenty of options for including site data in your releases.

The last thing we want to include in our release package is a collection of scripts and README-type files that facilitate easy and automated install and configuration of the site. The README (that is, a simple Installation Guide text file) should take a user from clean machine all the way to a fully functional site. These instructions should include system prerequisites, accounts and passwords needed for the install script and/or web site, and the exact script(s) to execute to fully set up a new site, or to update an existing site.

Let's roll up our sleeves now and look at the details of a basic Drupal install script. Please note that the script content covered in the following sections are included in the Github repository that accompanies this book.

Note that these particular scripts were written on Linux Ubuntu.

Anatomy of an Install Script

In this section, we're going to create a first-time install script for creating our Drupal site database. In the next section, we will build a script that sets various options on the new site, including enabling feature sets.

Let's start our install script with some simple usage content:

```
usage()
{
cat << EOF
Usage: $0 [options]

Options:
  -?    Show this message
  -h host_name      Connect to the MySQL server on the given host.
                    Default is "localhost".
  -P port_num       The TCP/IP port number to use for the connection.
                    Default is the default MySQL port.
  -D db_name        The database to use for the Drupal installation.
  -u user_name      The MySQL user name for the Drupal installation.
  -p password       The password for the Drupal installation user.
  -n site_name      The name of the Drupal site.
  -a admin_user     The name of the Drupal admin user account.
  -A admin_pass     The password for the Drupal admin user.
```

```
 -r db_root        The root user for the MySQL server.
                   Default is "root".
 -R db_root_pass   The password for the MySQL root user.
EOF
}
```

Not much explanation needed here, so let's move on to the next section, that of defaulting a couple of the variables:

```
mysql_host="localhost"
mysql_port="3306"
mysql_root="root"
```

Next, we'll use the power of shell scripting to capture some named arguments from the command line:

```
while getopts "?h:P:D:u:p:n:a:A:r:R:" OPTION
do
    case $OPTION in
        ?)
            usage
            exit 1 ;;
        h)
            mysql_host=$OPTARG ;;
        P)
            mysql_port=$OPTARG  ;;
        D)
            app_database=$OPTARG  ;;
        u)
            app_username=$OPTARG  ;;
        p)
            app_password=$OPTARG  ;;
        n)
            site_name=$OPTARG  ;;
        a)
            site_admin=$OPTARG  ;;
        A)
            site_admin_password=$OPTARG  ;;
        r)
            mysql_root=$OPTARG  ;;
        R)
            mysql_root_password=$OPTARG ;;
    esac
done
```

Accepting arguments on the command line will allow us to more easily automate execution of the script, passing in parameters from an automation or build tool (that is, Jenkins).

Next, we will need to prompt the user for any arguments not already set, starting with a quick confirmation that the user intends to drop and recreate an existing database.

```
read -r -p "Create/recreate the database for this Drupal instance? [Y/n]: " OK
if [ "$OK" ] && [ "$OK" != "y" ] && [ "$OK" != "Y" ]; then exit; fi

if [ -z "$app_database" ];        then read -r -p "Drupal instance database: " app_database; fi
if [ -z "$app_username" ];        then read -r -p "Drupal DB username: " app_username; fi
if [ -z "$app_password" ];        then read -s -r -p "Drupal DB password: " app_password; echo; fi
if [ -z "$site_name" ];           then read -r -p "Drupal site name: " site_name; fi
if [ -z "$site_admin" ];          then read -r -p "Drupal admin username: " site_admin; fi
if [ -z "$site_admin_password" ]; then read -s -r -p "Drupal admin password: " site_admin_password;
echo; fi
if [ -z "$mysql_root_password" ]; then read -s -r -p "MySQL root password: " mysql_root_password;
echo; fi
```

Note that the password arguments include the -s option, which ensures that the entered value isn't echoed back to the user—and visible to other people that might be looking at the screen.

Finally, we create the MySQL HOST variable, and execute the Drush site-install command:

```
HOST="$HOST:$mysql_port"; fi
php -d sendmail_path=`which true` `which drush` si --site-name="$site_name" --db-url="mysql://$app_
username:$app_password@$HOST/$app_database" --account-name="$site_admin" --account-pass="$site_
admin_password" --clean-url=0 --db-su=$mysql_root --db-su-pw=$mysql_root_password -y \
    || exit 1;
```

The reason we use PHP to execute the command, instead of running Drush directly, is because, by default, the site-install command will fail if the sendmail utility isn't able to send an email from the new Drupal install. However, in most cases, we want to simply configure email parameters later on. Wrapping the Drush site-install command as we did here allows us to fake out Drush, making it think it using sendmail to send an email, when in reality it isn't doing anything at all.

Remember that this script will need to be executed from the root of the Drupal site. Forgetting to do so will result in an error thrown by Drush that includes the message "A Drupal installation directory could not be found."

The Configuration Script

Now it's time to write the script that will configure the site—that is, everything beyond the new database created by the Drush site-install command. Some things we want to configure may include:

- Create custom roles

- Enable feature set(s)

- Set the site's email address

- Import reference and other default data

- Create alternate home page

- Delete built-in fields (for example, Image, Tags) from content types

- Disable the admin overlay

To start our configuration script, let's add a new role: called "Restaurant Manager." In our K&B Restaurants site, this might be used to define permissions specific to managers.

```
drush user-add-role "Restaurant Managers" "restaurantmanagers" -y
```

Next, let's enable a pair of feature sets:

```
drush en kb_default_configuration -y
drush en kbr_default_data -y
```

Remember that the feature sets themselves are simply modules within the /sites/all/modules directory. So we can enable them the exact same way we would enable any module. Nice, eh?!?! And because the first feature set specifies dependent modules, then all other modules, such as views, rules, services, will be enabled with that one command.

Now let's set the site's front page to a Basic Page content item with a path alias "home":

```
drush vset site_frontpage "home" -y
```

You can use the Drush vset command to set nearly any configuration value in the system. To see all of the variables available, you can run the following command:

```
drush vget
```

This will return all variables and their current values. With any variable you see, you can use the Drush vset command to alter the value.

Lastly, let's disable the admin overlay and also delete the Tags field from the Article content type. While this isn't necessarily required for the K&B Restaurants site, you can use something similar in other sites you may build.

```
drush dis overlay -y
drush field-delete field_tags --bundle=article
```

At this point, you have the script content required to make a new Drupal site database and configuration values. To summarize, a new server would execute the following steps to create a new site:

1. Get the site code (directly from the version control repository or from a ZIP file)

2. Run the install script, passing in associated parameter values

3. Run the configuration script

All of the above is, as you've no doubt noticed, capable of being run fully from yet another script, automation tool, or build and deployment platform. This is essential for maintaining a software development environment that centers on continuous delivery.

Be sure to check out the K&B Restaurants code found in the Github repository associated with this book. It contains fully detailed and tested versions of the script content discussed in these last two sections.

Backup, Restore

Remember our good friend Drush? Well here is yet another use for it: backing up your site, and restoring the full site (code and data) from one of those backups. Enter the command drush archive-dump, and Drush will automatically back up all of your site's code and database and compress it into a single file written onto your server's file system.

If you wish to restore the site to how it was when this archive was made, just use the command drush archive-restore archive-file.tar.gz and it will restore the site automatically for you—including all code and then entire database.

This will come in handy on several occasions. For instance, it will enable you to keep a series of archive files that you can use to revert your site to pretty much any time in the past, as we will describe in the business continuity, archiving section. The other obvious use of this is to secure the site's state before performing an update. You never know what could happen during an update, but you know for sure that you shouldn't just expect it to go smoothly.

Here's our strategy before performing any update or upgrade on the production server. This includes your own releases, and also core and module security updates and full version upgrades.

1. Log in to the live site and put it in maintenance mode from the Configuration admin tab, Maintenance mode link. There are ways to release a Drupal site while keeping it up and running, but in case anything happens and you have to revert the release, user actions that have happened during the release would be lost without the users having any way to know about it. For instance, someone created an account while you were performing the release and you had an issue with the release so you reverted to the site's state before the release; this user account will be lost and the user will try to log in or restore his password in vain. Putting the site in maintenance mode will prevent such user interactions from happening, effectively blocking the site for the time of the release. You can also use the command `drush vset --exact maintenance_mode 0`.

2. Back up the site's state. It is more than a good idea, it's the law. You're going to change things on the production site; you must be able to revert those changes in case they break something. Yes, they were already released successfully on the QA server and maybe on staging or pre-prod, so you have sufficient reason to assume that it will work flawlessly. But please don't assume; back up! You can just create a backup on the server's file system, as it is different from your business continuity archiving strategy.

3. Run a status of the code against your version control solution. There should be no code change between your version on prod and the same version on your repository. So for instance if your prod version is 2.3.1 and you are releasing 2.3.4, you want to make sure that your prod version has not been changed from 2.3.1. If something was changed directly on production and not on the repository, it means that the changes you are about to release, made by your developers to the code, have been made independently from those changes made directly on prod. If that's the case, you will have to interrupt the release and proceed with the following steps:

   a. Document the changes to the code that have been made directly on prod.

   b. You're done with the production server, you can put your site out of maintenance mode. No need to restore your backup since no changes were made for this release.

   c. On your dev environment, add those changes to the development branch (or if the dev branch is not quite ready for a new release, update the branch next in line for a release and make sure those changes will find their way into the dev branch) and test them.

   d. Those changes will have to go the full release process again (QA, pre-prod, whatever you have there).

   e. Find out who made those changes and make them understand the benefits of proper version control.

4. If your working copy on the server is clean, you are ready to update the code to your release version using your version control solution. There should be no conflicts since you passed step 3.

5. Run `drush updatedb`, or go to your site and browse to `/update.php` to run the necessary database updates.

6. Execute post-release actions. Ideally, those would be scripted by the developers under a unique post-release file, and the release manager would just have to do $ ./post-release.sh (for a Linux-based system) to run those steps, that could be enabling a new module and applying a feature set, for instance.

7. Go on the site and disable the maintenance mode. Or use the command drush vset --exact maintenance_mode 0

You can also use this whole process for QA, staging, and pre-prod releases, and automated fully under one script that takes the target version to be released as an argument and does the following (to be adapted to your os and language of choice):

- drush command to put the site in maintenance mode

- drush command to back up the site to a given tarball location

- version control command to check if the current version is unchanged

  - if not, communicate the error (by sending an email about it, for instance) and exit the script

- execute pre-release script, which will:

  - check the current version from a version file and based on it, decide if there are actions to execute

  - execute the pre-release actions

- version control command to update the code to the version passed as an argument

- drush command to update the db

- execute post-release script, which will:

  - check if there are actions to execute based on the code version passed as an argument

  - execute the post-release actions

- drush command to turn off maintenance mode

Ideally, all of this would be automated with Jenkins. In that way, a simple button click from a specific build would handle the entire deployment of that build.

Browser Testing

Running unit tests automatically after each commit is a good practice, but the pinnacle of automated testing for web applications is browser testing, where you run automated tests on the site as it will display to its audience: the browser. Of course, if you plan on using Drupal solely as a REST service for a mobile application, browser testing will hardly be relevant. For the rest however, it will be of great service.

You can use a web browser automation tool, such as Selenium, to create and run browser tests automatically, after each release or even after each commit. Using the same platform will allow you to polish your smoke tests using a tool like Selenium to run a series of tasks your Drupal distribution is expected to be able to do: creating accounts, verifying their permissions, creating content, removing content, running imports and feature sets, and so forth.

This will allow you to also cut testing times by having your QA people focus on the actual new features you're implementing rather than wasting time in running smoke tests over and over after every release to see if no major feature has been broken. Over the years, we've come to realize that a major part of a good test engineer's job is writing code. The main difference being that they aren't writing code to create or fix features; they are writing code to break features.

Maintenance

Web applications need love! From being kept up-to-date to scheduling some maintenance or reporting jobs, they will use some maintenance scripting.

Cron (Batch) Jobs

Most web applications have periods of higher and lower activity, on a daily basis. We want to use a job scheduler, such as Cron, to schedule automated tasks during the downtime, typically at what corresponds to night time for your target audience.

Drupal has a feature called "Cron job" that will run a set of automated tasks, such as indexing the content of your site for searching, checking for changes in external data sources and use feeds to import them if any, contacting external services you have configured to let them know of changes in the site, and so forth. Information about Drupal's Cron job can be found at https://drupal.org/node/23714. Note that it isn't a "real" cron job triggered by your server at a given time; it is triggered when a user visits the site, if a certain amount of time has elapsed since the last time it got triggered. To make Drupal's cron an actual cron job, you can edit the crontab and add a call to the cron.php file, which will make your server's cron trigger Drupal's cron tasks. For instance, to trigger it every day at midnight:

```
crontab -e
0 0 * * *  /usr/bin/lynx -source http://www.yoursite.com/cron.php
```

Business Continuity

After your site is up and running and you have successfully delivered, your job is still not over. A few simple scripts and cron jobs can be set up to make sure complete disaster is avoided in case you lose your site code, data, or even your server(s).

Archive

Using the same Drush commands as in the release section for backup and restore, we can set up automated backups of full snapshots of the site. There are different and more optimized ways to configure backups in order to minimize the amount of data to be stored, but the following is a simple example script (to be adapted to your operating system and language of choice) that will back up your full site's code and data. This script can be called from a cron job or equivalent scheduler on a daily basis (say at 2:00 am).

- find the current day of the week (for example, Monday).

- delete the daily backup from last week (daily_monday_*).

- drush command to back up your data into your archive folder, named after the day of the week (daily_monday_2013_09_02).

- if the day is sunday:

  - find the place of it in the month (say 2d)

  - delete the weekly backup from the 2d sunday of the month (weekly_2_*)

  - copy the backup file and rename it after its place in the month (weekly_2_2013_09_08)

- if the place is 1:
  - find the month
  - delete the monthly backup from the same month (`monthly_sept_*`)
  - copy the backup file and rename it after the month (`monthly_sept_2013_09_01`)
- if the month is january:
  - find the year
  - copy the backup file and rename it after the year (`yearly_2013_01_06`)

This system is a good compromise between frequency of backups and storage required. The further away the backup you need, the less precision you are likely to require in the backup's date. So decreasing the granularity with time will let you keep backups from years ago while having a great precision for recent backups.

For business continuity purposes, you will want to copy the backup to a different server, located somewhere else in the city, state, country, or world, and run the preceding script on that system. So if you ever have something happen to your Drupal server and lose everything, restoring your site to yesterday's version will be as simple as having any other server with an AMP stack running, downloading Drush to it, and restoring your whole site in one command.

Summary

This chapter pretty well concludes our exploration of Drupal as an enterprise development platform. After spending nine chapters being introduced to Drupal, and learning how to install, configure, and maintain a Drupal site, as well as configure security and REST services, we've ended up in this chapter discussing several software development best practices within the context of a Drupal-based application.

The next and final chapter will be a brief presentation of tips and suggestions for navigating the corporate world with open source software, as well as help in selling Drupal as a viable platform both up and down your organization.

■ ■ ■

CHAPTER 11

Selling Drupal in Your Enterprise

You made it! By now, you've no doubt realized that, if nothing else, you need to build some prototype applications with Drupal. Or, maybe you've been completely and totally convinced, and you're already making magic with Drupal. We certainly have.

In this last brief chapter, we want to help you understand and deal with various concerns, fears, and organizational opportunities that will surely arise from trying to insert Drupal—a community-built and supported open source platform—into your company's development process and toolset. People get comfortable with their tools, with their processes, and with everything they know. So trying to upend all that comfort can be difficult. Especially if you're in the camp of .NET-driven software teams that have always shied away from non-Microsoft or open source technology. But don't quit now!

Over the next few pages, we will show you how to discuss:

- Selling Drupal to your engineering folks as an excellent platform of choice (instead of always building apps from scratch)

- Getting sales and execs on board with your newfound vision

- Understanding and planning for open source considerations

The hard work has already been done throughout the last 300+ pages. So let's close out this wonderful time of exploration with some practical organization tips and recommendations.

Navigating Open Source Software in the Enterprise

Before starting this short jog through open source licensing and Drupal, we need to say that we are not lawyers. Please consult your own legal team before making any definitive decisions regarding licensing and Drupal. That said, the licensing FAQ on the Drupal.org site is a great place to start: https://drupal.org/licensing/faq.

For many people, "open source" is still an obscure term that doesn't seem to jive or work well with "enterprise." So let's spend the next minute or two discussing some specific areas of concern.

Generally speaking, open source software, such as Drupal, is not only free to use, but also has its source code publicly and freely available, and can be modified and redistributed at will. This leads to a few misconceptions, the two main ones being that open source software is not usable for applications that require a decent level of security, and that you will have to distribute the applications you build with it—for free—to anyone who requests it.

Let's start with the easy part. Drupal is quite secure. With literally thousands of eyes looking at its code and the code of its modules daily, security vulnerabilities are identified much quicker than most (if not all) proprietary commercial software. Patches are released quickly when the dedicated Drupal security team finds or is made aware of an issue. Some very prestigious entities out there are trusting Drupal for their web sites, including the White House (http://www.whitehouse.gov) and NASA (http://www.nasa.gov).

Now to the second and more contentious issue: licensing. There are different types of open source licences and it is important to read and understand the terms of Drupal's.

Drupal uses the GNU General Public Licence (GPL) version 2: http://www.gnu.org/licenses/old-licenses/gpl-2.0.html. This license requires that if you modify a piece of software that is under GLP license, your final modified product will be under GPL licence as well. This leads to the belief that you will have to give away the source of your Drupal-based site to anyone who requests it. We've heard this line several times and tried to come up with a brief highlight of what you have and don't have to do with regard to Drupal being under GPLv2.

- You do *not* have to give anyone access to the source of a software you are not distributing. This means that if what you produce is a web site, a backend, or any type of platform that runs on your server or any type of server that is not the user's, you do not need to release anything to anyone. Indeed, in this situation, the user is not provided with the site's software but with services the site is producing. You're the one using the code, they just use the site, and they cannot request your source for themselves.

- Copyrighted content remains copyrighted. The logos, brands, trademarks, text, images, styles, and other elements you author for the site are your own and *not* subject to the license. The license applies to the code, not to the content. This also means that whatever custom configuration, views, rules, and content types you create are your (or your company's) intellectual property. So for instance, if you are selling a Drupal site to users for them to run it (which means they can have access to the source code under the terms of the GPL licence), they still can't steal your logo, content, or even your specific content types. Only the code is under GPL—not your configuration of the code.

So, what work would you be required to distribute by the GPLv2? And in what circumstance?

There is only *one* case where you would have to distribute code for a Drupal-based application you made. It requires the following two conditions:

- The code uses the Drupal PHP API and it is built to work "on top of" Drupal—that is, it is a module or a profile;

- AND, a copy of the software is distributed to users or clients (typically for them to run on their own servers).

In this situation, because you distribute a copy of the software to users, they benefit from the licence for themselves and they have the right to use, modify, and redistribute the code for free.

This *doesn't* mean, however, that you are required to provide them with your Drupal database, which holds custom configuration for the site, or with your custom themes or feature sets. Drupal core and public modules being already publicly available, only your custom modules and profiles would become "public" (assuming you didn't give in to the bad practice of directly hacking Drupal's core or modules). As a general rule, those shouldn't contain proprietary attributes to begin with. Instead, they should provide a specific service that is then configured from the site (see where we're going here?) with your proprietary attributes.

For instance, if your custom module is designed to interact with your proprietary platform, don't put interaction specifics in the code. Instead, make a module that enables customizable interaction with a customizable endpoint, and configure it to be your proprietary interaction with your proprietary platform. You will be able (and probably should, if it doesn't exist already) to release this module without worrying about proprietary information leaking, and the community will gain a cool module! In other words, create a bridge between the stuff that is under GPL and the stuff you want to keep to yourself. This is common practice for commercial software built on GPL-based libraries and platforms.

Convincing the Higher-Ups

When it comes to selling the Drupal platform to your superiors and other such decision makers, it is actually quite easy. As we've been exploring throughout this book, using Drupal as an enterprise development platform easily reduces the time and resources required to build web applications and service backends. And clearly, promises of lower costs and greater margins are like music to executive ears!

We suggest pitching Drupal on a small project at first, one that sits well within the "happy path" of web sites and Drupal modules. And offer to provide a quick proof of concept, before committing to Drupal as your platform of choice. We are confident that you will quickly see how much time and money you can save your organization, and will likely move on to building the application for real on Drupal.

You may also need to talk with executives and managers about training for your team. The recommended approach here is to discuss it in terms of ROI: invest some energy and resources into a week or two of training for your developers and designers, and expect a large return on that investment in the way of cutting costs and increasing margins.

Convincing Your Team and Peers

As any seasoned software engineer, architect, manager, or salesman knows, a good idea on its own is just that—a good idea. Sometimes the hardest part is getting other people in your organization to give you the time and resources to try something. Sure, after reading this book, you're at least interested to see whether or not you can indeed cut time and cost, and create a more repeatable development process around web applications and mobile backends. But, at the end of the day, you may need to convince a few others. In this section,n we're going to briefly offer some tips and conversation topics to help you sell the idea of Drupal as an enterprise development platform to others in your organization.

The Developers

Just because you and your executive and sales team(s) are convinced about the benefits of leveraging Drupal to improve margin and competitiveness doesn't mean your development team will be ecstatic about investing time and effort into a new platform. Especially if the platform is not in their language or database of choice. Some developers are happy to learn new languages, platforms, and tools. But others are reluctant to invest time in technologies that they think do not match their career goals. And, honestly, that's healthy. But you have the advantage of helping the developers put another rapid-application-development tool in their tool belt.

"I don't like PHP," you might hear; or "I'm a .NET or Java developer; this is not for me." A great way to get people to take a look at Drupal is to start by telling them that *you don't expect them to become a PHP developer*. Most of the time, there will be no custom code required, and they can spend most of their time being Drupal architects and business process engineers, instead of producing code by the ton. It can be a good way to find support, as many developers like "higher-level" tasks such as defining content types and rules, even if it's not in their language or platform of predilection.

Everybody has a toolbox of software they use for this or that: IDEs, editors, various software clients, and so forth. Why not add a CMS like Drupal to it? Rather than seeing it as a career change, people should see it as a new tool to add to their toolbox, on their resume. And it's quite a sharp tool once you start getting familiar with it and learn how to best leverage its power.

The Sales Side

Salespeople and project managers may not be your ideal technical audience. And they can sometimes commit to customer requests that seem minor, but are actually a tremendous amount of work. With Drupal, however, it is quite easy for non-technical people to understand the range of things Drupal can do out of the box, and understand the difference between features provided by stable modules and features that will require a lot of custom work.

One of the goals of using Drupal as your platform of choice, particularly as opposed to developing from scratch, is to cut costs and do things cheaper and quicker. Your salespeople will not only understand that very well, they will become quite efficient at identifying good use cases and sales opportunities for Drupal (one of those many projects where everything can be done with Drupal core and stable modules, without any custom code, for instance). As we've seen, your sales people and project managers will be researching modules themselves in no time, to see if they exist and what they can do to help their clients. When a potential application's features and capabilities can be researched by a project manager, using only a browser and the `Drupal.org` site, those sales opportunities and the promises they make will take on a new dimension of truth and realism.

This will also allow them to directly invite a Drupal architect (a solutions architect specializing in Drupal solutions) into the RFP process and get back to the prospect the next day, with most of the solution already in mind, if not even a proof of concept already built. When we talk about projects moving fast with Drupal, we mean the whole thing—from the RFP and the proposal, through development, through testing, through deployment, and into maintenance. And you simply can't overestimate the value in a rapid and confident response to sales opportunities.

Use the Wheel, Don't Reinvent It

We can honestly say that writing this book, sharing with you the story of Drupal and its tremendous power as an enterprise development platform, has been an awesome experience. We've personally seen in many projects and various clients how much time and money we're able to save by starting with Drupal—as opposed to writing web applications or services or mobile backends from scratch.

Take the mobile team at the consulting company where we work, for example. A great bunch of hard-core super-talented iOS and Android developers who, on more than one project, have needed a simple RESTful backend to which they could synchronize application data. And more often than not, that same backend needs to provide an easy-to-use administrative interface where site admins can manage users and other resources and objects. Not to mention the need for just plain old web pages where non-admin users can use the application; all the things any standard web site would support.

But these guys don't want to be distracted by writing basic services and web sites, especially when they are typically the same from project to project. There's no value in that team over and over building sites that include:

- Data model/content types with strongly-typed fields

- Validation for the content's fields

- Business rules that are triggered by a wide variety of events, resulting in custom actions being executed

- Menus and other navigation

- Users, roles, and permissions

- Custom screen layouts

- Client-specific themes and styles

- Imports and exports

- Video, image, and document uploads and organization

- REST-based JSON-formatted services

- Integration with Android and iOS push notifications

- Built-in packaging and deployment

... to name a few capabilities.

HOW MUCH CODE?!?!

Just the other day, the group manager for our mobile team was sputtering about having to write a bit of PHP code for a module that didn't quite meet their requirements. Like we've said many times in this book, Drupal's architecture was created to allow for extensibility of core and module behavior, so we really needed to only write a couple dozen lines of code—because we were simply plugging into the Drupal platform.

So my response to the complaints about the module not doing 100% of what they needed, and having to write 20-odd lines of code? It went something like: "well, you had to spend a couple hours writing and testing a few lines of code against a well architected extensible platform. I suppose you could have written the entire site and REST backend from scratch, and ended up with thousands of lines of custom code!"

And then there are the "normal" web application projects, where the client doesn't care at all what platform or technology we use, as long as we meet the requirements and do it cost-effectively. Where historically we would have built a .NET or Java web application from the ground up using various packages and libraries, we are instead starting at between 50- and 80-percent complete, relative to building these sites from scratch.

Another by-product of using Drupal is that our design team—the folks that work in PhotoShop and HTML/JavaScript editors all day—can both prototype and build out their designs very quickly. As we covered in Chapter 10, the Drupal architecture lends itself very well to engineering and design teams working together but not stepping on each other's toes.

In the end, will Drupal meet all your needs for every web application? We doubt it! But we hope you find, like us, that Drupal can easily replace coded-from-scratch applications for a large portion of the web sites and service backends you create, cutting time and cost along the way.

Remember: TAMFT, there's a module for that!!

Index

■ V

■ W, X, Y, Z

Get the eBook for only $10!

Now you can take the weightless companion with you anywhere, anytime. Your purchase of this book entitles you to 3 electronic versions for only $10.

This Apress title will prove so indispensible that you'll want to carry it with you everywhere, which is why we are offering the eBook in 3 formats for only $10 if you have already purchased the print book.

Convenient and fully searchable, the PDF version enables you to easily find and copy code—or perform examples by quickly toggling between instructions and applications. The MOBI format is ideal for your Kindle, while the ePUB can be utilized on a variety of mobile devices.

Go to www.apress.com/promo/tendollars to purchase your companion eBook.

CPSIA information can be obtained at www.ICGtesting.com
Printed in the USA
LVOW09s1253231113

362555LV00005B/348/P